D0205743

The Secrets War

The Office of Strategic Services in World War II

Edited by George C. Chalou

National Archives and Records Administration

Washington, DC

Published for the
National Archives and Records Administration
by the National Archives Trust Fund Board
1992

Library of Congress Cataloging-in-Publication Data

The Secrets war : the Office of Strategic Services in World War II /
    edited by George C. Chalou.
        p.   cm.
    Proceedings of a conference sponsored by and held at the National
    Archives in Washington, D.C., July 11-12, 1991.
        Includes index.
        ISBN 0-911333-91-6
        1. United States. Office of Strategic Services—Congresses.
    2. World War, 1939-1945—Secret service—United States.   3. United
    States. National Archives and Records Administration—Congresses.
    4. Chalou, George C.   I. United States. National Archives and
    Records Administration.
    D810.S7S38   1992
    940.54'8673—dc20   91-45158
                                                            CIP

The paper used in this publication meets the minimum requirements of the American
National Standard for Permanence of Paper for Printed Library Materials Z39.48-1984.

CONTENTS

THE OSS AROUND THE GLOBE

I Spy

The Mediterranean and the Balkans

The OSS in Western Europe

The OSS in Asia

THE LEGACY OF THE OSS, 1945–91

PREFACE

The National Archives conference "The Secrets War: The Office of Strategic Services in World War II" was a long time in the making—50 years, as a matter of fact. For it was on July 11, 1941, that President Franklin D. Roosevelt appointed William J. Donovan to be Coordinator of Information. A year later, the Office of Strategic Services (OSS) was established to continue and extend what was begun just 50 years ago from the date of this conference.

This preface to the conference proceedings is my opportunity to encourage every reader to participate in the conference by enjoying the outstanding collection of presentations published in this volume. The National Archives is publishing these papers so that a wider audience can appreciate the contributions of this wartime intelligence organization.

The OSS was an intelligent solution to an intelligence crisis. Without timely and accurate information, the United States could not comprehend—let alone cope with—the worsening world situation. Without a central agency for collecting and processing information, the United States could not spend its human resources and treasure wisely in the prosecution of the war when it came. For us looking back, the coordination and initiative represented by the OSS may seem inevitable, but only a powerful vision and considerable hard work brought it about. The OSS represents a remarkable chapter in American intelligence history.

Personally, I know the OSS only by reputation. But what a reputation! Fortunately the OSS lives on not just in the memories of those who joined Donovan's entourage but also in the thousands of feet of important records that it generated during its 4 years of existence. These records reveal information—much of it previously unavailable—about virtually every aspect of the Second World War. Moreover, these records help us to gain an understanding of and appreciation for the administration and development of this nation's first modern national intelligence agency. The United States is the first country to make records of this character available.

Many of the contributors to this conference volume have already mined these records, finding new insights into the activities and importance of the OSS. As the years pass, countless other researchers will follow, and the records of the OSS will continue to enlighten those who seek to comprehend our history. They are an indispensable part of the National Archives holdings on the Second World War—holdings that were already second to none but are now further enriched by the addition of the OSS records.

On behalf of the National Archives, I am most pleased that we hosted the first major scholarly conference on the OSS. It is part of a broader effort that the National Archives is making during this, the 50th anniversary of United States participation in World War II. I am further pleased that we are also able to share, through this publication, the fruits of this significant and memorable conference.

Don W. Wilson
Archivist of the United States

INTRODUCTION

The National Archives and Records Administration serves many users of this nation's rich documentary heritage, and it supports a wide range of federal and public programs designed to reach a variety of audiences. The National Archives has maintained a special relationship with the scholarly community that stretches back to its founding and the pioneering efforts of J. Franklin Jameson and others who worked hard for its birth. Their efforts were successful, and today it is the legal mandate of this institution to select from the federal bureaucracy that small percentage of records that have enduring value to the government, the research community, and its citizens.

To continue this dialogue with the research community, the National Archives held 16 scholarly conferences between 1967 and 1979. These meetings were organized around a certain theme or major event in American history. The results of the conferences were published for the National Archives by Ohio University Press and, later, by Howard University Press.

This conference, "The Secrets War: The Office of Strategic Services in World War II," was held on July 11 and 12, 1991, at the National Archives in Washington. It differed from previous conferences because it focused on one organization that had a short but exciting life under its adventuresome leader, William Donovan. This prominent Republican attorney was named by President Franklin Roosevelt to be the Coordinator of Information (COI) on July 11, 1941, and continued as its head when the organization was renamed the Office of Strategic Services (OSS) in 1942. Through the war years the OSS served the intelligence needs of the United States but suddenly met its demise by order of President Harry S. Truman in the fall of 1945.

By bringing together veterans of the OSS, scholars of the OSS and World War II, and archivists expert in the records of the OSS and the war, the National Archives organized a program that served as a special half-century retrospective of this unique intelligence organization. Although the subject matter differed from previous conferences, the objectives of bringing together the users and the keepers and promoting a fruitful dialogue over a fascinating body of records remains as valid as in 1967.

The National Archives is grateful to the Central Intelligence Agency for its cooperation in the transfer and release of these records. Throughout the 1980s, declassification review of the OSS materials took place in the CIA. The transfer, processing, and writing of finding aids for these records followed in the National Archives and continues today with the help of National Archives volunteers under the guidance of project archivists. The large body of documents created and maintained by COI and the OSS and now in the National Archives are known in the aggregate as Record Group 226 for archival administrative purposes. But they have far greater meaning than that. They are the recorded testament of this nation's first modern intelligence organization, tempered and hardened in the heat of World War II. The National Archives takes pride in making available this intelligence treasury and the fruits of this conference to the international research community.

It is necessary to provide some commentary on the origin, program sessions, and events associated with the 2-day conference. The idea for a scholarly conference on the Office of Strategic Services goes back to early 1989, when I mentioned my proposal to the Archivist of the United States, Don W. Wilson. This thought was based upon my past work in military records and my sojourn in the reference branch where OSS operational records were first being made available. It was clear that these records were rich in historical content, providing a great deal of information about our wartime intelligence activities but also adding useful documentation about other aspects of World War II. After further consideration the National Archives decided that such a conference would benefit the research community and fit into general plans being developed in the agency for commemorating the 50th anniversary of the Second World War.

At that point, Dr. Wilson appointed me OSS Conference Director and named a special OSS Conference Steering Committee to assist in the program aspects of the conference. The committee consisted of Ray S. Cline, United States Global Strategy Council; Wayne S. Cole, University of Maryland; Elizabeth P. McIntosh, Veterans of OSS; J. Kenneth McDonald, Central Intelligence Agency; and Lawrence McDonald, John Vernon, and myself of the National Archives. This advisory committee met periodically to shape the program and to recommend speakers, commentators, and chairs. Final decisions, however, on the format, program, and arrangements were the responsibility of the National Archives.

After some discussion, the steering committee agreed that the OSS itself would be the primary focus of the conference but that some aspects of the larger war effort would need to be included. The committee was unanimous that the conference was first and foremost a scholarly one but also agreed that the participation of veterans of the OSS who were currently doing research and writing would enrich the meeting. It was decided that speakers would be asked to participate after topics were selected and that the use of archival materials—especially OSS records—would be a major consideration.

Many themes for sessions were discussed at the meetings of the committee, and gradually a selection took place. The historical context at the time of the establishment of the agency was important as well as the legacy of the OSS, and it was decided by the steering committee that both needed treatment. The committee also recommended that sessions be balanced between the operations of OSS headquarters and those overseas. Because of the many field units and activities scattered around the world, the group thought that one morning of the conference should be devoted to concurrent sessions examining OSS operations in the Mediterranean and the Balkans, western Europe, and Asia. A thematic session based upon the experiences of OSS veterans who conducted espionage was added. After approval of the draft program and suggested speakers by the National Archives, the Archivist invited all program participants to participate in the conference.

In addition to the sessions—each of which is prefaced by an introductory statement—it should be noted that some of the presentations are slightly longer in the volume and that each speaker was afforded an opportunity to make minor additions or corrections before publication. A decision was made by the National Archives that introductory remarks and commentary would not be included in the publication. For those readers who are interested, the audio recordings of conference sessions have been accessioned in Record Group 64, Records of the National Archives and Records Administration, and are available for use in the Motion Picture and Sound Recording Research Room (G-13) in the National Archives Building.

An attractive exhibit that captured highlights of the OSS welcomed attendees as they entered the Pennsylvania Avenue Lobby of the National Archives on the opening day of the conference. Marilyn Paul of the Office of Public Programs was the curator for this three-panel exhibit, which presented reproductions of over 30 visual and textual documents from the 4,000 cubic feet of OSS records in the National Archives. The intelligence agency's contributions in information gathering, propaganda, and secret operations were featured.

Conference attendees and special guests were treated to a gala evening reception on July 11 in the Rotunda of the National Archives. This was a special time for OSS veterans to meet old friends and wartime colleagues, and it afforded scholars an opportunity to talk to people who actually created or were mentioned in the records. The mood of the reception crowd of about 300 was relaxed, and they were in no hurry to leave the Rotunda—the special shrine of the Declaration of Independence, Constitution, and the Bill of Rights.

In addition to the outstanding work of the OSS Conference Steering Committee, there were many National Archives staff members and volunteers who assisted during the conference. Staff members of the Office of Public Programs were especially helpful in completing many of the logistical tasks of the conference. As the conference drew near, essential policy guidance was furnished by an informal working group of Donn Neal and Ray Mosley of the Office of the Archivist, Linda N. Brown, Assistant Archivist for Public Programs, and myself. As conference director, I want to give special thanks to Michelle Cobb, Brenda Jones, Larry McDonald, and Robert Wolfe for their advice, assistance, and support during the planning and operation of the conference. Pat El-Ashry very ably assisted me in numerous ways in preparing for and managing this conference. Mrs. Helga Warren translated Fabrizio Calvi's paper from French to English. Henry J. Gwiazda directed the copyediting and production of the volume. Mary C. Ryan, Anne E. DeLong, John F. Lynch, and Sandra M. Tilley ably copyedited and proofread the text. Richard B. Smith monitored the composition and printing.

The National Archives would like to express appreciation to the foundation of the New York law firm of Donovan Leisure Newton & Irvine for its financial assistance in sponsoring the conference.

It is my personal hope that all users of this conference publication and those of us entrusted with this nation's documentary heritage will be brought a little closer together by means of such conferences. Such meetings will contribute to a deeper understanding of this nation's march to the present and the victories it celebrated as well as the losses it endured.

George C. Chalou
OSS Conference Director and Editor

THE WORLD
GOES TO WAR
1939–41

In the opening address of the conference, one of America's foremost diplomatic historians, Waldo Heinrichs, explained the many complexities facing the United States and its President, Franklin D. Roosevelt, as the world lurched toward war. Heinrichs deftly weaves together the various diplomatic, economic, political, and military issues facing the United States during this critical period. As events of the spring and summer of 1941 unfolded, military action came to dominate the scene as Germany thrust through Denmark and Norway and quickly swept through France—and sent its submarines westward, hungry for kills. On the other side of the globe, Japan became more determined to create a Pan-Asian empire. Less than 6 months later, at Pearl Harbor, Japan unleashed a devastating attack on the United States. Franklin Delano Roosevelt was now a wartime President.

The second major presentation focused on key decisions Roosevelt made relating to the nation's need for more accurate and timely information from around the world. In July 1941 the President named William J. Donovan to head a new intelligence office as Coordinator of Information. Professor Robin Winks examines how and why Donovan recruited talented men and women to serve in his new organization. Winks deftly explains, by blending both analysis and example, the reasons why this charming New York attorney and talent hunter extraordinaire was such a successful recruiter. In large measure Donovan reasoned that his recruits' brains and high motivation would lead to a successful collection and analysis of information. Winks points out that although the "best and the brightest" came from many colleges and universities, the Ivy League schools—especially Yale—provided more than their share to the OSS.

The prominent European historian Gordon A. Craig chaired the session, introduced the two speakers, and provided a short commentary based upon his experiences in the OSS and COI.

THE UNITED STATES PREPARES FOR WAR*

Waldo Heinrichs

It seems a contradiction in terms to present a paper entitled "The U.S. Prepares for War" when that war began with Pearl Harbor, the very symbol of unpreparedness. On that day 50 years ago, the line of burly battleships featured on newsreels of the 1930s, which was supposed to be ever on guard against foreign threats, was sunk, beached, or sent limping home for repairs. In a larger historical perspective, Pearl Harbor and ensuing disasters in the Pacific were the price we paid for two decades of head-in-the-sand isolationism, of shirking leadership in world security to stop aggression before it got rolling, of miserly military appropriations that left the United States with at best two combat-ready divisions as late as the spring of 1941—in short, the price we paid for our inability to grapple with the hard, unpleasant facts of international life surrounding us.

There is much truth in this picture of myopia, but much truth is missing. The victory at Midway in June 1942 did not just happen. The aircraft carriers *Yorktown, Enterprise,* and *Hornet,* which sank four Japanese carriers, were built or started, and their tactics developed, in the isolationist 1930s. The attacking Japanese fleet was met in strength because for many years the U.S. Navy had been training selected intelligence officers in cryptanalysis and Japanese language, and some of these had penetrated the Japanese fleet code far enough to estimate correctly where, when, and how the attack would occur.

Obviously preparations for war were inadequate, but they were not inconsiderable. Indeed by 1941 they were extensive and accelerating, and given the dire threats facing the nation by then, urgent and sometimes frantic. Furthermore, preparations were never straightforward but subject

---

*This paper is drawn from the author's *Threshold of War: Franklin D. Roosevelt and American Entry Into World War II* (New York, 1988), to which the reader is referred for sources.

to conflicting demands, shifting priorities, and unknown variables. This was the context, one of crisis and rapid expansion, from which the Office of Strategic Services (OSS) emerged.

The United States had every reason to prepare as early and as powerfully as it could. Today we see German and Japanese expansion as much more complex than it was seen in the first postwar histories; but the menace to American security posed by these two powers in the modern analysis is no less great. The Nazi system was essentially acquisitive, depending on ever more space and resources. According to Gerhard Weinberg, Hitler anticipated ultimate war with the United States and was planning, indeed had started to build, 56,000-ton battleships and a bomber, the ME 262, capable of hitting New York from the Azores.

Japanese expansion was less singleminded but no less dynamic. The dominant military sought imperial self-sufficiency in resources for what they took to be an age of total war, but the army and navy had different versions of this resource empire—one northward against the Soviet Union, the other toward southeast Asia—and were fiercely competitive in securing existing war production and determining the direction and pace of advance. The lack of any central authority determining ends and means led to an inchoate expansionism, each venture creating the need for further steps, and violent changes in world politics providing the opportunities.

American officials were concerned with these threats, but for much of the 1930s they appeared remote and hypothetical. The French Army with its allies far outnumbered the Wehrmacht, and between the United States and Germany stood, as always, the Royal Navy. Italy's alignment with Germany seemed by no means definitive, and a German-Soviet pact was impossible to conceive of. Japan's aggression seemed confined to East Asia, where America's interests were judged to be marginal. From 1937 onward, Japan's expansionist energies were being spent in war with China. It was difficult to believe that Japan, so deficient in war resources, would be so foolish as to attack the United States, which so overshadowed it economically. Above all, it was difficult to believe so soon after the ghastly carnage of the Great War that nations would march to war again or that their people would let them.

Complacency was not the dominant mood of the 1930s. It was a time of devastating economic crisis that shriveled the internationalism of the 1920s. Nations turned inward to deal with the collapse of investment values, bank closings, and mass unemployment. Governments were more concerned with economic and political viability than with distant aggression. Central to the concerns of President Franklin D. Roosevelt were recovery and reform, and he could hardly afford to alienate the significant segment of his New Deal coalition that was at once reformist and isolationist. Even so, American rearmament, at least in seapower, was by no means negligible: built, building, or authorized in the programs of 1933 through 1939 (*before* the huge program of 1940) were 6 battleships, 3 carriers, 10 cruisers, 42 submarines, and 118 destroyers. In November 1938 the President called for production of 10,000 military airplanes, as much for boosting American production facilities as for arming the British and French.

In the latter thirties, as war clouds gathered, Roosevelt did what he could within the constraints of neutrality legislation and powerful isolationism to warn aggressors and encourage the democracies. These efforts included secret naval talks with the British, beginnings of military aid to China, development of hemispheric solidarity and defense, and ending commercial treaty relations with Japan, opening the way to embargo. None of these efforts deterred aggression. When the blow of Nazi conquest struck in May–June 1940, the United States was not preparing for war in any serious or comprehensive way. On the contrary, it expected, by selling arms to its friends, to avoid war.

The German conquest of Denmark, Norway, the Low Countries, and France in the spring of 1940 changed all that. Besieging Britain, German power spilled out of Europe, U-boats and occasionally capital ships ranged into the western Atlantic. Nazi hegemony in Europe, the peril to Britain, and this naval challenge in the American front yard ended the era of what we now call "free security." The Japanese, taking advantage of European weakness, moved into Southeast Asia, forcing on the hapless French an agreement for stationing troops in northern Indochina. They also entered into an alliance with Germany and Italy. This Axis pact aimed at deterring the United States from both directions, hemming it into the Western Hemisphere. In Japan some saw the alliance as opening the way to an insuperable coalition of the Axis powers with the Soviet Union. It is hard to imagine so few months bringing such a frightening reversal of fortunes for the United States.

The crisis played to Franklin D. Roosevelt's strengths, his calmness and buoyancy in the face of adversity, his experience in rearmament from World War I, his innovativeness and yet caution, and his feel for power internationally and domestically. His distinctive decision-making style suited the moment as well. On issues of urgency and importance to himself, he dealt with officials according to the task at hand and the relevant competence of the individual rather than by formal bureaucratic lines of authority. For example, to design new patrol lines and sectors for the Atlantic Fleet in April 1941, he brought its commander, Adm. Ernest J. King, to Hyde Park for the weekend. While the President's unorthodox methods caused confusion and uncertainty in ordinary times, they provided flexibility and adaptability in a time of radical change such as the government of the United States was entering. In 1940 the departments dealing with external affairs would have seemed relatively familiar to an official of the 19th century. The State Department, for example, in its Victorian setting next to the White House, ran a Foreign Service of some 700 officers. By the end of the war it would all have seemed entirely strange.

Decision making in 1940–41 was extraordinarily difficult for Roosevelt. Political circumstances were especially constraining, given the President's bid for an unprecedented third term and the virulence of the isolationist bloc. Where the rationale was convincingly the enhancement of American defense—as in the destroyers-for-bases agreement, the two-ocean navy program, the positioning of the fleet at Hawaii, conscription, and restrictions on export of strategic goods to Japan—he could move ahead. Otherwise he felt compelled to hedge, postpone, or, on occasion, engage in falsehood. Reelection was immediately followed by Britain's payment crisis and the President's inspired solution to it, Lend-Lease, which again required extraordinary political circumspection to secure passage through Congress. It was not until March 1941 that he felt free to look ahead and confront the large questions of strategy and preparation for war. When he did, he found most questions unanswerable.

The questions were fundamental. They would shape the envelope and parameters of rearmament. If the United States had to fight, what kind of a war would it be? Would it be with Germany alone? Could Japan be detached from the Axis? Would intervention in the Battle of the Atlantic necessarily lead to war with Germany, and would that automatically involve Japan? What would be the consequences for Britain's survival if Japan moved against Britain's imperial lifelines and war resources in Southeast Asia, and what should the United States do about it? Which way would the German Army strike in the coming campaign season? Cross-channel invasion of England? Northwest Africa, the Atlantic islands, and Dakar? Suez and the Persian Gulf? Or Russia? If Germany attacked Russia, would Russia survive, or, given the gloomy predictions, how long would it survive?

One must remember that as of the spring of 1941 the Wehrmacht was awesome. Hitler had struck down his enemies one by one, swiftly and completely. He had never made a mistake. Preliminaries to the main event of 1941—the lightning conquest of Greece and Yugoslavia and the airborne seizure of Crete—only strengthened this image of insuperable power.

All these questions bore on what kind of war the United States might face. Who would be the enemy, and who would be left as an ally? Would it be a war to invade Europe, or Pacific islands, or both, or in the worst case, a war to defend the Western Hemisphere? Should the nation ready itself for immediate war, sacrificing time-consuming weapons like battleships, or build for the longer pull? How much arms production should be planned for the American military and how much for which allies? The steel industry was reaching full capacity. How many new plants should be constructed? How much steel should be diverted for that construction from current production of tanks and ship hulls? How big should the American Army be, and how big could it be without diverting skilled labor from war production?

Knowing what Hitler planned to do in 1941 was a necessary first step in answering these questions, yet the President and his advisers were uncertain until early June, and some were still unsure on the eve of the German invasion of the Soviet Union. It has long been taken as a fact that the United States did have foreknowledge of the German attack on Russia as early as March, but from my investigation of the sources for that assertion and relevant intelligence material, I believe it to be incorrect. To be sure, American military attachés gained abundant information from train watchers that Germany was gathering large forces in the East, and they estimated with considerable accuracy the number of divisions. Nevertheless, officials concluded at first that Hitler would not be so foolhardy as to attack Russia before finishing off Britain, and later that the concentration in the East was aimed at intimidating the Soviet Union into making large economic concessions in the Ukraine and Caucasus and that Stalin, with his fawning attitude toward Germany, would concede. That Hitler would attack in any case only became clear, or much clearer, early in June with the MAGIC intercept of messages from the Japanese Ambassador in Berlin recounting conversations with Hitler and Ribbentrop. From F. H. Hinsley's account of British intelligence, London, too, was slow in reaching the correct conclusion.

Lacking assurance of what the summer held in store for Europe, Roosevelt hung uncertainly between transatlantic and transpacific threats. After passage of Lend-Lease, he hoped to assist in the Battle of the Atlantic, where Britain was suffering devastating losses from German U-boats and raiders. But even modest plans for intervening were shelved upon the signing of the Soviet-Japanese neutrality pact. The President felt he could not afford to weaken the Pacific Fleet by sending battleship reinforcements to the Atlantic just at the moment when Japan might feel emboldened to move southward.

Roosevelt especially feared a German thrust into northwest Africa with seizure of the Azores, Canaries, and Cape Verde Islands and Dakar. It would take a mere handful of divisions. Some have argued that he conjured up this Nazi threat to the Americas as a means of justifying intervention in the Atlantic, but his fears seem genuine (he reported dreaming of a "light" German air raid on New York at this time), and these fears were reinforced by a variety of reports, mostly unfounded, of German infiltration into North Africa and evidence in May 1941 of German pressure on Vichy to secure access to Dakar. Not knowing Hitler's intentions, Roosevelt dwelt on the most dangerous possibilities. He ordered preparations for the occupation of the Azores. His dispatch of troops to Iceland, though of complex origin, can also be seen in terms of defending the Atlantic.

The President was groping in the dark. He had no idea what was going to happen in Europe, and the Soviet-Japanese pact had come as an unpleasant surprise. He could not move east or west; he was pinioned by the Axis alliance. "When I don't know how to move I stay put," he said on a similar occasion. But staying put when so much hung on moving ahead was costly. For days at a time in May and June he was sick in bed, suffering, according to his secretary, Marguerite LeHand, more from exasperation than anything else.

A better intelligence system might have made a more accurate forecast, but one cannot be sure, for it was enormously difficult to gain information in these totalitarian societies. The American ambassadors and ministers in Europe were mostly experienced diplomats, and they were assisted by professionals of the Foreign Service who would become leading lights of American diplomacy after the war, but the dispatches and cables from Europe were meager fare, heavy with rumor and short on analysis.

A better system might have paid attention to the comment of the assistant military attaché in Moscow who noted that Hitler would not really engage in a two-front war by attacking Russia because Britain lacked the capability of invading the continent. It might have registered dissatisfaction when the military attaché in Berlin, after a meticulous account of Germany's strength in the East, concluded that it would probably invade Britain anyway. A better system might have encouraged a look at *Mein Kampf.*

The fact is that the United States had no system of intelligence. Each agency—the Office of Naval Intelligence, the Military Intelligence Division, the State Department—was a separate empire of knowledge. No means existed for gathering and evaluating information from different sources at the national level. MAGIC material came to a select few in raw form as decrypted radio messages that had to be read on the spot and handed back, the aching mind retaining what it could. Let me suggest that the paralyzing uncertainties of the spring of 1941 brought to the forefront the need for a comprehensive and analytical intelligence system and formed the immediate background for the appointment of a Coordinator of Information.

The German attack on the Soviet Union was a catalyst for revolutionary change in American foreign policy. Most observers predicted a quick German victory in 1 to 3 months, and indeed in the first weeks the advance of Panzer columns was spectacular. But as July passed, Russian resistance became stronger and German momentum slowed. It now became possible to conceive of the Russians hanging on until the autumn rains and winter and thus into 1942, and this made all the difference in the world to President Roosevelt.

Before the attack on Russia, Roosevelt worked for the survival of Britain but had to consider the possibility of invasion and British defeat, which would leave America standing alone in a totalitarian world. Reentry into Europe and defeat of Germany were hard to imagine. Now a coalition could form with the power and position to accomplish that. Now allies were vital, and American policy moved from a nationalist to an internationalist framework. If the German attack on Russia turned out to be more than just a diversion, the President wrote June 26, it would "mean the liberation of Europe from Nazi domination."

The new character and pace of decision making were evident immediately. Gone were the hesitation and indecision of the spring. On July 9 the President asked the Secretaries of War and the Navy to prepare an estimate of the production required to defeat the nation's potential enemies. Their answer in September was the Victory Program, which consolidated the arms requirements of Britain and the United States and for the first time set forth the outer boundaries of a war economy. Aid to Russia quickened. At first American coffers and supply were opened hesitatingly and then with increasing liberality. By the end of August the President deemed it of "paramount importance to the safety and security of America" to provide the Russians with a "reasonable" supply of arms. In September, in order to meet the Soviet demand for 500 tanks a month, the U.S. Army agreed to stretch out the equipping of the 3d, 4th, and 5th Armored Divisions and 15 tank battalions and to postpone activation of the 6th Armored Division.

At the same time, British-American relations reached a new stage of intimacy. They had been getting steadily closer in the winter of 1940–41, "becoming thicker, more tangled and more secure," in the words of David Reynolds. Secret British-American military staff conversations coordinated American strategic planning, represented by the Navy's Plan Dog memorandum and the Rainbow 5 war plan, with British strategy. The two nations agreed that if the United States joined in the war, both would concentrate on the defeat of Germany and maintain a defensive posture toward Japan. Technical, supply, and observer missions mushroomed. American naval observers went aboard British warships and British aboard American. The two nations exchanged secret technical data, intelligence, and cryptographic materials. Americans provided the British with two replicas of Japan's diplomatic cipher machine so they could obtain their own MAGIC decrypts.

Before August 1941, President Roosevelt was prepared to assist in the Battle of the Atlantic in every way possible except commitment of the Atlantic Fleet to use of force. One reason for this was that the fleet was still not ready to accept the responsibility of escorting convoys. Another reason was that planners found it impossible to segregate American escort operations; they would have to fit into an essentially British scheme, but the President as of July was not prepared to enter into formal undertakings with foreign authorities for the operation of American naval forces. That would have to await the establishment of common peace aims with the British government and thereby the political basis for risking and waging war, which in turn would have to await the Atlantic Conference between Roosevelt and Churchill at Argentia on August 9–12, 1941.

Reports had been circulating that the British were making a secret deal with the Russians providing territorial concessions in eastern Europe as an inducement for Russia to continue the war. The British were also said to be making territorial and economic arrangements with governments-in-exile in London. These contradicted basic American principles of self-determination, the open door, and nonrecognition of territorial change achieved by force. Roosevelt feared such agreements would set precedents that would undermine the political foundations upon which the anti-Axis forces could most effectively wage war and which he required to lead the American people into war if necessary. The first item of business at Argentia was establishing to American satisfaction that no such commitments had been made. The British did so. The resulting Atlantic Charter was a restatement of Wilsonian principles that would serve as an international standard to which free and subjugated peoples could repair. Its strength lay in the sharp contrast it drew between the multilateral world vision of the democracies and the self-serving aims of the Axis, and it thereby advanced the President's aim of building a coalition.

Political understanding having been achieved, intervention in the Battle of the Atlantic followed. American destroyers began escorting fast convoys in the western Atlantic in September, as soon as the complex deployments were completed. The U.S. Navy took over responsibility for guarding Denmark Strait between Iceland and Greenland against breakout by German capital ships, deploying six battleships and two aircraft carriers to Argentia and Iceland for the purpose. Shoot-on-sight orders were issued for a generously defined western Atlantic.

The same decisiveness Roosevelt displayed in European questions he manifested in regard to Japan. Japan's response to Hitler's attack on the Soviet Union was a decision to prosecute the southward advance, even at the risk of war with Britain and the United States, by securing bases in southern Indochina—that is, Cambodia and Cochin China—which would provide launching points for air attack and invasion of Malaya. Japan would also build up its Manchurian army to 850,000 so that if Russia collapsed or withdrew a sizable portion of its Far Eastern army to face the Germans, Japan could strike northwards. On July 24 Japanese troops landed at Saigon. The United States responded by freezing Japanese assets, embargoing oil shipments to Japan, and reinforcing the Philippines, particularly with long-range bombers. This hard line carried over into diplomacy: in the Hull-Nomura conversations of the fall of 1941 one finds no evidence that the United States was prepared to make significant concessions. The function of diplomacy was to gain time.

It is difficult to understand why Roosevelt took this hard line when he knew that an oil embargo was likely to provoke Japan into seizing Dutch and British oil resources in Southeast Asia. Why would he provoke war when he was risking war by intervention on the Atlantic and when British-American strategy called for concentration against Germany and defense in the Pacific? These have proved to be very hard questions to answer. As is often the case in probing Roosevelt's intentions, the evidence is sparse and inference is necessary.

What has been suggested so far is that in the wake of the German attack on the Soviet Union, Roosevelt left hesitation, and an essentially hemispheric policy, behind and began to operate within the framework of an international alliance for the defeat of Germany and Italy. This had implications for Japan. In mid-August the German offensive in Russia resumed with enormous gains. A vital question from the beginning had been whether Stalin would be able to draw reinforcement from his Siberian troops facing the Japanese. It became ever more urgent. Thus Japan's designs became twice linked to Europe, once by way of Britain's interests in Southeast Asia and again by way of Russia's reinforcement pool in Siberia. Before the German invasion of Russia, East Asian problems had been connected to European, but they had also been separate and distinctive. Now they fitted primarily into a global scheme of politics in Roosevelt's mind.

From this perspective he probably concluded that inaction would gain him nothing. Japan would be given no reason to desist from aggressive designs northward or southward. China would be discouraged and perhaps encircled, and the United States, embarking on a leadership role in world affairs, would look weak and helpless. Again from this perspective, a diplomatic settlement with Japan would remove the threat to Southeast Asia, and perhaps detach Japan from the Axis, but only at the expense of China, where Japan insisted on retaining troops. The United States could hardly urge allies, particularly the Soviets, to stand firm in Europe when it was pursuing appeasement in East Asia. And surely it would be unwise to help Japan out of a war that absorbed much of its expansive energy. Finally, a settlement that would provide Japan stability in the south might encourage it to attack northward.

This sort of reasoning, which is represented in policy papers, led to the hard line. In this analysis the Soviet-German war seemed to have intensified Japanese expansionism, opportunism, and unpredictability. Whether Japan went north or south, it threatened the improving world balance of forces. This careening expansionism had to be stopped. Japan had to be boxed in, contained, immobilized. So Roosevelt, I believe, decided to apply maximum pressure. Not a drop of oil. Let Japan's oil supplies dry up and its capacity for military operations anywhere shrink. Reinforce the Philippines. Create such uncertainty and concern among Japanese decision makers regarding the south and relations with America that they did not dare go north.

The planned reinforcement of the Philippines was very sizable for the America of that day: arriving by March 1942 would be 165 B-17 and B-24 bombers, 54 dive-bombers, and an additional 130 fighters, together with infantry, field artillery, tank, antiaircraft, and engineering units. The Navy sent a squadron of modern submarines. The British planned to send six battleships and a carrier to Singapore. The American big bombers, it was envisaged, would operate from Darwin, Singapore, the Dutch East Indies, and the Philippines, providing crucial deterrence against a Japanese attack southward. That they might also deter an attack northward is well documented. The bombers' range, their ability to bomb Japan from the Philippines and fly on to bases in Siberia promised to hold the Japanese in check. Army Chief of Staff Gen. George C. Marshall saw the air buildup as a way to "restrain Japan from advance into Malaysia or Eastern Siberia." By acting rapidly, the United States might give Japan "a complete pause." To Secretary of War Henry L. Stimson, this was the nation's "big stick," which revolutionized strategy in the Pacific. It would provide "immense powers of warning to Japan as well as of assurance to Russia." Secretary of State Cordell Hull believed that the air reinforcement had "really given a punch to his own diplomacy in the Far East and . . . opened the door to Vladivostok." The Army War Plans Division advised a continuation of pressures "with a view to rendering Japan incapable of offensive operations against Russia or against possessions of the associated powers in the Far East."

This thinking proved illusory. Most of the reinforcements did not arrive in time. Japan took the oil embargo as a deadly threat and on September 6 decided on war with Britain and the United States unless diplomacy met its essential requirements. It had decided as early as August 10 not to attack the Soviet Union in 1941, and Stalin learned this from his spies in Tokyo. Nevertheless, the story of the hard line against Japan is instructive. It illustrates the extent to which Roosevelt and his aides had escaped from a hemispheric mentality and begun to think in global terms. That was essential preparation for prosecution of the war.

Roosevelt went far to bring the American people out of their isolationist mentality to acceptance of rearmament and measures short of war. He recognized that the intense partisanship of the New Deal years and the elections had made himself a major issue, and so he stayed in the background during legislative battles, mustering his forces from behind the scenes. In speeches he eloquently pointed out the growing dangers without force-feeding his message, letting the situation and the facts educate the people. His Fireside Chats were masterful exercises in democratic leadership—plain, somber, yet reassuring. One could walk up the street on a summery evening and hear most of the President's talk over the radio through open doors as one passed from home to home.

In spite of bitter-end isolationism, polls indicated that the people followed closely behind the President, and he had his reasons—military unreadiness and uncertainty about what lay in store—not to go faster. The idea that the President was way out ahead trying to pull the American people along is mistaken. Roosevelt wanted to avoid war as long as possible not only because he wished to rearm as much as possible before the fight, but also because he knew that war would greatly increase the priority of American military demands when the crucial immediate need as he saw it was to provide the Soviet Union and Britain with sufficient arms to hold the German war machine at bay. The Roosevelt administration's record in preparing the nation for war—at least in fundamentals—was impressive. The President understood the vast capability of the American economy and set production targets commensurate with it, however forbidding they seemed at the moment. He had a keen sense of timing and sequencing in his decisions concerning preparing for war. The small size of ready forces masked very large military potential under construction and in training. A comprehensive war economy plan finally set production targets and established priorities in allocation of resources. The American public, on the whole, understood the threat and was supportive of the President's actions. The Army and Navy had agreed upon a strategy for prosecution of the war, as had the British and Americans. The President had formed a coalition powerful enough to defeat Germany and was devoting vital American resources to sustaining it. A much weaker group was forming to contain Japan, which at least emphasized Japan's isolation and provided a framework for common action in the future. Finally, a multilateral vision of the world had been proclaimed to fly as a banner in the free world camp.

GETTING THE RIGHT STUFF: FDR, Donovan, and the Quest for Professional Intelligence

Robin W. Winks

One should never be doing only one thing, and one should always have at least three agendas, only one of them hidden. This slightly revised observation, taken from a paper prepared on academic politics, applies well to the work of intelligence and surely to what I have to say this morning. For I have taken the title upon which George Chalou and I agreed to have at least two meanings: "getting the right stuff," somewhat in the manner of Tom Wolfe, as "recruiting the right kind of people"; and "getting the right stuff," as in "obtaining the necessary information." But since we are gathered here largely as historians, I will also discuss a third meaning, which relates to research in the field and recruiting as it is conducted today. This discussion of "the right stuff" will, at the end, bring us from July 11, 1941, 50 years ago today, the date on which President Franklin D. Roosevelt appointed William J. Donovan as Coordinator of Information (COI), to the present.

Little hard research has been done on how the Coordinator of Information and the Director of the Office of Strategic Services (OSS) defined "the right kind of people" or how—beyond personal contacts and word of mouth—they recruited or how what were in effect referrals from G-2 (Army Intelligence) truly worked. Our information is more anecdotal than one would wish. The massive, thorough, and very perceptive analytical bibliography compiled by George C. Constantinides, *Intelligence and Espionage* (Boulder, CO, 1983), contains no index entries under recruiting or personnel, though the book does (without the index revealing the fact) pass comment now and then on personality types. Indeed, most dictionaries, encyclopedias, and indexes to intelligence that contain an entry under recruitment are referring to the tradecraft of bringing someone over from "the other side." The Federal Bureau of Investigation's (FBI) definition of "recruitment," the "process of enlisting an individual to work for an intelligence or counterintelligence service," is bland and elastic enough, though a little unnerving in that it contains nothing about "appropriate individuals" or assessing that appropriateness as part of the recruiting process.[1]

Of course, the question hardly arises with respect to the early OSS, for people were eager to work for it, especially in Europe or Washington. The OSS offered an opportunity to do what was widely regarded, at least in university circles, as an important job, which drew upon a candidate's education, experience, and general background, with a whiff of danger (and sometimes a good bit more than a whiff). A job with the OSS most likely assured a posting to an interesting and cosmopolitan place, such as London, Bern, Paris, later Milan, or even Cairo or Istanbul, and an escape from the assumed tedium of spending the war typing up supply requisitions in some overheated stateside military post. The OSS appealed to a good number of men of action who had excelled on the football field, but any examination of photographs of groups of OSS men shows a disproportionate number who wore glasses. These were "the bad eyes brigade," people not lacking in courage or a desire to contribute to the war effort but acutely aware that a simple matter of a heavy rain might incapacitate them at a crucial moment. They composed disproportionately the largest unit, the Research and Analysis Branch (R&A).

A relatively casual swing through the growing body of OSS memoir literature tells us something, though only anecdotally, about the people who thought of themselves as "the right stuff." In 1941 Sherman Kent left his assistant professorship (at $3,500 a year) at Yale to become William L. Langer's number two in setting up the Office of Research and Analysis at the new COI/OSS (at something like $5,000 a year). The salary differential alone might help explain the shift, and Kent admits this was an incentive, but his account suggests other motives as well. He admired FDR and Donovan, he thought the mission of founding the country's first secret intelligence organization important and intellectually stimulating, he thought that propaganda in wartime was acceptable within limits but did not trust the politicians to set those limits appropriately, and he would be working directly with men he liked and would be able to recruit other men that he liked. He also had excellent contacts, for surely few young assistant professors of history anywhere could, as Kent did, simply run up to Cape Cod to confer with Charles Seymour, the revered historian of Versailles and of Woodrow Wilson and not incidentally president of Yale University, to have "a long talk" about whether he should join up. The "right stuff" that Kent, in turn, recruited turned out to be people he already knew and respected, who worked in French history (his own academic field) or with whom he had crossed friendly swords at conventions of fellow historians. Of the first 15 people he met in the OSS, 5 were from Yale, 4 from Harvard, 2 each from Columbia and Williams, 1 from the University of Virginia, and 1 from "one of the mid-west universities," which one he did not, just then, recall. This was not snobbishness on Kent's part, for at base he was a rude Jacksonian Democrat, but rather a reflection of reality. Of course he knew no one from Sam Houston State or Whittier College or Ball State; an examination of the 1941 program for the American Historical Association's annual conference of scholarly papers shows almost precisely the same distribution for speakers. Kent was merely recruiting according to the canons of the profession as it then was.[2]

Donald Downes, whose rather checkered career in the OSS, and especially in Secret Intelligence (SI), could still benefit from a good bit of probing, says in his recently released papers that the OSS needed people who understood the chicanery of Europeans and would not blush at what they might discover but who retained a high spark of idealism: the ideal combination of high-mindedness and tempered cynicism that, Downes wrote elsewhere, Yale had prepared him for.[3]

The postwar University of Pennsylvania archaeologist and field anthropologist Carleton S. Coon, on the other hand, admitted on page 3 of his memoir, *A North Africa Story* (Ipswich, MA, 1980), that he had always wanted "to travel in strange mountains, stir up tribes, and destroy the enemy by secret and unorthodox means"—that is, to be a kind of Richard Hannay, though far out beyond the Thirty-nine Steps of Broadstairs, and that joining the OSS meant that he never had to be "completely grown up." This may not sound much of a recommendation, but I am reminded of Ursula LeGuin's remark that the successful adult is merely the child who has survived (that is, has ignored the Biblical injunction to put away childish things) and that deciding what one wants to be when one grows up is a kind of death many people quite rightly resist. As vituperative as Coon is about most of his colleagues in his recollections, it is clear that he enjoyed being a curmudgeon among them.

R. Taylor Cole, who went from Louisiana State University to the Harvard graduate school (and who, after the war, enjoyed a distinguished career at Duke University) joined the Office of War Information (OWI), which soon palled, and was then invited over to the OSS with the thought that since he had co-authored *The Swiss Bureaucracy*, he might prove useful to Allen Dulles, who was organizing a staff for Bern. By the time the OWI would let Cole loose, however, Switzerland was closed down to new entries, so Cole wound up with SI (where the quite young lieutenant Richard Helms was a coworker) and was sent off to Stockholm. Foreign travel, the enticement of friends, and boredom with the routine chores of OWI drew Cole to the OSS in, it would appear, about equal measure.

Louis E. Keefer of the Army Specialized Training Program (ASTP), the alumni of which went in some significant measure to OSS assignments, author of *Scholars in Foxholes* (Jefferson, NC, 1988), suggests that the Army was eager to make use of the college educated and that the ASTP was created largely because "the right people" (his term) favored it. By early 1943, units were functioning in 22 colleges and universities, and more were added later that year. Over 37,500 trainees passed through Oklahoma A&M, yet I cannot assuredly trace a single one of them to the OSS; Yale, on the other hand, trained 7,000, of which a good number found themselves in the OSS, especially in the Pacific.

Max Corvo's *The OSS in Italy* (New York, 1990) covers 1942 to 1945. Corvo, it seems clear, gravitated to the OSS and it to him because he possessed knowledge, contacts of a different kind, and well-expressed anti-Fascist sentiments that translated into a valuable and desirable expertise. Early in 1942 he was, as he says, "to my great disappointment" (p. 3), assigned as a trainee for clerical duties at Camp Lee, VA. He did not wish to spend the war as a file clerk; he wanted to fight Fascists, preferably in Italy, and by June of 1942, he had formulated a plan for subversive warfare against Sicily, which the camp intelligence chief had the good judgment to forward up through G-2. In short, for him the system worked, and he was recruited because he was imaginative and, more important, because he possessed the requisite skills and some of the knowledge then needed by SI. Such knowledge might come, as it did for Corvo, through experience, reading, and family ties or, as for Kent, through the university, but in the end what mattered most was that a candidate already be in possession of a good bit of "the right stuff" in both senses of the phrase.

In relation to the size of its graduating classes, Yale appears to have contributed more members to intelligence work in 1943 than any other college or university in the nation. Harvard appears to have been a close second. This is not to suggest that Yale or Harvard graduates were more patriotic or more eager to escape the battlefield for the quiet channels of research or the dark streets of London, but rather that by 1943 something of a critical mass of contacts had grown up so that R&A, at least, continued to draw upon known sources and to use the old boy network. Toward the end of the war the OSS was beginning to be dominated by Army officers who had no love for the bad eyes brigade, but this shift most influenced SI and SO (Special Operations), X-2 (or counter intelligence) only a little, and R&A hardly at all. So the mass grew larger, and while a recruit might be drawn in from a remote point in the West—a young political scientist from the University of Colorado, for example—a bit of background research quickly shows that, in this instance, Columbia was the common denominator, since the recruit had been trained at the graduate school there.

There is, then, a myth about the Ivy Leaguers that should be remarked upon here. The picture given to us in much spy fiction and some spy fact goes roughly like this: smooth Ivy Leaguers were naturally favored in the OSS, for a secret intelligence organization obviously wanted men from institutions that had well-developed athletic programs and was especially strong in sports in which the delicate balance between teamwork and individuality—crew, swimming, track and field, for example—loomed large. It wanted men from institutions that built upon and developed social contacts and sophistication, and from which, in high probability, the graduate had sallied forth on one or more grand tours of Europe, so that were this figure of brain and brawn to be parachuted in behind the lines in France, he would not make a fool of himself by not knowing which wine to drink; they wanted recruits who had gone to a university that still required mastery of a foreign language for graduation, as the Ivy League did and most of the country did not.

There certainly was some truth in this picture. Some of these items were likely to be true of a majority of the candidates. But few people were expected to parachute behind enemy lines, and to reveal the truth, while there was a requirement that all graduates study a foreign language, if a somewhat unsystematic examination of the test scores and final papers of non-language majors at one Ivy League university may be taken as symptomatic, one would not want to count on the parachutee being able to pronounce the difference between a Chateauneuf-du-Pape and a St. Estephe, much less taste the difference. This composite represents what Ivy Leaguers liked to think of themselves, and what sometimes credulous non–Ivy Leaguers believed to be true, and to that extent it shaped perceptions of the OSS, but the stereotype was true of only a minority of graduates.

Consider these short observations from a general handbook on Ivy League institutions:

Of Yale: "The Yale man . . . excels at numerous tests of physical prowess," to wit, golf, squash, hockey, and polo. The first intercollegiate athletic event, a crew race between Yale and Harvard in 1852, and the fact that Yale had produced more football victories and more All-American players than any other institution clearly indicated where the true meeting of brain and brawn still occurred. Yale College students produced the oldest college daily, in time out of a building put up for them by Henry S. Luce and Briton Hadden, and it was widely believed that *Time* magazine contrived to mention Yale at least once in every issue. Each year, on the last Thursday of May, 135 juniors were inducted into the famous senior societies. The number of inductees was kept a dark secret, and the members were said to rise and leave the room if their society was mentioned (a strange way, I have often thought, to conceal the fact that one was a member of said society). Surely Skull and Bones was a match for OSS, CIA, and KGB combined.

Or of Princeton: It was solemnly reported that the school, possessed the oldest college literary and debating society, the Whig-Cliosophic, in whose debates no fewer than 200 U.S. Representatives, 100 Federal and State Supreme Court Justices, and 65 Senators (not to speak of 2 U.S. Presidents) had participated. The Woodrow Wilson School obviously trained the elite of the nation's Foreign Service.

To these kinds of boasts, calculated to attract new applicants, justify the costs on over-burdened parents, and to enhance a public image, Harvard, in the same composite publication, responded with the simple declarative line, "Harvard is unmatched at any American university."[4]

Before I leave this question of who were "the right stuff" and where they came from, I must admit to an obvious omission: the chaps and the lads and the young men who would drop from the night sky while conjugating their French verbs did not, by definition, include women. These collegiate institutions were all male, and the OSS was very heavily so: male, and for the most part, rather Waspish, though there was room for a good number of Jews, especially from western Europe, who formed part of the intellectual core of, in particular, R&A, as demonstrated by Barry Katz in his study of Franz Neumann, Herbert Marcuse, Otto Kirchheimer, Leonard Krieger, Felix Gilbert, and others.[5]

Though the OSS wanted the best and the brightest, it was slow to see women as belonging to these ranks. I have interviewed dozens of women who worked for the OSS and hope to interview far more; most told me of professional frustrations and sexual harassment. That was then and this is now, someone may rightly remark; one would not expect a new government agency to depart far from the cultural norms of the time. Many women with doctorates, some former professors and even departmental heads, found themselves working for far younger men who lacked advanced degrees. Some 700 women worked in the OSS overseas; a few rose to relatively high positions, as head of R&A, Ceylon (where the presence of 56 women made for the largest Far Eastern group), or chief of Morale Operations (MO), Southeast Asia Command, or in Naples. One whose story I am still tracking received such high commendations from Donovan and from her recruiter that they purged her file lest her "excellent, dangerous, and significant work" were to be revealed after the war. But of the 26,000 OSS personnel and of the 4,002 college-educated women, there were overwhelming numbers of filing clerks, librarians, and secretaries. After all, when Donovan told Margaret Griggs, who was placed in charge of hiring women, to get the "right types" for COI, one definition of right type apparently was a Smith graduate from the Social Register who could pass a filing exam.

Even so, as Katherine Breaks has demonstrated in a well-argued Yale senior thesis, the OSS was not, within the context of place and time, at all regressive. Women were, at least at times, recognized to be "the right stuff" and to be delivering good information; the agency could not be characterized as progressive, and most women did not play the role of those in France, where women who worked for the OSS and with the Resistance became a substantial force in their own right. (Indeed, a French scholar, Denise Breton, has argued that they won popular support for women's suffrage this way.) Nor were they used as intensively as by the Special Operations Executive (SOE), which M.R.D. Foot shows us put 53 women (out of 500 agents) into France, but as Ms. Breaks makes clear through her research, the women of the OSS were given opportunities that, often enough, they seized with alacrity.[6] Later the Office of National Estimates (ONE), originally run by OSS alumni William Langer and Sherman Kent and established within the new CIA in 1950, continued the realities of upper-echelon research-and-evaluation groups. In 1964 the Inspector General's study of CIA recruitment noted that there were, in ONE, "no black, Jewish or woman professionals, and only a few Catholics."[6]

What then was "the right stuff"? On the whole, William Colby's description in *Honorable Men: My Life in the CIA* (New York, 1978), p. 77, still serves well, even though he was writing of the agency in 1950. Intelligence work was viewed as glamorous, fashionable, and patriotic; the agency was felt to be at the vanguard of a liberating American democracy intent upon protecting the free world from the Soviet Union; it was filled with "politically liberal young men and women from the finest Ivy League campuses and the most impeccable social and establishment backgrounds." These words would not all be taken as praise today, nor do I think that Colby meant them as such, but they seem reasonably accurate with some important reservations. R&A had always recruited out of the Ivy League, and—since some researchers hold that at least 80 percent of all intelligence came out of R&A, with SI and SO coming in with quantitatively as little as 5 percent—it little matters if SI and SO were less Ivy in their personnel. In any case "Ivy League" is, in fact, usually used as a blanket term for all so-called elite institutions (the Ivy League as such did not even exist at the time), including the service academies and those colleges and universities referred to as the little Ivies, the Seven Sisters, and the public Ivies.

Though numerically these expanded groups were highly significant, heads of units were often from distinctly non–Ivy League institutions. Connections might get one a job, but generally only knowledge and performance moved one up the ladder. In any case, the man at the top of that ladder was an Irish American who, though a Columbia Law School graduate and friend of FDR, had nonetheless attended Niagara College, a small Dominican institution outside Buffalo, for his first 3 years. Further, one must be careful even with presumably well-researched works lest a careless reading foster new myths. In 1987 I wrote in *Cloak and Gown: Scholars in the Secret War, 1939–1961* (New York), p. 34, that 42 members of Yale's class of 1943 "entered intelligence work," a statement I have seen translated in at least a dozen recent books and articles into the flat assertion that they all went into the OSS, even though I thought I had made it clear that there were many other forms of intelligence work at the time.

Finally, "the right stuff"—a phrase redolent of class distinctions and likely thereby to embrace such figures as Philby, Burgess, and Blunt when one is speaking of the British—must also embrace loyalty. American fascination with the Cambridge spies arises, in part, I am sure, from our puzzlement over how men from such backgrounds could betray their country. There is the added fascination (and for many, the partial exoneration) arising from the fact that these men committed treason for reasons of conscience. This seems right, some argue, when set against the tawdry American traitors who sold their country's secrets merely so they might buy a better car or a bigger boat. But my definition of "the right stuff" requires a sense of loyalty, a sense that should not be confused by the notion that it is better to betray one's country than betray one's friends. When one betrays one's country, one does betray one's friends.

What of our second meaning of "the right stuff"? Once again some words of background will help us. Our two definitions of "right stuff" are not easily separable.

The OSS was an American equivalent of four, or more, British organizations that operated during World War II. I speak of MI6 (or SIS) (the Secret Intelligence Service), SOE, PWE (the Political Warfare Executive), and the Foreign Office's Research Department. Further, it is well known that the British tended to think that quite different types of people were needed for each of these organizations, not to speak of MI5, which was responsible for internal security.

Most histories of the OSS—certainly those of R. Harris Smith and Bradley F. Smith—make it clear that Donovan's organization was huge, incoherent, and divisive. Put into a comparative context, however, the various branches of the OSS appear a veritable dovecote of harmony compared to the way in which British intelligence organizations carped at one another. If one reads Donovan's papers at Carlisle, one comes away with the conviction that most of all he wanted good men (and some women), and he wanted them quickly. Any theories of social standing or of educational background, which might with hindsight be thought to compose his definition of "the right stuff" to get "the right stuff," must be weighed against his impatience and desire for instant action. Haste seems, at least on the Donovan record, to have been the driving force toward recruiting from a small number of institutions.

There was another notion at work, one much remarked upon and debated in the literature of intelligence, and this was the thought that the OSS would have to lean on the British, at least in its initial phases. Certainly the British thought this, and it was not unreasonable that FDR did so as well, though it is not clear whether he and Donovan thought the reliance would be on British expertise or simply on the ties of friendship built up by Donovan's journey to Britain in 1940 as FDR's personal envoy, the warm greeting he was given by Churchill and others, and Donovan's declaration that Britain would survive the great air battle (while the U.S. Ambassador was predicting the opposite). Donovan had also made a good impression on the British during a second trip, early in 1941, to the Middle East and the Balkans, where—despite some political naivete and some social gaucheness, much remarked upon later by those who would wish to diminish his accomplishments, but who miss the real point of his mission—he also sang the praises of the British and assured anyone who would listen that Britain would not only survive but would remain a major player in the respective regions after the war. One suspects, then, that the expected ties with the British were meant to be more familial than operational and that the British at least assumed that their analysis would be the more sophisticated one—that is, that they would be producing most of "the right stuff."

Of course, we also know that any notions about an unquestioning Anglo-American harmony on the intelligence front that may have prevailed in 1940 and 1941 were much weakened by 1943, the year of the OSS's proportionately greatest growth, so that one may assume that finding someone who would mix with ease with the British was no longer so important. When Yale's Professor Norman Holmes Pearson was recruited in 1941, he was sent to London because his recruiter was under the misapprehension that Pearson had been a Rhodes Scholar and that this would go down well with the British. Nonetheless, Pearson knew "the right stuff" when he saw it; his briefings were legendary. His recognition of "the wrong stuff" in Kim Philby was astute, and though in X-2, he wrote fine analyses when asked to do so. That Pearson did get along famously had relatively little to do with his Yale background, however, and nearly everything to do with his fascination with the British literati, his knowledge of the arts and letters, and his willingness to foray out into the darkened streets of London when the city was under attack by buzz bombs in search of the very culture that the British upper class thought the war was being waged to save. He might well have acquired his interest in British poets, in Hilda Doolittle and Bryher and T. S. Eliot, had he been a student at Illinois, but then the British would have dismissed him as a climber, an intellectual parvenu, rather than one to "The Wasteland" born. The Americans were not unsophisticated in their understanding of how to play on British snobbery.

As historian Elisabeth Barker has remarked, after the OSS and SOE carved up the world in June of 1942, relations ought to have gotten better, but instead they grew worse.[7] While British saw the OSS as filled with raw types who might function reasonably well in western Europe, they were intent upon retaining control in the Middle East and the Balkans (that is to say, upon the flanks of their empire), and they felt any Americans of ethnic descent from these areas who were allowed to meddle in intelligence matters were likely to have a decidedly non-British agenda. In this they no doubt were correct.

The Americans considered the British to be entirely too set in their ways, and increasingly they were recruiting individuals who did have non-British agendas of their own. By 1943, when the British began to shift from Mihailovic in Yugoslavia to Tito, Donovan was one such himself. Donovan sent out an independent mission to Turkey without informing the British and began his own effort to push Bulgaria out of the war. Soon Donovan was refusing to share with the British information gained from his Hungarian contacts through Istanbul. Further, once Stalin got wind of Allen Dulles's exploration of a separate peace in northern Italy, he began to doubt the value of the intelligence information being supplied to him from the West.

This means that three powerful factors were at work redefining "the right stuff." First, as American policy began to deviate from British, as Churchill reminded Americans that he had not been chosen as His Majesty's first minister in order to preside over the dissolution of the British Empire, and as attitudes toward the British became substantially and visibly less respectful, "the right stuff" began increasingly to mean data and conclusions that differed from the British. Second, as the military exerted more authority within and over the OSS, short-range military needs began to crowd out long-range and more contemplative studies. Third, as it became increasingly apparent that the Soviet Union was highly likely to pose a threat in postwar Europe, "the right stuff" came to be less about generic and quasi-academic inquiries into the nature of Pacific Island social structures and more about the capabilities and intentions of Joseph Stalin. Just as there is a real past and a past of the intellect, a construction, there is real intelligence, which focuses even-handedly upon all, since a friend today may be a foe tomorrow, and there is the intelligence of political and ideological demand.

Several writers have suggested that Donovan, attracted more to the derring-do of the branches, lost interest in R&A, but it does not follow that he lost interest in the product or that he thought that product unimportant. He, like the lay public, found tales of sabotage more interesting than analyses of steel production. It would be a mistake to conclude that he turned his back on R&A—he could, after all, afford to be relaxed about R&A, for he knew it was in good hands—or that R&A did not contribute significantly to policy, especially in postwar planning. We simply do not know.

We do know that these "most distinguished scholars" who were recruited were not the most distinguished at the time—they were too young—but one may reasonably believe that their experience in the OSS helped make them so.

This is, perhaps, the place to rehearse the idealized definition of good intelligence, of "the right stuff," and of how to get to it. Intelligence is analyzed information, that is, it is both the body of evidence and the conclusions to be drawn from that evidence. But most customers are more interested in the conclusions than in the evidence itself, so that the end product seldom reveals the process by which the conclusions have been reached. In theory the path to those conclusions is rigorous, schematic, and clear. One first seeks out the information needed to respond to a question. Herein lies a problem, of course, since the customer must know how to ask good questions and must be patient enough to allow for searching out data that, though potentially relevant, may prove quite irrelevant. One may not prejudge the answer to the question by prejudging the data. But human nature being what it is, the persons responsible for seeking the data—whether, as most often was the case in World War II, by reading thousands of index cards and hundreds of reels of microfilm and culling through old newspapers, trade magazines, or intercepts or—less often— by risking one's life to go into the field and observe troop movements or sleep with a general—must not be the persons who verify the accuracy of that data, for risk and eyestrain may combine to make those persons want the data to be true. In the ideal schema, others test and verify the data under the pressure of a deadline but nonetheless with adequate time to carry out the most essential cross-checks. This second group of individuals, however, must not be the persons who decide what the data actually mean, for having devoted much time to them, these persons will want the data to mean something, and they may mean nothing.

A third group turns to analysis of meaning as distinct from analysis of credibility. This group produces what the lay public might regard as conclusions, a confusion similar to the one arising from mistaking a history textbook for history. In any case, those who tell the consumer what the information, now intelligence, actually means must not be the same persons who decide what to do with the information, since the information will, once again, as at each previous stage, have been contaminated by human desire: that is, those who believe they know what the information means may wish for a particular action to result from their hard work, when the best action might well be no action at all. Thus, another group, those who make policy, will determine what to do with all this "right stuff." Finally, this last group must not be tainted by partisan political considerations, must not tell the consumer what the consumer wants to hear but instead what the process has yielded, as contrary to political hopes as that may be. It follows, of course, that the director of an intelligence agency must never be a personal friend of the President of the United States unless that director has superhuman self-discipline and no political ambitions at all.

Thus goes the theory. Experienced professionals will consider stating it in these terms to be an academic waste of time, since all well know that the theory, sound as it may be, cannot be put into invariable practice. One cannot always wait for four quite different teams to deal with a body of data to prevent its contamination by human ambition. Seldom do the inquiries that matter most allow time to seek out all the relevant data, and one can never know that all data are in hand. However much integrity a director may have, policy will turn upon political realities, budgetary realities, time-constraint realities, and on the quality of the information and the quality of those analyzing it. Intelligence theory is one thing; intelligence practice is quite another. Though theory may well describe a goal to strive for devoutly, that goal will almost never be attained. The problem with the analogy so often drawn between the work of the academic scholar and the intelligence professional is that the latter has an impatient and hungry customer awaiting the product while the academic is fortunate indeed if anyone cares about the product enough to even read it, not to speak of acting upon it.

Thus, "the right stuff," when we speak of the right information, differs from consumer to consumer, from place to place, time to time, task to task. Donovan quite rightly said that the activities of the OSS were an "adjunct to military strategy." This meant two things at the least: that his intelligence agency ought not itself to engage in military affairs, and that it should both gather reliable information and plant unreliable stories and rumors that would do damage to the enemy. From this tension—the need to establish the reliability of that which was coming in while twisting to propaganda purposes that which went out was to an extent far beyond the relatively benign operations of the Office of War Information—arose the classic schizophrenia of the OSS. Disinformation was not mere mud slinging, of course: Roosevelt and Donovan were both appalled when the OWI allowed a commentator to refer to Victor Emmanuel of Italy as a "moronic little king"—this most decidedly was not "the right stuff." Roosevelt had a good notion of what he wanted, though he had little time to be specific, much less theoretical—at one meeting with the Assistant Director of the Budget in the summer of 1942, the President had to deal with rubber conservation, gasoline rationing, the construction of the St. Lawrence Seaway, rehabilitation legislation, the future of overseas air transport, the merger of domestic communication systems, and training personnel for postwar overseas military governments of occupation, as well as with the OSS—and he left it to Donovan to define intelligence in operational terms. Nor did it bother FDR that he might, as consumer, receive three or more operational definitions of "the right stuff," since the FBI was in charge of domestic counterintelligence, and despite Donovan's protests, South America continued for most purposes to be under Nelson Rockefeller, the Coordinator of Inter-American Affairs.[8]

And so "the right stuff" became what Donovan said it was, what the bad eyes brigade in R&A deemed it to be, and increasingly what the primary consumer, the Joint Chiefs of Staff, said they found it to be.

One problem with intelligence history is that we cannot truly know the precise sequence of cause and effect, get at an unvarnished story, or rely upon the available documentation without extraordinary efforts that go well beyond normal historical inquiry. One need not rehearse the obvious problems: sources that have been destroyed, surviving sources that were intended to mislead, potential informants bound by law or their own convictions to silence, the risk that the apparently cooperative interviewee is running one along false trails, both official and deliberate and unofficial and inadvertent contamination of evidence, the temptations to embellish or enhance the story, and an elongated period of government closure. All these problems occur with any historical subject, of course, but with intelligence history, they occur in spades.

Beyond these standard source problems is a far greater problem. Recently the diplomatic historian John Lewis Gaddis, commenting on "Intelligence, Espionage, and Cold War Origins" (*Diplomatic History* XIII [Spring 1989]: 191–212), noted five areas of intelligence history requiring far closer examination than they have so far received. One of these areas is the pursuit of the historians' damaging "So What?" questions: What difference did it make, to cite three tidbits of information from the wartime OSS files, that Hitler most likely had only one testicle, that Sicilians were still using 16th-century vulgarism, or that the dimensions of narrow-gauge railway tracks were not the same in all parts of the British Empire. One may easily imagine replies to the second and third "So Whats?": Certainly an agent attempting to operate as a Sicilian had best get the local vulgarities right; certainly an invading force that intended to capture and use a local narrow-gauge line had better know whether equipment liberated in one former colony could be employed in another. But beyond such obvious practicalities, can it be *proved* that an intelligence operation contributed in any significant way to a military victory? Can one conceivably quantify the extent of that contribution? May one draw the historian's customary distinction between "proximate," "necessary," and "sufficient" causation? Can we even demonstrate that a government's actions were taken on the basis of information it had (or did not have) when, especially with the advance of satellite surveillance, one knows that far more data are gathered in than can be productively analyzed? In short, how does an intelligence historian demonstrate that "the right stuff" was obtained? was recognized to be "the right stuff"? that "the right stuff" survived the scrutiny of the skeptics, of those who viewed it as a plant, or of those who thought it insignificant though accurate? How does one then unequivocally show that this "right stuff" moved through channels to the most appropriate consumer and then resulted in what, with historians' hindsight, might be viewed as the right decisions? In truth, we cannot, or at least not very often, apply the usual canons of certitude, thereby opening the door to much speculative, romanticized, and essentially anecdotal history (or contrarily, to yet another study of organizational charts and bureaucratic management, political science, or civics often operating in the guise of history), and thus to history that tends to discredit the field and discourage further research.

To be sure, there are exceptions to this cautionary tale. We know that ULTRA made a difference and that military histories of World War II, and especially of 1944 and 1945, written without knowledge of the work done at Bletchley may well need serious revision. We do not know, however, *what* difference ULTRA made. We certainly know that the French Resistance produced valuable intelligence information, though we know far less well how that information was used. We know that early R&A reports—especially the first reports ground out under the heaviest of pressures and the closest of deadlines by Langer and Kent's R&A team in preparation for Operation Torch—were praised and applied, though even with this example the only result we can document was that a jubilant Donovan was able to justify R&A's methodology to effect a substantial budget increase.

Indeed, those who are intensely skeptical about the value of intelligence organizations argue that we can never know whether the vast expenses are worthwhile, and intelligence professionals often feed this skepticism by pointing out (rightly, but not helpfully) that the public (in which include the out-of-house historian) will never know of the fully successful operation. True, in-house historians such as Sherman Kent, who helped launch the in-house journal, *Studies in Intelligence*, have demonstrated that most information a democratic society seeks to classify and keep as secret may, with the application of the research methods of a good graduate student and access to a major university library, be ferreted out. Tom Clancy's novels have shown this very nicely. If, as Kent (and the British historian A.J.P. Taylor) have argued, "of the things our state must know about other states some 90 percent may be discovered through overt means"—a figure Kent later raised to 95 percent—one may reasonably ask about the nature of "the right stuff," gathered at great expense and some risk, that composes the other 5 to 10 percent. An intelligence professional will, most likely, reply that this residue is key to having the advantage over a real or potential enemy and that it is worth the candle, but since it is precisely this residue of information that is routinely denied to the historian and yet precisely this residue that must be examined in order to know whether "the right stuff" was caught in the net, one has great difficulties in meeting a "proof of effectiveness" test.

What do the official histories tell us? Arthur B. Darling's early in-house history of the CIA to 1950, now freely available, is a useful if sanitized administrative history that makes no attempt to deal with issues of effectiveness.[9] With one exception, the generally unpublished branch histories, some of them remarkably frank (especially on personnel) in their unrevised forms, provide little data by which one might judge the "rightness" of the "stuff." The articles that have appeared in *Studies in Intelligence* come rather closer to meeting the historian's needs, but they often seem strained. A summary document that rests in the National Archives, with the limiting and somewhat dry title "Certain Accomplishments of the Office of Strategic Services," prepared at a time when the OSS was seeking to justify itself and thus further the possibilities of its postwar survival, is decidedly guarded and (let us admit it) unconvincing. That, for example, Africa-SI, by agreement with X-2, was able to identify 85 members of a German and Italian support organization in Lourenço Marques or that SI was instrumental in having 12 Germans and Italians expelled from Mozambique is most likely true and is certainly interesting, but we have no way of knowing—despite excellent research by Douglas Wheeler on intelligence matters in Portugal and its colonies—how significant this was.[10]

Despite the picture that emerges from Anthony Cave Brown's *The Last Hero: Wild Bill Donovan* (New York, 1982), with its frequent implications that Donovan inflated his agency's role, I think there is good evidence to the contrary. To be sure, Donovan tried to orchestrate a flow of favorable public information about the more romantic side of OSS work, with articles in *Life*, the *Saturday Evening Post*, and elsewhere, on the importance of spies, especially when the Joint Chiefs and Congress had revealed their intention to terminate the OSS, but when he was not dealing with an eager public, he was at least as circumspect about inflated claims as any other head of an agency in the Roosevelt-to-Truman transition period. Consider, by way of example, the penciled notes he attached to Conyers Read's draft history of SO. Read was a distinguished historian of Elizabethan Britain, a professor at the University of Pennsylvania, and a teacher of historical research methods, and his in-house history was, on the face of it, relatively restrained. Still, Donovan penciled in so many corrections and qualifications, they required eight pages of type simply to list. When, for instance, Read wrote that M. Preston Goodfellow, head of SO, assumed personal responsibility for "several million dollars worth of materiel," Donovan commented that the claim was "ridiculous," and when Read gave the OSS credit for inventing various plastic devices for dirty tricks, Donovan noted that the British had already done this and the OSS merely pushed things along. Read concluded that the "Tolstoy" mission was valuable as a reconnaissance of Tibet, and Donovan said that "on the contrary there was no immediate practical value" to the mission. Where Read loosely wrote that SOE worked "under" American command in North Africa, Donovan changed the language to "in collaboration with," and again, as Read rhapsodized over booby traps, limpets, knockout drops, and the like, Donovan noted that the OSS must not "act as if we originated this." In sum, Donovan appears to have been intent upon preventing inflation of the in-house official record and to have understood that, at the bottom line, "the right stuff" must always prove to be the true stuff.[11]

Still, it is evident that a good bit of "the right stuff" did come from agencies other than ULTRA. The invasion of North Africa was, surely, eased by the R&A report for Operation Torch and by information collected in the field on hostile Vichyite forces. Surely the existence of an OSS source in Corsica during the nearly 4 weeks the Germans held out there made some difference. Presumably the existence of an OSS unit hidden in Rome during the assault on Anzio was important. How important remains the historian's question.

On the whole one learns more about the OSS's "right stuff," in that one gains an understanding of how non-OSS individuals felt about the centrality of OSS operations to the war effort, through reading between the lines in Thomas F. Troy's carefully studied history of the establishment of the CIA, *Donovan and the CIA* (Frederick, MD, 1981), than in most more widely angled books. There are any number of stories in Anthony Cave Brown's *The Last Hero* that suggest that the OSS, or some specific branch of it, did or did not get "the right stuff." Without fuller study, fuller access, and fuller understanding, we are likely for some time to have to conclude that the probabilities are that, in a given operation or out of a given station and within a given time frame, the OSS most definitely gathered what a post-action evaluation would regard as "the right stuff," and in another given operation, station, or time, it did not. Too often the right answer to the question "So What?" is that we do not know.

History is, in the long run, the history of what people believed to be true rather than what the professional historian's laborious research may have shown the truth to have been, for people are motivated by what they believe to be true, not by the truth the researcher discovers long after. In this sense all of history is the study of thought, even when that thought is confused and ill informed, even dead wrong. Thus, if people believed in the 1940s that "the right stuff" came from the Ivy League or consisted of crateology—using the dimensions of crates shipped on Axis rail lines or aboard vessels to estimate the nature of the shipment—then that is the case, and Monday morning quarterbacking, while important and interesting and certainly instructive on how to improve intelligence, is in some measure irrelevant to understanding actions and their motivations at R&A or in SO or SI in 1944 or 1945.

But the real strength of our question, "So What?," and of the assumption that we might learn for the present from the past, cannot be swept completely aside by the truism that what people believed to be true was what most mattered. I conclude, therefore, with a brief moment of reflection on the question: Are we getting "the right stuff" *now*? Whether we obtained the right information in a timely fashion and analyzed it in a productive way during the Persian Gulf war—a subject of much journalistic discussion—is not for the historian to judge, for the question is too recent and at base too tendentious for analysis just now. No doubt in due course we will have some reasonably solid answers (the gist of which will be "Sometimes") but we cannot know this yet. So my reflections are limited to the question: Are we getting "the right stuff" now in the sense of getting the right people to analyze the right information?

Broadly I would say the answer is clearly no. This unhappy conclusion arises from four interlocking conditions.

First, academia by and large no longer cooperates with the intelligence community. Those who know little of university life, having long been separated from it, may ascribe this to the notion of "political correctness," the idea that an abusive political left holds sway upon our campuses. This is, in my view, true of only a tiny number of institutions and, by and large, not of institutions from which intelligence agencies are likely to recruit. Rather, the separation of intelligence from academic life began at some point during the revelations about the Bay of Pigs and accelerated, as might be expected, during the period of campus unrest in the midst of the Vietnam war. There is an order from President Nixon that instructed the Central Intelligence Agency not to recruit from Ivy League institutions (to which Stanford was added as an honorary member), since they were, the President thought, the primary fomenters of discontent, and to focus more on the great middle western universities, the sectarian colleges, and California, excluding Palo Alto. Some believe this directive to be fraudulent, and in the form circulated quite possibly it is, but the spirit of the directive, however worded, is undoubtedly a correct statement of the President's point of view. Conformity was, naturally enough, the result; there were enough prescient people inside the CIA who were quietly questioning the wisdom of the war, and one hardly wanted to recruit more who would tip the balance. Thus the agency cut itself off from the campuses precisely at the moment when university administrators were happy to be freed of yet one more destabilizing influence which, after all, they could not count upon to behave any more than the students could be counted upon to tug their forelocks in the future. The fault was mutual, though each side to the broken symbiotic relationship blamed the other.

Second, academia lost its interest in being helpful to the intelligence community at the point when it had become all too apparent that the covert actions tail was wagging the intelligence dog. Academics believed in research and analysis, in an intelligence agency that sought out "the right stuff" and delivered the goods (which is to say, delivered national estimates and daily briefing papers untainted by partisan party political urgencies). They also concluded that the agency was no longer getting or delivering "the right stuff." Further, they believed that an intelligence agency was essentially an educational institution and that paramilitary covert operations contaminated the entire agency. (I believe that there might be some hope of healing this breach if such operations, to the extent that they can be legitimized, were run exclusively from the Department of Defense.) Believing this, academics washed their hands of the various agencies, and while some continued contract work, the great majority simply backed away. A convenient date, certainly an intellectually convincing one, for this backing away is September 1973, when the presumably elitist Office of National Estimates, to which academics could relate, ceased to function.

Third, increasingly apprehensive about academics or individuals recommended by academics or even individuals recruited from the type of institution that would permit open and violent protesting of war, the intelligence agencies began to make their recruiting, screening, clearance processes so convoluted that one might read the whole 10 volumes of the original Proust while awaiting an answer to a simple question. Clearance time crept upward to 18 months, and even 2 years was not unknown. But no young person who is able, eager, and curious is willing to sit out such a long bureaucratic delay. The agency was attempting to recruit within a high demand group, the members of which could go off to law school, medical school, the Peace Corps, or the Department of State in the time the agency was still trying to find out if a student ever smoked a joint. Even if the potential recruit remained faithful to the idea of serving his or her country, the agency could not make clear what the prospective assignment would be. Those who remained constant through all this silliness were least likely to question, to shout "Enough already"; they were also most likely to have ideological reasons for wanting to work in intelligence or not to have the same range of options. And people with ideological convictions are, by definition, incompetent in research and analysis more often than competent.

Fourth, the agency began to recruit the people who badly wanted to join up. Anecdotally, I admit to having suggested to some young men and women at Yale that they at least consider intelligence work. These were the students of steady mind, clear-eyed about society and their place in it, with excellent academic records, superlative research skills, well spoken, skillful when writing, observant and quiet when appropriate, yet always ready to ask me, in seminar, "Yes, but so what—sir?" And I noticed that nearly all applied and not one entered. Some few came back to tell me they had found the process curious, stupid, degrading, or simply off-putting, and perhaps the agency intended this to remove arrogant candidates. It is my belief that if so, the agency also removed the self-assured, the confident, the questioning, and the adventurous—precisely the qualities that had been so attractive to the OSS—in the process.[13]

Of course, the people with whom I spoke tended to be in disciplines that would have attracted them to HUMINT,* and the agency was tilting ever more toward SIGINT,** in part because it is the nature of our society to spend its money on bigger and better toys, in part because one could sell a reluctant Congress on satellites where one could not, apparently, sell it on training programs in Farsi, and in part because a new symbiosis was developing with those disciplines and institutions strong in computer science and mathematics and (dare I say it) a little weak in social concerns. Recruiting has turned, then, toward disciplines that tend to be attractive to those who are less likely to ask "So What?" and more likely to deliver a good computer program. The result was an unparalleled technical capacity to eavesdrop on conversations in Red Square or, if we so chose, in a village outside Madras, where one day Rajiv Gandhi would meet his end.

---

*Human intelligence.
**Signals (or electronic) intelligence.

But unless I am badly misinformed, such eavesdropping would do us little good, since we have, neither in the CIA or in the State Department, a single full-time employee who speaks the full range of languages of southern India. Too bad for those humanities and history students who once filled the ranks of the OSS and, reasonably often and reasonably well, delivered "the right stuff"; they appear not to be wanted any longer.

There is also the plain silliness that envelops even—or perhaps most of all—professionals. Recently a former student of mine applied for intelligence work and all went swimmingly until the polygraph test. This she "failed," at the hands of some markedly unreflective males who apparently gave no thought to gender issues or to how a person leaving the soft cushion of an excellent job to venture into the unknown might react with some small show of emotion while being fluttered. Failing once, she took the test a second time, for there was one question on which (quite wrongly, to my almost certain knowledge) these flutterers concluded that the candidate was lying.[14] On the second occasion they expressed anger and dismay that she had, shortly before coming in, taken two Advil for a sore knee. "What is the trouble with you?" they shouted. "You took two Advil the last time, too."

Well, I hope we are getting "the right stuff," but it will not be through this process or by way of recommendations from friendly critics such as myself, for I will not submit any students of mine to such "wrong stuff" in the future. Of course, I would never survive the polygraph either: I react emotionally to certain questions, and in any case, I took two Advil this morning myself.

NOTES

1. Leo D. Carl, *International Dictionary of Intelligence* (McLean, VA, 1990), p. 346.
2. Yale University Library Archives, Sherman Kent Papers: ms. autobiography. Edited by Tony Arnold, the memoir is soon to be published as *The Reminiscences of Sherman Kent*, with an introduction by the present writer.
3. Donald Downes Papers, in the author's possession pending transfer to the World War II Collection, Yale University Library.
4. These comments are drawn from Andrew P. Tobias, Arnold L. Bartz, and Caspar W. Weinberger, Jr., *The Ivy League Guidebook* (New York, 1969), pp. 99ff.
5. Barry M. Katz, *Foreign Intelligence: Research and Analysis in the Office of Strategic Services, 1942–1945* (Cambridge, MA, 1989).
6. Denise Breton, *Les Femmes dans la resistance* (Paris, 1977), p. 229, as cited in Katherine Breaks, "The Ladies of the OSS: The Apron Strings of Intelligence in World War II," B.A. thesis, Yale University, 1991, p. 460. Foot's figure appears in his *SOE in France: An Account of the Work of the British Special Operations Executive in France, 1940–1944* (London, 1966), pp. 465–469.
7. Barker, *British Policy in South-East Europe in the Second World War* (London, 1976), p. 119.

8. See John Morton Blum, *V was for Victory: Politics and American Culture during World War II* (New York, 1976), p. 34; James MacGregor Burns, *Roosevelt: The Soldier of Freedom* (New York, 1970), p. 383; and Frank Freidel, *Franklin D. Roosevelt: A Rendezvous with Destiny* (Boston, 1990), p. 436.

9. Arthur B. Darling, *The Central Intelligence Agency: An Instrument of Government to 1950* (University Park, PA, 1990).

10. See "Certain Accomplishments of the Office of Strategic Services," in Branch Histories, Records of the Office of Strategic Services (RG 226), National Archives.

11. See Wayne Nelson to Files, Dec. 18, 1946, attached to Read's Branch History of SO, Folder 58, Box 76, Entry 99, RG 226, National Archives.

12. On the demise of ONE, see Lawrence Freedman, *U.S. Intelligence and the Soviet Strategic Threat* (Boulder, CO, 1977), pp. 31–54.

13. On the earlier principles of recruiting, as described in this paper, consult Allen Dulles, *The Craft of Intelligence* (New York, 1962); and H.H.A. Cooper and Lawrence J. Redlinger, "Finding the Right Stuff," in *Making Spies: A Spotter's Handbook* (Boulder, CO, 1986), for some observations that are, to my mind, frequently wrong. Tim Heald's *Old Boy Networks* (New York, 1984) is useful here. The classic formulation of the WASP stereotype is analyzed in E. Digby Baltzell, *The Protestant Establishment: Aristocracy & Caste in America* (New York, 1964). While some social historians have suggested that Baltzell first formulated the term WASP in this book, many of us can recall usage of the term in the 1950s.

14. I am aware that the CIA does not rely solely on polygraph tests when recruiting and that such tests are generally not admitted as legal evidence in a court of law. After I spoke, a person who is very familiar with polygraph results declared that no candidate would be rejected on such evidence alone. I trust that this is so. In the instance to which I refer, the candidate was, nonetheless, told that failure to pass the polygraph test was the reason for rejection.

THE OSS: FROM HOME AND ABROAD

Donovan valued the importance of the collection of information from both domestic and foreign sources and the evaluation of that information. The Research and Analysis Branch was an essential part of that effort. Over time the R&A staff grew domestically and eventually established offices overseas. Professor Barry Katz has studied the R&A organization carefully, and during the second session of the conference on Thursday, July 11, he presented an overview of its creation, growth, leadership, and accomplishments. As Katz noted, Donovan and the successive heads of the R&A Branch worked hard to pluck the almost 900 people needed to discover and analyze strategic information needed by the United States.

London was the largest overseas station of the OSS and was responsible for many field operations. During the war, the young economist Walt W. Rostow joined the OSS and was sent to London to join the Enemy Objectives Unit (EOU). This small but select unit was staffed to evaluate and prioritize German targets for Allied bombing missions. Rostow's recollections of his experiences are acute, and his careful assessment of what a dedicated group can accomplish when working together came through forcefully in this presentation. The second speaker, Arthur M. Schlesinger, Jr., joined the London R&A operation in 1944, just weeks after the Normandy invasion, where, as he recalls, he was greeted in London by the German V-1 attacks and its sinister buzz overhead. His main task was editing the *European Political Report*, a classified weekly report of "irrelevance to immediate military needs" but valuable in assessing the role of European resistance movements. His recollections and asides on leading personalities provided the conference audience valuable additions to the documents of the London R&A.

The third presenter on intelligence activity in London is Sir Robin Brook, who had a major role in the direction of the Special Operations Executive

(SOE) in Western Europe. Brook explained that SOE was a wartime organization that adapted to the needs of economic and military warfare. The speaker explained that through clandestine operations, agents and small teams were flown into occupied areas and worked with the resistance groups or created small networks known as "reseaux." Brook made clear to the audience that in the merger of SOE and the OSS in late 1942, the "newcomers" started as deputies. Three-person special teams, called Jedburghs, usually included an OSS agent. Some met death upon landing, while others provided effective assistance to resistance groups.

Harold A. Deutsch, a prominent historian who held several positions in the Research and Analysis Branch, also did duty in London. As chair of the Thursday afternoon plenary session, Professor Deutsch introduced the four distinguished speakers and provided commentary at the end of the session. Deutsch challenged the audience to think about "what if this or that" had happened during the course of the war. He urged students of World War II to at least consider such questions in their research and writing.

THE OSS AND THE DEVELOPMENT OF THE RESEARCH AND ANALYSIS BRANCH

Barry M. Katz

The Office of Strategic Services (OSS) produced more than its share of drama and intrigue: intrepid agents dropped from the sky behind enemy lines, paddled ashore in rubber dinghies, and secreted away the famous OSS L tablet in the event of capture. An oft-quoted quip of Gen. William J. Donovan places these exploits in perspective, however: "We did not rely on the 'seductive blonde' or the 'phoney moustache'," he remarked after the war. "The major part of our intelligence was the result of good old-fashioned intellectual sweat."[1] Out of this concept grew the Research and Analysis Branch (R&A).

Donovan's belief in the intellectual core of modern intelligence work commanded his attention even before he was named to the position of Coordinator of Information (COI) in July 1941. In June of that year he reported to the President on a lengthy tour of the Mediterranean in a "Memorandum of Establishment of Service of Strategic Information." Whether or not the United States was drawn militarily into the war, it seemed clear that a running evaluation of the American strategic situation was vital, and Donovan urged that a corps of "carefully selected trained minds," with knowledge of languages and research techniques, be assembled in Washington for this purpose.[2]

The United States, it will be recalled, alone among the great powers, had approached the war with no single, centralized agency responsible for the collection, interpretation, and dissemination throughout the government of information bearing upon national security. With virtually no usable precedent before him, Donovan had to raise virtually from scratch an army of analysts possessed of the expertise that would enable them to operate at the same level of professionalism as the services of Britain, Nazi Germany, and the U.S.S.R. Perhaps his single greatest innovation was to recognize that this pool of talent existed, ready-made, as it were, within the nation's colleges, universities, and research institutes.

In contrast to the operational branches of Donovan's organization, which were empowered to seek out information from clandestine sources, the theory behind the Research and Analysis Branch was that in modern warfare, reliable estimates of the enemy's capabilities were of greater value than knowledge of the enemy's plans. Intelligence of this sort, moreover, was more likely to be buried in trade journals, technical reports, local newspapers, encyclopedia articles, and textbooks than in spools of microfilm hidden in the heel of an enemy agent's shoe. To ferret out such published information and to assemble it into a coherent and meaningful picture, however, required specialized training that could hardly be provided under the emergency conditions of war.

Faced with this situation, Donovan's first act was to summon to Washington James Phinney Baxter, president of Williams College and an authority on modern diplomatic history. Baxter and his successor, William L. Langer of Harvard, consulted widely within the academic community. A mounting sense of urgency, the abominable nature of the Nazi regime, and the opportunity to contribute to the impending war effort on the basis of their academic skills, not in spite of them, provided a sufficient lure. Before the end of its first year, by which time the COI had evolved into the wartime OSS, R&A had come to house a community of scholars of unparalleled distinction. By the end of the war, R&A had grown into a professional corps of some 900 scholars, respected for their intellectual credentials and for the creativity with which they applied the methods of modern scholarship to the discovery and analysis of data.

During his 4-year tenure as Chief of R&A, Langer directed his recruiting efforts in three directions. Although his mandate was viewed with some suspicion by officials in Washington, the eastern academic establishment proved responsive to his call. From Harvard, Langer drew upon such distinguished colleagues as economist Edward S. Mason and historian Crane Brinton; the military historian Edward Mead Earle joined them from Princeton's Institute for Advanced Study; Yale contributed Sherman Kent, who would build the sprawling Europe-Africa Division of R&A; and Columbia released its pioneering Sovietologist Geroid T. Robinson.

The senior academicians of the branch in turn appealed to their own students, assistants, and proteges in a second recruiting drive, which netted an extraordinary pool of younger talent: Carl E. Schorske, H. Stuart Hughes, Leonard Krieger, Gordon Craig, Arthur Schlesinger, Jr., and Franklin Ford were among the 40 professional historians who collectively would redirect the course of postwar historiography; a generation of aggressive young economists, including Walt W. Rostow, Moses Abramowitz, Carl Kaysen, Sidney Alexander, and Paul Sweezy, began what would become distinguished careers in the Economics Subdivision; sociologists Edward Shils, Morris Janowitz, and Barrington Moore joined the effort, along with a host of others whose names are familiar within their disciplines and beyond. Altogether at least seven future presidents of the American Historical Association, five future presidents of the American Economic Association, and two Nobel Laureates would lend their specialized skills to the wartime tasks of research and analysis.

In the spring of 1943, by which time the tide had begun to turn in favor of the Allies, R&A began a third recruiting drive of a sort unprecedented either in war or peace. Recognizing that the refugee community in America offered a unique pool of linguistic fluency, regional expertise, and sensitivity to cultural and political nuance, R&A began to identify scholars who had been driven into American exile by the Fascist regimes. More interested in intellectual acumen than political conformity, the Central European Section hired Marxist theorists Franz Neumann, Herbert Marcuse, and Otto Kirchheimer. Felix Gilbert and Hajo Holborn, heirs to the Meinecke tradition of intellectual historiography, joined the branch, and future Nobel Laureate Wassily Leontief, petroleum expert Walter Levy, and the radical political economist Paul Baran helped produce estimates of German and Soviet economic capabilities.

The "faculty" assembled in R&A included prominent scholars from disciplines including anthropology, classics, economics, geography, history, linguistics, psychology, and sociology. Despite—or, perhaps, because of—the extraordinary academic qualifications of this group, the history of research and analysis within the OSS was not wholly untroubled. Internally, Langer had constantly to be alert to smoldering tensions inherited from university life. These differences arose above all from the mutual unfamiliarity of the concepts, theories, and methods of the different disciplines and from the received division of academic labor that segregated "regionalists" from "functionalists." The demands of total war, however, in which "the traditional distinctions between political, economic, and military data have become almost entirely blurred,"[3] forced the scholars of R&A into a collaborative interdisciplinary enterprise of a type never before seen in the world of scholarship.

On its external flank, the branch had to contend with the insistence, provoked in some measure by Donovan's expansive reach, that intelligence gathering and analysis must be entirely independent of the policy-making process. "There is no future in R&A as a pressure group," Langer's staff was warned. Their sole purpose was to transform raw intelligence data into concise, factual, and rigorously objective analyses for the use of appropriate government agencies and "not to suggest, recommend, or in any way determine the strategy or the tactical decisions of the war." The OSS had entered a crowded field, and R&A's only hope of exerting an influence was by winning a reputation for the objectivity, integrity, and disinterested professionalism of its work.[4]

Driven by these two imperatives—the transcendence of the conventionalized academic division of labor and the standard of strict neutrality and objectivity—R&A produced some 2,000 reports on a bewildering range of topics relating to every theater of war. The German-born theorists of the Central European Section scrutinized 40 daily newspapers for points of potential vulnerability in Axis and Axis-dominated countries; an interdisciplinary team of economists, geographers, sociologists, and literary scholars collaborated in producing remarkably accurate estimates of the capacity of the Soviet Union to absorb the German invasion; the Enemy Objectives Unit, a group of London-based economists under the command of Charles P. Kindleberger, developed a theory of strategic bombardment designed to cripple the capacity of the Germans to field a highly mechanized, fuel-dependent army.

As the war progressed, R&A units followed the advancing front and set up bases in North Africa, France, Italy, and finally in the heart of occupied Germany itself, from which analysts reported on the shifting constellation of political forces. From Washington, London, and Wiesbaden, R&A researchers prepared massive amounts of documentation pertaining to the military occupation and denazification of Germany, and for the war crimes research staff. The vast body of material prepared by scholars of the eminence of John King Fairbank, Gregory Bateson, Cora DuBois, and Charles Fahs still provides some of the most detailed documentation of the Far Eastern theaters of operation.[5]

From Washington, London, and a dozen OSS outposts overseas, R&A scholar-analysts followed the course of the war and helped to lay the foundations for the peace that would follow. In the last analysis, however, and despite an exceptionally high level of achievement under the most demanding of circumstances, political and bureaucratic forces conspired to limit the effectiveness of the branch. Feelings of frustration were widespread, clients had actively to be sought, and it was always cause for celebration within R&A when an assistant undersecretary or colonel happened across one of the reports and had a kind word to say.

If the course of the war was not dramatically altered by R&A—the "Chairborne Division," as it came to be known around Washington—neither should it be too readily assumed that its principal legacy was the institutionalization of intelligence in the postwar era. Although a number of prominent R&A veterans transferred to the Central Intelligence Agency in 1947, in reality there were as many discontinuities as continuities between the two services. R&A to some extent earned its reputation as a hotbed of academic radicalism, and the changed circumstances of the incipient cold war imparted a different and inhospitable air to what Allen Dulles called "the craft of intelligence."

Despite Donovan's pleas that the talent assembled in the branch "should not be dispersed,"[6] the scholars of R&A fled in droves back to their universities to take up unfinished manuscripts and doctoral dissertations and to apply their newfound skills to teaching and research. Indeed, it is not to the war or to the CIA that we must look for the decisive impact of the Research and Analysis Branch, but to that ultimate *de*-centralized intelligence agency, the American academic establishment. Sovietology; the Area Studies movement, a peculiarly historical and philosophical current within the economics profession; and collaborative, interdisciplinary research programs of every sort can be traced back to the wartime headquarters of the branch at 23d and E Streets NE.

Just as the Manhattan Project transformed the postwar conduct of science, virtually no field within the humanities and social sciences was unaffected by the *levée en masse* of the scholarly community. Although their impact upon the war was less explosive, in the OSS two generations of scholars learned to adapt their essentially academic skills to the practical exigencies of history. In addition, they learned there an ethic of engagement and the lesson that the responsibilities of the intellectual do not end at the door of the classroom, the library, or the archive.

NOTES

1. Quoted in Corey Ford, *Donovan of OSS* (Boston, 1970), p. 148.
2. A selection of documents pertaining to COI/OSS can be found in the appendix to Thomas F. Troy, *Donovan and the CIA: A History of the Establishment of the Central Intelligence Agency* (Frederick, MD, 1981).
3. "Functions of the Research and Analysis Branch," Folder 24, Box 2, Entry 145, Records of the Office of Strategic Services, Record Group 226, National Archives and Records Administration, Washington, DC (hereinafter cited as RG 226, NA).
4. "Draft of Proposed Guide to Preparation of Political Reports," Projects Committee Correspondence, Box 5, Entry 37, RG 226, NA.
5. For a more detailed survey of the full range of R&A activities, see Barry M. Katz, *Foreign Intelligence: Research and Analysis in the Office of Strategic Services, 1942–1945* (Cambridge, MA, 1989), and the relevant chapters in Bradley F. Smith, *The Shadow Warriors: OSS and the Origins of the CIA* (New York, 1983), and Robin W. Winks, *Cloak and Gown: Scholars in the Secret War, 1939–1961* (New York, 1987).
6. Donovan to President Roosevelt, Nov. 18, 1944, in *War Report of the OSS*, vol. 1, intro. by Kermit Roosevelt (New York, 1976), pp. 115–116 (exhibit W-43).

THE LONDON OPERATION:
Recollections of an Economist[1]

Walt W. Rostow

The Setting

My assigned title is too broad. These recollections are confined narrowly to the Enemy Objectives Unit known affectionately or otherwise as EOU. EOU was formally part of the Economic Warfare Division of the American Embassy and housed in 40 Berkeley Square. But its door was barred to all but the American Ambassador and a few designated Air Force officers. Of the 15 professionals who served in EOU at one time or another over its 32 months of active life, all were from the Office of Strategic Services (OSS) except 2 who came from the Board of Economic Warfare. (See Appendix B, "EOU Personnel.")

EOU was, in effect, the child of an Air Corps colonel named Richard D'Oyly Hughes. Hughes was a British Army officer who followed the love of his life, Frances Robertson Chase, from India's northwest frontier to St. Louis, where he married and promptly became an American citizen in the early 1930s. He was one of those selfless men of high intelligence, integrity, and dedication who play important roles in great enterprises but, operating at a middle level of authority, leave few traces in the formal records. Chief planner for the American Air Forces in Europe, his unpressed uniform bedecked with distinguished British decorations, he became a truly major figure in the Allied effort.

In 1942 Hughes found himself in London, wholly dependent on British sources of intelligence, without an independent staff capable of evaluating the flow of material on which planning had to be based. He induced Ambassador John G. Winant and Gen. Dwight D. Eisenhower to request that appropriately trained civilians be sent to London to work, in fact for Hughes, but formally within the Embassy. After some bureaucratic infighting, the first contingent, consisting of Chandler Morse, the unit's chief, Rosalene Honerkamp, its secretary, and me, arrived in London on September 13, 1942, after a languid Sikorsky flying boat journey from New York to Bottwood Bay (Newfoundland) to Shannon harbor in Ireland—and then on to London in a plywood DeHaviland.

The previous experience of those who served EOU and its outposts converged in a quite particular way with Hughes's intellectual biases. As a professional soldier, a product of Wellington and Sandhurst, Hughes had long been trained in the principles of concentration of effort at the enemy's most vulnerable point and of prompt and maximum followthrough when a breakthrough was achieved. The members of EOU were mainly trained as economists—reflecting the assumption that the broad objective of the strategic bombing offensive was to weaken the German war economy. Our task, then, was to develop and apply criteria for the selection of one target system versus another, one target within a system versus another, and if the target was large enough and bombing precise enough, one aiming point versus another. The intellectual level of development of these criteria was quite primitive when EOU arrived in London. To put no fine point upon it, the United States had committed itself to a massive daylight precision bombing program without developing the doctrine and techniques of target selection or the intelligence required to underpin the exercise, or as we shall see, without perceiving initially what it would require to conduct precision bombing operations against the opposition of the German single-engined fighter force.

A Doctrine Emerges

Hughes properly took a little time to size up the small but overactive young crew he had called in from Washington at long distance—a bit like a colonel in the field trying to figure out a batch of lieutenants sent from headquarters. He initially put EOU to work not on high-flown theories of target selection but on a narrowly focused and painstaking task: aiming-point reports. These were analyses of particular German industrial plants or installations designed to establish the most vulnerable point of attack. The aiming-point reports were an invaluable education, requiring visits to the nearest equivalent plants in Britain as well as detailed exploitation of virtually all the intelligence London could provide, not merely about the plant itself but also on the economic sector of which it was a part and the role of that sector in the German war effort.

After testing us with the discipline of aiming-point reports (of which we ultimately produced some 285), Hughes unleashed EOU toward the close of 1942 on the principles and practice of target selection. This was the doctrine we evolved. We sought target systems where the destruction of the minimum number of targets would have the greatest, most prompt, and most long-lasting direct military effect on the battlefield. Each of the modifiers carried weight. One had to ask, in assessing the results of an attack, how large its effect would be within its own sector of the economy or military system, how quickly its effect would be felt in frontline strength, how long the effect would last, and what its direct military (as opposed to economic) consequences would be. The application of these criteria was serious, rigorous intellectual business. It required, among other things, taking fully into account the extent to which the military effect of an attack could be cushioned by the Germans, notably by diverting civilian output or services to military purposes or buying time for repair by drawing down stocks of finished or unfinished products. In all this our knowledge as economists of the structure of production, buttressed by what we had learned from the aiming-point reports, converged with the classic military principles Hughes and his best senior colleagues brought to the task. The EOU view was, then, a doctrine of warfare, not of economics or politics.

Once EOU developed its doctrine and as D-day approached, a good proportion of its personnel diffused in what was known as Operation Octopus to assist (or, as some thought, subvert) the 21st and 12th Army Groups, the Allied Expeditionary Air Force, G-2, SHAEF, and the British Air Ministry. Aside from its umbilical ties to the 8th and 15th Air Forces, EOU probably had its greatest operational impact through Operation Octopus. Clearly, its mode of operation violated every textbook rule of administration. Located for almost 2 years in British air intelligence, for example, I was simultaneously in the chains of command of Gen. William J. Donovan, Gen. Carl Spaatz, Air Vice-Marshal Frank Inglis, and Ambassador John Winant; but it made good sense at the time and worked quite well.

A Doctrine Tested in Three Bureaucratic Battles

The doctrine that emerged from the interplay of EOU, Hughes, and the top U.S. Air Corps command was not unchallenged. There were three critical intervals of head-on high-level policy conflict involving clashes of personality, vested interest, and unforeseen events, as well as doctrine. EOU played a role in all three bureaucratic battles, which quite literally determined the shape of the air war in Europe.

The first came in the second half of 1943. With great courage Gen. Frederick L. Anderson, chief of Bomber Command of the 8th Air Force, took the bold initiative of attacking aircraft production, then concentrated in central Germany, before long-range fighters were available to protect the bombers. The unexpected attacks began in July. Under forced draft, German single-engined fighter production at well-known plants—expanding before our eyes in reconnaissance photos—had risen from 381 in January to 1,050 in July, and first-line fighter strength rose in proportion.[2] Allied air supremacy on D-day was clearly endangered if the German expansion plan was permitted to come to fruition. The American attacks forced the Germans to disperse their production, and December production was reduced to only 560. But U.S. bomber losses in the summer and autumn were heavy and generated much criticism in Washington as well as London.

British supporters of area bombing of cities thought the time was thus ripe for a full-court press. They argued that a decisive Wagnerian crisis in German morale could be brought about if the U.S. bombers would abandon daylight bombing and join the RAF in night attacks. Those holding this view often argued that it was the break in German morale that caused capitulation in November 1918.

With a large flow of long-range fighters in sight, the American military establishment was not about to abandon its deeply rooted commitment to daylight precision operations. EOU played its part in the defense of American doctrine by asserting that the German acceptance of defeat in 1918 was based on the situation in the field. A typical paper argued that "collapse will come this time also from the top, and as a result of the military and military supply situation literally defined. I see no evidence or reason to believe that area bombing, whatever its great virtues as a generalized drain on the structure of Germany and its military potential, is capable of precipitating a decisive crisis."[3]

The issue was settled, as often in public policy, by an event, not an argument. In the week beginning February 20, 1944, the whole U.S. bomber force, conforming to a long-laid plan, was dispatched to attack German aircraft production from one end of Europe to the other. It was estimated that about 100 U.S. bombers and crews would be lost. The number lost was only 22. The weather miraculously held clear until February 25, and General Anderson, pursuing basic military doctrine, despite the exhaustion of the crews and protests from the bomb division commanders, exploited the breakthrough relentlessly until the winter weather closed in. The German single-engined fighter force never recovered from its unlikely defeat by the American long-range fighters. It was during these days—known widely as The Big Week—in effect, that a mature United States Air Force emerged.

From the perspective of those immediately engaged, The Big Week in February 1944 was Murphy's Law in reverse or intervention by Higher Authority. But not atypically, success led directly to more trouble: the second and third great conflicts over bombing policy, both related to the appropriate use of air power before D-day and in the wake of the Allied landings. Both involved intense debate in which, at the bureaucratic level, General Spaatz was squared off against Eisenhower's deputy, Air Chief Marshal Arthur Tedder, and part of the RAF, and at the intellectual level, EOU was squared off against Tedder's one-man brain trust, Solly Zuckerman. Zuckerman was a scholar of the sexual and social life of apes who, under the curious but not atypical imperatives of war, became an expert on the physical effects of bombing, which he applied in the Mediterranean, and then a bombing strategist. There are Americans (and some British) who to the end of their days regarded (or will regard) the last year of the struggle in Europe as a war against Solly Zuckerman rather than Adolf Hitler.

Stated with reasonable objectivity, the first controversy was about bombing policy before D-day. Even before The Big Week in February had ended, Hughes and EOU were at work on a plan to exploit air supremacy over Germany. A plan to bomb German oil production was drawn up, approved by Spaatz as early as March 5, and went forward to Eisenhower and Tedder. The judgment underlying the plan was that a radical reduction in oil supplies was the optimum way to reduce by strategic bombing the fighting capability of the German ground and air forces. Meanwhile, Zuckerman, basing his judgment on his (highly debatable) view of lessons of the air war in the Mediterranean, persuaded Tedder to support concentrated attacks on western European railway marshalling yards, postponing the whole question of oil until after D-day.

Spaatz took the view that attacks on marshalling yards would have diffuse generalized effects but would not interdict military supplies because the minimum essential lines could be repaired overnight and the Germans would not engage their beleaguered fighter force to defend marshalling yards. Thus, his primary and overriding responsibility would be at risk, that is, Allied air supremacy on D-day.

The battle between Spaatz and Tedder was promptly joined by their passionate intellectual spear carriers. The crisis and what proved to be interim resolution came at a historic meeting on March 25, 1944, chaired by Air Chief Marshal Charles Portal, representing the Combined Chiefs of Staff; but the decisive voice was Eisenhower's. He decided in favor of Tedder and marshalling yards on the grounds that the latter would provide some immediate help in the landings and their aftermath, whereas the military effects of the oil attacks might be delayed.

But that was not the end of the matter. On April 5, the 15th Air Force successfully attacked Ploesti, exploiting a comic mistake by SHAEF headquarters. To block oil attacks in the Mediterranean theater as well as western Europe, SHAEF confined the Mediterranean air forces to marshalling yard targets, although the connection with the Normandy landings of the marshalling yards of southern Europe was a bit obscure; but SHAEF failed to omit Ploesti, which was on the standard marshalling yard list because there were small marshalling yards outside each refinery. The error was noted and exploited. The attack—in effect, on the refineries—was successful, and significant immediate effects on the German oil supply could be detected.

On May 12 the American bombers in Britain attacked a substantial group of oil targets in central Germany including the most important at Leuna. Eisenhower had given Spaatz 2 pre–D-day good weather days on oil when the latter threatened to resign. The Germans were not defending the marshalling yards, and their fighter force was expanding again. Spaatz felt he might not be able to fulfill his overriding D-day responsibility: to assure Allied air supremacy. ULTRA intercept intelligence promptly and unambiguously provided evidence of German panic as they elevated the defense of their oil production to overriding priority—above even factories producing single-engined fighters. The evidence was sufficient to convince Tedder that the oil attacks should be promptly pursued. (What Tedder actually said in response to the ULTRA reports was: "I guess we'll have to give the customer what he wants.")

Almost 2 valuable months were lost in reversing Eisenhower's March decision, but when German aircraft production began to rise in dispersed factories later in 1944, there was insufficient aircraft fuel to train the pilots and fly the planes. From a peak of 180,000 metric tons production in March 1944—before the insubordinate attack on Ploesti—aircraft fuel production was down to an incredible 10,000 tons by September. (Overall, oil supplies were reduced from 981,000 to 281,000 tons.)[4]

The third battle that tested EOU doctrine was over the optimum tactical targets in support of D-day. Tedder and Zuckerman again argued that marshalling yards would suffice; EOU argued for isolating the Normandy battlefield by taking out three rings of bridges, above all the Seine-Loire complex. The weight of the American air force and, ultimately, Generals Bradley and Montgomery's respective ground force headquarters was thrown behind the bridge concept. The technical argument hinged on how many tons of bombs were required to render a bridge unusable for, say, 3 weeks. Zuckerman argued that 1,200 tons per bridge (600-1,200 sorties) were necessary. On the basis of Mediterranean experience, EOU thought less than one-third of that tonnage would suffice. Again the issue was settled by a somewhat adventitious event.

On a day when bad weather was predicted in Germany, with good weather predicted in France, the Americans proposed a test with some 3,000 aircraft broken into flights of 60. With that force we could have attacked virtually every bridge on our three-tiered list. On getting word of the proposed enterprise, the marshalling yard advocates were furious, and the massive test was called off. By way of compromise, and after some extraordinary shenanigans involving 10 Downing Street (where Prime Minister Winston Churchill and Lord Cherwell maintained a strong dislike of the marshalling yard strategy), experimental attacks were permitted on May 7, 1944, on 6 Seine bridges by a total of fewer than 50 P-47 fighter-bombers each carrying two 1,000-pound bombs with delayed fuses. There was nothing in prior experience to indicate they would do the bridges any harm. In a statistical sport, three bridges were badly damaged, and a fourth (at Vernon) was dropped into the Seine by six P-47s with accuracy not to be seen again until the war in the Persian Gulf. The extraordinary success of the experiment was a matter of luck—except that the fighter-bomber group chosen for the experiment had been practicing low-level attacks on bridges in Texas, a fact not widely circulated before the event. The post-attack photograph of the submerged Vernon bridge was on every general officer's desk the next morning; Tedder capitulated in the face of hard but not quite statistically reputable evidence, and the Seine-Loire bridge attacks were approved. By D-day the interdiction of the Seine was complete, and Germany's reinforcement of its armies in Normandy, from the Calais area and elsewhere, was significantly impeded. Having ferried across the Seine, German forces were fed into the battle piecemeal and brutally harassed by virtually unimpeded Allied fighters and fighter-bombers.

Thus, within 6 days, from Vernon to Leuna (May 7–May 12), the American air forces won back a good deal of what they had lost by Eisenhower's decision of February 25.

The EOU Role in Perspective

Even on this authentically nostalgic occasion I would underline with all the emphasis I can muster that the role of EOU should not be overemphasized. We contributed a useful piece to an enormous mosaic of Allied effort.

Looking back, I can see again the faces not only of Hughes, Anderson, and Spaatz but also of the key figures in British intelligence on whom the American effort was based—as able, imaginative, and dedicated a group of men and women as was ever assembled. They backed the precision bombing effort not only as good allies but also because the intelligence requirements were more exacting and challenging than for the area bombing of cities or marshalling yards, where all that was really required was an automobile road map. Moreover, there was Portal's bombing policy staff. Led by Air Commodore Sidney Bufton, these young men with one or more tours of operations supported the American precision bombing effort unswervingly against strong nationalistic appeals. In addition there was Thomas Hitchcock, a polo-playing American air attaché in London, who made a critical contribution to the improbable conversion of the Mustang into a long-range fighter. The long-range fighter, which won virtually total air supremacy over Germany, proved essential to validating the American commitment to precision bombing. That validation and the air supremacy it provided was essential to the Normandy landings, the consolidation of the bridgehead, and the attacks on oil, which not only virtually grounded the German Air Force but also radically reduced the mobility of German ground forces on the western and eastern fronts in the last year of the war.

Gen. Adolf Galland, chief of the German fighter force, summed up an extended analysis (see appendix A), as follows: "The raids of the allied air fleets on the German petrol supply installations was the most important of the combined factors which brought about the collapse of Germany."

Air Chief Marshal Sir Arthur Harris, commander of the RAF bomber force, was a redoubtable opponent of the oil offensive and referred to its advocates (including EOU) as "the oily boys." Against his will, the RAF was forced into the oil offensive and played an effective role. Harris's final word (see appendix A) is a bit grudging—but on the whole a gracious capitulation: "I still do not think it was reasonable at that time, to expect that the [oil] campaign would succeed; what the Allied strategists did was to bet on an outsider, and it happened to win the race."

But above all, there were the air crews who flew up from the peaceful British countryside, assembled, and in a matter of minutes found themselves for much of the air war plunged into an inferno of antiaircraft fire and lethal air combat—some dying or going into captivity; others limping home carrying dead or wounded; all undergoing traumatic strain carried gracefully or otherwise for the rest of their lives.

Let me quote a bit from the commanding colonel's austere after-battle report on the attack on the bridge at Vernon, the photograph of which settled a not trivial bureaucratic battle:

> While the force orbited at 10,000 feet above the break in the overcast, the first man initiated the attack on the target. He drove for the deck south of Vernon, leveled out over the town and drove straight for north abutment at deck level and full throttle. His flight path was about 25 degrees off axis of bridge and point of aim was intersection of bridge and foundation supporting north end of the steel span. The bombs were released at point blank range and he pulled up over the bridge, breaking left with evasive maneuvers on the deck. . . . During the attack, the bombers were the target of the most intense light flak they have yet encountered.

I do not believe the members of EOU, caught up in exciting headquarters' business, ever forgot for long those for whom we were ultimately working. After all, they were of our generation.

Some Final Observations

EOU will always be associated with the name of Charles Kindleberger as well as Richard Hughes. Kindleberger took over from Chandler Morse as chief of the unit in February 1943. He left in May 1944 ultimately to join Gen. Omar Bradley's staff. Like the rest of us engaged in Operation Octopus, he kept closely in touch with 40 Berkeley Square. His character and style suffused the outfit to the end. His rule in exercising authority was: "Tough upwards, soft downwards." Despite our modest military ranks, we spoke our minds to higher authority. We all learned that one could debate quite amicably with general officers if advocacy was interspersed with a sufficient number of "Sirs." But beneath the fraternal spirit that marked EOU and the texture of humor which suffused virtually all talk in the family, Kindleberger quietly exercised discretion and compassion on behalf of his subordinates when required. Above all he is, as I once wrote, a man of "fierce integrity." He insisted on a self-critical integrity among us, perhaps best illustrated by his insistence in the autumn of 1944, after a sustained period of advocacy, that we pause, draw back, and reexamine skeptically our logic and the factual evidence for the policy positions we held.

What, finally, can one say of the longer run impact of EOU and the OSS of which EOU was a component? I would make only three casual concluding observations.

First, it was an irreversible experience of public service that helped shape the lives of its members. As nearly as I can calculate, virtually all of us subsequently spent some time in government.

Second, a lesson was driven home that affected those of us who were economists, as most of us were. We learned that theories—no matter how elegant or attractive—had to be forcefully disciplined against the facts before a policy decision is reached.

Finally, EOU contributed in a small way to rectify in the long run the situation Franklin Roosevelt confronted as war approached in mid-1941, a situation that led him to evoke Donovan as *deus ex machina*. The situation was that American military intelligence, specially G-2, was grossly inadequate, the military services put overriding priority on operational virtuosity and consigned their least competent permanent officers to intelligence, and there was no way the situation could be rapidly changed from the top. As on other occasions, Roosevelt brought into play the principle of competition—not Adam Smith's Hidden Hand, but the not-so-Hidden Foot of Donovan and his merry men and women.[5]

After deciding OSS was irrepressible, the Army turned to the best East Coast law offices to remake G-2. The Navy, already quite competent at assembling order-of-battle data, gradually drew on similar intellectual resources to build up its deficient analytic capabilities.

Even more important, the kind of able military men who rose to command under the pressure of a great and initially desperate war, learned that they needed intellectuals and that not only physical and social scientists but all manner of bright, enterprising civilians could work well in a military setting, where innovation in thought and hardware was essential for survival. Thus, the link was forged that yielded not only the CIA, but also RAND, the AEC, and all the other institutionalized links between intellectual life and national security that persist down to the present.

APPENDIX A

Some Ex Post Views of the U.S. Bombing Offensive in Europe

Note: the following passage, including quotations, are from my *Pre-Invasion Bombing Strategy: General Eisenhower's Decision of March 25, 1944* (Austin, TX, 1981), pp. 78-80.

Albert Speer's memoir opens its 24th chapter with this rather Wagnerian passage: "On May 8, 1944, I returned to Berlin to resume my work. I shall never forget the date May 12, four days later. On that day the technological war was decided. Until then we had managed to produce approximately as many weapons as the armed forces needed, in spite of their considerable losses. But with the attack of nine hundred and thirty-five daylight bombers of the American Eighth Air Force upon several fuel plants in central and eastern Germany, a new era in the air war began. It meant the end of German armaments production."[6] Speer's earlier testimony, comparing the relative strategic results of oil and transportation attacks, is more precise: "As a result of the loss in the fuel industry it was no longer possible even in December 1944 and January 1945 to make use of the reduced armaments production in the battle. The loss of fuel had, in my opinion, therefore, a more decisive effect on the course of the war than the difficulties in armaments and communications."[7]

Galland [commander of the German fighter force] elaborates Speer's view as follows:

The most successful operation of the entire Allied strategical air warfare was against the German fuel supply. This was actually the fatal blow for the Luftwaffe! Looking back, it is difficult to understand why the Allies started this undertaking so late, after they had suffered such heavy losses in other operations. . . .

As early as June, 1944, the month the invasion started, we felt very badly the effects of the consolidated offensive. Fuel production suddenly sank so low that it could no longer satisfy the urgent demands. Speer, when interrogated by the Allies, stated that from June on, it had been impossible to get enough aviation fuel. While it was possible with the greatest effort to keep up at least a minimum production of motor and diesel fuel, the repair work on the plants where normal fuel was converted to octane constituted difficulties which were impossible to overcome. The enemy soon found out how much time we needed for reconstruction and for resuming production. Shortly before this date was reached under tremendous strain came the next devastating raid.

By applying the strictest economy measures and my using the reserves of the OKW (Western High Command), it was possible to continue the fuel supply to the army during the summer months of 1944. Yet from September on, the shortage of petrol was unbearable. The Luftwaffe was the first to be hit by this shortage. Instead of the minimum of 160,000 tons monthly, only 30,000 tons of octane could be allotted. Air force operations were thereby made virtually impossible! For the army similarly disastrous conditions did not arise before the winter.

The raids of the Allied air fleets on the German petrol supply installations was the most important of the combined factors which brought about the collapse of Germany.[8]

Postwar analysts and historians are indeed virtually unanimous in their verdict that the attack on oil represented the most effective use of strategic air power in the European theater, although it absorbed less than 10 percent of the tonnage dropped by USSTAF (United States Strategic Air Forces) in the period January 1944–May 1945, as opposed to 43 percent allocated to land transport. It is hard to avoid the conclusion that the oil offensive should have been begun at the earliest possible time, in the wake of The Big Week of late February; it is clear that it could have been pursued without significant loss to the pre–D-day transport attacks, including the bridges and rail lines; and it should have been pursued relentlessly by the RAF Bomber Command as well as the 8th and 15th Air Forces. In his own way Harris, long a redoubtable opponent of oil, is generous in retrospect as well as justly proud of the contribution ultimately made to the oil offensive by his command:

> In the spring of 1944 the Americans began a series of attacks against German synthetic oil plants, and a week after D-Day Bomber Command was directed to take part in the same campaign by attacking the ten synthetic oil plants situated in the Ruhr. At the time, I was altogether opposed to this further diversion, which, as I saw it, would only prolong the respite which the German industrial cities had gained from the use of doing the enemy enormous harm for the sake of prosecuting a new scheme the success of which was far from assured. In the event, of course, the offensive against oil was a complete success, and it could not have been so without the co-operation of Bomber Command, but I still do not think that it was reasonable, at that time, to expect that the campaign would succeed; what the Allied strategists did was to bet on an outsider, and it happened to win the race.[9]

APPENDIX B

EOU PERSONNEL

NAME	AGENCY	DATE OF ARRIVAL	DATE OF LEAVING	OUTSIDE ATTACHMENT
Rosalene Honerkamp	OSS	Sept. 42	Oct. 44	—
Chandler Morse	OSS	Sept. 42	Mar. 43	—
Maj. W. W. Rostow, AUS	OSS	Sept. 42	Apr. 45	Air Ministry Aug. 43–Apr. 45
John De Wilde	BEW	Oct. 42	May 43	—
Capt. Harold J. Barnett, Inf	OSS	Oct. 42	—	OSS Washington Apr.–Nov. 43; G-2 SHAEF, Apr.–Aug. 44
Capt. William A. Salant, FA	OSS	Nov. 42	—	MAAF Nov. 43
Maj. Charles P. Kindleberger, AUS	OSS	Feb. 43	—	21st Army Group May–July 44; 12 Army Group July 44
Irwin N. Pincus	BEW	Apr. 43	—	—
Edward Mayer	OSS	May 43	Dec. 43	—
1st Lt. Carl Kaysen, AC	USSTAF	June 43	—	RE 8 July 43– Jan. 44; AEAF Jan.–July 44
Ruth Ellerman	BEW	June 43	Oct. 44	—
Pvt. Phillip Combs	OSS	Nov. 43	Oct. 44	MAAF throughout
T4g. Warren C. Baum	OSS	Dec. 43	—	Air Ministry throughout
Lt.(jg.) James Tyson, USNR	OSS	Dec. 43	—	MAAF Feb.– Apr. 44
1st Lt. Mark Kahn, AC	OSS	Feb. 44	—	—
2d Lt. Robert Rosa, AUS	OSS	Feb. 44	—	12th Army Group Aug. 44
Nancy House	OSS	Jan. 45	Apr. 45	—

NOTES

1. This essay draws upon my unpublished history of EOU ("Economic Outpost with Economic Warfare Division," vol. 5, *War Diary of the OSS London: The Enemy Objectives Unit [EOU] To April 30, 1945*, located in the National Archives in Washington, DC), as well as on my *Pre-Invasion Bombing Strategy: General Eisenhower's Decision of March 25, 1944* (Austin, TX, 1981). The latter contains a bibliographical note (pp. 139–140) as well as a collection of reproduced primary documents.

2. The source for these official German figures is *U.S. Strategic Bombing Survey, Overall Economic Effects Division*, "The Effects of Strategic Bombing on the German War Economy," Oct. 31, 1945, p. 156. The German single-engined fighter production plan, which British intelligence acquired in 1943, called for a leveling off at about 2,000 per month at the end of 1943.

3. This passage is from a memorandum of mine in the British Air Ministry, dated November 14, 1943, addressed to an influential advocate of area bombing, but widely circulated.

4. Source: *U.S. Strategic Bombing Survey*, Table 41, p. 179, from official German sources.

5. I owe the concept of the Hidden Foot to a fellow economist: Burton Klein, *Prices, Wages, and Business Cycles: A Dynamic Theory* (Elmsford, NY, 1984).

6. Albert Speer, *Inside the Third Reich* (New York, 1970), p. 346.

7. Quoted in Sir Charles Webster and Noble Frankland, *Strategic Air Offensive against Germany*, 4 vols. (London, 1961), 3: 239–240. See also, five of Speer's reports to Hitler on the effects of the attacks on oil in ibid., 4: 321–340. For a recent brief review of the oil offensive, with special emphasis on its consequences for oil storage facilities and stocks, see Edmund Dews, *POL Storage as a Target for Air Attack: Evidence from the World War II Allied Air Campaigns against Enemy Oil Installations*, RAND Note N-1523-PA&E (Santa Monica, CA, June 1980).

8. Adolf Galland, *The First and the Last* (New York, 1954), pp. 224–226.

9. Sir Arthur Harris, *Bomber Offensive* (London, 1947), p. 220.

THE LONDON
OPERATION:
Recollections of a Historian

Arthur Schlesinger, Jr.

It is a joy to take part in this alumni reunion—an occasion marred only by the thought of so many cherished friends and colleagues who are no longer with us. But the events we are recalling, or trying to recall, took place, after all, nearly half a century ago. It is lucky that so many veterans of the Research and Analysis Branch (R&A) of the Office of Strategic Services (OSS) are still around to supplement and correct diverse and vagrant memories of what was for all of us a most exhilarating time of our lives.

In preparing for this conference, I had hoped to be able to draw on letters written to my wife and to my parents from London in 1944. Given wartime security restrictions, such letters would say little about the OSS but would be helpful in evoking the atmosphere of the time. I believe that these letters still exist in storage somewhere, but I have been unable thus far to lay my hands on them. Accordingly I have had to rely on OSS records released to me some years ago under the Freedom of Information Act, on the London diaries of our commanding officer, Col. David K. E. Bruce and of my R&A colleague Richard Brown Baker, on Barry M. Katz's incisive but inevitably selective historical essay, on Robin Winks's witty and informative account of the OSS as a wholly owned Yale subsidiary, and on that most indispensable but treacherous of instruments, my own sadly fallible memory.[1]

I came to Washington in early 1942 to join the Writers Bureau of the Domestic Branch of the Office of War Information (OWI), occupying a desk vacated a few weeks earlier by my friend from the Harvard Society of Fellows, McGeorge Bundy. The chief of the bureau was the biographer Henry Pringle, and among my associates were Sam Lubell; Philip Hamburger; W. McNeil Lowry; Hodding Carter, Sr., and his wife, Betty; Chester and Barbara Kerr; and others. Some of our work, especially a pamphlet on the treatment of Negroes (as black Americans called themselves in

1942), was bitterly criticized on Capitol Hill as New Deal propaganda. Republican gains in the 1942 congressional elections led the President and the OWI Director Elmer Davis to rein the writers in. A Republican was appointed head of the Domestic Branch, bringing a covey of advertising men in his wake—all this prompting one of our group, the artist Francis H. Brennan, to design a satiric poster for the new regime entitled "Four Delicious Freedoms." A number of us, led by Henry Pringle, resigned in protest in April 1943.

James Phinney Baxter and W. L. Langer had already raided the Harvard history department for the R&A Branch of the OSS, and Donald McKay, another Harvard friend, now recruited me. In May I joined the R&A Central Intelligence Staff at what seemed then the munificent salary of $3,800 a year. My boss was yet another Harvard friend, the medievalist S. Everett Gleason, who later collaborated with Bill Langer in the classic history of FDR's foreign policy before Pearl Harbor and still later ran the secretariat of the National Security Council. My job was to edit a classified publication of strictly limited circulation called *The PW Weekly*—PW standing for psychological warfare.

The PW Weekly was compiled from reports and memorandums produced by R&A's regional desks. It was dutifully sent to high officials from the White House down. I have come upon no evidence that the publication had any influence or even that any top officials ever found time to read it. It played a useful role within the OSS, however, by providing an outlet for the work of the regional desks and thereby sustaining the morale of the analysts. Also, our condensation and (often) rewriting of sometimes opaque research memorandums may on occasion have helped analysts clarify their own thoughts. I had a fairly free editorial hand, except when I clashed with the Stalinist views of the chief of the Latin-American section, and I greatly enjoyed my daily tours of the desks, especially my contact with those two great teachers and seductive personalities Felix Gilbert and Franz Neumann.

My plan, however, was to get overseas. Gleason, in a November 1943 memorandum to Langer, reported that I was asking to be sent to London. Allan Evans, another Harvard medievalist had set up an R&A London outpost in the weeks after Pearl Harbor. Crane Brinton, still another Harvardian, arrived in early 1942. Gradually R&A had developed connections with British intelligence agencies. Its main impact in 1943 came from the remarkable group of economists—Charles Kindleberger, Walt Rostow, William Salant, Carl Kaysen, and others—who formed the Enemy Objectives Unit and had decisive influence on Allied bombing strategy. Next to the economists, with their brilliant fusion of analytical and quantitative techniques and their intimate involvement in military operations, historians and political scientists seemed a bunch of dilettantes.

Langer in Washington was, I think, increasingly dissatisfied with the London R&A operation. Crane Brinton's notable qualities as a historian—his ironical skepticism about the capacity of human beings to control their destiny—made him a diffident administrator. In February 1944 the economist Chandler Morse was appointed head of R&A/London in tribute both to the primacy of economists in R&A work and to Morse's own forceful and well-organized personality. Morse was sympathetic to political analysis but had to deal with a certain condescension in economists. According to Rostow's *R&A War Diary*, he had to wean his professional colleagues "away from the analytical and statistical studies of which they had been so proud, and to interest them in the larger but vaguer and more subjective type of analysis which was familiar to the political staff."[2] The arrival of Harold Deutsch in February greatly strengthened R&A political analysis.

I agitated all through the winter of 1943–44 for a London assignment and sought to prove my expendability by helping recruit people who could take over my duties—Ray Cline from Army Cryptography and Sebastian di Grazia, whose book on Machiavelli won the Pulitzer Prize in 1990. R&A/London was now in a time of hectic expansion, tenfold, Barry Katz writes in his book.[3] In May 1944 Harold Deutsch sent a message to Washington requesting my inclusion in the group of analysts about to depart for London. The message reads: "Mr Schlesinger will be assigned . . . to one of the most important posts in the R&A Branch, being that of Chief Editor and Project Supervisor on the Political Staff. In this capacity, he will edit and, in many cases, direct the composition of projects, which will be directly concerned with the servicing of psychological warfare operations during the anticipated invasion."[4]

Deutsch, I imagine, put in the business about psychological warfare as a selling point in Washington. His interest, and mine too, lay in political analysis. I felt, even then, that long-range psychological warfare was overrated as a factor in winning wars. In any case, the British in the Political Warfare Executive (PWE) and the Special Operations Executive (SOE) were far more skilled practitioners in that arcane field than we were, and tactical psychological warfare—the deception plans that were so important in masking the invasion, for example—were the business of the military and of the operational intelligence branches, not of R&A.

In late June I set sail on the old *Queen Elizabeth*, crossing out of convoy in zigzag course in 6 days from New York to Greenock, a Scottish port on the Clyde near Glasgow. There were 16,000 persons on board: Army, Red Cross, a smattering of civilians and Glenn Miller's band. Twelve of us slept in a stateroom built for two. One of my cabin mates was a young man who showed what seemed inordinate and, in the circumstances, rather dismaying interest in the fate of the *Titanic*. His was a name to remember—Walter Lord.

I arrived in London 3 weeks after D-day and 2 weeks after the Germans had begun their V-1 assault on Britain. As the OSS delegation debouched from the Glasgow train and settled for a night in the Euston Station hotel, we heard for the first time the wail of the siren, that awful sinister buzz overhead, the even more sinister silence as the motor cut off and the bomb hurtled toward the city—then the explosion, accompanied by an involuntary surge of relief that it had landed somewhere else. This became a familiar sequence in the weeks to come.

R&A by this time was established in a handsome Georgian mansion at 68 Brook Street, catercorner from Claridge's. The building was rather rundown in the 5th year of the war; I always walk by it when I go to London and am glad to report that it looks in sparkling condition today. I shared an office on the second floor with a group of analysts and secretaries. Large windows gave us an excellent view of incoming buzz bombs. We all did regular night duty as fire guards, which meant sleeping on cots in the office and taking one's turn for a couple of hours on the roof. The barrage by night and by day meant that one lived at a higher pitch of tension than ever before and gave life a grim humor and, as one survived, constant exhilaration. "I am not worried about one of those bombs having my name on it," a friend said to me as a doodlebug roared overhead. "The one I'm worried about is labeled: 'To whom it may concern.'"

We were a block away from Grosvenor Square, where the American Embassy occupied the stately building that is today the Canadian Embassy, on the opposite end of the square from Edward Durrell Stone's awful modern structure that now flies the American flag. Grosvenor and Berkeley Squares formed an American enclave in the middle of the West End.

My main work was editing a classified weekly publication, the *European Political Report*. R&A that summer was in a mild state of administrative turmoil. New people were arriving every week. Strong personalities were competing to hold on to or acquire domains of authorities. The suspense of the invasion, the buzz-bomb bombardment, soon the replacement of V-1 by the without-warning V-2—all this stretched nerves and irascibilities.

Richard Baker noted in his journal a talk in mid-July with another R&A colleague, newspaperman Ben Crisman: "We hashed over the faults of our branch. . . . Neither he nor I quite see the sense in many things. I have for some time felt myself rudderless in a swelling sea. Despite the lack of a clear sense of direction, we are constantly badgered by ridiculous administrative orders. We are supposed to be an assemblage of scholars and political analysts, but in fact we are a herd of baffled people under a barrage of silly orders from a top-heavy hierarchy of ambitious egotists."[5]

I don't recall the situation in quite such tragic terms, and very likely Baker and Crisman were responding to passing frustrations. Still there was a real problem, perhaps less one of administration than of function. Political analysis simply did not quite fit into the critical requirements of that tense summer. With one exception, our work had the glaring defect of irrelevance to immediate military needs. It did not, save for that one exception, contribute directly, as economic analysis did, to the goal topmost in everyone's mind—victory over the Nazis. Reading David Bruce's London journal, I am struck at the extent to which operational urgencies crowded R&A out of the sight of our courteous and exceedingly capable commanding officer.

Of course R&A analysts could contribute to postwar planning, especially via Ambassador John R. Winant, Philip Moseley, and the European Advisory Commission. Felix Gilbert was thus evidently responsible for the zonal division of Berlin.[6] But there were frustrations here too. The center of postwar planning was Washington, where Leo Pasvolsky and his State Department team were making preparations for Dumbarton Oaks, the War Department was training officers for the military occupation of Germany, and the Justice Department was brooding about war crimes tribunals—all, it must be said, with assistance from R&A/Washington.

The exception to military irrelevance lay in the R&A/London assessment of European resistance movements. The FFI (Forces Françaises de l'Intérieur) were already giving invaluable assistance to the Anglo-American invasion, and the flow of military and political intelligence back to London was steadily increasing. The question of the present and future role of resistance groups became a major concern and caused serious, if generally subterranean, debate. The issue, not often explicitly drawn, was the role of Communists in the resistance and the hope of some, and the fear of others, that Communists might use the resistance as a means of vaulting into postwar power in France and Italy.

Most in R&A/London believed in the vital importance of preserving the Grand Alliance after the war for the sake of world peace. They feared that premature suspicion of Communist purposes would revive Soviet mistrust and undermine the hope of postwar amity. There were also those in Gen. William J. Donovan's ecumenical organization who had a Marxist faith in the benevolence of the Soviet Union and in the desirability of Communist revolution.

I was less hopeful about postwar felicities. I had been a longtime anti-Stalinist, and, though I flinched when OSS rightwingers in Wiesbaden in the spring of 1945 talked of using Nazis to combat the anticipated spread of communism, I did not believe that the OSS should go out of its way to strengthen the Communist position in Western Europe. Later in Paris in the winter of 1944–45, when Allen Dulles sent Noel Field to us with the recommendation that the OSS help subsidize Field and his Comité Allemagne pour l'Ouest, Bert Jolis and I, after interviewing Field, strongly and successfully opposed Dulles's recommendation.

My concern was much strengthened in the summer of 1944 by talks with British Labour Party figures, especially Aneurin Bevan. Bevan lived in Cliveden Place, around the corner from the house I shared with OSS colleagues in Eaton Terrace. He detested American capitalism but relished Americans and was especially appreciative of the bottles of whiskey that his OSS friends produced from the Navy wine mess. With his lilting Welsh intonations, Bevan was a fascinating conversationalist, and he would hold young Americans spellbound with his speculations about the world after the war.

Bevan doubted that the Grand Alliance would last and predicted that the struggle for postwar Europe would be between the Democratic Socialists and the Communists. This remained an abiding theme for him in spite of his equally abiding apprehension that Britain would end up as capitalist America's poodle. "The Communist Party," Bevan wrote in 1951, "is the sworn and inveterate enemy of the Socialist and Democratic Parties. When it associates with them it does so as a preliminary to destroying them."[7]

The internal R&A debate was subdued, but I believe it occupied the minds of analysts more than the documents might suggest. For obvious reasons, France was an object of special concern. We studied reports, interrogations, documents, and manifestos to find out all we could about Combat, Liberation, the Front National, the Francs-Tireurs et Partisans; their composition, authority, and political direction; and their relations with General Charles de Gaulle and his intelligence chief, "Colonel Passy" (André Dewavrin), in London. Most of us had been uncomfortable with the chilly U.S. policy toward de Gaulle and the French Committee of National Liberation (FCNL), and the decision in July 1944 to recognize the FCNL was greeted with heartfelt relief. We also tried to size up resistance movements in Italy, the Low Countries, and Denmark and to observe the exiled opposition to Franco in Spain. This in my recollection was the most interesting and useful part of R&A/London's political work.

I would like to raise another issue perhaps that is more in our minds today than it was in the summer of 1944: the OSS and the Holocaust. Much has been written in recent years about the alleged indifference of the American and British governments to reports of the Nazi decision, presumably made in 1941, to exterminate the Jews. I have asked myself and I have asked R&A colleagues when we first became aware of such a program of total extermination as something beyond the well-recognized viciousness of the concentration camps. The OSS should have received the best possible intelligence, and the German-Jewish refugees who played so influential a role in R&A would surely not have been inclined to overlook or minimize such intelligence.

Yet my recollection is that, even in the summer of 1944 as we read with horror the mounting flow of information about concentration camps, we still thought in terms of an incremental increase in persecution rather than of a new and terrible decision for extermination. Barry Katz writes of R&A's central European analysts: "Although they had reported regularly on incidences [sic] of official violence and terrorism, on mass deportations, and on the network of Nazi concentration camps, their papers prior to their work on the Nuremberg indictments yield no unambiguous evidence that they had grasped these as elements of a systematic policy of genocide." Katz traces this failure to Franz Neumann's theory that the war against the Jews was not an end in itself but the means to a larger end, "the 'spearhead' for general oppression," the first step toward the real goal—the destruction of civil society.[8] If this OSS myopia is so, and it accords with my own recollections, then it is hard to condemn Franklin Roosevelt for not grasping what the R&A German experts also failed to grasp.

As the summer of 1944 wore on, I found myself increasingly concerned about the uses of the R&A output. The *European Political Report*, I knew, was somewhat read in English as well as American intelligence agencies; after the war R.H.S. Crossman of PWE told me that he had first encountered my name in that connection. But one never knew whether R&A political analysis really made any difference to anything.

In the winter of 1943–44 William J. Casey had arrived with a vague commission from General Donovan to help Colonel Bruce by setting up a London secretariat. Casey too grew concerned with the problem of distribution and came up with the notion of a joint SI/R&A Reports Board to centralize the dissemination process. Casey and I became friends and, despite acute political disagreements, stayed friends of a sort till the end of his life. By September I was scheduled to be a deputy chief of the new SIRA Reports Board.

The chief was an old friend from Harvard—Philip Horton, whom I had known as curator of the poetry collection at Widener Library. Horton showed an unexpected and uncommon proficiency at intelligence collection, worked for CIA for a while after the war, and finally became executive editor of *The Reporter*. I was to be his deputy for political intelligence; Harry Rositzke, another student of literature who later went on to a distinguished career in CIA, had the far more important job of deputy for military intelligence. The SIRA Reports Board did not go into full operation until we all went to Paris in late September 1944, but that is another story.

My conclusions are, I fear, banal: that in time of war military and economic intelligence are more important than political intelligence, even though political intelligence bears more vitally on the peace to come. As Winston Churchill told the House of Commons on Armistice Day in 1942, "The problems of victory are more agreeable than those of defeat, but they are no less difficult." Unfortunately you have to win the war first.

My second conclusion is equally banal: that intelligence is only as effective as its dissemination. So is my third conclusion: even the best-designed dissemination system cannot persuade busy people to read political analysis unless it affects the decisions they are about to make.

Perhaps the greatest impact of the political analysis work in R&A/London was on the analysts themselves: in forcing us to think under pressure about fundamental questions of political culture and social structure, about human depravity and human heroism, and, I must add, in leaving rich memories of fellowship forged in the year of the buzz bomb.

NOTES

1. David K. E. Bruce, *OSS Against the Reich: The World War II Diaries*, ed. Nelson D. Lankford (Kent, OH, 1991); Richard Brown Baker, *The Year of the Buzz Bomb: A Journal of London, 1944* (New York, 1952); Barry M. Katz, *Foreign Intelligence: Research and Analysis in the Office of Strategic Services, 1942–1945* (Cambridge, MA, 1989); and Robin W. Winks, *Cloak and Gown: Scholars in the Secret War, 1939–1961* (New York, 1987).
2. Katz, *Foreign Intelligence*, p. 125.
3. Ibid.
4. Harold C. Deutsch to William A. Kimbel, May 6, 1944.
5. Baker, *Year of the Buzz Bomb*, p. 49.
6. Katz, *Foreign Intelligence*, pp. 83–84.
7. Aneurin Bevan, "Foreword," in Denis Healey, ed., *The Curtain Falls* (London, 1951).
8. Katz, *Foreign Intelligence*, pp. 55, 176, 213 (n. 74).

THE LONDON OPERATION: The British View

Sir Robin Brook

I should preface my address by pointing out that it is given entirely personally, entirely based on my own recollections. I have no documents, so it must be regarded on the basis of reminiscence rather than of record.

The Special Operations Executive (SOE) was a wartime improvisation based on secondary sections of the British War Office and Secret Service, extended to cover the enormous sphere of the Second World War and gradually adapted to fit in with the plans for economic and military warfare as they developed.

Its joint origins engendered dual capacities: Phase 1—the clandestine operations through agents, either singly or through networks known as "reseaux"; and Phase 2—the paramilitary operations through agents working under secrecy but more exposed and apt to be in uniform. The former was required in the early stages for the formation of cells and the buildup of resistance among occupied populations, while the latter was more appropriate for close cooperation with invading troops in conjunction with the Special Air Service (SAS) and Operational Groups (OGs).

Late in 1942, two changes of momentous significance occurred—the German occupation of southern France (ZNO), as a reaction by the Germans to the Allied invasion of French North Africa, and the integration of the OSS as an equal partner into the relevant SOE staff structure, which accordingly received a great reinforcement of personnel and resources. At that time, the SOE incumbents were inevitably the more experienced and, in the resultant SOE/OSS, retained their posts while the newcomers started as deputies.

My own deputy was a clever lawyer of Belgian origin—Paul van der Stricht; we got on very well, and his Canadian-born wife later resided in my house, a residence that was not only most convenient for SOE HQ in Baker Street but also housed several other distinguished lodgers including the minister's principal private secretary, Hugh Gaitskill (later Chancellor of the Exchequer and leader of the opposition in the House of Commons); Gaitskill's assistant and private secretary, Pat Hancock (later ambassador); and SOE's Arthur Knight (later chairman of Courtaulds).

The OSS arrived on the scene when the first phase of activity had succeeded after many losses and some mistakes in covering France (except in the east) with fairly comprehensive networks of varying effectiveness and intensity. Those composed the bulk—but not the whole—of my area, the western European (D/R) region of SOE.

The cooperation with the OSS in London went deeper, being based on integration with scope for the different operational styles of SOE, the OSS, and FFI (Forces Françaises de l'Intérieur). Command, planning, operations, and communications were integrated, and special aspects of activity were developed on top of the basic spread of sabotage through the regions and the network of agents. The basic plan of disruption of transport and communications was intensified and expanded but specially fortified by the introduction of field liaison units with the armies and of teams called "Jedburghs." These teams were in theory tripartite but in practice mainly bipartite. The tripartite concept meant three members from three different participating countries. The original idea, for example, mandated that a Jedburgh team working in France would have one American, one British, and one French member. Likewise, a team working in Italy would be composed of an American, a British, and an Italian member. In practice, however, only 10 of about 100 Jedburgh teams had members from three participating countries. Jedburgh teams were frequently unable to find a local representative. In many cases, particularly because of U.S. preference, the Jedburgh teams had one British and two American members or one British and two French members. These teams acted as focal units (in uniform) from D-day onward for contact, communication, and control with Resistance forces within the orbit of the invading troops. A special training school was set up for the months before D-day.

These two late developments, liaison units and Jedburgh teams (planned in 1943 and executed in 1944), proved effective almost beyond expectation. The liaison units provided contact, identification, and almost instant response, with tangible results (involving regular military forces and special SOE and OSS forces), especially in the prolonged campaign for the reoccupation of Holland. The Jedburghs, which required and received candidates of exceptional nerve and courage, took charge and procured deliveries in many areas and, as anticipated, proved a great stimulus to morale.

Both these activities depended from my establishment as Regional Director within Special Force Headquarters (SFHQ), which had superseded SOE/SO. At these stages and later on, the intervention of the Maquis (French Resistance fighters) made a sharp difference in the calls for help from the field. These requests were two-edged from the point of view of the planners and the deliverers because most of the people were not really Resistance in the specialized sense. They were resisting deportation to Germany but getting into local tangles, attracting German attention, and calling for and demanding supplies to an extent that was disruptive rather than productive. They had to be dealt with because they were there. My organization indicated to me that the total resistance in Western Europe by mid-1944 numbered 550,000. And I suppose that a quarter of those were Maquis, who were out of touch with orders, behind with communications, and totally deficient in stores and money. This complicated the issue, yet the change in the air situation made it possible to help them, whereas up to the spring of 1944, it had been almost impossible. The moment air control over Europe was fully established and daylight deliveries on a massive scale became possible, the intelligence services could take the Maquis more seriously and consider them customers-members. But until that moment, SFHQ had to resist Maquis appeals in order to maintain the limited services it could supply to the reseaux and build up for the drops of Jedburghs and to Jedburghs. In addition there were the needs of D-day and its aftermath. Almost my final responsibility before going overseas with SHAEF was to give the D-day exposition (attended by Gen. William J. Donovan) of the disposition of our joint resources, the plans, and the performance to date.

The OSS of course covered Secret Intelligence (SI) as well as Special Operations (SO), and their combined head was David Bruce, a most distinguished man with whom I formed a lasting friendship, which included a common interest in wine and visiting him in China when he was the U.S. representative before diplomatic relations were established.

Although I was responsible in SOE and therefore in SO for Western Europe, France was always the most important component and, with the predominance of invasion planning and preparations, inevitably took priority in SOE/SO operations.

There were several sections involved in France, but the three principal ones were "F," the section directly operated from England; "RF," which was for liaison with the Free French, who depended on us for supplies and communications; and "AMF," which operated from newly occupied North Africa. The first two sections worked to directives from COSSAC and later from SHAEF, while the third took its brief from Allied Force Headquarters (AFHQ) through a staff unit called Special Planning and Operations Center (SPOC), rather surprisingly under command of a "Mr. Brook in London"!

By this time, SOE and the British Foreign Office were fully convinced that Charles de Gaulle's position in France was too strong to be bypassed; this provided the only divergence I recall from the formal policy of the OSS, which was tied by Cordell Hull's and therefore Roosevelt's commitment to Vichy and distrust of de Gaulle, but this policy eventually dissolved, although having meanwhile led to American cooperation with Darlan.

De Gaulle himself, however, never acknowledged our right to run the independent "F" section, which nevertheless was acceptable to the Resistance and to French public opinion. The healing of this breach was finally consummated with the dedication by our patron, the Queen Mother, of the memorial to their 104 lost agents, which I attended on May 6 at Valencay.

The monument consists of two pillars that are shaped to curve around a large global light, which is a symbol of the moon. Although most of you may realize the importance of the moon in our lives, the symbolism does act as a regular reminder to the local people and any visitors that the whole of the clandestine phase depended on the possibility of operating night-flying aircraft, with night-trained pilots, and with tested grounds so that in the dark or semidark the pilots could find the reception committee and then either drop out at a very slow pace and run across the field or, later on, put down small aircraft on the landing ground. Valencay was chosen as a place for the memorial because it was one of two areas in France that was large enough to accommodate planes larger than Mosquitoes (the tiniest aircraft involved in the operations). I do not suppose many of you have traveled on a Mosquito—I do not recommend it! (Later on, the pilots were able to use Hudsons, which could carry more people and supplies.)

I was fortunate in my area that the breach with de Gaulle was the only serious political controversy, but those of you who have read the current memoirs of top KGB defector Gordievsky will have realized how crucial is the overriding political element in subversive activities, as my colleagues in Yugoslavia and Greece also found.

Owing to the imminence of the Torch landings, AMF under the recent Chairman of the Special Forces Club in London, Sir Brooks Richards (then Lt. Cdr. RNVR), had to act quickly. Both the tempo and the terrain on both sides of the Mediterranean gave full scope for the qualities and temperament of the OSS. Political events, too, proved favorable for de Gaulle, both with regard to the local situation and his fuller recognition by the United Kingdom and the United States. The contribution of the OSS was correspondingly greater in this theater, both in the buildup and in the execution of the Torch landing later.

Meanwhile, the major effort was concentrated in support of the prospective main landing, Operation Overlord. A proportion of this effort was diverted—from our point of view, wasted—in support of the amazingly successful deception plan to persuade the OKW and particularly Hitler that the main landing was still to come, *north* of the Somme.

The achievements of SFHQ in support of the invasion, including the fulfillment of the vast majority of the thousands of railway and communication cuts (the latter, by forcing enemy units onto the air, being even more significant than anticipated) have been well documented by Professor M.R.D. Foot and others.

The respective commanders in chief have given their appreciations, so I need say no more than that those results far exceeded the expectations of the military and came fully up to our own. They also, more important for the longer term, provided an indispensable stimulus to national morale and recovery in the occupied and oppressed nations.

Shortly afterward, General Eisenhower handed over responsibility inside France to General Koenig, with his HQ styled as Etat-Major, Forces Françaises de l'Intérieur (EMFFI), and this particular phase of my activities came to an end.

I followed with SHAEF to Versailles, Rheims, and Frankfurt with responsibilities partly operational, partly liaison within both G-3 and G-2. For some of those aspects my OSS opposite number was Col. Frank Canfield. Operations, in the main, were fully devolved onto field commanders, but SHAEF (G-3 Ops C) did take responsibility for one wide-ranging scheme, code-named "Vicarage," for contacting and dropping units into prisoner-of-war camps to avert the massacres of prisoners that were sometimes threatened. Communication was established with almost every POW camp and often duplicated, but in the end blackmail within the camps and the suddenness of the German collapse superseded most of the consummation.

Once we split up into Zones of Occupation in Germany, we went our several ways. But I was glad to exchange visits and views with Frank Wisner in his Ribbentrop mansion and Allen Dulles—whom I had known before and for whom I had a high regard—in Berlin. The almost open house that Dulles kept for the so-called "resisters" was remarkable and stimulating though a source of some difference of attitude as to their value! But by this time it was more of an agreeable aftermath.

I expect it is well realized what a strange place Berlin was at that time. And Allen Dulles really believed in a German resistance that might have accomplished something. I think we were a little bit skeptical, but it certainly was an enlivening side of life in Berlin. Otherwise it was very desolate to contemplate—and I had a slightly personal interest in the fate of an Olympic stadium, where I had competed only a few years before. Also, many of the secret archives had been discarded and were being used by the Russians as a substitute for toilet paper. It was a very unusual situation, in which our recent deadly enemy's complicated security arrangements were spread before us. I do not know what advantage the OSS was able to take of that situation or whether it turned out to be as important as it sounded. But somewhere, presumably, there are remains, not of our archives, but of their archives.

OSS: A REVIEW OF RECORDS, RESEARCH, AND LITERATURE

The third plenary session's panel was chaired by J. Kenneth McDonald, Chief Historian of the Central Intelligence Agency. Lawrence McDonald of the National Archives has spent several years processing the OSS records transferred from the Central Intelligence Agency and directs a team of volunteers who are preparing finding aids to the records. He made the first presentation. Panelist Richard Breitman is professor of history at the American University in Washington, DC. Breitman's several books include extensive use of World War II–era records in the National Archives. His presentation related primarily to the research use of OSS records and the utility of the various OSS finding aids. During his remarks, he praised the assistance of reference archivists for their many suggestions to him during his research. George Constantinides, a retired intelligence officer and bibliographer of intelligence literature, surveyed the entire genre of nonfiction relating to the OSS. This comprehensive survey included incisive and thoughtful assessments of the accuracy and utility of these publications. Constantinides also suggested areas where future research and publication were needed. During the discussion period that followed, the question of why British-originated material within OSS records was not declassified was raised. McDonald explained that it was the practice of the National Archives to obtain guidance from the British government concerning such material.

THE OSS AND
ITS RECORDS

Lawrence H. McDonald

July 11, 1991, is the 50th anniversary of the establishment of the Office of Coordinator of Information (COI) and of the appointment of William Donovan to serve as its director. The National Archives, and all of us attending this conference, also celebrate an acquisition of unprecedented significance, the accessioning of the records of the Office of Strategic Services.

The process of transferring, arranging, and describing these invaluable records has been under way now for more than a decade. Never before has a national intelligence agency released its records for research. Though the Central Intelligence Agency continues to declassify and transfer records remaining in its Office of Strategic Services (OSS) Archives, the National Archives has already received close to 5,000 cubic feet of OSS records and opened them for scholarly investigation.

After the OSS was terminated at the end of World War II, almost all the OSS records were eventually transferred to one of two agencies: the State Department or the Central Intelligence Agency. In 1975 and 1976 the National Archives opened over 1,100 cubic feet of OSS records received from the State Department for research. Of the more than 6,000 cubic feet of records in the OSS Archives of the Central Intelligence Agency, the CIA has, since 1980, transferred more than 3,200 cubic feet of records to the National Archives. Once they are declared inactive, only a small part of the records generated by federal agencies can be permanently preserved. The records of the OSS are a special case; most of them, with the exception of 2,000 cubic feet found to be of no historical value, will be assigned for permanent retention at the National Archives.[1]

OSS records draw heavy reference because this vast assortment of files reveals information never before available about one of the great defining moments in modern history, the Second World War. They offer the researcher a kind of précis of that war, providing a wealth of research ma-

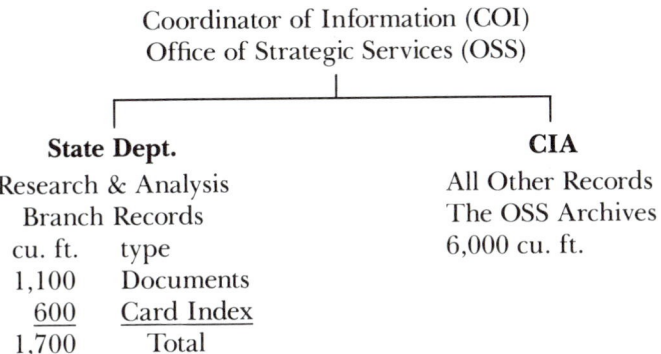

COI, OSS TEXTUAL RECORDS (1945)

Coordinator of Information (COI)
Office of Strategic Services (OSS)

State Dept.	CIA
Research & Analysis	All Other Records
Branch Records	The OSS Archives
cu. ft. type	6,000 cu. ft.
1,100 Documents	
600 Card Index	
1,700 Total	

After the OSS was closed down on October 1, 1945, its records were divided. Some 1,700 cubic feet of OSS R&A records were transferred to the State Department. The rest, amounting to more than 6,000 cubic feet, were eventually transferred to the CIA.

terial on every theater of the war in the form of intelligence files or of records on all aspects of covert operations in combat and behind enemy lines.

The OSS gathered *intelligence* on conditions in practically every country on earth, but it was not allowed to conduct covert *operations* in the Pacific theater, which Gen. Douglas MacArthur made entirely his own. At the insistence of J. Edgar Hoover and Nelson Rockefeller, the Coordinator of Inter-American Affairs, no OSS operations were allowed in Latin America. Hoover also brought domestic surveillance under the authority of the Federal Bureau of Investigation, barring OSS counterintelligence operations within the United States. For these reasons the records of OSS covert action operations are almost entirely confined to Europe, Asia, and North Africa.

Even so, the OSS established more than 40 different overseas offices during World War II, extending from Casablanca to Shanghai and from Stockholm to Pretoria, and the OSS Research and Analysis Branch (R&A) made intelligence analysis of conditions within practically every nation in the world. One could write a history of the Second World War from the intelligence files of the OSS alone. In short, researchers use the OSS records more heavily than almost any other 20th-century military records in the National Archives.

OSS files provide a record of America's first national intelligence agency, founded belatedly in the crucible of war, long after other great powers had accorded foreign intelligence and covert operations a distinct and permanent role within their political systems. As predecessor to the Central Intelligence Agency, the OSS not only passed on to the CIA its records, methods, and experience, but it provided a training ground for many of the CIA's eminent intelligence officers. Four of the CIA's fourteen directors—Allen Dulles, Richard Helms, William Colby, and William Casey—have been OSS veterans. Indeed, the ranks of OSS veterans furnish a roster of many of the best and brightest in nearly every field in American life.

President Roosevelt established the Office of Coordinator of Information to collect, correlate, and disseminate all intelligence relating to national security. He appointed the charismatic William J. Donovan, who served as a dollar-a-year man, as chief of this civilian agency. The U.S. Army, Navy, State Department, FBI, Secret Service, Immigration and Naturalization Service, Customs Service, and Treasury Department all had offices for foreign intelligence. The COI was to synthesize and disseminate intelligence acquired from all these agencies.

The President's draft of the original order establishing the new centralized intelligence agency gave Donovan military authority and stipulated that the new agency was to have the name Coordinator of Strategic Information. Opposition from the Army and Navy to the idea of a centralized intelligence organization was so strong that the President revised the draft and changed the name to Coordinator of Information. Reluctantly the military accepted, but an underlying opposition remained. Donovan's critics found him personally ambitious; some dismissed him as an enthusiastic amateur.

Adversaries rightly believed that COI would bear the stamp of Donovan's dynamic personality. Donovan served with great distinction in World War I as an officer in the 42d Division, the "Rainbow Division." Awarded the Medal of Honor, the Distinguished Service Cross, the Distinguished Service Medal, and the Croix de Guerre, "Wild Bill," as he was known to the troops, returned from France one of the most highly decorated American soldiers.[2] After the war, Donovan served in the Coolidge administration as Assistant Attorney General for the Antitrust Division. Returning to private practice in 1929, he founded the firm of Donovan Leisure Newton and Irvine in New York City. Before America marched to war again, he was a millionaire.

Donovan's reputation for reckless bravery followed him into World War II. He went ashore with the troops at Anzio. He met with OSS Detachment 101 guerrillas behind enemy lines in Burma. On D-day, he and David K. E. Bruce went in with the invasion force. When he and Bruce found themselves pinned down by a German machine gun on Utah Beach, Donovan informed Bruce that they could not allow themselves to be taken alive and asked him if he was carrying his suicide pill, the L tablet. Bruce confessed he had neglected to bring the poison tablet with him. Donovan searched his pockets for his own L tablets but found none. Then he said, "Ah well, no matter for the pills. If the Germans take us, I'll shoot you

COI, OSS, AND THEIR SUCCESSORS

Agency	Established	Personnel	Budget
Coordinator of Information (COI)	11 July 1941	c. 1,600	$12,953,832
Office of Strategic Services (OSS)	13 June 1942	12,718	$115,547,232 (1942-46)
Strategic Services Unit (SSU)	27 Sept. 1945	9,028	$11,858,683 (FY 1947)
Central Intelligence Group (CIG)	22 Jan. 1946		
Central Intelligence Agency (CIA)	18 Sept. 1947		

The Coordinator of Information (COI) was the first of a series of U.S. intelligence agencies that eventually transferred its functions, records, and staff to the CIA.

first as your commanding officer, then I'll shoot myself, so there's nothing to worry about."[3]

He was, as President Eisenhower described him, "the last hero," and he loved the excitement of war. Roger Hilsman writes that, having seen the horror of war at first hand, many combatants would settle for an honorable wound and safe passage back to their home and country for the duration of the war.[4] Though not a war-lover, Donovan, by contrast, seemed eager for American intervention in the war against the Axis.

An Irish American and an interventionist Republican, Donovan made a welcome addition to the bipartisan war coalition that President Roosevelt desired. Donovan already had the support of such administration contacts and fellow Republicans as Secretary of the Navy Frank Knox and Secretary of War Henry Stimson.

Donovan's energy and enthusiasm affected every branch and unit in COI.[5] To spread American propaganda by means of radio broadcasts and publications, the Foreign Information Service (FIS) was established in July 1941. FIS was the major psychological warfare instrument of COI, and with its listening outposts, it also became an effective source of intelligence. The Oral Intelligence Unit interviewed recent travelers, who brought COI information from all parts of the world. The work of this unit would later be taken over by the OSS Survey of Foreign Experts. American ethnic groups and organizations were tapped for information concerning their countries of origin in Europe and the Mediterranean by the Foreign Nationalities Branch. The Visual Presentation Branch prepared films and illustrations for documentary presentation and assembled pictorial records of strategic value.

The collection of intelligence by undercover agents outside the Americas was predicated on an agreement with the Army and Navy that their espionage services would be consolidated under the Coordinator of Information. But the President's order establishing COI did not give this new agency a definitive charter. The President and Donovan agreed that there would be no directive in writing concerning specific functions. And Donovan developed COI in action more than in theory. Though there had been no authorization for them, a section in Donovan's office, designated "Special Activities–K and L Funds," was established to manage COI's own espionage, sabotage, subversive activities, and guerrilla units.

During his mission to England in the summer of 1940, Donovan had learned much of British methods of unorthodox warfare. In November 1941, Donovan placed a branch office in London, which would work closely with the British Special Operations Executive in training American covert action teams. The London office grew from a staff of 50 to 2,000 personnel during the course of the war and became the prototype of OSS offices throughout the world.[6]

But COI failed to win the support of the intelligence-gathering agencies. J. Edgar Hoover described COI as "Roosevelt's folly." When COI agents made a clandestine raid on the Spanish Embassy in Washington to photograph documents, Hoover, eager to protect his own territory, ordered several FBI squad cars to the embassy, sirens blaring, forcing the COI agents to take flight. Assistant Secretary of State Adolf Berle disdained all espionage as "paranoid work." Army and Navy intelligence chiefs, jealous of their won prerogatives, offered little cooperation and, in some cases, deliberately withheld information from COI.

COI was also divided within. The chief of FIS was Robert Sherwood, a Roosevelt speechwriter who won four Pulitzer prizes. He believed that FIS should broadcast only white propaganda, the open dissemination of the truth, but Donovan wanted to make use of black propaganda as well. Black propaganda deliberately falsifies its source, purporting to emanate from the enemy, for instance, but actually originating in the OSS Morale Operations Branch (MO).

Sherwood conceded the usefulness of black propaganda in some situations. Many others in FIS rejected it entirely. Black propaganda, they believed, would poison the wellsprings of information from which all, friend or foe, would drink deeply. It would bring every Allied statement about the war under suspicion.

The pros and cons of disinformation and deception notwithstanding, Robert Sherwood and most of the top FIS officials were not comfortable with Donovan and the military men in COI, whom they regarded as reactionaries.[7] When Donovan injured his knee in an automobile accident and was temporarily disabled, Sherwood joined with Librarian of Congress Archibald MacLeish and Budget Director Harold Smith to heighten the chorus of those urging the President to dismantle COI. But Donovan also had advocates at home and abroad. He profited much from the advice and support of a British naval intelligence officer stationed in Washington, Ian Fleming, later to become the author of the James Bond espionage novels.[8] Fleming provided Donovan with valuable information on the structure and operation of the British intelligence system and encouraged COI to develop the closest possible liaison with MI6.

Still more important to the vital connection between COI (and later the OSS) and the masterful British intelligence and covert operations was Sir William "Little Bill" Stephenson, Britain's wartime intelligence chief in the United States, who generously supplied Donovan with highly classified information concerning the superior methods and organization of the British Secret Intelligence Service. Knowing Donovan to be an Anglophile and an ardent interventionist, Little Bill made Wild Bill an indispensable channel for the exchange of top secret information and warmly assisted his efforts to design COI/OSS under British influence and direction. "There

SSU ARRANGEMENT OF THE OSS ARCHIVES

A—**Locations:**

Algiers	Caserta	Madrid
Amzon	Chungking	New Delhi
Angola	Costa Rica	New York
Athens	Dakar	Norway
Austria	Denmark	Oslo
Barcelona	Heidelberg	Pacific Coast Area
Bari	Holland	Paris
Belgium	Honolulu	Prague
Bern	Iceland	Pretoria
Bucharest	Istanbul	Rome
Burma	Kandy	Shanghi
Calcutta	Kunming	7th Army
Cairo	Lisbon	Singapore
Casablanca	London	Stockholm
		Washington

B—**Office**

Budget and Finance	Office of Strategic Services
Camouflage Division	Operations Group
Censorship Division	Operational Supply
Communications	Personnel
Counterintelligence	Personnel Procurement Branch
Cover and Documentation	Pictorial Records
Director's Office	Planning Group
Division of Oral Intelligence	Planning Staff
Emergency Rescue Equipment	Property Board
Field Experimental Unit	Registry
Field Photographic Branch	Reproductions Branch
Finance	Research and Analysis
Foreign Nationalities Branch	Research and Development
General Counsel	Schools and Training
George Office	Secretariat
Headquarters	Security
Headquarters and	Services
Headquarters Detachment	Secret Intelligence
History Office	7th Army
History Project	Special Funds
Intelligence Service	Special Funds Division Finance
Maritime Unit	Special Operations
Medical Service	Special Projects
Morale Operations	Survey of Foreign Experts
Naval Command	Strategic Service Operations

B—Office *Continued*
Technical Services Staff
Theater Office
Transportation

Visual Presentation
X-2

C—Category
Administrative (AD)
Equipment (EQ)
Financial (FIN)
Index
Intelligence (INT)
Maps
Miscellaneous (MISC)
Other

Operational (OP)
Personalities (PTS)
Personnel (PERS)
Photographs and Motion Pictures
(PHOTO)
Projects (PRO)
Propaganda (PROPA)
Radio and Cable (R&C)
Research (RES)

After World War II, the Strategic Services Unit (SSU), a group of OSS veterans, arranged most OSS records according to these OSS locations, offices, and file categories.

is no doubt that we can achieve more through Donovan than any other individual," said Stephenson. "He is receptive and can be trusted to represent our needs in the right way."[9]

President Roosevelt resolved the matter. On June 13, 1942, he abolished COI and established by military order the Office of Strategic Services under the jurisdiction of the Joint Chiefs of Staff (JCS). COI's records and all its functions, except Sherwood's foreign information activities, which were assigned to the Office of War Information, were transferred to the OSS. JCS Directive No. 67, dated June 23, 1942, described and empowered the OSS to prepare intelligence studies, to plan and execute subversive activities, and to collect information through espionage. JCS 155/4/D, dated December 23, 1942, further authorized the OSS to carry out psychological warfare in direct support of military operations. It defined psychological warfare to include propaganda, economic warfare, sabotage, guerrilla warfare, counterespionage, contact with underground groups in enemy-controlled territory, and contact with foreign-nationality groups in the United States.

COI had been a small civilian agency composed of little more than a handful of branches and offices. Before the close of World War II, the OSS, a semimilitary agency, would develop more than 40 branches and units with a well-chosen staff of almost 13,000 men and women. Modeled closely on the British systems of intelligence and covert operations, the OSS combined the functions assigned to four British organizations—the Secret Intelligence Service (MI6), Special Operations Executive (SOE), Political Warfare Executive (PWE), and the Foreign Office Research Department—

OSS WASHINGTON DIRECTOR'S OFFICE RECORDS FRAGMENTS

CIA JOB	Received at NA	Boxes	Contents	SSU Arrangement (LOC)
78 - 713c	3 Jan. 1980	1 - 7	Miscellaneous records	WASH-DIR OFF-OP-267
57 - 114	23 April 1985	1 - 10	Combined Intel. Committee minutes, reports, etc.	WASH-DIR OFF-AD-76
56 - 31	3 Sept. 1985	120 - 121	Radio and Cables (Thai)	WASH-DIR OFF-R&C-1-4
79 - 461	12 Mar. 1986	1 - 9	Correspondence with Navy, State, and War Depts. and with FDR and HST	WASH-DIR OFF-AD-81
81 - 815	22 July 1986	538 - 739	All other records from Gen. Donovan's office	WASH-DIR OFF-AD-1-75 (57-114) AD-77-78 (79-461) EQ-1-3 FIN-1-6 INT-1-17 OP-1-267 PERS-1-31 PHOTO-1 PRO-1-2 (56-31) RES-1-6 (78-713c)
80 - 452	12 July 1991	1 - 5	Boston Series (Fritz Kolbe)	WASH-DIR OFF-INT-11

In the years following World War II, the system of arrangement imposed on OSS records by SSU was largely lost, and the records were scattered in fragments throughout the CIA's archives. The records of the Washington Director's Office, shown here, had to be reconstructed from fragments transferred to the National Archives in six different shipments.

into one agency.[10] The OSS not only added operational units to carry on clandestine warfare and sabotage but also assumed full responsibility for the entire intelligence cycle including direction and planning of intelligence requirements; collection of intelligence; evaluation, analysis, integration, and interpretation; and dissemination or distribution of the final product to appropriate offices, called customers.

The OSS assigned the collection of covert intelligence primarily to its Foreign Nationalities Branch (FNB) and its Secret Intelligence Branch (SI). On December 22, 1941, President Roosevelt approved a plan to establish FNB within COI. FNB was to provide a new field of political intelligence by organizing contact with political refugees and with those important groups in the United States that were of recent foreign extraction and therefore retained distinctive ties with their countries of origin. The FNB staff was small, limited to only 40 or 50 people, but immigrant groups in the United States, eager to show their loyalty to the American war effort, voluntarily provided information concerning Europe and the nations of the Mediterranean area. Exploiting this cost-efficient advantage, FNB was to measure the mood and exploit the intelligence sources of non-Asian foreign-language groups.[11] FNB records provide a mine of information concerning the hopes and fears, the loyalties and bitterness of first-generation Americans at midcentury.

Far more important in the collection of intelligence was the OSS Secret Intelligence Branch. SI produced almost a sixth of all the records in the OSS Archives of the Central Intelligence Agency, more than any other OSS unit except Research and Analysis. SI records are scattered throughout Record Group 226, but most SI intelligence is concentrated in a large regional file, the Washington Registry Office SI Branch Field Files, which consists of some 450 cubic feet of records.[12]

The special task of SI was espionage, the collection of intelligence by clandestine means primarily from human sources. Espionage is distinct from other forms of intelligence collection such as communications interception, cryptanalysis, photographic interpretation, and other methods of intelligence acquisition. But though the OSS Foreign Broadcast Quarterly Corporation (FBQ) occasionally recorded radio intercepts and the OSS London Office's Enemy Objectives Unit (EOU) employed photographic interpretation to plan strategic bombing, espionage was the main source of OSS intelligence.[13]

Most of the intelligence collection for the French Riviera campaign, in August 1944, was the work of the OSS, especially the OSS field offices in Caserta and Algiers, which gathered intelligence on everything, as William Casey said, "down to the location of every last pillbox or pylon." Some of the most significant intelligence gathering was the product of OSS offices in neutral capitals.[14] The OSS Lisbon and Madrid offices were established early, and the OSS Istanbul office was located in a famous seat of intrigue.

OSS RECORDS AT THE NATIONAL ARCHIVES

Textual Records		Quantity
Research and Analysis Br. (State Dept.)	Reports, etc.	1,100 cubic feet
	Card Indexes	+ 600
		1,700
OSS Archives of the Central Intelligence Agency		+ 3,200
		4,900

Other Record Types	Quantity
Maps and Charts	7,648 items
Motion Pictures	367 reels
Sound Recordings	27 items
Still Pictures	11,933 images

A survey of the OSS textual records and other OSS record types now in the National Archives.

OSS Stockholm sent agents into Norway and Denmark. In Switzerland, a memorable contribution to determining the progress of German nuclear and bacteriological research was made by an OSS officer, Moe Berg, who spoke six languages. But Moe Berg will be remembered at least as well for his years in the American League as catcher for the Washington Senators and the Boston Red Sox.[15]

The work of Allen Dulles's Bern office was outstanding. During World War I, Dulles had served as an American espionage agent in Switzerland, where he was once approached by Russian revolutionary N. Lenin. Dulles failed to meet with Lenin, to whom the Germans had just offered transportation to the Finland Station and safe return to Russia. As director of the OSS Bern office, however, Dulles rarely failed to take advantage of sound intelligence provided by unsolicited walk-ins. At great personal risk, German anti-Nazis Fritz Dolbe, Fritz Molden, Hans Bernd Gisevius, and others brought Dulles vital intelligence concerning German order-of-battle, aircraft defenses, submarine production, the V-1 and V-2 rockets, and other matters. At first, British MI6 experts Harold "Kim" Philby and Sir Claude Dansey dismissed much of the intelligence collected by the OSS Bern office as the fabrications of German plants spiced with just enough truth to make them seem plausible. Time would show that Philby was a Soviet agent, and careful appraisal and analysis would establish the quality and reliability of the OSS Bern production.[16]

Without proper evaluation, the best intelligence collection may be dismissed as so many meaningless facts. The swarm of unprocessed information, sometimes haphazard and indiscriminate, generated by collection may lead to an intelligence glut more confusing than enlightening. Sorting out the raw data produced by SI and other OSS units, integrating it into a coherent pattern, analyzing it and preparing finished intelligence in the form of reports, studies, and memorandums in response to anticipated customer requests—these were the functions of the OSS Research and Analysis Branch. The R&A staff selected the pertinent material from the mass of fragments and details furnished by clandestine sources and incorporated it with information drawn from overt intelligence—the periodicals, books, monographs, and other publications and records available in our open society. At least 80 or 90 percent of the intelligence exploited by R&A derived from open sources available at places like the Library of Congress and the National Archives, where the OSS maintained small offices.[17]

The Director of the R&A Branch throughout most of the war was Professor William L. Langer of Harvard University, an eminent historian renowned for his scholarly monographs and familiar to students of history as editor of the Langer series on the rise of modern Europe. The exceptional style and scholarship often typical of R&A reports and memorandums is not surprising when one considered that Langer appointed some

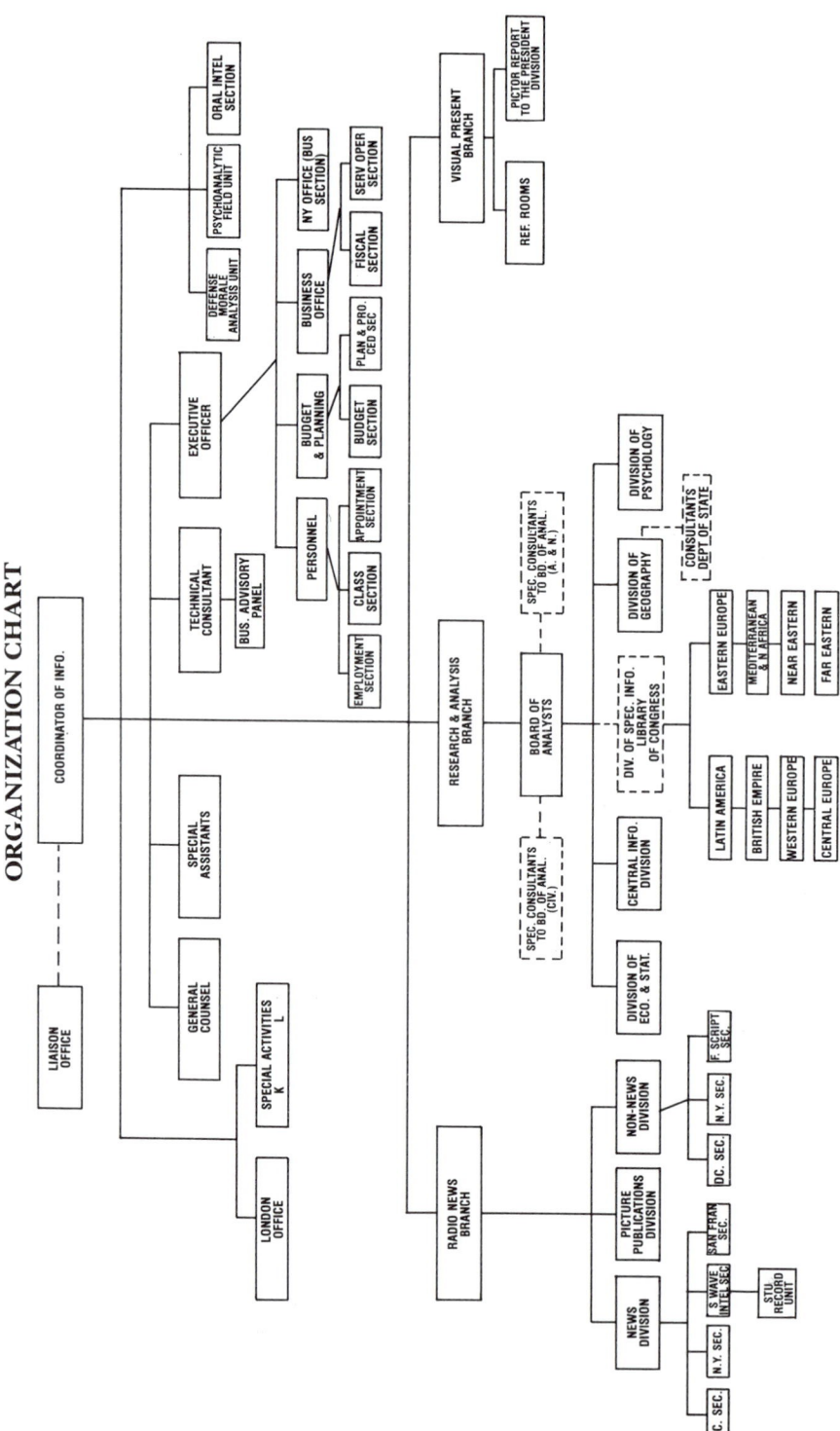

ORGANIZATION CHART

COI organizational chart, October 10, 1941.

The Office of Coordinator of Information had a relatively small staff and existed for only 11 months, but its organizational chart included many of the finest historians, economists, and social scientists in the United States. Among them, to mention only a few, were Crane Brinton, Harold Deutsch, Hajo Holborn, Ray Cline, H. Stuart Hughes, Arthur Schlesinger, Jr., Herbert Marcuse, Carl Schorske, Walt Rostow, John K. Fairbank, and Charles Kindleberger. Five of the R&A economists later became presidents of the American Economic Association; seven of the historians became presidents of the American Historical Association.[18]

In 1946 the State Department, which had taken over the bulk of the R&A files after the war, began releasing R&A records amounting to some 1,700 cubic feet of documents to the National Archives. Like the files of other OSS units, R&A records include correspondence, cables, minutes of meetings, progress reports, budget studies, press clippings, foreign publications files, POW interrogations, target information, and a large map collection. The largest series by far, however, consist of informational intelligence reports on political, economic, military, and morale matters for almost every nation in the world. The reports series were organized as a straight numerical file—every document being assigned the next consecutive number, whatever its subject or provenance, as received—by the R&A Central Information Division (CID) Library under Wilmarth S. Lewis. They are accessible only through the card index developed by the CID Library.

Protecting the security of OSS intelligence collection, analysis, and operations against enemy intelligence was the function of the OSS Counterintelligence Branch (X-2). Counterintelligence exposed and counteracted enemy espionage. Penetration, as James Jesus Angleton observed, is the essence of counterintelligence. OSS X-2 worked its way inside the Axis intelligence systems while preventing enemy penetration of OSS operations.

Before D-day, British Counterintelligence (MI5) captured practically every German spy whom the Reich had sent into Britain, some 120 agents in all, and forced them to turn against their Nazi masters. These doubled agents identified other German spies, revealed the methods of the German intelligence services, provided the Allies with German codes and ciphers, and sent carefully contrived disinformation back to Germany. This Double-Cross System, made famous by Sir John Masterman's monograph of the same name, was the work of the Twenty Committee (XX), to which Norman Holmes Pearson, the Chief of OSS London X-2, was assigned as liaison.[19]

The revelation after the war of massive Soviet penetration of Britain's Secret Intelligence Service at the highest level severely weakened the credibility of all British intelligence services despite postwar efforts to recover the confidence of their allies by enforcement of the Official Secrets Act. In the wilderness of mirrors that was World War II espionage, James Angleton, known to his colleagues in the intelligence community as the Delphic

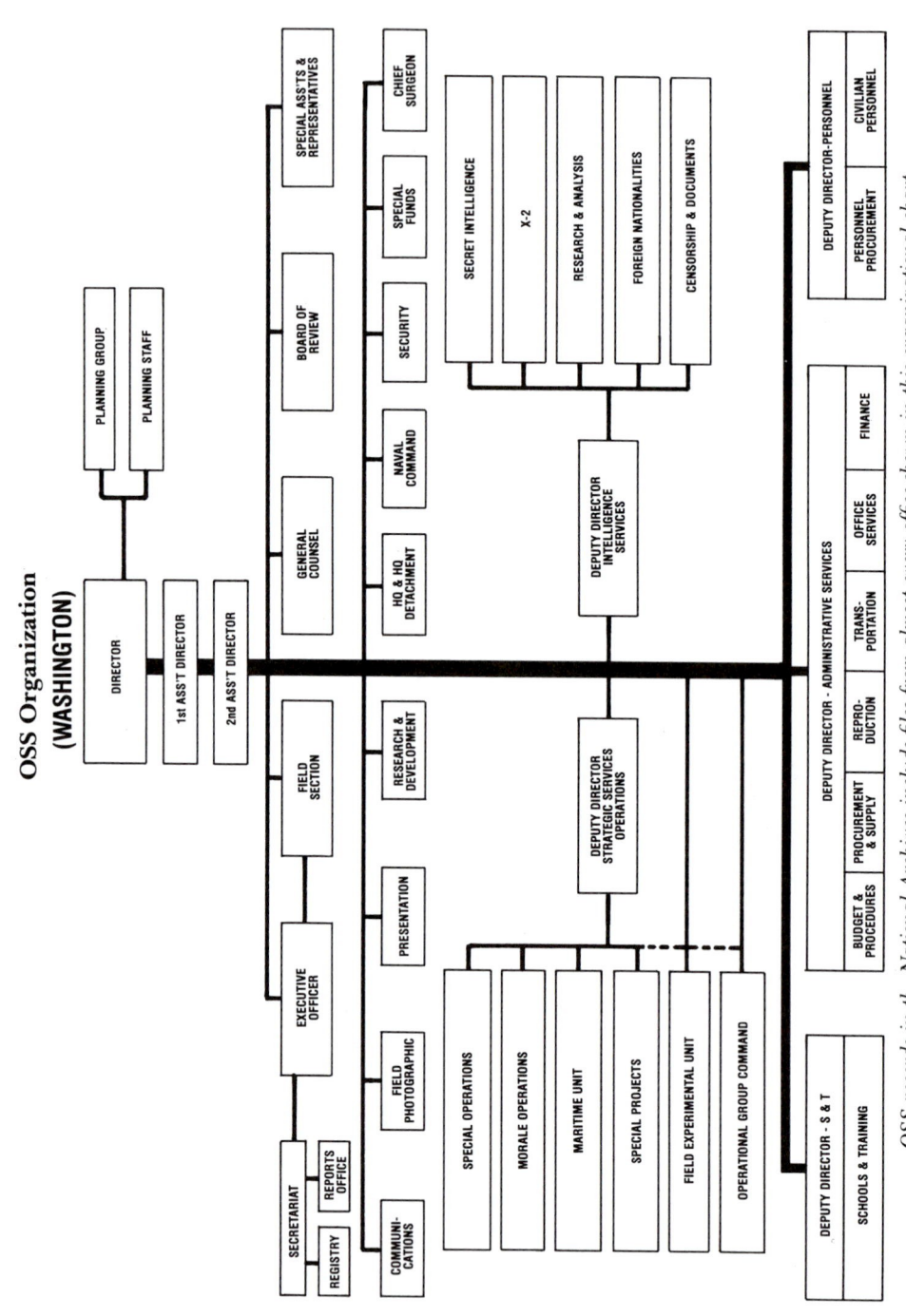

OSS Organization (WASHINGTON)

OSS records in the National Archives include files from almost every office charge in this organizational chart.

Oracle, may have already discovered the treachery of Kim Philby and the Cambridge Apostles Guy Burgess and Sir Anthony Blunt before the war ended. That the OSS was also the target of Soviet penetration is certain. Ardent Marxists and Communists, like the Lincoln Brigade veterans and emigré scholars, were among the most competent and dedicated anti-Fascists, and Donovan knowingly appointed them to positions in the OSS. "I'd put Stalin on the OSS payroll if I thought it would help us defeat Hitler," said Donovan.[20]

The reality or the extent of penetration of the OSS by Soviet moles or other infiltration remains largely an unanswered question. The CIA did not originally offer to transfer financial, personnel, and counterintelligence files from its OSS Archives to the National Archives. The CIA at first withheld financial files in case of legal investigation; personnel files were withheld in order that the CIA might service the requests of OSS veterans. Counterintelligence files, being among the most security sensitive of OSS records, were withheld to protect intelligence methods and security, especially the identity of informants. After careful review of these records, however, the CIA has begun releasing most of them. The watchlist, vetting, safe haven, personalities, and intelligence files and other material in X-2 records may yet provide the answers to some of our questions.[21]

General Donovan believed that the principal contribution of the OSS would be strategic intelligence, which is the basis for the formation of national policy. This primarily would be the final product of collection, analysis, and synthesis by the FNB, SI, R&A, and X-2.[22] Some of the most valuable information contributed by the OSS, however, was the tactical or field intelligence often provided by the OSS Special Operations Branch (SO) teams working behind enemy lines with resistance groups. The foremost concern of SO teams and missions was liaison with the resistance, providing weapons and supplies to the indigenous underground forces, training them, and planning and coordinating their sabotage with Allied operations. SO teams also secured target information and assisted in the rescue of downed Allied airmen.

Outstanding among the SO missions in Europe were the Jedburgh teams. The Jedburghs were specially trained three-man teams parachuted into France, Belgium, and Holland on and after D-day. Each team consisted of two officers and a radio operator. One officer was a native of the country to which the team was sent, and the other British or American. Working closely with the British Special Operations Executive (SOE), SO sent 87 Jedburgh teams and 19 OSS Operation Groups, or guerrilla units, into France alone.[23]

In June 1944, as the Allied invasion of France began, a wave of popular support for the army of liberation swept across Europe. Resistance forces, assisted by the Jedburghs, crippled German efforts to counterattack by cutting rails, destroying bridges, mining roads, cutting off telecommuni-

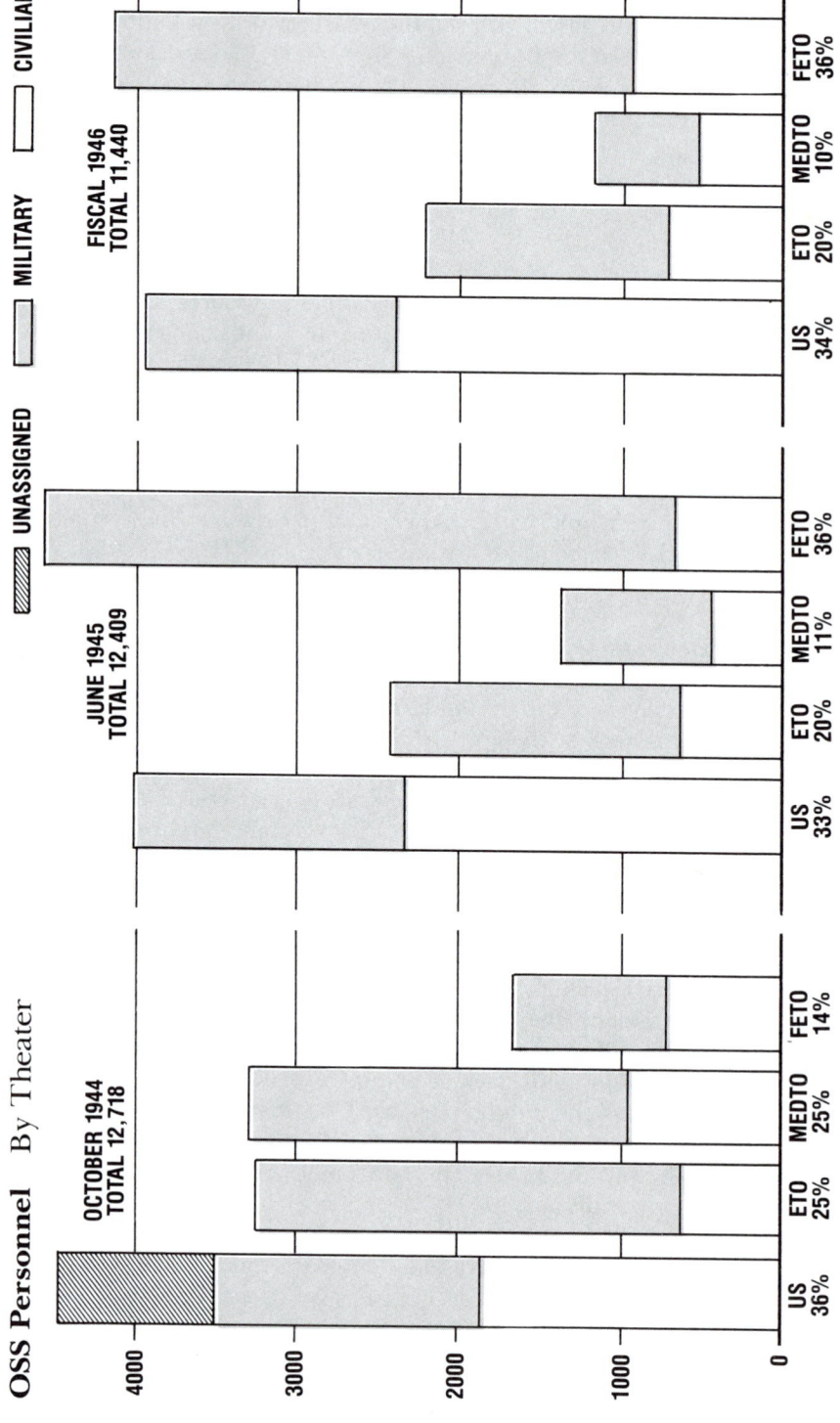

OSS Personnel By Theater

cations, and sabotaging German vehicles. As a consequence, the German response to the Allied invasion was delayed by 48 hours. So successful were the Jedburgh teams that General Eisenhower requested additional SO support for resistance groups and for acquisition of tactical intelligence.[24]

Even before V–E Day, many of the Jedburghs were transferred to the China theater, where Jedburgh methods of training, organizing, supplying, and leading indigenous troops were applied with the same success as in Europe. SO teams inflicted heavy losses on imperial forces by sudden strike and withdraw tactics, destroying communications and transportation and isolating Japanese units. Vital to Japan's control of the Chinese interior was the mile-long bridge that crossed the Hwang-Ho (Yellow) River near Kaifeng. This double-track bridge was the thread that joined the Japanese armies of north and south China. Against all odds, Jed veterans and a brave band of Chinese guerrillas under the command of Col. Frank Mills and Maj. Paul Cyr mined the great Hwang-Ho bridge. On August 9, 1945, the day Nagasaki was bombed, SO Mission Jackal blew away two large spans in the bridge just as a Japanese troop train was passing over. The entire train, carrying some 2,000 Japanese soldiers, was dragged to the bottom of the Hwang-Ho.[25]

The destruction of the Hwang-Ho bridge was one of the many achievements of SO Detachment 202 in the China theater. Preeminent as the model for successful guerrilla operations and the predecessor of the Green Berets was the famed SO Detachment 101, which did much to win the war for the Burma Road. To reestablish contact with Chiang Kai-shek's Nationalist army, the Allies had to wrest control of the Ledo-Burma Road away from Japan's 15th Army and open the highway from the Lashio railhead to Kunming. Enlisting the support of native peoples like the Kachins, Karens, and Chinese in Burma, some 1,000 officers and men of Detachment 101 formed a guerrilla army more than 10,000 strong that fought savage jungle warfare against determined Japanese troops. The monsoon rains fell upon them in sheets. Leeches crawled through the eyelets of their boots; they poured the water and blood out of them at the end of the day. Cholera, plague, and typhus were a constant threat. Malaria and bacillary dysentery were unavoidable. Fighting under some of the worst combat conditions in the war, Detachment 101 perfected the art of guerrilla warfare, harassing the enemy with strike and evasion tactics, baiting them into reckless retaliation against the native population, and inflaming the smoldering embers of resentment into a conflagration of hate against the Japanese occupation of Burma. Before the war ended, Detachment 101 destroyed Japanese forces many times their numbers.[26]

Less than 3 weeks after V–J Day, President Truman signed the order terminating the OSS, effective October 1, 1945. When the OSS finally closed its doors, custody of all its records was assigned to one of two

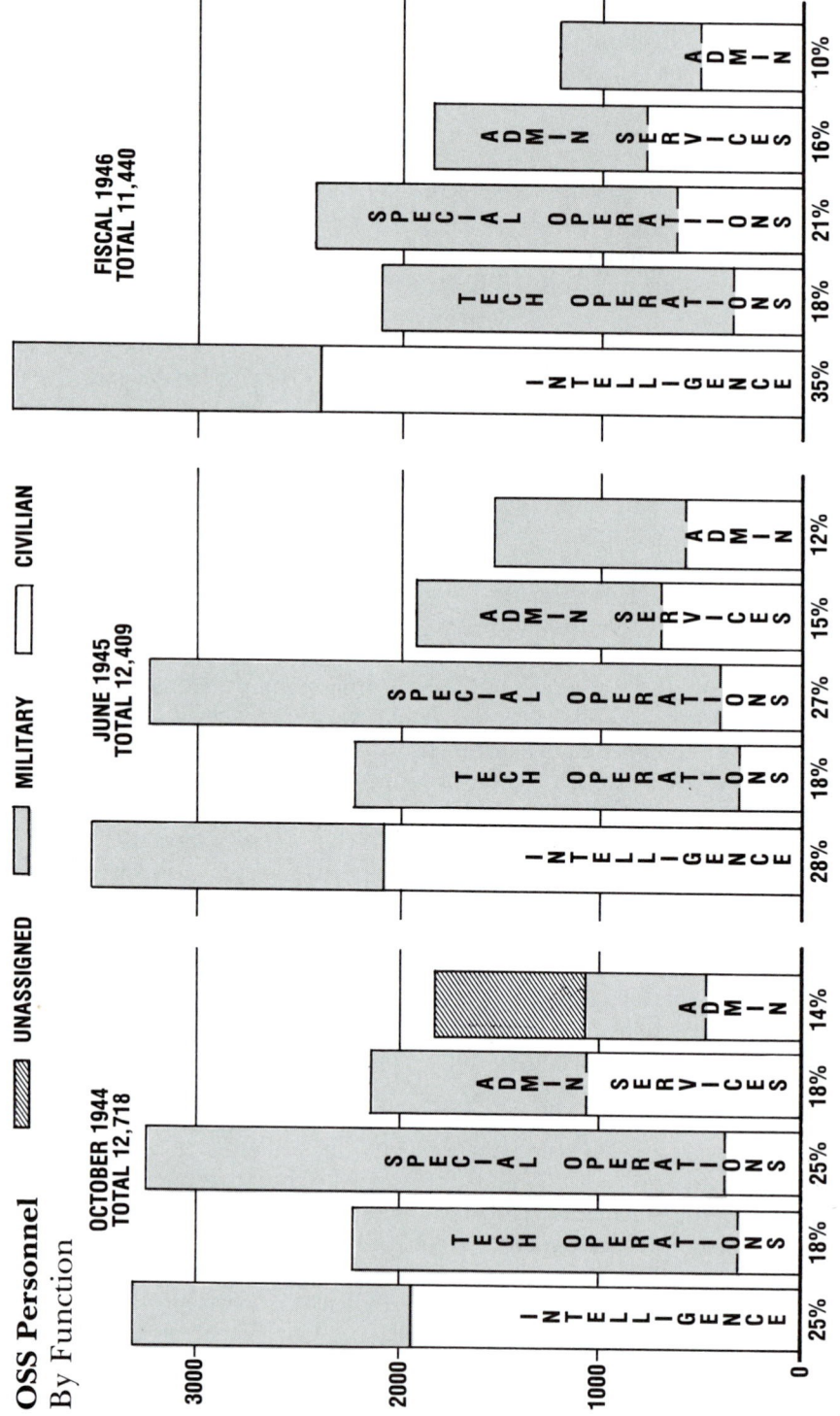

OSS Personnel By Function

agencies. As mentioned earlier, 1,700 cubic feet of reports and other files from the CID Library of the Research and Analysis Branch were sent to the State Department. All other OSS records were transferred to the Strategic Services Unit (SSU), a War Department office made up of veterans drawn from the OSS Secret Intelligence and Counterintelligence branches. Half the records acquired by SSU consisted of the files of the New York, San Francisco, and especially the Washington OSS offices; the other half comprised the records of all OSS overseas offices. Bringing together more than 6,000 cubic feet of records from the home offices and from OSS outposts all over the world, the SSU carefully arranged them according to point of origin, thereunder by OSS branch or unit, and thereunder by file type. To this day every file folder received by SSU bears the mark of this fundamental system of arrangement. Having labeled each folder, the SSU then shelved the records alphabetically, beginning with the Algiers Office and ending with the Washington Office.

In 1947 the Central Intelligence Agency assumed custody of the OSS records so carefully arranged by the SSU. After years of hard use at the CIA, the SSU's original system of arrangement was largely lost, the various series often becoming mixed due to frequent relocation and reshelving. The records of General Donovan's Washington office, for instance, were gradually broken up and interfiled in five different and unrelated series. In the 1950s the CIA reorganized its OSS Archives and created a complicated set of finding aids in the form of multiple card indexes, which it integrated with the indexes to its own CIA records. The CIA's system of access and control, though workable, was necessarily complex, often requiring a tripartite search to locate a single document.

In 1980 the CIA began transferring its OSS Archives to the National Archives, becoming the first national intelligence agency ever to release its once-classified records for research. Of the 6,000 cubic feet in the OSS Archives of the Central Intelligence Agency, the CIA has so far transferred more than 3,000 cubic feet to the National Archives. In addition, following the National Archives appraisal, the CIA was allowed to destroy 2,000 cubic feet that were determined to have no value for research. The CIA is in the process of reviewing the records remaining in its OSS Archives and transferring them to the National Archives.

Reasons of security made it necessary for the CIA to retain all of the finding aids. With the generous help of volunteer workers, the National Archives has been creating its own finding aids for the CIA's OSS Archives. Descriptive lists are now available for most of the OSS records at the National Archives, and the lists have been computerized to improve access and control.

Thanks to years of work by the NARA projects volunteers, we now have folder lists for most of the records accessioned from the CIA's OSS Archives, and as we computerized these lists, we have reconstituted, intellectually, the original series arrangement.

The underlying issue here involves the methods and purpose of description and arrangement of the CIA's OSS Archives accessioned so far. The nine different computer printouts compiled for OSS records received at the National Archives are abstracts of the folder lists, which were composed according to a standard format by the OSS projects volunteers. The computer printouts are as follows:

1. Point of Origin: Also displays branch, record type/serial, and associated location (where included).

2. Branch: Also displays record type/serial, point of origin, and associated location.

3. Associated Location: Also displays point of origin, branch, and record type/serial.

4. Area: Also displays point of origin, branch, record type/serial, and associated location.

5. Code/Project Name: Also displays point of origin, branch, record type/serial, and personal name (where included).

6. Personal Name: Also displays point of origin, branch, and record type/serial.

7. Notes: Also displays point of origin, branch, and record type/serial.

8. Record Type: Also displays point of origin, branch, and associated location (where included).

9. Entry: Also displays box and folder number, point of origin, area, associated location, code/project name, and personal name.

The development of these printouts is an ongoing process even now. Our first objective after compiling folder lists had to be bringing the scattered fragments of the series back together by means of computer arrangement. As a consequence, most of our time and effort has been devoted to building up our printouts for Point of Origin (#1), Branch (#2), and Record Type (#8) in order to determine what the National Archives had received and where it was. This was essential to establish control over the OSS Archives, and we gave this task primary consideration.

The subject index is a recent creation as opposed to numbers 1, 2, and 8. It is still quite small (151 pages) compared to the 1, 2, and 8 printouts (1,020 pages each). But the National Archives is steadily working at it.

The Personal Name File (#6) printout has grown by almost 25 percent since May 1991 to 611 pages. But this printout is also relatively new.

The Code/Project Name (#5) printout is also a highly useful finding aid, which has given many researchers who already have some knowledge of code names a significant practical advantage.

The printout for Associated Location (#3) will be generally indispensable for researching the records of the CIA's OSS Archives. Half the entries that appear in the Point of Origin (#1) printout are OSS home

Fiscal 1945

OSS APPROPRIATION $ 7,000,000
ARMY-NAVY CONTRIBUTION 89,000,000
TOTAL OSS OBLIGATION 96,000,000
(SUPPLIES DELIVERED, IN WAREHOUSE, EN ROUTE, AND ORDERED)

OSS Supply Obligations
Distributed by Theater

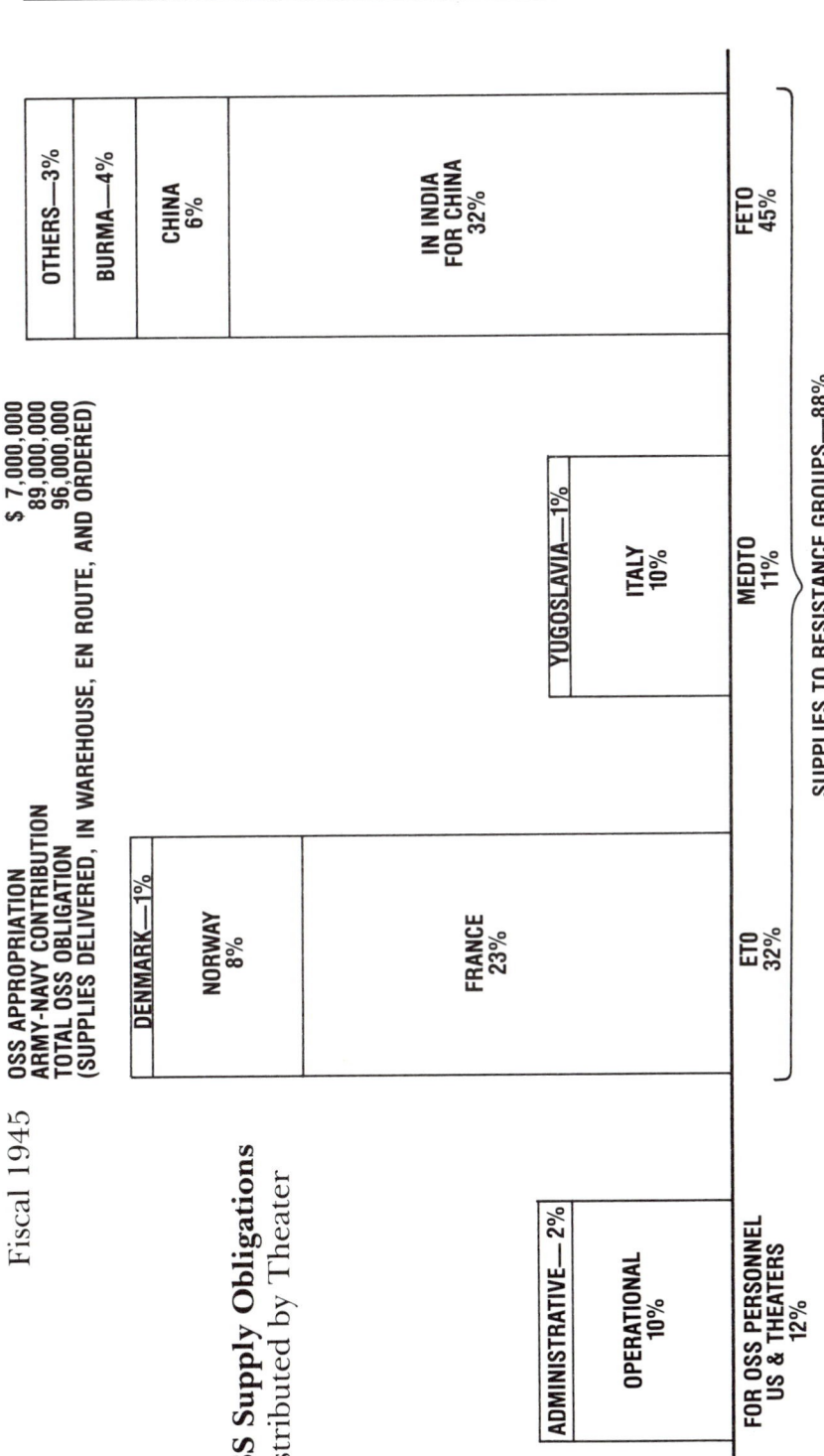

By fiscal year 1945 the OSS commitment of supplies shifted dramatically to the Far East Theater of Operations (FETO).

office locations, especially the Washington Office. These home office records provide information on OSS operations and intelligence all over the
world. The Associated Location (#3) and Area File (#4) printouts tell us
to what part of the world these home office records relate. The OSS overseas offices also maintained files on intelligence and operations for areas
other than the host country. Printouts #3 and #4 indicate, for instance,
London Office records regarding France and Spain, Cairo Office records
regarding Greece and the Balkans, and Calcutta Office records regarding
Japan, Thailand, the Philippines, and Burma. Most researchers will probably want to make use of printouts #3 and #4.

We have come to the end of our account of the OSS and its records
without really finishing the story. We have not discussed the work of the
OSS offices like the Planning Group, Maritime Unit, Schools and Training, the Field Photo Branch, or the many other branches and units within
the OSS. A glance at the descriptive lists written for the OSS records
reveals a nearly endless collection of files touching on every aspect of the
war including interrogation of POWs; the edible Aunt Jemima explosive
powder and other OSS special weapons and devices; the Dixie Mission to
Maoist Yenan; the correspondence of John Ford and John Steinbeck concerning nisei Japanese; the tragic death of John Birch and the beginning
of the cold war; the OSS and Syngman Rhee; early OSS contacts in Vietnam and Southeast Asia; the sizeable OSS R&D collection of press extracts
translated from German newspapers; the files of the R&A Jewish desk;
the OSS Censorship and Documentation Branch collection of passports
and credentials; manuals on disguises, guerrilla warfare, and lock-picking;
analyses of Hitler's speeches; the Breakers cables and reports on German
efforts to overthrow Hitler; the OSS General Counsel and the war crimes
trials; the Soviet Karkov trials; and Palestine.

Even this list can hardly begin to suggest the many files of interest in
this rich and varied group of records. Writers and scholars the world over
will continue to plumb the depths of OSS records for many years to come.

NOTES

1. A critical survey of literature on intelligence can be found in George C. Constantinides, *Intelligence and Espionage: An Analytical Bibliography* (Boulder, CO,
   1983). An official history of the OSS was prepared by the SSU History Project.
   This was published in two volumes in 1976 with introductions by Kermit
   Roosevelt: volume 1, *War Report of the OSS*, and volume 2, *The Overseas Targets*.
2. *American Decorations: A List of Awards of the Congressional Medal of Honor, the
   Distinguished Service Cross, the Distinguished Service Medal Awarded under Authority
   of the Congress of the United States, 1862–1926* (Washington, DC, 1927), pp. 256,
   697.
3. Richard Dunlop, *Donovan: America's Master Spy* (Chicago, 1982), p. 439. General Donovan's arrangements for Overlord appear in the OSS cable files, Wash-

ington—Registry Office—Radio and Cables—49, Folder 1026, Box 159, Entry 134, Records of the Office of Strategic Services, Record Group 226, National Archives and Records Administration, Washington, DC (hereinafter cited as RG 226, NA).

4. Roger Hilsman, *American Guerrilla: My War Behind Japanese Lines* (Washington, DC, 1990), pp. 95–105.

5. Walter Karig published one of the earliest accounts of Donovan's work as Coordinator of Information in his article "The Most Mysterious Man in Washington" in *Liberty* magazine, Jan. 3, 1942. The article was filed in the COI/OSS Central Files, Folder 39 (8345), Box 65, Entry 92, RG 226, NA.

6. Arthur B. Darling, *The Central Intelligence Agency: An Instrument of Government to 1950* (University Park, PA, 1990), pp. 10–20.

7. Kermit Roosevelt, *War Report of the OSS*, p. 34.

8. Some of Ian Fleming's correspondence with the OSS appears in London—Secret Intelligence Branch—Operational Files—45, Folder 393, Box 318, Entry 190, RG 226, NA. Thomas F. Troy, *Donovan and the CIA: A History of the Establishment of the Central Intelligence Agency* (Frederick, MD, 1981), pp. 81–82.

9. R. Harris Smith, *OSS: The Secret History of America's First Central Intelligence Agency* (Berkeley, 1972), p. 33.

10. Robin W. Winks, *Cloak and Gown: Scholars in the Secret War, 1939–1961* (New York, 1987), pp. 60–61.

11. OSS New York Office—Foreign Nationalities Branch—Administrative Files—1, Box 1, Entry 100, RG 226, NA, contains personnel lists, budget requests, and basic documents.

12. Entries 108 and 108A, RG 226, NA.

13. Concerning FBQ, see Folder 24402, Box 397, Entry 92, RG 226, NA. Concerning the R&A EOU, see Entry 91, London War Diaries in *History of the London Office of the OSS*, National Archives Microfilm Publication M1623, roll 3, RG 226.

    The historian David Kahn maintains the superiority of cryptanalysis over espionage in his book *The Codebreakers: The Story of Secret Writing* (New York, 1973), p. 273. However, it is significant, as Christopher Andrew points out, that without espionage, the Allies might have taken many years to break the all-important codes generated by the German code machine Enigma. Christopher Andrew, *Secret Service: The Making of the British Intelligence Community* (London, 1985), pp. 448–457.

14. William Casey, *The Secret War Against Hitler* (Washington, DC, 1988), pp. 48–54, 132.

15. Moe Berg's personnel file appears in the COI/OSS Central Files, OSS folder 19487, Folder 1, Box 313, Entry 92, RG 226, NA.

16. OSS Bern Office records in Entries 125 and 190, RG 226, NA, are often annotated in Allen Dulles's own hand. John Ranelagh, *The Agency: The Rise and Decline of the CIA* (New York, 1987), pp. 72–78. The OSS Survey of Foreign Experts and the George Office also had the function of intelligence gathering.

17. Winks, *Cloak and Gown*, pp. 474–476.

18. Barry M. Katz, *Foreign Intelligence: Research and Analysis in the Office of Strategic Services, 1942–1945* (Cambridge, MA, 1989), p. 203, n. 15.

19. Winks, *Cloak and Gown*, pp. 280–291. Not all SI efforts to penetrate Germany were successful, as William Casey's wartime report demonstrates, London— Secret Intelligence Branch—Operational Files—9 and 21, Folders 82A and 94, Box 300, Entry 190, RG 226, NA. Most of the SI agents sent into Germany were never heard from again.

20. R. Harris Smith, *OSS*, pp. 10–11. A memorandum of DeWitt Clinton of February 27, 1946, discusses penetration of OSS briefly; COI/OSS Central Files, Folder 32, Box 120, Entry 92, RG 226, NA.

21. A history of OSS X-2 for the European Theater of Operations is found in Folder 493, Box 58, Entry 144, RG 226, NA. For OSS concern about Communists in their ranks, see Folder 260, Box 38, Entry 144, RG 226, NA.

22. In the perennial debate over the importance of analysis as opposed to collection, Donovan also tended to give priority to analysis. Kandy—Registry Office—Operational Files—18, Folder 2097, Box 116, Entry 154, RG 226, NA.

23. History of the OSS in London, War Diary, SO Branch, OSS London, vol. 4, book 1, Jedburghs, pp. i–xxv, Box 24, Entry 91, RG 226, NA. The London War Diaries are the most thorough history of any OSS overseas office, consisting of more than 14 cubic feet of records. It is readily available on National Archives Microfilm Publication M1623. Concerning the Special Operations Branch, see rolls 6–7; concerning the Jedburghs, see roll 8. The OSS Operational Group Command (OG) developed out of the SO Branch. OG teams were larger than those of SO, usually composed of about 20 to 30 men. Unlike SO teams, the OG teams often engaged small enemy units in direct combat. The London War Diaries describe OG operations in vol. 4-A, M1623, roll 9. The origin of the name Jedburgh is uncertain. It appears as early as July 7, 1942, in an SOE directive. It apparently derives from British infiltration during the Boer War in South Africa. See Fabrizio Calvi, *OSS, La guerre secrète en France, 1942–1945: Les services spéciaux Americains, la Résistance et la Gestapo* (Paris, 1990), p. 359.

24. London War Diary, SO Branch, OSS London, vol. 4, book 1, Jedburghs, Box 24, Entry 91, RG 226, NA. Bradley F. Smith, *Shadow Warriors: OSS and the Origins of the CIA* (New York, 1983), pp. 290–293.

25. Many citations for Mission Jackal, SO Detachment 202 in China Theater, and the Jedburgh missions in Europe can be found in the Code and Project Names printout, which is based on descriptive lists written for the OSS Archives of the Central Intelligence Agency.

26. Hilsman, *American Guerrilla*, pp. 67–227.

RESEARCH IN OSS RECORDS:
One Historian's Concerns

Richard Breitman

In most of my previous searches in the Archives, I have not been looking specifically for operations or officials of the Office of Strategic Services (OSS) but rather at the targets or areas of OSS interest—for example, subjects of OSS surveillance or informants used by the OSS. Perhaps because of this orientation, I have had to look a little longer and come back a few more times than most researchers, and I acquired unjustifiedly the reputation of being an expert on OSS records. I have found and am finding useful information in OSS records about Nazi officials or about anti-Nazis. That OSS records even today can teach me and others something about the Nazi regime reveals something about the quality of OSS intelligence amassed under pressure during the war.

Some of you in the audience, I know, are still interested in unearthing information from OSS records and writing about it. So I have a chance now to repay at least one old debt and provide some guidance about how one goes about using OSS records. For our purposes, let us quickly divide the OSS records into two categories: the Research and Analysis Branch (R&A) records transferred by the Department of State in the late 1940s, and the remainder of the OSS records, which came to the National Archives from the CIA from 1979 to 1991.

For the R&A records, what I have to say is not all that encouraging. They are useful. There are certain basic agency-created indexes available, but they are not very good for historical research. The end result is that you will have to spend a lot of time either with the index you are interested in or in systematically plowing through the documents themselves. As always, a knowledgeable archivist can help you a good deal, but from the index you cannot quickly and simply find specific information you are seeking. I once spent 4 solid weeks using the OSS-created card index to OSS records on Germany (plain number file and XL file). That was the *index*, and I had to use the index before I could get any documents.

For the CIA's OSS Archives, which is now the large majority of the OSS records, the situation is much better, and it is much better because Larry McDonald and his crew of volunteers have compiled a set of finding aids on computer printouts that enable you in some cases to locate very quickly what you need. All of his finding aids will give you a specific entry, a box number, and a folder number, as well as other information.

Because I had conducted a good deal of my research before these finding aids were available, I went back earlier this week with Larry and did a little test. Sometimes the best way to see how the system works is through an example. I took a subject of more than hypothetical interest, namely, peace feelers or peace negotiations between the Nazi regime and the Soviet government in Stockholm during the middle of World War II, and I said to Larry: "Let's see what we can find through the finding aids." There is a subject index, and we tried a number of possibilities: peace feelers, peace negotiations, Nazi-Soviet, Russia-Germany, other things, all of no help. There are simply not enough entries in the subject finding aid to handle a topic like that, although if you happen to be interested in a topic that is listed, say, war crimes, you will very quickly get help.

I also had the names of six individuals whom I knew to be involved in these peace feelers, and we tried the name finding aid. I quickly found three hits: Three of the individuals whom I had listed were in fact in the name index, and I now had particular entries, boxes, and folders I could go to right away. Why only three? The reason that the other three were not there was not because there is no information about them, but rather because the name index is compiled from folder lists. These three individuals who were listed were either interrogated directly or were the subjects of OSS inquiries, and files were set up on them. The remaining three had no such files.*

I happen to know that there are mentions of the other three individuals in some OSS documents, but they do not appear in the name index. So the name index is really an index to the information in the folder lists, not to all the information (names) contained in the documents themselves.

The best tool turned out to be the location index (or point-of-origin finding aid) because it quickly showed me the locations of all the secret intelligence or counterintelligence records that emanated from Stockholm. That listing narrowed down my search immediately to 11 boxes. Once I

---

*Editor's Note: According to OSS project archivist Lawrence McDonald, the computer-generated indexes of personal names (#6) and the subject index (#7) are quite new at this time, and it will be some time before these indexes are complete, given the volume of OSS documentation yet to be extracted and entered. For further information relating to OSS finding aids and research in these records, see the paper by Lawrence H. McDonald in this section of the volume.

had those 11 boxes, I could look at the folder lists, and they could give me additional details on the contents of those boxes. Within a relatively short period of time, I had reduced my search to perhaps a day or two's work. I would not necessarily find everything through looking at 11 boxes or fewer, but I would certainly find the bulk of what was likely to be relevant and useful. So these finding aids are invaluable time-savers.

If I wanted to be diligent about the topic, I would use some of the other, more unusual finding aids: the associated location finding aid, for example. I might talk to the archivist, who might know of related material elsewhere, or look at the rather detailed inventory to the Donovan Papers, which are not yet included in the OSS finding aids. The finding aids and these other methods, however, by no means solve all of the problems of research in OSS records.

Let me spend a few minutes on some of the problems. The problem of classification of records remains quite serious. Maybe I am particularly unlucky, but I seem to run into an inordinate number of withdrawal slips indicating that particular folders or documents within particular folders are still classified. The public does not have access to them because either the CIA or the National Archives has specifically decided to deny access under provisions of the Freedom of Information Act allowing for exceptions. In most cases, the withdrawal slips indicate that release of the information would either damage national security or adversely affect American relations with foreign countries.

I know that there is considerable support for exceptions to the Freedom of Information Act, but I find it rather hard to convince myself that material that is almost 50 years old, or in some cases more than 50 years old, might somehow affect national security or American foreign relations. I do think a great deal of time could be saved—time within the CIA, time within the National Archives, time for researchers—if the government were to decide that after a certain number of decades, all such material simply should be declassified. I am willing to leave open the number of decades, but I think that this automatic declassification would be of benefit not only to researchers but also to taxpayers.

Then there are some particular areas that are missing from the records either because the material is still classified or because it was never recorded on paper in the first place. For example, we know only a small amount about how the system of assigning code names and code numbers worked and how reports from particularly reliable informants, as opposed to reports from less reliable informants, were handled. This whole area is not well reflected in the files. In passing, I should say that we know relatively little about the identities of people with code names and code numbers unless those individuals have come forward and identified themselves or unless scholars have been able to decipher the material. A list of most of the code names and numbers for OSS officials is available, but there is not one for the informants and foreign agents working for the OSS.

Another area where much remains to be done is in the relations between the OSS and the British or other intelligence agencies. I know that my friend and colleague Brad Smith is working in this area, but he has agreed with me that the records in this area are not as complete as they could be. Those who are giving us oral testimony about the OSS's relationship with other intelligence agencies will undoubtedly help future researchers.

In spite of all the good things I have said about Larry McDonald's finding aids, I do want to put in a pitch for proceeding in another manner. If you have the time, I would urge you to look at an entire series (or several series) of records and go through it document by document, preferably in chronological order. The reason is that, even if you are only interested in one narrow subject, you will learn what the flow of information was like at that time, from where information was coming, what range of subjects was covered, and how your subject was related (or unrelated) to other subjects in the files. You will have a much better grasp of how your subject fits into other things, which I think is important in the historian's analysis. Even if you end up photocopying the same documents you might have located more quickly through use of the finding aids, you will understand them better and be able to write more knowledgeably about them.

Something else happens when you look at a broader range of material. You find things that you either did not expect or were not looking for at all but which quickly arouse your interest. The process of accident in historical investigation is much underestimated. My colleagues tell me that this is also true in scientific research, that you learn valuable lessons often by accident. It causes you to rethink your topic or to choose your next research topic in a different manner.

As an example of this process of finding information by accident, I would like to read something that happens to relate to the question raised earlier by Professor Arthur Schlesinger, that is, how much the OSS knew of the Holocaust. I was looking for some information about Allied intelligence in the Middle East, and I ran across the following document, which was not very well identified—it was undated, but with a little work I was able to date it.

Under the heading "Belzec, the Slaughter House," the author wrote:

> In the uniform of a Polish policeman I visited the sorting camp near Belzec. It is a huge barracks, only about half of which is covered with a roof. When I was there about five thousand men and women were in the camp. However[,] every few hours new transports of Jews, men and women, young and old, would arrive for the last journey toward death.

The OSS received the first eyewitness account of Nazi exterminations. At liberation, the Belsen camp pictured here held 60,000 Jews and political prisoners. (208-YE-1A-19)

It is humanly impossible to convey the impression that these five thousand people made upon me. They are no longer in the image of men. Skeletons with eyes dead with resignation, naked, frightened, they are in constant motion with convulsive nervous movements. A child is lying with its face towards the roof. It is in the last agony of death. But no one pays any attention to it. Amidst this indistinguishable mass I spot an old man completely nude. He had probably been stripped of his rags. No one looked at him. He makes no impression on the people who surround him. The guards keep on shooting at the throng. Corpses are scattered everywhere. Convulsively moving men step over the corpses, barely noticing the dead. Every few minutes the guards pick a number of men to clear the dead which are piled up alongside the fence. This, too, is done without any emotion, without a single expression on their faces as though they are completely oblivious of what they are doing. These are no longer normal beings, but one large convulsive mass breathing its last . . . .

A long train thus packed with several thousand men, women, and children is switched to a siding where it remains from two to eight days. The doors are never opened. Those inside suffer inhuman agony. They have to perform natural functions over the heads of the others. Many cars are painted with lime which begins to burn from the dampness of the human urine and increases the tortures of the barefoot and the nude.

Because there are not enough cars to kill the Jews in this relatively inexpensive manner, many of them are taken to nearby Belzec where they are murdered by poison gases or by the application of electric currents. The corpses are burned near Belzec. Thus within an area of fifty kilometers huge stakes are burning day and night.

This document actually is the first eyewitness account of the extermination operations near a camp to reach the West. Because I have some passing acquaintance with the subject, I knew that this was a record of the experiences of Jan Karski, a Polish underground figure who came to London in November 1942 and reported on his experiences there.

Karski's information, along with additional material supplied by others, moved the Polish government-in-exile to pressure the Allied governments to issue a declaration denouncing the Nazi policy of exterminating Jews. Such an Allied declaration was made public on December 17, 1942. Rabbi Stephen Wise and other American Jewish leaders presented separate evidence of a Nazi plan to exterminate Jews to President Roosevelt in a personal meeting at the White House on December 8, 1942. In other words, it would have been hard for FDR not to have noticed this situation.

I am not going to repeat what I have written elsewhere about Roosevelt. I guess I should say in passing that I have been criticized by some for being too lenient on Roosevelt and criticized by others for being too critical, so I find myself in a relatively comfortable middle position.

The substance of Jan Karski's report in London was known previously and approximately through Karski's memoirs and recollections, but the details were unknown. We now have a contemporary record of his report. It is the kind of thing one can find unexpectedly in the OSS records if one takes the time to look through records systematically.

THE OSS:
A Brief Review
of Literature

George C. Constantinides

Shortly after World War II, former Secretary of State James Byrnes observed from long experience that a government agency was the closest thing to immortal life on this earth. On the face of it, this seemed an odd and inappropriate comment to make when many a temporary U.S. agency had been or was in the process of being dismantled, the Office of Strategic Services (OSS) being one. And yet, students of intelligence history detect some truth in Byrnes's remark in view of the OSS's spiritual durability. They and those who have followed developments in our postwar national security organization agree that, as one writer put it, the OSS was the direct lineal ancestor of the CIA. It is this genetic connection with today's intelligence that, more than anything else, explains continued interest in the OSS itself as an organization. Accounts of individual or group derring-do and operational accomplishments will, no doubt, regularly attract and fascinate the general public. The Countess of Romanones's professed adventures in *The Spy Wore Red* are a most recent example. Their secondary contribution to keeping interest in the OSS alive, however, will inevitably diminish with the passage of time.

There is one school of thought that has not reconciled itself entirely to the transfer of OSS intelligence philosophy and concepts (especially of covert action) into the postwar era. As a result, it has played a role in perpetuating attention to the OSS. Representative of this group is the scholar who reveled in the belief that Henry Kissinger had finally managed to get rid of William Donovan's "one hundred professors" in 1973. As he saw it, these undesirable leftovers were removed when William Colby dismantled the Office of National Estimates (ONE). But hard to match is the passion exhibited by another academic in 1990 when he wrote the following: "Harry Truman had killed the OSS in 1945 but failed to drive a wooden stake through its heart; it rose again as the CIA."*

Finally, interest in the OSS has benefited from the recent explosion of curiosity about intelligence subjects in general. This has resulted in a steady flow of literature long after the end of the OSS's short life that is out of proportion to its overall contribution to Allied victory. Though some may disagree, most will accept Barry Katz's judgment expressed in his *Foreign Intelligence* that the organization "in general exercised little influence on the actual conduct of the war."

By my count, 62 English-language works of nonfiction on the OSS have been published as of the end of June 1991. These are books fitting my definition as those devoted exclusively or substantively to the subject. Excluded by my criteria, for instance, are the autobiography of William Langer and the biography of William Casey. Both of these were disappointing to those looking for material of these luminaries' OSS days. The books I include divide very conveniently for a reviewer into two periods, 1945–70 and 1970 to the present. The first period witnessed the appearance of 23 books, 6 of which were published between 1945 and 1947. All but two were authored or coauthored by OSS veterans or persons with some OSS connection. The exceptions were Klein's *The Counterfeit Traitor* about Eric Erickson, whom William Casey in his history called the most valuable OSS agent in Stockholm, and Andersen's *The Dark City*.

A slight majority of the books of this period comprised personal accounts by veterans of wartime experiences. The remainder was largely collections of anecdotes of OSS operations. Both types are said to have received encouragement from Gen. William Donovan, who wished some of the OSS saga told. The declassification of some records prior to the OSS's termination provided material for the collections of operational vignettes such as Ford and MacBain's *Cloak and Dagger* and Alsop and Braden's *Sub Rosa*. It is apparent that much of the literature of this era is of an embryonic quality and some, like Louis Huot's *Guns For Tito*, with its obvious gaps and political dyslexia, of indifferent quality or historical value. Allen Dulles's *The Secret Surrender* is at the other end of the quality spectrum. So too is Peers and Brelis's *Behind the Burma Road*, which, like Dulles's book, is a firsthand account of important events.

The first of the books by former OSS members critical of some aspect of the organization appeared during this period. I term these the literature of discontent, though they were in content much more than that. Donald Downes's *The Scarlet Thread* and Peter Tompkins's *A Spy in Rome* were the initial two of this category. They differ from later critical studies by nonaffiliated authors in that they are not attacks against the institution or

---

*Charles D. Ameringer, *U.S. Foreign Intelligence: The Secret Side of American History* (Lexington, MA: Lexington Books, 1990).

intelligence activities per se; rather, they express disagreement or personal unhappiness with some policy or portion, particularly with some of the management. Tompkins fumed against the "Johnny-come-latelys," official views, and the "Italo-American Mafiosi" in the OSS. Downes directed his barbs at what he called the "amateurs," "cast-offs," and "stupid sons of the rich and famous" in the organization. The literary wit and worldly disdain employed by that critic of British intelligence, Malcolm Muggeridge, are not their only weapons of choice. All the same, they served to balance somewhat the largely favorable portrait of the OSS projected by most writers during that time period.

Five others must be singled out for various reasons. Aldo Icardi's *American Master Spy* is in a category of its own. The author's main motive in writing it was to give his version of the Holohan murder case in Italy, which became a cause célèbre. As of this date, it is the only book that deals with it as a central subject, albeit ex parte. Elizabeth MacDonald's *Undercover Girl* had a number of firsts that distinguish it, among which was the revelation of the work of Allied black radios. Further, it made a pioneering protest against male attitudes toward women in substantive war duties. *Into Siam* by Nicol Smith and Blake Clark describes at first hand an operation unique for its operational conditions and the exalted level of its principal sources. Stanley Lovell's references to truth drugs in *Of Spies and Stratagems* later set off intense public concerns. Roger Hall's delightful *You're Stepping on My Cloak and Dagger* is the one humorous and light treatment done until now, to the best of my knowledge. It had at least 13 printings by 1957 and will still amuse.

The 1970s represent a watershed. That decade witnessed the start of works with a wider perspective and more comprehensive treatment and, in some instances, with a different thrust. At the same time, the output of personal accounts by OSS veterans continued, and these were, in fact, still a majority. It was a veteran, Edward Hymoff, nevertheless, who was one of the first to express an adverse opinion in writing about the literature's trend up to then. In his *OSS in World War II*, he gave a harsh opinion of previous works; he dismissed the greater part of what had been written on the subject as of little consequence.

His effort, comprised mainly of old or additional anecdotes, did not significantly rectify the situation. New entrants who began to take an interest in the subject included professional writers, academics, and scholars. Undoubtedly stimulating their interest was the opportunity to exploit available new sources. These were the declassified portions of the OSS Archives, access provided by the Freedom of Information Act and the newly released in-house history of the OSS. In addition to these, there was a more relaxed access to personal journals and recollections of some principal figures in the organization.

Former CIA analyst R. Harris Smith showed how the latter material could be tapped. His *OSS*, written in 1972 and thus prior to the release of OSS archives, is, in my view, a transitional work. It is wider in scope and has a different focus. Backstage maneuvering and bureaucratic wrangling occupy much of his story, as do operational faux pas and failures. Smith is revisionist not merely in this respect. He also draws some large lessons, among which is the belief that many cold war developments were traceable ultimately to General Donovan.

We must recall that this was the epoch when American intelligence, and especially its postwar covert action activities, were under vigorous attack. Bradley Smith was one whose views suited this climate and who took fullest advantage of the new sources of information mentioned. In two books (one of which, *Operation Sunrise*, he co-authored), he made no secret about his feelings and dislike of covert actions (secret shenanigans he calls them) and links them historically to the OSS. The CIA, he claims, tried to have pro-OSS books produced. He goes even further in *The Shadow Warriors*, a probing, disputed, wide-ranging work; he not only tries to evaluate the OSS's effectiveness but raises a number of provocative questions concerning the rationale for the OSS's adoption of covert actions. Arguably, he goes beyond anything intended by earlier critics or by Archimedes Patti in *Why Vietnam?* or Max Corvo's *The OSS in Italy*. While both of these cite various dysfunctions, Patti stresses policy errors. Neither questions the basic premises of the OSS.

To keep matters in perspective, books critical of the OSS to any degree were still a minority. Laudatory or noncontroversial ones by OSS veterans continued to appear—as a matter of fact, at twice the rate as during the first period. The one book that stands apart is that of Jane Foster, who was indicted as a Soviet agent and Communist. Evasive and unconvincing, it warrants mention only because of special and negative reasons. A handful of books represent notable exceptions to the personal histories of narrow scope. William Casey and James G. Rogers left us accounts of headquarters and of operations from the broader perspective of senior positions. Rogers's journal gives us an indication of what richness remains to be tapped in personal papers; it is also a fascinating peek into a segment of the capital's wartime social power structure. David Bruce's diary, however, just published under the title *OSS Against the Reich*, is exceedingly discreet on matters of substance.

Nonveterans made no mean contribution to the better literature. Take books about General Donovan. Of the four so far, the two by veterans (Corey Ford's *Donovan of OSS* and Richard Dunlop's *Donovan*) are largely panegyrics. Anthony Cave Brown's *The Last Hero*, though flawed, was an improvement. Based on the general's private papers, it contained new or clarifying material. Thomas Troy's *Donovan and the CIA* is the most scholarly to date. Its official sponsorship meant the author was able to use unrivaled archival material to probe a particular subject.

Other works worthy of note must include Robin Winks's *Cloak and Gown*. Though some grumbled that it leaves the impression that Yale won the intelligence war, it broke new ground in examining the links between academia and American intelligence. Its profile of James Angleton is the most carefully crafted up to that time, and it contains, along with R. Harris Smith, one of the best bibliographies on the OSS. Barry Katz's *Foreign Intelligence*, published in 1989 and mentioned earlier, has the distinction of being the first full-length study devoted to the Research and Analysis Branch (R&A). It is one of six books on the OSS published by a university press. Joseph Persico's *Piercing the Reich* greatly expanded on the little that had appeared about intelligence operations into the Reich itself. Its preface contains a good resumé of the new source material that was available and which its author mined.

One cannot reexamine the literature of the last 20 years without arriving at a new appreciation of the official histories of the OSS, which were released in 1976. In my earlier estimation, I did not stress properly their true merits and their significance. By concentrating too much on details and faults or gaps, I left to my book's introduction recognition of the historic nature of their publication. The only precedence for the release of secrets of an intelligence organization had been the British government's history of the Special Operations Executive (SOE) in France. Researchers would do well to regard these histories both as a mine of information and facts and for leads into new areas of inquiry.

Persico, for one, credits the histories for providing the incentive for his book on operations into Germany. To illustrate the point further, take the mention made of the activities of the Special Counterintelligence Units of X-2 (SCIs). A fascinating, full story of their work waits to be told. To the best of my knowledge, only one person, Akeley Quirk in his short memoirs published in 1981, has written a firsthand account of experiences with such a unit. Happily, the young intelligence scholar Timothy Naftali is in the process of writing a history of X-2 and SCI. There are other areas for further research and for writing that I believe will be of general or special interest. R&A certainly deserves more than a single study in view of its pioneering work in the war and its influence on postwar research methodology in academia and in intelligence. Katz expresses astonishment that R&A had been completely overlooked by historians. Nor has the exact contribution of the OSS to Allied knowledge of German nuclear plans and intentions been fully looked into. There is only passing mention of this subject in the OSS operational history, while the 1974 biography of Moe Berg by a trio of authors makes claims that still await verification. Even William Casey's more authoritative chapter on the matter seems to need updating and possible revision in light of newer information. Professor Winks's opinion that a major book is needed about the OSS's work with Italian resistance is quite right. One can also argue that Donovan's years with COI and the OSS have not been exhaustively treated, since the most authoritative work, Troy's, is not concerned with operational management. If Persico is correct that the Labor Branch was virtually the only source of American intelligence on conditions in Germany until 1944, that branch should be a productive area for research.

Finally, there is the need to verify some of the accounts of accomplishments found in anecdotal collections and personal histories (or combinations like those of Robert Alcorn). Although of secondary priority, we must keep in mind that we are still sorting out claims and myths in works about previous wars. Civil War intelligence is a very good case in point. That potentially conflicting claims can be expected to crop up is attested to by the contents of a recent book.** Gen. M.Z. Slowikowski, who headed Polish intelligence in North Africa in 1942, has written that he forwarded voluminous intelligence produced by his extensive network to London via the American pouch. He "presumes" the Americans in Africa read his network's intelligence. He does not stop there but charges that certain unidentified American officials deliberately distorted history by attributing all Allied intelligence operations in French North Africa to themselves. He thus raises serious questions concerning the exact credit for information on which estimates and plans for the North African invasion were based. Since that invasion is regarded as the OSS's first major success, here indeed is a matter worthy of a talented and hearty researcher.

**M.Z. Slowikowski, *In The Secret Service* (London: The Windrus Press, 1988).

Published Books on the OSS

1940s

Alsop, Stewart, and Thomas Braden. *Sub Rosa: The OSS and American Espionage.* New York: Reynal & Hitchcock, 1946.

Ford, Corey, and Alastair MacBain. *Cloak and Dagger: The Secret Story of OSS.* New York: Grosset & Dunlop, 1945.

Huot, Louis. *Guns for Tito.* New York: L. B. Fischer, 1945.

Legendre, Gertrude. *The Sands Ceased to Run.* New York: William-Frederick, 1947.

MacDonald, Elizabeth P. *Undercover Girl.* New York: Macmillan, 1947.

Smith, Nicol, and Blake Clark. *Into Siam, Underground Kingdom.* New York: Bobbs-Merrill, 1945.

Gardner, John, et al. *Assessment of Men: Selection of Personnel for the Office of Strategic Services.* New York: Rinehart, 1948.

1950s

Andersen, Hartvig. *The Dark City: A True Account of Adventures of a Secret Agent in Berlin.* New York: Rinehart, 1954.

Downes, Donald C. *The Scarlet Thread: Adventures in Wartime Espionage.* New York: British Book Center, 1953.

Hall, Roger. *You're Stepping on My Cloak and Dagger.* New York: W.W. Norton, 1957.

Icardi, Aldo. *Aldo Icardi: American Master Spy.* Pittsburgh, PA: Stalwart Enterprises, 1954.

Klein, Alexander. *The Counterfeit Traitor.* New York: Henry Holt, 1958.

Morgan, William. *Spies and Saboteurs.* London: Gollancz, 1955.

————. *The OSS and I.* New York: W.W. Norton, 1957.

1960s

Alcorn, Robert. *No Bugles for Spies: Tales of the OSS.* New York: David McKay, 1962.

————. *No Banners, No Bands: More Tales of the OSS.* New York: David McKay, 1965.

Barrett, Neil H. *Chinghpaw.* New York: Vantage Press, 1962.

Duke, Florimond, and Charles M. Swaart. *Name, Rank, and Serial Number.* New York: Meredith Press, 1969.

Dulles, Allen. *The Secret Surrender.* New York: Harper and Row, 1966.

Frillman, Paul, and Graham Peck. *China: The Remembered Life.* Boston: Houghton Mifflin, 1968.

Lovell, Stanley. *Of Spies & Strategems.* Englewood Cliffs, NJ: Prentice Hall, 1963.

Peers, William R., and Dean Brelis. *Behind the Burma Road: The Story of America's Most Successful Guerrilla Force.* Boston: Little, Brown, 1963.

Tompkins, Peter. *A Spy in Rome.* New York: Simon and Schuster, 1962.

1970s

Booth, Waller B. *Mission Marcel-Proust: The Story of an Unusual OSS Undertaking.* Philadelphia: Dorrence & Co., 1972.

Caldwell, Oliver J. *A Secret War: Americans in China.* Carbondale, Southern Illinois University Press, 1972.

Cave Brown, Anthony. *The Secret War Report of the OSS.* New York: Berkeley, 1976.

Dreux, W. *No Bridges Blown*. South Bend, IN: University of Notre Dame Press, 1973.

Dunlop, Richard. *Behind Japanese Lines: With the OSS in Burma*. Chicago: Rand McNally, 1979.

Ford, Corey. *Donovan of OSS*. Boston: Little, Brown, 1970.

Hymoff, Edward. *The OSS in World War II*. New York: Ballantine Books, 1972.

Kaufman, Louis, Barbara Fitzgerald, and Tom Sewell. *Moe Berg: Athlete, Scholar, Spy*. Boston: Little, Brown, 1974.

Moon, Thomas N., and Carl F. Eifler. *The Deadliest Colonel*. New York: Vantage Press, 1975.

OSS Special Weapons, Devices, and Equipment. Wickenberg, AZ: Normount Technical Publications, 1975.

Persico, Joseph E. *Piercing the Reich: The Penetration of Nazi Germany by American Secret Agents During World War II*. New York: Viking Press, 1979.

Smith, Bradley F., and Elena Agarossi. *Operation Sunrise: The Secret Surrender*. New York: Basic Books, 1979.

Smith, R. Harris. *OSS: The Secret History of America's First Central Intelligence Agency*. New York: Dell Publishers, 1972.

U.S. War Department, SSU Unit, *War Report of the OSS*. 2 vols. New York: Walker & Co., 1976.

1980s

Bancroft, Mary. *Autobiography of a Spy*. New York: Morrow, 1983.

Casey, William. *The Secret War Against Hitler*. New York: Regnery Gateway, 1988.

Cassidy, William L., ed. *History of the Schools & Training Branch, Office of Strategic Services*. San Francisco: Kingfisher, 1983.

Cave Brown, Anthony. *The Last Hero: Wild Bill Donovan*. New York: Times Books, 1982.

Coon, Carleton S. *A North Africa Story: The Anthropologist as OSS Agent, 1941–1943*. Ipswich, MA: Gambit, 1980.

De Champlain, Hélène. *The Secret War of Helene De Champlain*. London: W.H. Allen, 1980.

Dunlop, Richard. *Donovan, America's Master Spy*. Chicago: Rand McNally, 1982.

Foster, Jane. *An Unamerican Lady*. London: Sidgwick and Jackson, 1980.

Katz, Barry M. *Foreign Intelligence: Research and Analysis in the Office of Strategic Services, 1942–1945*. Cambridge, MA: Harvard University Press, 1989.

Ladd, James D., H. Keith Melton, and Peter Mason. *Clandestine Warfare: Weapons and Equipment of the SOE and OSS*. London: Blandford Press, 1988.

Patti, Archimedes. *Why Viet Nam? Prelude to America's Albatross*. Berkeley: University of California Press, 1980.

Quirk, Akeley. *Recollections of WWII: OSS SCI Unit 6th Army Group*. Fullerton, CA: Sultana Press, 1981.

Romanones, Aline, Countess of. *The Spy Wore Red: My Adventures as an Undercover Agent*. New York: Random House, 1987.

Smith, Bradley F. *The Shadow Warriors: OSS and the Origins of the CIA*. New York: Basic Books, 1983.

Troy, Thomas. *Donovan and the CIA*. Washington, DC: Central Intelligence Agency, 1980.

Troy, Thomas, ed. *Wartime Washington: The Secret OSS Journal of James Grafton Rogers.* Frederick, MD: University Publications of America, 1987.

Winks, Robin W. *Cloak & Gown: Scholars in the Secret War, 1939–1961.* New York: Morrow, 1987.

1990s

Brunner, John W. *The OSS Crossbows.* Williamstown, NJ: Phillips Publications, 1990.

Corvo, Max. *The OSS in Italy, 1942–1945.* New York: Praeger, 1990.

Hilsman, Roger. *American Guerrilla: My War Behind Japanese Lines.* Washington: Brassey's (U.S.), 1990.

Lankford, Nelson D., ed. *OSS Against the Reich: The World War II Diaries of David K. E. Bruce.* Kent, OH: Kent State University Press, 1991.

Melton, H. Keith. *OSS Special Weapons & Equipment: Spy Devices of World War II.* New York: Sterling, 1991.

Moon, Thomas. *This Grim and Savage Game.* Los Angeles: Burning Gate Press, 1991.

Quigley, Martin S. *Peace Without Hiroshima: Secret Action at the Vatican in the Spring of 1945.* Lanham, MD: Madison Books, 1991.

The author wishes to acknowledge the valuable assistance provided by Walter Pforzheimer and especially Hayden Peake in compiling the above list.

THE OSS AROUND THE GLOBE

✦ I Spy

The first of four concurrent sessions, "I Spy," was held in the National Archives Theater on Friday morning, July 12. This session was designed to provide first-person accounts of espionage by OSS veterans who operated in three different countries. Aline, the Countess of Romanones, was sent undercover in 1943 to Madrid, Spain, to help rejuvenate that Secret Intelligence (SI) operation. The second espionage agent, Peter Tompkins, was selected by Donovan to land on the seacoast of Italy and help the Italian partisans sabotage German operations and report intelligence. Helene Deschamps-Adams was a young French freedom fighter of the Resistance who decided to work for the OSS behind German lines in France. Although there are celebrated espionage novels that have captivated millions of readers, these three speakers pointed out that much of what they did was demanding, dangerous, and sometimes disappointing. All three have written of their espionage experiences. Another OSS veteran, S. Peter Karlow, provided important commentary on how agents got their information out and how that information and its source was rated within the OSS. David Kahn, the well-known author of *The Codebreakers* and *Hitler's Spies*, also provided valuable commentary, chaired the session, and conducted the discussion.

THE OSS IN SPAIN DURING WORLD WAR II

Aline, Countess of Romanones

From January 1944 through August 1945, I served in Madrid with the Office of Strategic Services (OSS). Our small and inexperienced cadre consisted of 12 to 15 people (typically 3 women and 9 to 12 men) in a small office under the nominal cover of the "American Oil Mission," in a building some blocks away from the U.S. Embassy. The Madrid station's principal responsibilities included strategic deception—misleading the Germans about the landing area for Operation Anvil, the Allied landing in southern France—reporting military order of battle and industrial intelligence on the German war machine, counterintelligence on German covert operations run through Spain, and monitoring the channeling of art treasures and other valuables from Europe to safe havens in Latin America.

Madrid was probably the most hostile environment for an OSS station anywhere in the world. Although determined to remain neutral, Spain was under strong German influence. Without German assistance, the Nationalists could probably not have won the civil war that had ended 4½ years before. In 1944 Spain and Portugal were, along with Sweden and Switzerland, the only countries on the Continent not under direct Nazi domination. The other three neutrals were basically pro-Allies, but in Spain there were over 600 German intelligence agents and many Japanese and Italian agents as well. We and the British were a pitifully small force by comparison. German access to the Spanish government, especially the military and security agencies, was virtually unlimited, and what they could not get through formal liaison they could acquire through their recruited agents, who honeycombed these institutions. We were shot at, abducted, threatened, and robbed by German assets who could act almost with impunity. And if that wasn't enough, we encountered an almost equally hostile attitude from the U.S. Embassy staff and the Department of State. Fortunately we were too busy to think much about these obstacles, and in fact, there was little we could have done to overcome them. The rest of this paper will follow my career in the OSS from its beginning through the postwar period in order to give a clearer idea of what it was like to spend a year and a half in the hottest foxhole for staff intelligence operatives in Europe at the time.

My experience as a member of the OSS in Spain was similar, I suspect, to that of others in our group in Madrid. When recruited in September 1943, I was unaware that the work would be intelligence, despite the mysterious attitude of the man who informed me that tests for overseas work with the War Department would necessitate my using a false name and address when reporting for work in Washington, DC. About a month before, I had met a man at a dinner in New York who heard me complain about being too young for overseas war service; he promised to help. I did not know then that my background and affiliations, as well those of my parents and grandparents, would be investigated. There were no restrictions, and recruits for sensitive work were carefully examined.

The training received at the Farm, a country estate about 20 miles outside of Washington, was the same for men and women. During my weeks there, 1 other woman and about 30 men of different ages and nationalities were being prepared for intelligence work. Although students were predominantly Americans, there were Yugoslavs, a Belgian, several Frenchmen, and a German or two. Frequently someone would come back from Europe and give us a lecture on working "out in the field," but for the most part our training covered handling weapons, self-defense, detailed European geography, Morse code, coding, memory tricks, surveillance, organizing networks, recruiting agents, and anything else that our instructors had ever read in a spy story or seen in a movie. We were even taught how to roll a newspaper into a fine point to serve as a stabbing knife.

When I was informed that I would be going to Spain, I was advised to study that country and two other countries as well, so that my companions at the school would not know which was to be my destination. We used code names to protect the secrecy of our identities, and we were constantly reminded that intelligence was a secret business and that we were not to trust anyone. Students were transferred to other schools if they could not put up with the grueling routine or if they had divulged their identities, and replacement recruits arrived every 2 weeks.

When being readied to fly to Spain, I was told that there had been a triple agent working for our group who had blown the covers of many of our people and that I would be sent with a number-one priority because help was needed urgently. I left at night on a Pan American clipper from Long Island Sound, the only woman among about 32 men, on my way to Lisbon. These flight departures were kept secret and obliged passengers to remain on call in different hotels in the neighborhood for several days before. Years later Gregory Thomas, our Chief of Station (COS) in Madrid, and I laughed about my being sent in company of four-star generals of the European High Command in comfort and style, while he had been transferred to Spain on a merchant ship that took weeks. On the same flight were two colleagues of the OSS, William Larrimore Mellon, a specialist on Basque problems, and James MacMillan, our financial man. We spent several days in Lisbon, learning the latest developments with the OSS there, and then took a small plane to Madrid. We were the only passengers, and they forgot to close the door, which was almost blown off. When we landed at the small Madrid Barajas Airport, the only other aircraft there was a German Junker whose large black and red swastika on the wing made us realize we were getting nearer to the enemy.

In Madrid the offices of the Secret Intelligence (SI) department of the OSS were on the second floor of a low apartment building on the Calle Alcala Galiano, number 4. Later we moved for greater security to the attic of the American Ambassador's residence on the Calle Eduardo Dato; this palace had been rented from the Duke of Montellano.

We were made to realize from the start that the OSS's remaining in Spain depended on not irritating the ambassador, who was striving to get us out of the country. But despite our efforts not to, most of us got into trouble now and then. We were all handling two or three or four jobs at the same time: one inside the office and the other jobs outside. We were told to avoid becoming friendly with American Embassy personnel because they did not have our security training and could unwittingly endanger our cover. Later I learned that Secretary of State Cordell Hull and the American Ambassador in Spain both worried that the OSS would usurp the State Department's terrain. They also resented the fact that OSS employees received higher salaries than State Department personnel. After the war, when the OSS was disbanded and most of our staff was sent back to Washington, we were told we had been overpaid and were obliged to pay the government back. My entire savings went into a check to the government, and recently one of my former colleagues informed me that his debt had been calculated to amount to so much that he had to pay back money from other sources long after the war ended. Rumors in Washington about graft and corruption inside OSS ranks were unwarranted in the case of Spain because Gregory Thomas ran the station with care and efficiency.

Most of us organized chains (agents nets), as we had been taught, as soon after arrival as possible, and we had been trained to keep all our activities secret from each other. For the head of my chain I used a Spanish Communist who had been the private secretary of one of the ministers of the Republican government. She was supposed to select one woman in whom she would have total confidence, since her life depended on this, and that women would select another, and so on, until 15 women had been recruited. That way I knew only one other member of the chain, the last woman only knew one; the others knew two, but no more, so that if one were to be caught the chain would not be uncovered in its entirety. These women were chosen to be located inside suspects' offices as charwomen, secretaries, or maids.

We preserved the appearance of normal office hours as closely as possible, but any serious surveillance must have shown that we were doing more than occupying ourselves with deliveries of oil to Spain. In fact, Spain received no oil deliveries for much of 1944 due to pressure on the Spanish government to stop tungsten shipments to Germany. Also, many of us had to work nights. Our radio man, Ben Turpin, made contact with our agents dropped behind enemy lines often after midnight, and either Robert Dunev or myself were on call at night to decode urgent incoming messages.

All coding was done by hand; there were no electronic devices, and our typewriters were manual. The system consisted of strips, each containing 25 to 30 units of 5 letters. The strips had chronological identification codes, and there were different sets for each day of each month. It required memorizing letter combinations, and no strips were alike. Ciphering had been one of the classes we were taught at the Farm; we were taught many different types, but the others were for individual use. Outside the code room my work entailed organizing the aforementioned women's chain, uncovering certain pro-Nazi sympathizers and agents inside Spanish society, putting up the women couriers from France who brought us information on German troop movements, serving as the contact between an outside Mexican agent and our COS, and handling other urgencies that arose. Double agents abounded and we recruited Germans, Italians, and Spaniards who were working for the Gestapo to double for us.

We were told to trust only Spanish nationals who had been on the Republican side in the Spanish Civil War of 1936–39 (Nazi Germany supplied Franco's forces with airplanes and war materiel), and therefore we had close association with many Spanish Communists. This did not improve our relations with the Spanish government. The Soviet military supported the Republic and aided Spanish Communists occupying Madrid during the 3-year war. The Soviets also confiscated all the gold in the Spanish treasury at war's end, leaving the country destitute.

There was more work than could be handled by the small OSS force in Spain. German companies had branches all over Spain, which were perfect covers for espionage. Many South American embassies were abetting the Nazis. The Japanese ran their worldwide intelligence center, referred to as MAGIC, from Madrid with a powerful radio transmitter that could reach Tokyo, even relaying data about American ship departures with troops for the South Pacific. We rarely had time to note what we were doing. When we did write accounts of our activities, they were often too brief and usually inadequate. This was especially the case during the months before the German capitulation. Several years ago I was looking up records of stolen paintings moved through Spain to South America and could find no account of shipments that I had known about personally.

Nor did we document the several predicaments in which we embroiled ourselves while serving in Spain. I traveled to Malaga at one point to deliver microfilm to an agent, and the police arrested me upon my arrival there as well as on my way back to Madrid. Robert Dunev once had to be rescued by the Spanish secret police (he fortunately had run an agent in the secret police) when the Germans were about to drug him and take him to Berlin. Mellon was captured by frontier patrols in the Pyrenees and barely escaped with his life. These events grew more frequent in the months before D-day, as both sides planned the battles that would end the war in Europe, and they gave Ambassador Hayes reason to be irritated. Fortunately, Gregory Thomas, who knew Spain and its language well, kept peace with the embassy and the State Department.

Agents in Spain had help from outside the OSS. The Maquis, including Spanish Communists who lived in southern France since the end of the Spanish war, sabotaged German assets and brought us maps of the enemy's coastal armaments—mines in the bays and on land, roadblocks, antiaircraft guns, and camouflaged pillboxes. SI Spain's office was able to warn the Anvil planning staff not to attack in the Marseilles area because of the gigantic defense the Germans had readied there. By the time the invasion took place, the U.S. military knew the location of every German defense weapon and troop. After the Anvil landing, SI Spain continued to inform minute by minute on the German Panzer units' sizes and positions.

In August 1945, a cable came in from Washington ordering the immediate return of all OSS employees in Spain and the termination of all networks that had been working for us. It was a hasty move and created much distress among our staff. That same week, I received a surprise. An OSS official from Washington visited and informed me that I was the only one of our SI group to be kept on for work in a supersecret organization inside Spain. I was told that this would depend on my being able to get my visa extended to permit me to remain in the country. A cable showing I had a serious job, to reopen offices of the American firm of John J. Ryan and Sons in Madrid, was provided for me to use to justify a prolongation of my visa. Convincing Walter Butterworth, the Acting Ambassador at the time, that I would not be engaging in espionage was not a comfortable experience since I had been told to maintain the head woman of my chain to work as my secretary, and I thought espionage was exactly what I would be doing. Butterworth was not easy to convince and asked me to swear on a Bible, which I was able to do since I believed I would be working for some other intelligence department of the U.S. government. For several months I received my pay from John J. Ryan and Sons. I opened an office in Madrid and obtained bona fide sales to Catalan manufacturers. Then I was abruptly ordered to leave for Paris, where I was told I would work with a company called World Commerce Inc. I took for granted that this was my new cover. I worked with Jack Okie there, who had been in the Lisbon SI station. We did more or less the same work in Paris as in Madrid— opened offices, initiated business with French firms, and handled the barter of products between Czechoslovakia and Sweden. Again, abruptly, 6 months later I was asked to proceed to Zurich, where I opened bank accounts for World Commerce and established an office there for the same company.

My boss at this time was Frank Ryan, who had been the Chief of SI for Spain and Portugal in Washington. I had the impression that I would eventually be organizing networks for information on Soviet intelligence activities. I was scheduled to move to Prague to open offices there when I married. Only 40 years later did I learn that this company was not openly being used as a cover for U.S. government intelligence, even though everybody I saw and worked with during the 2 years in that job had been an OSS agent in one country or another. The company's set-up seems to have been a precursor to the Iran-Contra situation, where sales from private companies were used to bolster pro-U.S. groups in a foreign country.

After the war the Spanish nationals who had been hired during those years, who were Communists, remained on in the Embassy in Madrid and with time placed their sons and daughters and grandchildren in the Embassy. I knew them and recognized them over the years, especially since my house was near the American Embassy and I saw them often. Until 1976 the Communist Party was outlawed in Spain, and I warned the different American Ambassadors frequently that the existence of Spanish Communists in the U.S. Embassy could be embarrassing. Also, anyone who had known the OSS personnel recognized CIA employees, because they employed the same chauffeurs and could be seen being driven around Madrid. Some of these employees may have ceased to be Communists, but many are today still members of Spain's Communist Party. I have encountered them during elections in surveillance with me at the election table.

Several years ago when I was preparing a book about the OSS in Spain, I asked a German friend if he had ever heard of a beautiful German woman who had been working in German intelligence in Madrid during the war. (I prefer not to mention her name for reasons that will become clear.) I remembered her well because she had had much influence with a pro-Nazi section of the government and the military and had been stiff competition. My German friend laughed and told me that he knew her well, and that I would have no difficulty in contacting her since she currently lived in Washington, DC, and was married to a CIA man. He informed me that the lady had been a widow with two children when she escaped from Spain to South America at war's end. She married a Columbian there and had several children. That husband died, and she married a CIA man she had met in Bogota and came to live in the United States.

When I contacted this woman in Washington, her CIA husband had died several months before; she kindly invited me for lunch at her home, and we enjoyed recalling many details of those war years and the people who took part in them, learning for the first time particulars that clarified many doubts we each had. She claimed to have been connected with the Abwehr when it was taken over by the Gestapo and said her work was restricted to obtaining intelligence in Madrid. She told me she had tried to commit suicide at the end of the war, but that Ramon Serrano Suner, General Franco's brother-in-law, and the Minister of Agriculture, Miguel Primo de Rivera, saved her and helped her go to South America where she could rebuild her life. Although it was 40 years later, she was still attractive, attractive enough to impress many at a dinner I attended with her and to remarry very shortly after that a distinguished American. She is still living in the United States today.

My experience in Spain has shown me that written reports are the opinion of the person composing them; they are often insufficient, sometimes not exact. It is difficult often to register happenings in periods of great activity when agents are too busy to have time to keep records. When I examined OSS Spain files recently, I found much missing; it is to be hoped that more information will appear when uncataloged boxes recently arrived in the National Archives will be cataloged, but some of the most harrowing events will probably remain unknown.

ARE HUMAN SPIES SUPERFLUOUS?

Peter Tompkins

If you had lived as long as I under Nazi-Fascist domination, or under an administration that believed that history is made by shredding government documents, you would cherish, as I do, this institution, the National Archives. It supports the pen against the sword.

There is a misguided notion that human spies are no longer essential, outmoded by sophisticated electronic equipment. Not so. Even the Office of Strategic Services' (OSS) William Colby, former Director of Central Intelligence, recently had to admit that during Operation Desert Storm, had we had an agent in Saddam Hussein's bed, we might have been better informed as to his whereabouts and his intentions.

Another canard is perpetuated by devotees of ULTRA, the system that broke the German codes in World War II. They attribute to ULTRA wonders that were in fact provided by human spies. I do not wish to denigrate ULTRA. When I was studying the subject, I even felt sorry, for the first and only time in my life, for Hitler. Had it not been for ULTRA, Churchill and Roosevelt might not have been so privy to Hitler's every strategic move.

With tactics it was different. ULTRA, though correct, could be dangerously slow in distribution. As an example I give you Operation Shingle, with which I have considerably familiarity. In January 1944 the Allies, held up at Cassino, landed at two small port towns south of Rome on the Tyrrhenian coast of Italy, Anzio and Nettuno.

The landings were designed to capture from the Germans the Alban Hills south of Rome, astride field Marshall Kesselring's only communication routes to his 10th Army on the Cassino front. The operation was so important that both Churchill and Hitler took a personal hand in directing the battles. The danger to each adversary was of such magnitude, according to the senior military historian of the U.S. Army's Chief of Military

History, Martin Blumenson, that the outcome of the war itself hung in the balance.

Espionage and Italian partisans played a crucial role in avoiding disaster for the Allies and turning the tide against the Germans.

Allied commanders needed to know firsthand what the Germans were doing on the other side of the lines and how to coordinate partisan activities to coincide with the expected German retreat and liberation of the first Axis capital. To handle this job, General Donovan, Roosevelt's chief intelligence gatherer, cleared it with Gen. Mark Clark, commander of the U.S. 5th Army, for an American OSS officer to be smuggled into Rome just before the landings. When I volunteered, both generals agreed.

My qualifications, if any, were that I spoke Italian like a native, had been a war correspondent in Rome for the *New York Herald Tribune* barely 3 years earlier, and for some months had been recruiting and training anti-Fascist agents in Allied Italy to be infiltrated by parachute or submarine to spy on the Germans throughout northern Italy.

On the morning of January 20 I flew off ahead of the invasion fleet to land at Bastia in Corsica. At dusk I sailed eastward in a captured Italian torpedo boat, heading through the brisk, moonless night toward a spot on the Tyrrhenian coast about 100 miles north of Rome, where I was put ashore in a rubber boat.

From the beach I made my way into Rome—with some trouble and several scary moments, especially when the Feldgendarmerie was checking my self-made identification documents. In those early days of the OSS we still had no false documents service in the field. Somehow I managed to arrive safely in the enemy capital early on January 21, the day before the landings.

In Rome I got in touch with a young anti-Fascist police officer. He had come on foot from Naples, working his way through the fighting lines, and had brought a secret OSS radio code-named VITTORIA. This he placed at my disposal along with his services, which proved, as things turned out, to be very devoted: he was later monstrously tortured by sadistic Fascists and cold-bloodedly executed by the Nazis, though he easily could have saved himself had he chosen to betray me. The Italian government posthumously awarded him the highest military medal. His name was Maurizio Giglio.

Giglio introduced me to the Socialist member of the military junta of the Roman Committee of National Liberation, Franco Malfatti. Malfatti was just my age, 24, and until recently was Italy's Permanent Undersecretary of State for Foreign Affairs. He cheerfully agreed to deploy his 500 men to help me fulfill my mission.

Soon we had men and women watching every road in and out of the capital, 24 hours a day, and as you know, all roads lead to Rome. Malfatti, of Austrian origin, had a direct source in Field Marshal Kesselring's headquarters, making us privy to the German daily situation maps.

Another 24-year-old, Giuliano Vassalli, recently Minister of Justice in Italy, had just made a daring raid on the main jail and had liberated two future Presidents of Italy, Giuseppe Saragat and Sandro Pertini. He introduced me to the heads of the Roman resistance with whom we organized activities to coincide with the expected Allied advance.

On January 22, at 5 minutes after midnight, 250 ships of the Allied assault force dropped anchor off Anzio. The sea was calm, the night black. Ten minutes before H-hour, rocket-launchers opened a barrage on the landing beaches. When the roar of several thousand rounds subsided, there was silence on the darkened shore.

Landing craft headed for the beaches virtually uncontested. "We achieved," wrote Gen. John P. Lucas, in command of the invading Allied VI Corps, "what is certainly one of the most complete surprises in History. I could not believe my eyes when I stood on the bridge and saw no machinegun or other fire on the beach."

As dawn rose, the calm plain of Latium stretched inland toward the Alban Hills, rising 3,000 feet to their summits, a bare 20 miles away. Churchill's strategy was about to pay off. Kesselring's whole 10th Army was threatened with destruction.

At 10 a.m. on the morning of the landings, I sat disguised as a military policeman astride a motorcycle near Mussolini's former office in Piazza Venezia, watching truckloads of heavily armored German paratroopers in their camouflaged black and tan uniforms speeding south toward the beachhead.

From the building on Rome's main drag, the Corso Umberto, from which I dispatched my first secret message by radio, I could see Germans in the Hotel Plaza hurriedly packing to leave. Himmler's personal representative in Rome, Col. Eugen Dollmann, later admitted living some anxious moments at Kesselring's headquarters that January morning when "evacuation of the capital and retreat hung by a thread." According to Dollmann, Kesselring confided that he had no doubt that the heads of the resistance were preparing at last to come out of their hiding places and that American tanks would be able to give a hand to the insurgents in the city. Dollmann quotes Kesselring as saying that "only a miracle could save us."

Gen. Mark Wayne Clark, commander of the 5th Army, and Gen. Sir Harold Alexander, Commander of the 15th Army Group, provided that miracle. What ensued is to this day one of the most controversial episodes of the war. Suddenly everything changed. The liberation of Rome was indefinitely postponed. The OSS base pleaded for information on every German move. Our signals over radio VITTORIA, drafted by me in

English for immediate action on the beachhead, began to be broadcast as many as five times a day—at that time far and away the largest and most dangerous volume of intelligence sent by secret radio in Italy. From Kesselring's own situation maps we began to inform the Allied Command of just when, where, and in what force the Germans were moving, massing, or planning attack and where they were hiding gas, ammunition, or supplies. The messages are all here in these archives, easily checked.

On the morning of January 24, my Socialist sources informed me that all available German troops within a 90-kilometer radius of Rome had been ordered south, moving through Rome the night of January 22–23. Among them were three battalions of paratroopers and units of the 90th Panzer Grenadier Division, plus five divisional artillery groups. Units of the 29th and 3d Panzer Grenadier Divisions were reported transferred from the Garigliano front, moving toward the beachhead. Units of the Hermann Göring Division were moving toward Albano. Two more motorized divisions were reported transferred from Tuscany to the beachhead, to be replaced by two divisions from north Italy, one of which was already on its way.

Kesselring nevertheless estimated that if the Allies launched an attack on January 24, he still had too few forces to oppose them. The road to the Alban Hills was open; beyond them Rome could not be defended. Every German general in the area agreed they must withdraw. But no attack materialized.

By the evening of the 24th the Germans believed "the greatest crisis had been overcome." If the Allies now failed to interdict German railway traffic, Kesselring hoped to build up his forces around the beachhead faster than the Allies.

Hitler, hoping the Allies would not recognize and exploit the weakness of the German position, took immediate steps to strengthen Kesselring's forces. From France he ordered the 715th Infantry Division plus a company of Panther tanks immediately to the beachhead. From the Balkans he ordered the 114th Infantry Division, and from Germany, two Panzer Grenadier regiments with supplementary armored units.

Ralph Bennett, in his recent scholarly book, *ULTRA and Mediterranean Strategy*, says Kesselring improvised defense measures with astonishing speed and skill, throwing every unit he could lay hands on into the fray. Bennett notes correctly that several of these measures were discovered in good time, but not by ULTRA. Bennett says, "This was not the kind of work at which ULTRA usually excelled, and its reports were not of outstanding quality."

Malfatti's sources, on the other hand, were timely and exact. On January 28 I sent this message over the secret radio: "UNITS TWO ARMORED DIVISIONS THROUGH BRENNER TWENTYTHIRD TO FIFTH, BOLOGNA VERONA LARGEST CENTERS. BOMB RAILWAY

BRIDGE ON PO RIVER. TERNI CIVITACASTELLANA VERY BUSY. TWO DIVISIONS ALONG COAST SPEZIA CIVITAVECCHIA. FEW DEFENSES OSTIA FREGENE AREA. GROSSETO AND CASTIGLIONE TRASIMENO AIRPORTS ACTIVE. AIRBORNE UNITS ARRIVED GUIDONIA NIGHT TWENTYSIXTH."

That same day, January 28, Hitler issued an order in which he stressed the tremendous importance he attached to eliminating the beachhead. Not only was this to be a "battle for Rome" and for the fate of the 10th Army, but its importance would far transcend the Italian theater. Hitler believed that if the Germans succeeded in destroying the Anzio beachhead, it would prompt the Allies to postpone their invasion of northwest Europe. Speed and daring were therefore essential.

At his headquarters in East Prussia, Hitler received Kesselring's chief of staff, General von Westphal, and approved a plan to counterattack the beachhead. From then on Hitler took a direct interest in the Anzio situation, including tactical details of attack on a very narrow front.

This made us feel we were jousting in person with Der Führer. On January 29 we radioed warning of an imminent German attack against the beachhead from their Pratica di Mare (I Parachute Corps bases on the Allied left flank), with a feint from Albano-Genzano (in the center of their line). We scheduled the attack for the 29th and estimated 200 to 300 antitank guns constituted the German defense in the Appian area.

It took a while for my OSS colleagues on the beachhead to convince VI Corps that the information was from an American officer behind the lines, but they managed to get the warning phoned to the various threatened Allied units. I have a copy of the annotated orders as they went out, spread over a period of 20 minutes.

That same day, January 29, our information was confirmed by the Journal of the German 14th Army: "The main mission of the Fourteenth Army is to annihilate the beachhead which the enemy is reinforcing. The attack is to be made as soon as possible, depending on the arrival of the necessary forces, which is being delayed as the railroad system in Italy has been crippled by enemy raids."

In answer to our signal, precision bombing by the Allied air forces scored a direct hit on the I Parachute Corps command post at Pratica di Mare, temporarily knocking out the entire corps's communications network and paralyzing its means of directing artillery fire.

The German Army journal reported: "Enemy area bombing of Combat Group 'Graesser' destroyed the artillery communications net, and all fire direction charts for the action—planned to reduce the bulge north of Aprilia—were lost. The attack has been postponed 24 hours as it needs the total support of artillery."

On February 1 I was happy to lead my message with, "NICE GOING BOMBING PRATICA DI MARE."

Ralph Bennett chooses to give ULTRA credit for our intelligence. But his error is palpable from his own text. "Next," he writes, "came a major success in the decrypting of Kesselring's orders of the 24th which outlined his plan of campaign so clearly that the signal was given high priority *even though it could not be sent until 2 February* [italics mine]."

That was 3 days *after* the attacks had been reported by us and acted upon by the Allies. There was nothing wrong with ULTRA's intelligence. Quite the contrary. It just was not timely in the field. To confirm these facts I recently checked the ULTRA signals meticulously in London's Public Record Office.

By January 30 Gen. John P. Lucas, commanding VI Corps, had at last managed to mount an offensive of his own. As the advantage lay with the attacker, his three-division attack threw the Germans off balance, and their own offensive had to be postponed. Unfortunately, Lucas had delayed so long that by the morning of the 30th, the German 715th Infantry Division had arrived from France and the 26th Panzer from the Adriatic—just as we had warned. Slipped into the line by Kesselring, they caused the U.S. 3d Division, especially the Rangers, heavy losses.

Still, the Germans were only able to halt the VI Corps attack with the greatest effort and at the expense of some 5,000 casualties. From the German point of view, their own defensive stand was nothing short of miraculous.

On February 2—the same day London was issuing its passé ULTRA signal—I radioed: "FORCE NOW FACING BEACHHEAD CALLED FOURTEENTH ARMY TO CONSIST TWO ARMY CORPS PLUS TWO DIVS RESERVE X ACTUALLY IN LINE FIFTYFIVE THOUSAND MEN IN FOUR DIVS X GOERING X NINETIETH X SIXTYFIFTH AND UNKNOWN X CORPS ALSO HAVE STRONG UNITS ANTI-TANK GUNS X OTHER FOUR DIVS COMING DOWN INCLUDE THREE FIVE SIX AT CIVITACASTELLANA X IN SPITE BOMBING GERMANS PLANNING NEW ATTACK FROM PRATICA DI MARE X."

This was received at the beachhead that same day. The ULTRA signal covering the earlier January 29 attack had not even arrived at Caserta. Yet Mr. Bennett praises ULTRA, and I quote: "A still greater intelligence triumph was in store. Hard on the heels of these orders came those of January 28, signalled [from London] soon after midday of 3 February. Kesselring detailed his plan for a large scale counterattack on the bridgehead timed to start on *February 1* [italics mine]." Our message had gone out 4 days earlier on January 29, and the action was long since over.

F. H. Hinsley, in his definitive *British Intelligence in the Second World War*, points out that it was not until February 5 that ULTRA decrypts showed that I Parachute Corps was commanding the German right wing (Pratica di Mare), and the 76th Panzer Corps was commanding the left. We had sent these details 3 days earlier. Yet Bennett says: "This ULTRA intelligence formed the high point of ULTRA's contribution to the defense of Anzio and reached Clark and Alexander in plenty of time to warn them of what was afoot."

It arrived, as it happens, several days too late, but it helpfully confirmed our own reports.

In his official history of the campaign, Blumenson describes how, on receipt of intelligence from our secret radio in Rome on February 2, Alexander and Clark ordered Lucas in the nick of time to dig in and resist a powerful German counterattack with freshly arrived reinforcements.

In his book *Command Missions*, Gen. Lucian Prescott, commander of the 3d Division, wrote: "Early the following morning (February 3) General Lucas called me to say that the Army had just informed him it had secret intelligence that the Germans were in far greater strength than we had thought and were preparing to launch a counterattack to drive the beachhead into the sea. We were to stop all attacks, dig in for defense and hold the Corps beachhead line at all costs."

February 3 dawned cold and cloudy. VI Corps was busy laying minefields, stringing barbed wire, digging trenches, and waiting for the enemy, whose orders from Hitler were to eradicate the "abscess" south of Rome."

War correspondent Wynford Vaughan-Thomas, who was on the beachhead, vividly describes the situation in his book *Anzio*: "The intelligence reports arrived with the monotonous persistence of the messengers in a Greek tragedy, bringing no comfort but only further confirmation of a steady German buildup. . . . The fighting of 3–4 February gave a warning to VI Corps that soon they would be fighting for their lives."

Under heavy skies and intermittent rain, without air support, the British slowly fell back. By noon of February 4 their situation was critical. Reserves had to be thrown in with troops straight off the landing ships. By midnight the British had lost their salient and suffered some 1,400 casualties, but the main line still held.

Thereafter, says Bennett somewhat cavalierly: "There was no Ultra of importance about the second preliminary stage (for Hitler's main attack) which between 7–13 February recaptured Aprilia as a jumping off point for the main German effort codenamed *Fischfang*."

We, on the other hand, radioed from Rome on February 6: "GERMANS PLANNING LAUNCH HEAVY ATTACK AGAINST BEACHHEAD FOUR HUNDRED HOURS OF SEVENTH."

Again Vaughan-Thomas gives an account of the results of our warning: "Our intelligence got wind through its sources in Rome that the night of the 7th was zero hour and there was a hurried stand-to along the Allied line. . . . The battle that was to lead to the crisis on the beachhead had begun."

But the Germans, surprised at unexpected Allied resistance, were again unable to push through their attack. On February 8 we ended a long message on German units and dispositions with the words, "PRACTICA DI MARE ATTACK STILL PLANNED."

Despite bad weather and strong wind, 2,000 Allied bombers struck against enemy assembly areas with remarkable accuracy, foiling this attack. That same day the German Army journal reported: "Due to strong enemy resistance and our heavy losses, the main attack which had been planned for 8 February had to be postponed. The attack will take place during the night of 8 to 9 February."

On February 9, 84 medium bombers on their way to attack supply dumps around Valmontone were diverted en route and dropped their loads on German troop assembly areas indicated by us near Campoleone. By this time a special liaison officer had been assigned to the OSS by the joint U.S. and British air force to enable its bombers, even when already airborne, to switch to urgent targets as we radioed them in.

That same February 9 we obtained a report directly from Hitler's Colonel Dollmann, and again we warned the base: "SS COLONEL SAYS OWING RETREAT RUSSIA MAXIMUM EFFORT WILL BE MADE ITALY."

That February 9 was the day Hitler approved Kesselring's plan to wipe out the beachhead. The German Army journal reported the decision: "On this day was promulgated the first order of the Fourteenth Army for the attack to wipe out the Nettuno Beachhead. The Fourteenth Army will attack the enemy beachhead on X day, 15 February 1944 at Y hour, with its main effort 1.5 Km west of Aprilia Nettuno Highway." Just where we kept pointing with our messages.

Hitler insisted that the beachhead be eliminated at any cost. If this could be accomplished, he considered the chances of a major invasion of Europe to be greatly reduced. Hitler even made plans beyond the elimination of the beachhead. Seconded by Kesselring, he envisaged using the victorious forces at Anzio for a major offensive on the 10th Army front to push the Allies back toward Naples.

That the Germans were anxious to keep the secret of their forthcoming offensive is evidenced by their journal of February 13: "The Fourteenth Army will attack on February 16. . . . The entire operation, especially date and time of attack is to be considered top secret. Officers of the High Command who are here in advisory capacity will be forbidden to communicate with their headquarters by telephone."

Yet February 15, the day before the actual attack, we radioed: "SPEZIA RIMINI LINE SEEMS EMPTIED FOR ATTEMPT SMASH BEACHHEAD BUT LACK OF GAS VERY SERIOUS X NAZIS FIGURE MAXIMUM EFFORT IN NEXT FEW DAYS X."

On February 16, as the world was soon to learn, the Germans launched their massive attack, which was to come within a hair of throwing the Allies into the sea. Hitler, personally directing the attack from his headquarters in East Prussia, issued a ringing order of the day. He expected his forces to eliminate the beachhead within 3 days. Kesselring was confident his forces would drive all the way to Anzio, then return in triumph to parade captured prisoners through the streets of Berlin.

Exactly on schedule on the morning of February 16, enemy guns opened up with the heaviest concentration of artillery fire against both sides of the Albano road. Out of the pall of smoke and dust came the assault waves of the 3d Panzer Grenadiers and the 715th Infantry. Enemy tanks in groups of four to eight fired at close range and then returned to replenish ammunition.

On the morning of February 17 we radioed: "ENEMY IS LESS OPTIMISTIC BUT STILL EXPECTING SUCCESSFUL BIG ATTACK WITH ARRIVING REINFORCEMENTS." We listed scores more targets, and, despite the overcast sky, 700 Allied bombers raided the attacking Germans. All other air missions were scrapped.

That evening the German 14th Army commander debated whether to discontinue the attack or commit his second wave of two divisions. He was in favor of calling off further efforts because of the enormous losses suffered by the first waves. By this time his 65th Division was down to less than 1,000 men. Kesselring, though in doubt about the outcome of the battle, was in favor of continuing. Hitler would sanction no let-up in any case. In the renewed attack, the Germans penetrated to a depth of almost 4 miles over a 4-mile front and were pounding the Final Beachhead Defense Line. The equivalent of six German divisions were pitted against four depleted American battalions.

In London, Churchill had no illusions about the battle. "All hung in the balance. . . . It was life or death." In Washington, Secretary of War Henry L. Stimson called a hurried press conference to plead with the American public not to give up hope over the Anzio situation.

On the night of February 17–18, the Germans mounted a supreme effort to push the Allies into the sea. On the 18th, from 8 a.m. to 8 p.m., the full strength of the Germans was loosed against the battered American battalions. But Allied bombers were out savaging their pinpointed targets, largely consisting of ammunition and gasoline stores and usually well hidden from Allied air reconnaissance, and the Germans found it increasingly difficult to keep supplies flowing to the beachhead. For 2 more days they tried vainly to reorganize their attacks.

On February 21 we radioed: "GERMANS ESTIMATE THAT IF PRESENT ALLOUT ATTACKS AGAINST BEACHHEAD FAIL THEY WILL NO LONGER BE ABLE TO REDUCE BEACHHEAD."

General von Westphal, Kesselring's Chief of Staff, attributed the German failure primarily to the strength of Allied intelligence and the weakness of that of the Germans. "The assault," wrote von Westphal, "found the enemy ready, so that the surprise which would have increased the prospects of success was absent. . . . German troops penetrated to within twelve kilometers of the beach, and some units still nearer. . . . Naturally they would have kept up the pressure if they had known how things were on the other side. But uncertainty of the conditions and intentions of the enemy is one of the characteristics of warfare. We now know that the allied command had in fact already decided on reembarcation when the German pressure suddenly and unexpectedly ceased."

As for an Allied appreciation of the intelligence collected by the Socialist partisans, which I sent out from Rome over secret radio VITTORIA, the intelligence officer in Alexander's headquarters responsible for handling our messages was to write of it the following account:

> Both the volume and quality of the information transmitted was of the highest possible type. The information was of direct and highly important military value. Confirmation of this can be made by consulting the cable files and by reference to VI Corps memoranda to OSS.

> Without the complete files, it is impossible to cite all the outstanding work done by this team. Perhaps the most valuable contribution of this station was acting as the only independent source of intelligence for the VI Corps and the Anzio Beachhead. Such important individual intelligence items as the first identification of parachute units, description and location of German heavy railway guns, warning as to precise time and direction of two German land attacks and a sea attack by "E" boats, show why this team received such praise and gratitude from VI Corps, 5th Army, the Navy, and the 12th Air Force. In addition, a consistently high level was maintained in the reporting of battle order, troop movements, enemy intentions, supply traffic, and dumps. Such was the value of the road traffic counts and air target selections by the VITTORIA team that Tactical Air Force appointed a special Liaison Officer to OSS for this work. Also, at the specific request of CI [Counter intelligence], G-2, valuable information of the enemy's organization and espionage activity was obtained and transmitted by this team.

> It is difficult to emphasize sufficiently the great value to American beachhead forces and Allied air forces of the work done by VITTORIA, always at tremendous risk. The records of VI Corps, Fifth Army, AAI [Allied Armies in Italy], 12 ASC [Air Support Command] and MATAF [Mediterranean Allied Tactical Air Force] are sufficient testimony of this value, as were the many verbal tributes of Colonel Langevin of VI Corps, General Howard of 5th Army, and Wing Commander Wiseman of TAF [Tactical Air Force].

All of this intelligence was, of course, gathered by Italian partisans at great risk and considerable sacrifice: 22 of our men were tortured and butchered in the Ardeatine Caves massacre alone.

To what extent these partisans contributed to saving the Anzio Beachhead remains for historians to settle. But among the papers of General Donovan—now collected in Carlisle, PA—is a one-page copy of a letter addressed to President Roosevelt as well as an identical message to the Joint Chiefs of Staff, in which the general reports the following:

An OSS unit hidden in Rome set up a 24-hour watching service on the 12 main highways out of the capital. Five times daily they radioed to the Anzio beach-head vital intelligence procured by their agents. These included a man employed in Field Marshal Kesselring's headquarters and another who was liaison officer between the Gestapo in Rome and the Italian secret police. At a critical moment in the battle the Rome team flashed word of an eminent German counterattack along the Anzio-Albano axis. This attack was hurled back only because G-2 at Anzio knew where and when it was due. Colonel Langevin, G-2 of the VI Corps stated that OSS might well be said to have saved the beachhead.

It is in my case the opinion of those against whom these efforts were directed (such as General von Westphal) that it was intelligence, or lack of it, that, in the final analysis, proved decisive at Anzio. And this intelligence was produced by humans, not by ULTRA. The reason this story may be little known is that considerable effort was exerted to see that it was shredded. The enemy does not always face you squarely. Luckily these archives stand to set the record straight.

BEHIND ENEMY LINES IN FRANCE

Helene Deschamps-Adams

My first visit to the National Archives was in July 1975, at the pre-Bicentennial exhibit entitled "Her Infinite Variety." I had the honor to represent the women of the Office of Strategic Services (OSS), and I am delighted to have been asked again to participate in this year's celebration of the 50th anniversary of World War II.

My talk today is about the French Underground versus the American OSS. It is a look back at the mission of an OSS field operative behind enemy lines.

It seems that no matter how noble a cause is, quite often politics, competitive rivalry, and fanatical doctrines find a way to infiltrate and erode many ideals. By the end of 1943, the regular Underground (FFI), the Communist Underground (FTP), the Secret Army (SA), the Maquis (guerrilla fighters), the pro–de Gaulle and pro-Giraud forces, and a large number of independent networks, or reseaux, were all functioning on their own, each trying to outdo the others and to show their powers.

Disenchanted by this political situation, I decided to leave the French Underground, with whom I had fought since the end of 1940, and join the American OSS as a field operative. My chief in the Resistance, Colonel Beaugard, referred me to a man called ARNAUD, one of the partisans' leaders in my area. I asked him to introduce me to an agent of the OSS who was operating in our sector.

ARNAUD was not enthusiastic the first time I mentioned my wish to work with the Americans. Hard-headed and pro–de Gaulle, the man could not understand my growing dissatisfaction with the infighting and petty squabbling among the partisans. "Fancy the damn foreigners, do you?" ARNAUD grunted angrily. After much reluctance, however, he agreed to arrange a meeting.

PETIT-JEAN was the code name of the key OSS agent in the southeast sector. The team was JACQUES and was part of the chain in the most successful OSS network in occupied France, code-named Penny Farthing.

Recruiting in the field was not prefaced by paperwork, investigations, oaths of allegiance, and other requirements necessary in normal times. One's word, and an introduction by a known Resistance leader, was sufficient, as patriotism and proven loyalty provided the initial recommendation. There were neither facilities nor time for checking the life history of each volunteer.

I had no special training and had not undergone any schooling. My espionage skill had been in the field of service, playing a dangerous game with the enemy. I received the code name ANICK.

I was paired with another OSS agent, code-named HELLOPS, and we covered the territory from Avignon to Montpellier to Marseilles. HELLOPS and I reported on German defense work and fortifications, on the strength and movement of enemy troops, and on the transport of equipment and ammunitions. We also covered airfield locations, and we bicycled along the Mediterranean shores to detect coastal defenses and locate German mines, antiaircraft, and camouflaged nests.

We were quite often handicapped in our missions by the Underground. The main factors were lack of communication, unwillingness to cooperate, and political affiliations, as you will hear in my narration of a mission I participated in during the landing in southern France in August 1944. These interferences did not come from every reseau, but they happened often enough to be a problem.

At the time of the landing, events were taking place at such a speed that it was sometimes hard to follow the changes that would make a positive occurrence turn into a most dreadful ending. I will exclude many details and give only the facts, but I have documents, decoded messages, passes, letters, and photographs to validate the report pertinent to this mission. Also, there are still living witnesses in the villages where the events took place.

At 11 a.m. on August 17, 1944, my adopted sister Jackie (who also was in the OSS) and I met PETIT-JEAN at the Café des Deux Garçons in Aix-en-Provence. Three days had already passed since the landing on the Mediterranean coast. Orders were given to locate units of the SS Panzer Division, which had come up from the Atlantic coast, near Bordeaux. We also had to estimate the strength of the German infantry escorting the tanks. Any details, no matter how small, should be reported, we were told. We had to leave immediately. PETIT-JEAN had to stay behind to meet BIBENDUM, the ringleader of the Parachute Drop Section, but he would meet us the next morning at 8 o'clock in the village of Pertuis, almost 30 kilometers from Aix. We then would move to Apt, meet our radio operator, and give him intelligence data.

As PETIT-JEAN was leaving the café, he intentionally left the local newspaper. Inside the folded pages were passes with falsified German seals and stamps, which would allow us to pass German posts without too many problems. There also were miniature printed booklets, giving information on enemy insignias, materiel, and troop descriptions, and he had added a few bills of French currency for an emergency.

By noon we were on our way with the only transportation available to French civilians—bicycles. Beyond the hamlet of Venelle, we spotted an enemy ammunition train camouflaged under tall plane trees. We immediately paused near the tracks, leaning busily over Jackie's bike, and while she forced some air into the tire, German guards came to investigate. Reassured that we were no threat, they offered help, while I methodically listed in my mind the number of boxcars and their location. We left again, heading toward Pertuis. Coming in the other direction was a German convoy composed of several trucks, light machine-gun vehicles, and a number of foot soldiers. At the same time, a P-47 aircraft appeared out of nowhere and began raking the convoy with machine-gun fire. We tossed our bikes into a ditch and threw ourselves into a sunflower field while the fighter plane made several dives, strafing the convoy. The German machine-gun vehicles were hit first, then several trucks and a number of men escorting the convoy. They must have been carrying fuel, because there were explosions everywhere, and a long column of black smoke ascended to the sky. The plane left, and taking advantage of the confusion, Jackie and I crossed the field until we reached the main road again, a kilometer or so beyond the convoy.

We knew that we had to cross a bridge across the Durance River. It was supposed to be guarded by German soldiers, but when we came near, there was not a soul around; the bridge had been bombed. In the thick mud of the riverbank, we could see the grim outline of a large bomb, which had failed to explode; its gray nose was pointing upward.

Leaving our bicycles on the riverside, we started crossing the bridge, moving with great difficulty along the damaged rail, holding on to one of the sagging cables.

As soon as we set foot on the other side, we were surrounded by a group of men in civilian clothes, carrying guns. They wore the French FFI armband. They searched us, found our papers with German stamps, and took us prisoner.

Forced to march to Pertuis with guns at our backs, we were taken to the city hall for interrogation. We tried to explain our mission to a Mr. Martin, the tobacconist in town and the man in charge. We told him who we actually were, talked about the American OSS, ARNAUD, Colonel Beaugard, and PETIT-JEAN, but they only laughed: "ARNAUD? PETIT-JEAN? the OSS? What kind of nonsense is this?"

The only purpose these men understood was to defend the land that belonged to them. They agreed to wait until morning, however, for the arrival of the man called PETIT-JEAN. They locked us in a pigsty for the night and placed a guard at the door.

Around 1 a.m. there was a violent scuffle outside, accompanied by vociferous shouts. The door flew open, and our guard was knocked down with the butt of a rifle. Men wearing the FTP Communist armband prodded us with the snouts of their weapons and ordered us to follow them to their camp on the other side of town.

We were prepared to cope with the Germans but not to be held captive by our own countrymen. First seized by the FFIs, now we were pawns of the FTPs!

Many examples of terrorism and gangsterism had been traced to the FTP Communists. Banks had been robbed, stores looted, and raids against the regular Underground, or FFI, were more political than patriotic. The OSS headquarters in Algiers had been warned and was well aware that its agents were often harmed by the FTPs, some of whom were fanatical supporters of Marxist dogmas. The FTPs considered the OSS the vanguard of an imperialist regime. In any event, whatever this group wanted of us was not very clear. Perhaps they thought we were important hostages, and they wanted to receive the credit for our capture. On the other hand, if we were, as we claimed, agents for American intelligence, they could use us as barter for future bargaining.

Less than an hour after our abduction, Martin, the FFI chief, presented himself to the rival camp. Martin was accompanied by a dozen men armed to the hilt and they looked furious. They launched a barrage of vile obscenities, dire threats, and vulgar, tight-fisted gestures. The Communist leader made the mistake of pointing his weapon at Martin, whose bodyguards disarmed him and kicked him savagely to his knees.

Following a long pause, the FTP man gave us back to the FFIs. "We'll meet again," he hissed angrily; "I'm not finished with you bitches," he warned.

Eight, nine, ten o'clock passed. PETIT-JEAN never came.

Brought back in front of a makeshift tribunal, the trial was conducted with dispatch. I knew by now our chance of survival was thin; the Underground had a reputation for carrying out its verdicts with speed and alacrity. Martin listened to the reading of the charges.

"You are collaborators," they stated. "The proof is undeniable. The papers you carried have German seals. You have been found guilty of treason. The penalty is death."

We were paraded through the town, past hundreds of hostile villagers. A sort of frenzy seemed to possess them. From the everyday housewives to the petit-bourgeois merchants, these "self-appointed patriots," who had never lifted a finger during the Occupation, cautiously hiding in their homes, were now out in the street, demanding justice, spitting at us as we walked by. They felt safe—the Americans had landed!

We reached a café-restaurant on the marketplace, and we were told to sit on a bench and wait. Neither of us could utter a word. What can be said when death awaits? I wanted to cry, but it was too late for that.

We were jarred from our nightmare by sharp-cut orders. The beaded curtain of the bar parted, and in came BIBENDUM, the ringleader of the Parachute Drop Section.

He came forward and made a broad gesture of relief. "I came in time!" he exclaimed. "Some FFIs on the road boasted to have captured two girls. I was with PETIT-JEAN early this morning. German snipers got him—a bullet through the heart—nothing I could do for him." He spoke rather matter-of-factly.

Martin showed up behind him, a bottle of red wine in one hand, glasses in the other. "No hard feelings!" he joshed, with a broad smile, as if an insignificant misunderstanding had just been settled.

We all sat, and after a lengthy meeting, we were advised by BIBENDUM to move ahead and pick up BERTRAND, our radioman in Apt, and from there go to St. Tropez on the Riviera, where the OSS had set up their temporary headquarters. "It's no use to continue this mission without PETIT-JEAN," said BIBENDUM.

The FFIs from Pertuis gave each of us a permanent Underground pass, and by 1 p.m. Jackie and I started on foot across the Luberon High Hills. Arriving at Apt, we inquired about our man at the inn indicated by BIBENDUM. "He left," we were told, "as soon as he heard of PETIT-JEAN's death; he thought everyone had been killed." Exhausted, we decided to stay overnight in Apt and start fresh the next morning.

We had been lying on our bed no longer than 1 hour when a violent explosion resounded. From our window, I saw a string of German tanks entering the town of Apt. It was one of the SS Panzer units we had been scouting. One of their guns blasted the side of a large building. People were running in all directions, screaming: "Les Boches sont là!—the Krauts are here," and we ran with them.

A tank rumbled past us, and soldiers jumped out of a Reichswehr troop carrier, shooting at will. In a narrow lane, Jackie unlocked a garden gate, and we ended up on Highway 100.

We met a group of Maquisards some kilometers further on. Around 6 p.m. an informant who had been able to escape from Apt reported that the town was under siege; the enemy was searching house to house for partisans, and looting was everywhere.

At dusk, Jackie and I were asked by the Maquisards to go forward and cross the German line after nightfall to summon American troops reported to be making their way inland. "The passage by the dark of night should be fairly easy," they insisted.

I agreed to go, for at least part of our mission would be achieved. We now had the location of a Panzer unit to report.

The Maquisards gave us a requisitioned little Simca car. Jackie insisted on going into the cramped back, and I sat with the driver. We had been driving without light for about 30 minutes when, taken by surprise, we encountered a German patrol moving along the road. Shots rang out in the dark, crackling, shattering noises of machine guns.

Hunched over the wheel, our driver barked, "Get down. The S.O.B.s have spotted us." I could hear voices cursing in German. Fragments of shattered glass showered inside the car.

No more than 15 minutes later, a second fusillade hit the car, coming from the right side of the road. This time, it was from a single automatic gun. It was then that I heard Jackie cry out, "I'm hit!"

Amid the gunfire and panic, it was impossible to find out how badly she had been wounded. The driver raced blindly ahead. We finally reached a safe intersection. When I groped back and looked, Jackie was dead.

There is no way to express how I felt. Devastated would perhaps be appropriate—and also guilty because that night I had agreed to go forward.

Perched on the hill was the village of Reillanne. The driver summoned the townspeople. One of them gave me a sheet with which to wrap Jackie's body. There was no coffin. We simply dug a hole and buried her.

The head of the FFIs from the village removed his beret and said out loud: "Jacqueline, young girl of France, you gave us your courage, your belief, your life. In the name of France, in the name of the Resistance, in the name of my men, thank you, and farewell."

Among the villagers standing by was the FTP Communist from Pertuis, holding his automatic weapon. We had met again.

Around 5 a.m., after I had arranged for a cross to be placed on Jackie's cursory grave, I was given a new driver with a motorcycle, and I was able to reach the American Task Force Butler, Armored Division, at Forcalquier. I gave my report on the Panzers, the ammunition train in Venelle, and the enemy soldiers roaming the countryside to the American G-2 officer. Then I left for the coast, where I joined the first group of G-2 Strategic Services Section agents who had landed. These agents were headed by Henry Hyde, the "MONSIEUR HENRI" of many messages dangerously decoded in various hidden corners. He was the chief of the French desk of the OSS and was attached to Allied Forces Headquarters in the Mediterranean theater.

August 20, 1944

In peacetime, St. Tropez, on the French Riviera, was just another quiet little harbor bathed in sunlight. In the middle of war, it was unrecognizable. I could hardly believe my eyes when, still grieving over Jackie's death and weary with travel, I came into town and had my first glimpse of the mass of American mechanized military power moving up the beach; landing ship tanks (LST), liberty ships, and 2½-ton cargo amphibious trucks (DUKWs) filled the harbor. Jeeps darted in all directions; trucks, tanks, men, cars were everywhere. The sky was dotted with barrage balloons protecting the landing against air attacks, and I could hear the deep thud of mines being exploded.

Lt. Gen. Alexander M. Patch, 7th Army Commander, gave tribute to the OSS units involved in passing information prior to this landing. "It was," said the general, "probably the fullest and most detailed work provided to G-2 Intelligence." I must say that I am proud to have been part of one of these units.

OSS headquarters and its initial 23 SSS G-2 male agents and one young woman, myself, were temporarily installed in St. Tropez at a villa which was the estate of René Clair, the famous French movie producer.

On August 24, at dawn, Henry Hyde gave his orders. All agents present were sent alone or in pairs to different destinations to gather new intelligence data on the retreating, yet implacable, fighting German Army.

I teamed with a Jedburgh named Patterson. "You are to enter the city of Marseilles to the East," Henry said. "The Underground has opened a breach in that area. The city is still occupied by the enemy, so watch it. Establish contact with the FFIs, get details on the German garrison defending the town and their approximate force. You'll get a radioman there."

We left the villa around 7 a.m. in a requisitioned Peugeot car, taking the inland route. In an open area, near the villages of LeLuc and LeMuy, we sighted several wrecked gliders that had been part of the Rugby Airborne Task Force.

At the bend of the road, a temporary prisoner-of-war camp came in sight. The German prisoners looked at us with grim, burning eyes and had ascetic, hungry faces. Some were wounded. A loner was standing near the barbed wire fence, holding a snapshot. He held it preciously between his fingers, smiling. His eyes raised slowly at our approach. They were the vacant eyes of a madman.

Patterson sensed my uneasiness. "Keep your pity for those who understand pity," he said dispassionately; and, remembering Jackie, I thought bitterly, "He's right. Why should I feel sorry? Wasn't it supposed to be a hunting game? Them, or us!"

When we reached Marseilles, the city was in a turmoil. Only a small area was liberated, but the 224th German Division was fighting desperately to hold on. Units from the American Armored Division were coming up, reinforced by two French battalions.

Our contact in Marseilles was Mimile, a nickname for Emile, a drug pusher and a pimp who proved to be of maximum usefulness on special raids. He was an expert with the knife and did silent, expedient work. His connections throughout all walks of life made him invaluable. His men, as he pompously called them, were a pack of ill-dressed mobsters who carried miscellaneous weapons ranging from small pistols to Sten guns and from World War I Lebel bolt action rifles to knives of all sizes. They brought up-to-the-minute information of all German movements in town.

Mimile's "business office," a narrow cubicle with no window, was on the third floor of a bar, near the Place Gambetta. When we entered the room, he was straddling a chair, waiting. He received us somewhat as Napoleon would have greeted one of his inferior officers.

"Who's the girl?" he asked scornfully.

"She works with me," Patterson replied in French, which he spoke fluently.

Patterson and I brought gifts to persuade Mimile to help us. He apparently felt we owed him the American Camel cigarettes we presented, but because gasoline was scarce, our promise of a few gallons put us in business.

During the next 2 days, French General de Monsabert, commanding the 3d Algerian Division, set up headquarters at the Hotel du Quinzième in town and started negotiations with German General Schaffer. They failed to come to any agreement.

Two battalions of Allied infantry, supported by tanks, and detachments of Algerian goums were in the process of attacking the city. By August 27 the harbor of Marseilles was mopped up. The surrounding forts surrendered. Patterson and I fed all this information through the radio operator provided by Mimile.

We were joined shortly after by other agents. The OSS headquarters in Marseilles was installed by Frank Schoonmaker at 3 rue Gabrielle, and Henry Hyde established his temporary command post in my own house in Aix-en-Provence. I went on to continue with the French campaign.

A monument has been erected by the grateful townspeople of Apt at the spot where Jackie was killed.

On the morning of August 30, my co-agent Patterson was called to Grenoble. Upon departure, he handed me a letter: "This is for Schoonmaker. He will take care of you while I'm gone."

Around 1 p.m., a Jeep took me to the OSS headquarters in Marseilles, and I went directly up the long flight of marble stairs to the second floor. Frank Schoonmaker leaned back in his chair and looked at me across his desk. I handed him the letter and his eyes ran rapidly over the paper.

"What do you want me to do?" I asked.

He hesitated. "You'll come up to Lyon with us," he said. "JEROME, one of our best agents, arrived from Montpellier this morning. You'll go with him."

Taking the phone, he gave a quick order. His glance at the Baby Ben clock on his desk indicated that he was anxious for me to be off.

The clouds that had been gathering during the morning had finally burst. JEROME was waiting for me under the archway, hunched in his oilskin poncho. We had never met before, and he was silent while driving to the petroleum, oil, and lubricant depot to fill the Jeep with gas and get another jerrican for the trip.

With all the roads jammed full of Allied military convoys, our progress was slow. Rain fell heavily. Midway to our destination, at La Coucourde, JEROME was forced to make an abrupt stop. We stared in disbelief at the scene of carnage stretching along the 10 miles ahead of us on Highway 7. Three German divisions, including the mighty 11th Panzer, had been totally eliminated on the east side of the Rhône River. The German losses were prodigious. The American field artillery had fired upon the retreating enemy considerably more than 75,000 rounds of ammunition. Long convoys were destroyed, and the entire area was covered with a mass of burned trucks, trains, and equipment. Eleven thousand German soldiers lay dead, decaying on the road. Fifteen hundred horses perished. The Germans had lost a total of 2,100 vehicles and six 380-millimeter railroad guns, the mighty long-range guns of which they were so proud.

When JEROME's Jeep was finally able to pass over this graveyard, the road was cluttered with helmets, skeletons of cars of all sizes, lost gas masks, hand grenades, and guns. Hundreds of bloated bodies of German soldiers were strewn along the roadside, still smoldering in the aftermath of battle. The men had died in bizarre positions, some cowering in heaps, crawling, sprinting, shooting, yelling, or even imploring Heaven with a plea. Rain was falling into their open mouths, running slowly over their gray, dead lips. Here and there, an outstretched hand had beckoned for help.

JEROME and I drove silently through the carnage, the stink of rotting flesh impregnating the air we breathed. Somehow, as if taken under a strange trance, my fixed eyes kept on staring at the horrifying sight.

"Sweet Jesus! What is the world coming to?" JEROME exclaimed bitterly.

"Please, push the accelerator," I begged, gagging.

He tried to speed away from the macabre scene, avoiding as best he could the shell craters yawning open on the highway. Then there was a thump, and the Jeep stopped moving. It was stuck in a mortar hole, and the front wheels were sliding in the mud.

A house was still standing, and from the road I could see the interior with its floors neatly sliced open like a layer cake, the colorful pink, blue, and yellow wallpaper, the paintings on the walls, a mirror reflecting the leaden sky. The dismantled walls were still standing, gray and wet, dripping black rivulets. Dirty water ran down the gutter. In the back of the building was what once had been a small vegetable garden, a few dry cabbages and bean stalks seeding to the ground.

The stench of a slaughterhouse stifled our breathing. A dead horse was lying on its back, and its four stiff legs were sticking up in the air. Its belly was so bloated that it had cracked open, letting out foul and putrid matter. Rats, attracted by the filth, squealed busily amongst the mounds of rubbish. Gasping at the sight and smell, I vomited.

"Damn it," JEROME swore under his breath. He got out. "Stop feeling sorry for yourself and help me, will you!" he shouted impatiently.

"I can't drive," I moaned, feeling another wave of nausea rising up.

"Hell, try anything. We'll rock the car back and forth. It's not that heavy. Take the right side."

As I came out of the vehicle, he collected some loose bricks scattered around and lined the edge of the muddy crater. "Now push. I'll take the other side."

With both hands gripping the car door, I used all of my strength to shove once, twice, three times. The machine hesitated at the brim and then rolled back into the hole. We tried again, and this time the wheels rolled over the edge, free. There were several minutes of wheel-spinning before the Jeep started to move, waddling off the road, splashing slush in all directions.

JEROME took a look around, a grim expression on his face. "Ye Gods! What a stink. Let's get the hell out of here!"

We both covered our mouths and noses, tightening handkerchiefs around our faces in an effort to muffle the fetid miasma polluting the air. The car groaned around the curve as we passed the ruins of war, and we were on our way again. Several kilometers ahead, near Loriol, close to the mouth of the Drôme River, our little car crossed a pontoon where a company of engineers worked hastily to repair the damage from the recent heavy shelling.

The battle of Montélimar had lasted 8 days before the Americans had succeeded in penetrating the town. The thoroughfare was deeply marked by the signs of fighting. Two tanks stood lonely and naked in a ditch, blackened by fire.

It was the middle of the night when we arrived at SSS G-2 quarters located in a chateau outside of Lyon: Chateau Gleisol. The residence, which had been Marshal Pétain's home for a short period of time, had become an incongruous mixture of former grandeur and an accumulation of military equipment, ranging from parachutes and radio transmitters to handguns and clothing. I was assigned a room by a man on duty at the billeting desk. It was elegant but damp and cold.

The following morning at breakfast, I saw people I had met at the landing: Poniatowsky, Duff, Bender, Guy, Millen, Parsons. An aura of transience hung over the premises. People were gone one day and back the next. New faces cropped up and disappeared periodically; no one ever asked questions. Everybody was friendly enough, drank straight scotch, vodka, or whiskey, and remained aloof with an "I don't give a damn" attitude.

I began to feel restless staying at the chateau. One day I was able to catch a ride to Lyon and shop for immediate necessities. On the black market, I found a wool dress, shoes, and a warm winter coat for the coming frost.

The gratification was temporary. The thrill and stimulation experienced from undertaking a mission was lacking, and I missed it. It could perhaps be compared to an addictive pattern that gripped me from inside with a twisting sensation, and after days of waiting or "fasting," it became intolerable. Living on the edge had become a habit, and I fervently hoped that my inactivity would not last much longer.

Early one morning, I was summoned to a study where Henry Hyde waited. The narrow hall at the end of the stairs dead-ended at what was called the "map room." I knocked and entered in a single motion. Henry was reading a report, and I knew the instant I saw him that he was preparing a mission.

It was a pleasant room, carpeted with beautiful oriental rugs and a rich oil painting over the marble mantel. There was a round central table covered with deep, green felt. The leather-bound books lining the hand-crafted shelves lent a worldly, lived-in ambience.

Henry was not talkative or relaxed. He looked weary, no doubt from the weight of fatigue and heavy responsibility. His personal secretary had not arrived yet, for OSS female personnel showed only after an area could be called "safe."

I had not seen him since the departure from St. Tropez, and yet he gave his orders without any friendly preamble. He was all business.

I tried to second-guess my assignment. I had heard that American troops were moving fast to the east.

"You are looking fit," remarked Henry from behind his desk.

"I'm fine."

"Good." He reached for a pack of cigarettes in his shirt pocket and drew one out. "You will leave by noon with BERTRAND, the radio operator, and go to the Jura plateau."

He paused for a while. I observed he was weighing me shrewdly. He struck a match and spoke between puffs of his cigarette.

"We need a report on German strength and movements," he told me, "anything that might be important to the military, such as bridges and road conditions, artillery posts, river crossings, an approximate number of enemy troops; you know what I need. It will be difficult terrain. Germans are all over. We are expecting a big move. You can do anything you think is necessary to obtain this information; it's your option, as long as we get what we need. An agent will contact you in Arbois when your mission is completed."

"BERTRAND will give you some funds. It will come in handy to pay off any informers. I am sorry you have to go," he added, giving me one of his famous smiles.

I walked out and closed the door behind me. Back in my room I prepared a small bag. Then, ready to leave, I went downstairs and checked the rest of my belongings at the storeroom. "I'll be back in a few days," I told the enlisted man in charge of the storage. "OK, Ma'am, and take it easy." He winked at me.

September 1944

The German opposition to the American advance had stepped up into savage resistance, particularly in the Jura and the Vosges sector. The uncertain front line was now perilous to cross, and the 7th Army G-2 was obliged to depend more and more on the OSS SI agents to obtain functional information from behind enemy lines.

In the Jura, American troops were advancing, and BERTRAND's battered Jeep passed convoy after convoy. The rain was streaming from the colorless sky, making the macadam gleam like glass. The Jeep slid along the road with a "pfuit" that sounded like the rustling of taffeta. Sometimes, we had to inch behind endless lines of Army trucks.

With the entire VI Corps advancing along the main highway, traffic became so heavy that halts were necessary to gain sufficient clearance between marching units. Blown-up bridges also forced us to detour over muddy trails and thick ridges. The foot soldiers had churned the soil on these roads into a quagmire.

The thoroughfare had now widened, permitting us to speed ahead. We had passed along an endless line of trucks when my eyes caught something unusual that didn't register immediately.

"BERTRAND," I said, "did you see something out of the ordinary back there?"

He nodded his head. "I think so." The Jeep came to a screeching halt, and we waited. Several vehicles drove by, their tarpaulins secured against the heavy downpour, and sure enough, there it was—in the middle of the convoy was a German car loaded with men! The Germans were trying to surrender with a white rag attached to the windshield, but nobody was paying attention to them.

BERTRAND drove ahead of the convoy and notified the military police directing the traffic to prepare a reception committee.

The humidity penetrated the car, making the seats sticky to the touch. BERTRAND was huddled up to the ears with his coat. I couldn't fall asleep, constantly overhearing his cursing. From the corner of my eye, I could see his shoulders shivering as rivulets of icy water streamed down from the canvas top.

He sneezed. When he did, the car skidded from side to side. We bogged down against a thick root embedded in the dark red clay. The spinning wheels threw soft mud against the plastic side windows and, mixed with the rain, clouded the view. The wipers could barely keep the windshield clear of the dirty water.

Opening the canvas, BERTRAND surveyed the road ahead and grunted. "Damn it! Where is this crummy place?" He blotted his wet face with his sleeve and turned the headlights on. A few kilometers along, a signpost indicated we were at last entering Arbois. It was about midnight by then.

Arbois was the little town where Louis Pasteur had once experimented with his rabies vaccine. At an inn situated at the crossroads, BERTRAND stopped the Jeep to inquire about lodging. He knocked at the door loudly.

A man with a sleepy voice answered through closed shutters. "Can't you see we're closed? This is not a night to wander around the village," he nagged. "The Germans are still at the other end of town. If you want a room, you can perhaps try Madame Massière, if you make it to her home. It's 25 rue Puget."

The wind and the rain encircled the woman's solitary house. BERTRAND slid on the loose stone steps that led to the front door. They were almost buried under a mass of unkept plants, and it gave the appearance of a tombstone.

Madame Massière was an old, wiry little widow who refused to let us in. Following a long palaver conducted through the shutters, she finally agreed to rent two rooms for a couple of days. She inched down the stairway in a white flannel nightdress to greet us.

I stretched the kink out of my back. My legs and arms were stiff, and my feet almost numb as I helped unload the car. It took a very short time. I slept the remainder of the night, and BERTRAND knocked at my door around 6 a.m.

As I dressed, I could smell burning wood and hot milk. Madame Massière had a bowl ready on the small kitchen table with a slice of dark bread for our breakfasts. She appeared content, even lighthearted with the new-found company, and she fussed over me, offering more hot milk.

A short while later, BERTRAND and I were ready to tackle our tough assignment. BERTRAND turned the key of the Jeep. The motor chugged, fought dampness, fired into life, and the car, driven cautiously, headed toward the outskirts of the village.

The weather had not changed. High, biting winds and a granite sky still presided. The ground was cloaked in a thick fog. Halting at a small grove on high ground, we got out of the Jeep and surveyed the lush pastures surrounding us. BERTRAND carried his well-traveled suitcase containing the radio and a map.

Crows were flapping above, only to settle with loud cawing a few trees on. Clouds were lying low over the region. From far away came the tolling of a church bell. A small herd of cows walked unhurriedly, single file, out to pasture. The atmosphere was peaceful.

Squatting over the army blanket I had spread on the ground, my companion folded open a map and begin the briefing. "We're on the border of enemy territory. Watch for it. The tightening of the lines has increased, and nonresident civilians crossing these lines are shot on the spot," he said, switching a large lump of chewing gum from the right to the left side of his jaw.

"What a start!" I mumbled. I moved closer, trying not to look too apprehensive.

His finger ran over the map. "As far as we know up to yesterday, the Krauts are all around there. These are the hills over there, behind you."

I turned around and distinguished the outline of several looming hills. From afar, the terrain already looked hostile and treacherous. BERTRAND continued, his breath smokey in the damp, icy air. "You'll be crossing a stream. It's shallow. Keep on going to your right and try to make yourself scarce. Head toward the safety of the forest."

I nodded, listening intently.

"You'll find some farms if you follow that path. The people are on our side. They'll feed you information about what's going on. Here's some cash for emergencies and here is your route. Look at it for a while. Good luck."

He handed me the map. I kept my eyes focused on the red pencil marks indicating the route to follow.

"By the way," he added, "your password is 'such bad weather.' The response will be 'for the past week.'"

He thought hard for a while; then, looking at me, he suggested, "I think it will be good to have a story ready in case you are caught. How about this? You are searching for members of your family who ran away from Arbois at the approach of battle. You are lost. Ask them to help you find your way back." He hesitated. "I think it will work."

"It sounds logical," I replied approvingly. I studied the map while he opened the suitcase.

BERTRAND checked his watch and waited silently without speaking. Then at the appointed time, he tried to get his signal through. His right finger twiddled the selector dial. With his left hand he corrected the volume. The air was so jammed with enemy traffic that he failed to raise anything.

"I should start getting on with the assignment," I told him dully as I stood up.

BERTRAND looked up at me with an uncertain, quizzical expression on his face. "Are you scared?" he asked.

At this point, I had seen and experienced more than a lifetime of hardships and challenges. I laughed inwardly, thinking of the proper young lady I had been taught to be at the finishing school. My language and my way of thinking had become stronger and far more liberated than expected of such a well-mannered young lady. I bit my lip, saying, "You're damn right I'm scared. Those Germans aren't just out there sightseeing!"

"Christ," he said, "don't get mad at me!"

I shrugged my shoulders. The tension was getting to me. "Oh, forget it. I'm nervous, and yes, I'm scared. I'll be back tomorrow about the same time—I hope, if everything is OK." I attempted to appear unfazed by the upcoming mission.

"See you."

I turned and walked away in the direction of the distant hills that rose above the icy, cold haze. A cloudburst bathed the countryside and made the trees faint shadows in the morning light.

I had been walking for about an hour through the hills, avoiding the country road and choosing instead to follow the dense edge of the forest so I could hide in case of emergency. A sudden noise of vehicles coming up the hill filled the air.

Gripped with fear, my heart pounded painfully. I took cover behind a large thicket, waiting for the intruders to come. Unseen, I watched a German troop carrier coming near, then, a few minutes later, a staff car appeared with a couple of high-ranking officers sprawled in the back seat. The machines rumbled past, roaring away, and I was about to come out of my hiding place when a motorcycle with a sidecar approached, ridden by a German soldier and a companion. I ran back into the woods until the sound of the motor disappeared.

Alone again, I surveyed the surroundings and noticed a small farm ahead. It was badly kept, the stone walls were crumbling at places. I could see a barn on the side. The hinges of its door were broken, the stalls were empty, and the animals were gone except for one cow who started to bridle nervously at my approach.

A short, stocky middle-aged man with an unkempt black beard covering his chin passed the corner of the main building. He turned his head instinctively in my direction as if he knew someone was there. After a minute of indecision, he opened the front door and went in.

I followed him and knocked at the entrance.

The panel opened cautiously, and the double barrel of a hunting gun greeted me. "*Qu'est-ce que vous voulez?*" "What do you want?" asked the man holding the weapon.

I peeked through the open door. "I am from Arbois. I'm searching for my family who left at the approach of battle. I'm lost. Can you help?"

The farmer watched me narrowly. "What's your name?"

"Helene Massière," I lied, purposely adopting my landlady's name.

"I don't know what you want, but I know you are not from around here."

In a last effort, I said, "I am lost, and it's *such bad weather.*"

The man's face relaxed and was now showing curiosity. "Yes, such bad weather for the past week," he replied.

He had completed the password. I extended my hand in recognition. He turned his head toward the back of the room.

"You can come out, Mathilde. Did you hear? She's one of us."

His wife came out from the other room with a trace of a smile on her face. "Sit down and rest," she invited, placing a bowl of fresh milk in front of me. She sat on a chair, rested her hands on her lap, and studied me. I could see she did not approve of my work nor my appearance. Frankly, I must have looked strange to her: disheveled and dirty, mud clinging to my shoes.

The man was fretting nervously. "You need information, don't you? A German convoy was here last night. I understand their language a little. They were talking about reaching Vesoul and trying to make a stand. They also mentioned blowing up one of the bridges on the Doubs River. It's all I can tell you." He paced back and forth while I drank my milk. "Listen, I have one contact for you. Tournaire is his name. He's a poacher. I'm sure he will help you." He gave me the directions. "Be careful," he added in parting, "the Germans are roaming around. They are everywhere."

The woman seemed anxious to see me go, and I did not blame her, for it was not possible these days to harbor strangers without becoming suspect in the eyes of the enemy. Wasting no time, after an effusive goodbye from the farmers, I started on my way.

Next I approached a brambly wooden fence surrounding a small cottage. I was about to cross the yard when a figure loomed from the far end of the trail, cycling along the dirt path. It was a man in his forties with a rubicund face, pink and smooth.

"Bonjour," the man greeted, coming near. A dead hare was limply bobbing from the handlebars of his bike. "*Vous voulez me voir?*" "You wanted to see me?"

"*Oui, j'ai perdu mon chemin.*" "I lost my way, and it's such bad weather."

The poacher looked at me, mumbling a few unintelligible words while dismounting his rusty bicycle. He finally answered, "For the past week." "Come," he said, opening the door.

The room we were in was dark, brightened only by the fire in the hearth. He added a log, then dropped the hare in the sink near the window.

Are you hungry?" he asked without looking.

"Something warm would be good. I have been on the go since early morning."

He brought out a bottle of plum liquor and filled two little glasses.

"This will keep you warm. It's 100 proof. I make it myself." He drank his own in one long gulp, then placed some *paté de campagne* and bread in front of me.

"*Alors,*" he started, sitting across the table, "what can I do for you? You've got the right password; who do you work for?"

I quickly swallowed my food. "I need information on German moves and installations in this area. I work for the Americans."

He expertly rolled a cigarette, placing the tobacco in the thin paper, then licking the edge before inserting it between his lips.

"I didn't know the Americans used woman agents." he shook his head disapprovingly. "*Chacun son goût!*" "To each his own!"

Quickly changing the subject, I asked, "Is there anything important you can give me?"

"Sure. I hear the Germans are moving a lot of troops toward Besançon and Luxeuil-les-Bains. I think they are trying to regroup behind their own border. Also, they have installed heavy artillery along the Doubs River. I was also told that one of their fuel depots outside of Besançon contains more than 700,000 liters of gasoline."

"Any news on the defense of Besançon?"

"I don't know anything about that, but I can take you to my Resistance friends. They have connections."

He got up. "Eat while I clean the rabbit, and we'll go."

Using a razor-sharp knife, Tournaire removed the fur of the animal, then cleaned the insides. The meat was placed aside in a dish.

I watched him rinse the blood off his knife and wash his hands. I also noticed the rifle resting against the kitchen chair, and I suddenly shivered at the thought that I really did not know this man. He could just as well have been a collaborator! Actually, code words were such a frail security.

To chase the thought from my mind, I studied my surroundings. The cottage was kept neat and clean, but the limited assortment of utensils indicated that there was no woman living here.

"Ready to go?" Tournaire inquired, adjusting his beret.

"Sure." I removed my cold feet from the warmth of the hearth, and we left on foot, following the thickly wooded, twisting road in the Jura hills.

It was a long, brisk walk until we reached a tiny hamlet of five or six houses scattered at the edge of a rather large, babbling creek. It was silent all around, and the commune appeared deserted. One of the houses was burning.

"Germans' work." The poacher pointed his finger at the flames.

The weather had not lifted. Rain clouds were drifting low over our heads. I was cold, and the humidity penetrated my clothes. A stray dog came sniffing at our feet, shyly wagging his tail. On the side of the road, up the creek, was what was left of the German motorcycle I had seen earlier that morning. The bodies of the two soldiers lay in the mud next to their machine.

I felt we were not alone, even though no sound or movement could be perceived. Soon I could hear the switching of branches, the breaking of twigs, but my companion did not appear concerned.

Four Resistance men suddenly appeared out of nowhere. They wore the FFI armband and carried automatic weapons.

"They must be the ones who killed the two Germans," I deduced.

One of them called, "Hey Tournaire, you brought your girlfriend along?" They laughed.

When they were close enough, the poacher took them aside, and I could vaguely hear him confide, "She's American. She needs information about the Krauts."

"We'll be glad to help," they declared, turning in my direction with broad, friendly smiles. And they did help.

I experienced many exhausting hours on the march, or in hiding. At times, I stopped at a friendly home long enough to gather intelligence and drink a glass of milk or munch on a piece of cheese. It was incredible how fast news traveled from farm to herdsmen and villagers, even though the distances were often great.

Now it was already late afternoon. I could make out a single-story house perhaps a hundred yards inside the woods. A gully cut across my path, and I jumped from rock to rock. I could now see better. The house was more like a large hovel with a dull, gray slate roof.

I stood listening to the whisper of the wind through the tall branches and to the faraway call of birds. I entered the lush verdure of the forest, making a wide detour around the house. The ground was covered with ferns, muffling the crunch of dry acorns under my feet.

A woman stepped out from the front door and began sweeping the porch. She was humming a soft, indistinct melody to herself. With a wave of her arm, she chased the mongrel dog which had stretched out along the top step. She continued to sweep the dirt aside. From the hovel, the wail of a baby brought the woman running back indoors.

I weighed the situation. It appeared normal enough. I stepped forward, and the dog let out a weak growl as I went by. When I passed the front door, the woman restrained a cry of surprise.

"You needn't worry. I won't hurt you. We are on the same side."

Seeing that I was unarmed, the woman relaxed a bit. I asked her where the men were. The peasant pointed a finger in the direction of the woods.

"Over there," she said.

"Can I come in and wait for them?"

She nodded her head while wiping the infant's nose. "Yes."

It was not unfriendly, so I went in and sat on a stool near a wooden table. The woman brought me a piece of country bread, and I dunked it in the bowl of soup placed in front of me. No conversation was exchanged.

A good half-hour passed before I heard voices and heavy steps approaching the front porch. The woman appeared unconcerned when the door opened and two men entered. The older one carried an axe on his shoulder, and the other brought logs into the frugal room.

They appeared startled upon seeing the stranger.

"My name is Sorbier," said the younger one, placing a log on the fire. "What can I do for you?"

"Perhaps help me," I responded, holding his unbreaking stare. "It's such bad weather," I recited, waiting for a reply.

The man's face unbent. "For the past week," he answered. He quickly came forward and we shook hands.

"This is my father, and my wife and son."

"Do you have any news for me?"

Sorbier shook his head negatively. "Our home has been raided many times in the past few days, and we do not have visitors from the outside. But Tournaire, the poacher near the creek, went exploring yesterday, and ..."

"Yes, I know, I have been there already."

"All I can tell you is that the German troops are scattered everywhere. You had better be on your guard."

As he spoke, noise resounded outside, and the dog began barking furiously.

The old man stood motionless for a few seconds, then he turned his head toward the door wondering what to do next. Sorbier quickly positioned himself in front of the dirty plate and placed the soup spoon between his fingers.

The wife was a faster thinker. "In there," she urged, and she pushed me into a cupboard in the wall that was used to store fruits. I lay on a pile of apples, afraid to move and have the fruits roll from under me. A sour, fermented odor filled my nostrils, and I pinched my nose not to sneeze.

Between the thin planks of wood hiding me, I saw the door thrust open with a kick of a boot, and three German soldiers stomped in. I caught a glimpse of Sorbier's emaciated face as he nervously rolled a thin cigarette paper between his fingers and inserted the homemade weed into his parted lips. I held my breath and caught an apple as it began rolling off the heap.

The German in charge was swaying and nearly incoherent from drinking. He moved forward clumsily, a machine pistol under his arm.

"*Manger, manger*; eat, eat," he repeated over and over again, gesturing with his finger to his mouth. The baby started cooing.

"Give them some food," Sorbier told his wife with urgency. "Give it all!"

The woman shakily handed them the loaf of bread and the potful of soup. They greedily filled their mess cans. Then the drunken noncommissioned officer jabbered an order, and they immediately looted the shelves, placing a few potatoes and dry cheese in their knapsacks.

Passing by the potbellied stove in the center of the room, they kicked it, fortunately not hard enough to topple it over.

"Auf Wiedersehen." They left with their spoils as abruptly as they had entered.

Nobody in the hut spoke a word.

The peasant wife knocked softly at the cupboard door, and I crawled out and stretched my stiff limbs.

"I'll be on my way now," I said, straightening my crumpled clothes. "I don't want to bring you any trouble. Thanks for the food."

They still could not speak, either stunned or disheartened by seeing their last rations taken away.

I left some small change on the table and closed the door quietly behind me.

My mission had not been futile. I had collected important information during the day. I was now on my way back, and after some hiking, the dying day's twilight spread among the trees. The vineyards were almost divested of their leaves in this part of France and took on the yellow and rusty tones announcing the sad splendor of autumn.

I had been walking steadily for a couple of hours. I passed behind a small dwelling, crossing pastures and apple orchards; ahead lay a rutted dirt road and farmstead. There I noticed a great stir of activity. A gust of wind whirled a cloud of leaves into the air. My view of the barn was screened temporarily. When the leaves settled, I felt the ambience of the farmland precarious. The yard and path leading to the village was full of men milling about and bellowing orders. I could perceive the familiar field-gray uniforms of the Wehrmacht. I was standing at the very place BERTRAND had warned me to avoid.

The metallic clanging of tanks jarred the air, and I hurriedly jumped into a muddy ditch, slush spattering my face. I popped my head over the embankment. Ahead, two Mark IV tanks were maneuvering heavily along the path, their big single guns erect as sinister sentinels.

Resigned, and to avoid detection, I remained low in the ditch until I could pass shrouded by the veil of darkness. I made a bed of dead leaves behind a dense grove of undergrowth. A well-trod path ran narrowly between two hedges, and I carefully studied my position before settling.

It had rained during most of the day, and I was drenched and cold. Clumps of mud clung to my shoes and coat. I grew progressively colder, and hunger poked at my ribs. Taking a piece of vitamin chocolate from my pocket, I munched on it slowly. My feet ached, and blisters were swelling my heels.

Exhausted, I let my head bow with fatigue and I nodded off. When I awoke, it was with an unpleasant abruptness. I glanced around. It was now pitch dark, and I immediately felt reassured. Rain fell steadily, whipping my face. Around me, the countryside was a gloomy carpet of mud and water. Ill-shaped trees bent over and twisted their branches, submitting to the first autumn assault.

The roar of artillery could be heard, resounding from the direction of the town of Dôle. The explosions came without interruption, and brilliant flares curved into the sky, glided, and vanished into the night. Parachute flares danced in the air, illuminating the ground.

My legs had cramped, and I stretched them carefully before getting up to start down the hill.

After sitting so long on the rain-soaked ground, my clothing was saturated all the way down to my panties and felt uncomfortably heavy.

Progress down the hill was painstakingly slow. As I reached a steeper path, I stopped dead in my tracks. My neck tensed.

There was a unmistakable scuffling of stones in the distance. It was fortunate my sense of hearing had become keen in the dark. The sound stopped for an endless minute. All I could hear was the absence of footsteps. Complete silence.

Not daring to move, I continued to listen and heard fresh noises ahead.

The icy slicing of the wind blew my hair and rippled my coat. It was bitterly cold, and somewhere out there was a German patrol.

Crouching down, I remained motionless and held my breath at intervals as I waited for the crack of a gun. In the orchard, apples fell from the trees and plopped onto the wet earth. The silence lengthened.

It became intolerable, squatting in total gloom like a cornered animal. I wiped the rain from my face as I rose and broke the rigidity of my posture.

I felt the urgency to move. I started down the hill once again, making my way through the orchard. I carefully avoided breaking twigs as I advanced along the uneven terrain. Then a snap: A sprig crushed under my weight.

The answering crack of a sub-machine-gun broke the silence.

"Tac, tac, tac," a flash lit the darkness. Collecting all of my energy, I vaulted over a low stone wall and landed within a short distance of a soldier. In that split second, I distinguished the outline of a German helmet.

My pulse was pounding. I realized it was useless to crouch now, for I knew just about where I was. I felt afraid of death, lost and alone, and I broke into a zig-zag run. My breath came in short, hard gasps through parched lips.

A second burst echoed from the hill, but I was already a good distance away, sheltered by the dark trees of the orchard. Branches slashed my legs as I raced in the direction of Arbois with my skirt tucked up tightly in my hands.

I tripped and fell over a rock and whimpered in pain, feeling the skin of my knee peel. Rolling back on my feet again, I continued to run.

Nearby, a rooster disoriented by the shelling and the flares lighting the sky started crowing long before dawn.

The orchard thinned, and I came out into the open.

The shelling had stopped, but the rain kept on falling. The dismal, muddy streets of Arbois were alive with men from the 143d Division leaving for combat. Some of the soldiers looked straight ahead with their jaws set, thumbs under the slings of their rifles, and faces void of expression; others were laughing or whistling halfheartedly.

I stood limply with my back against an iron fence. I felt dirty and drained. As I watched the soldiers go forward to the same front line I had just passed, one of the men called, "Hi, honey!"

He threw me his combat jacket. "Looks like you need it more than I will up there!"

Little did he know that the young girl to whom he donated his jacket was bringing back information that would perhaps save his life and those of his comrades.

The rest of the unit went down the street. I listened to the thud of their footsteps and the clanging of equipment. I felt sick. Fever flared up inside me, and I sat on the ground totally ragged.

The shops still had their iron shutters rolled down. It was very early. The few inhabitants in the street glared at me as they passed. Some stopped to stare, and others pointed at me. When the troops were completely out of sight, I stood up and walked to the far edge of Arbois, guided by the tall spire of a church in the distance.

BERTRAND was sitting quietly on the blanket with his radio and earphones adjusted. He had built a small fire to decrease the humidity, but it was not burning well. A thick, opaque smoke rose from the wet branches. "Welcome back," he muttered, disengaging his headset. He poked at the sputtering fire and pushed the wood that was burning onto a damp clump of not yet ignited. "How was it?" he asked.

"Muddy all the way!"

"Want a drink? You look like you could use one."

I nodded. He extracted a small flask from his pocket and handed it to me. I took a generous swig of cognac. The strength of the alcohol made me cough and shiver all over. The burning liquid felt good running down my throat.

I dropped down heavily beside him and drew a Lucky Strike from the pack he had placed in front of me. I watched the pale flames of the fire for a while, pleased with the warmth on my hands and face.

"We'll go back to our rooms as soon as I get through. You must be beat!" BERTRAND grinned as he removed some twigs embedded in my hair. "Do you have much for me?"

I shook my head affirmatively and took another sip. "Yes. The people in this area were quite talkative."

As I gave him the information, he began coding the message. Luckily, the air was clear enough with little interference. Plugging in the earphones, he listened to the static and muttered, "I'm getting it," and he got busy.

He received a reply and started the message. It went through:

OSS information helped the Allies to liberate France and reach Paris in August 1944. (208-YE-68)

Many obstacles on the road leading to Mouchard. Bridges blown around Dôle, and main road sown with explosives. Important enemy field depot located by FFIs some twenty kilometers east of Besançon. Heavy enemy artillery installed along the Doubs River. Bescançon occupied by an estimated 3,000 German troops. Luxeuil-Remiremont road heavily defended by enemy—Road from Luxeuil to Plombière still open.

Orders sputtered back immediately through the clattering static: "Wait. Contact man on his way. Out."

The fire faded to ashes; the branches collapsed inward with faint sparks. BERTRAND packed his gear, rolled the blanket, and we drove back to Arbois.

Madame Massière, our landlady, was a kind, thoughtful woman in her late 70s who was still bewildered by the war. She was sitting in the old-fashioned parlor, mending a threadbare knitted vest. When BERTRAND and I entered, she bit off the thread and set the garment down.

She took a look at me and was startled, seeing me disheveled and drenched to the bone. She chided me gently, saying, "Come in at once. You'll catch your death! Take that coat off this instant."

Rushing to the kitchen as fast as her old legs permitted, Madame Massière returned with a bowl of steaming soup. It was marvelously hot. I cradled the warm bowl in both hands and drank from it slowly. The woman fussed over me, meanwhile fluffing pillows and rearranging the cream-colored doily that covered the chair in which I sat next to the fireplace.

The flames blazed brightly and surged as if determined to clear the room of humidity and shadows. A small tabby cat that had curled up near the chair opened an eye and yawned indolently. My clothes smelled damp and musty, and the hem of my skirt started to steam with the heat.

After a while I took inventory of my bruises. My left knee had been badly cut during my flight through the orchard.

"Let me see," the old woman said, putting on her spectacles. I removed my hands and stretched my leg. Dirt and mud were all over the open wound and cuts. It was very sore.

Pulling open the drawer of a small cabinet, Madame Massière extracted dry leaves from a tin box and yellow powder from a bottle. Adding pharmaceutical oil of some sort, she ground the mixture in an enamel bowl with the back of a spoon and mixed it all together. I winced with pain when she applied the healing concoction to my skin. She bandaged the knee with a piece of cloth.

I was aching all over, and I sneezed several times while rubbing my drippy nose. "I don't suppose running in the rain did me much good," I said, trying to inject some humor into the situation. The landlady looked up at me with a feigned look of disapproval. She asked no questions. BERTRAND had removed his combat boots and socks, and stretched his feet to the fire.

After swallowing two aspirin, I took a hot water bottle from the kitchen and climbed the creaking staircase to my room. Poking his head through the bannister, BERTRAND shouted, "Our contact should arrive late tonight."

The contact man sent by Henry Hyde from Chateau Gleisol turned out to be Patterson, my co-agent during the landing in St. Tropez and the liberation of Marseilles. He had come to take me back to Lyon. BERTRAND was to stay behind and wait for another agent to replace me. Patterson told me I had to report to Henry Hyde and receive new assignments.

The drive from Arbois back to Lyon was fast, for there was almost no southbound traffic. We were hungry when we arrived in the city, and we decided to have lunch at a black-market restaurant.

In the early afternoon, we started in the direction of the chateau, past Notre Dame de Fourvière, the cathedral with the marvelous Byzantine architecture. On the steps of the church, a candle woman with a crinkled face smiled as we drove by.

Upon our arrival at Chateau Gleisol, I noticed immediately the change of atmosphere. It was more tame, more like a very industrious place would be, with a few women, secretaries I assumed, dressed in smart uniforms and carrying sheafs of paper in their hands. They gave me mocking looks at the site of my draggle-tailed coat, making me feel self-conscious.

No sooner had I checked at the billeting desk than I was called to Henry Hyde's study. I was depressed and disheartened. My cold was no better, and I had an excruciating headache. I wished that for once I could stay in one place for a while and nurse myself.

"Hello!" greeted Henry. He spoke as if we had last seen each other at lunchtime. "How was it? Have a hard time up there?"

Peeved, I reflected, "He makes it sound as if I had taken a trip to the Riviera!"

"No," I replied coolly, "very easy!" My voice had risen to a high pitch, and my nerves were on edge for I felt the pressure with which I had lived for the past 3 days. With effort I regained my composure and smiled thinly at him. "It rained all the way, and I've got a king-size cold."

I wished he would show a little compassion. He gave me his irrepressible grin instead. "You did a good job, I'm told."

His charm was still his forte, which he knew very few could resist. He leaned back in his chair. "Are you ready to go?"

"When am I leaving?" I was certain he would say tomorrow, or in a day or two.

"As soon as you have had a checkup at the dispensary. JEROME will drive you to the OSS station at Chateau Gaillard near Annemasse at the Swiss border, and he will continue to Thonon. I've notified him already, and he will be waiting for you downstairs. In Annemasse, report to Captain Mathews. Here are your orders."

"*Bonne chance*," he added.

Henry reached for an ashtray and tapped his cigarette. His face held the expression of a man satisfied with himself.

I was not disposed to discuss or argue and only left the room. The dispensary was in the right wing of the chateau, and I was directed immediately to the infirmary. The medic gave me an injection and some pills, then he cleaned and bandaged my knee. On my way out I stopped by the storeroom where I had left my bag and checked it out.

The Americans had mopped up France and were moving east into Germany. Because I did not speak German, I could not contribute to the gathering of intelligence on that front. I followed Henry's new orders, and I continued to work for the OSS, but my return from Arbois had ended my days as a field operative behind enemy lines.

The Mediterranean and the Balkans

The second of four concurrent sessions, "The Mediterranean and the Balkans," was held in Room 105, the Archivist's Reception Room, in the National Archives Building. This session was directed toward those OSS field operations that took place after Operation Torch, the Allied landing in November 1942 in North Africa. Although the presentations differed a great deal in scope of subject and timeframe, all the speakers had made extensive use of the operational records of the OSS. The first speaker, Arthur Funk, building upon his considerable research and writing relating to World War II, examined some recently opened OSS Algiers records to provide the audience new information on the OSS contribution to the invasion of southern France in August 1944. Max Corvo's presentation, delivered by his son William Corvo, was based upon Corvo's impressive contribution—in both Washington and overseas—to the Italian Secret Intelligence (SI) Branch's success. The sensitive account by this OSS veteran of Italian-American descent conveys the proud effort many gave to the cause. The third speaker was Dušan Biber, one of the foremost historians in the Balkans. Dr. Biber was able, after some difficulty because of political and military events, to leave Ljubljana, Slovenia, to deliver his paper on the special and somewhat mysterious OSS McDowell mission to the Yugoslav headquarters of Draža Mihailović, the leader of the group known as the Chetniks. The presentation by Timothy Naftali examined the role of James Angleton's early career as the chief of OSS X-2 (counterintelligence) operations in Italy. Naftali's paper was grounded in extensive use of OSS X-2 records opened for research between 1989 and 1991 and on interviews with Angleton's family and colleagues. New York attorney Henry Hyde—a key Donovan operative in North Africa and Europe and one who provided dynamic SI leadership in the field—chaired the session and provided commentary.

THE OSS IN ALGIERS

Arthur L. Funk

Even before the Operation Torch landings in North Africa in November 1942, agents of William "Wild Bill" Donovan—until June 1942 Coordinator of Information (COI) and thereafter head of the Office of Strategic Services (OSS)—had begun operations in the western Mediterranean. Posts had been established in Madrid, Lisbon, and Tangier. Through the Tangier post, Col. William Eddy kept in touch with Robert D. Murphy, President Franklin D. Roosevelt's personal representative in North Africa, and with his vice consuls in Morocco, Algeria, and Tunisia.

Some aspects of OSS operations have been very fully covered in written accounts, some not so fully. The pre-Torch period has been covered in Murphy's own memoirs, in William Langer's *Our Vichy Gamble*, and in Kermit Roosevelt's *OSS War Report*. A number of recent books provide interesting revelations—notably Gen. Rygor Slowikowski's *In the Secret Service: The Lighting of the Torch* (1988), Fabrizio Calvi's *OSS: La guerre secrète en France* (1989), and Anthony Cave Brown's *The Last Hero: Wild Bill Donovan* (1982). All of these books give information about the prelanding intelligence networks and communications that paved the way for the North African landings.[1] Furthermore, the papers of a conference on Torch, sponsored by the British Institute in Paris, have been published in the Spring 1989 issue of the Institute's *Franco-British Studies*. The papers and commentary, representing both scholars and participants, deal in part with the value of OSS material as made available to Washington and to the planners in London.[2] There is also an assessment of this period in David A. Walker's doctoral research (see *Journal of Contemporary History*, October 1987, for his article on "OSS and Operation TORCH").[3]

With the North African landings safely accomplished, Eddy moved the OSS office to Algiers, where Gen. Dwight D. Eisenhower established Allied Force Headquarters (AFHQ). At the same time, the British Special Operations Executive (SOE) established a mission in the Algiers area, code-named MASSINGHAM. As SOE ran a large operation out of Gibraltar, the British soon constructed facilities, such as radio transmitting equipment, and brought in planes, which at first permitted more in the way of operations than the Americans in the OSS could do. The principal base was at the Club des Pins, west of the city. Eisenhower called for close cooperation between the British and Americans—essentially between Eddy and Col. Douglas Dodds-Parker, who shortly after the landings succeeded the original incumbent as commander of MASSINGHAM. Some of the Club des Pins facilities were shared.[4]

In the last few years there has been a revival of the debate over the assassination of Adm. François of Darlan.[5] The OSS is involved because an OSS agent, the anthropologist Carleton Coon, was a training officer for the Corps Franc, of which the assassin, Fernand Bonnier de la Chapelle, was a member. It has been alleged that he used a Colt Woodsman pistol that Coon owned. SOE has been involved because the Corps Franc training was done at the Club des Pins under MASSINGHAM's sponsorship. It has been demonstrated convincingly in the recent Huan Coutau-Bégarie biography of Darlan, however, that the assassin used a Rubis 7.65 given to him by a friend, Mario Faivre. Although there will be continuous controversy, the evidence now available seems to exclude direct British and American involvement.

Shortly after Darlan's assassination, Gen. Henri Giraud, backed by the Americans, succeeded the admiral as High Commissioner for North Africa. He was already serving as commanding general of French forces.

The Allied presence in French North Africa enabled OSS agents to operate closer to southern Europe than before, but the complicated political situation made for difficulties. The Americans had based invasion plans on cooperation with Admiral Darlan and General Giraud. This relationship led to ties with former Vichy administrators and services that, while generally anti-German, represented the traditional French hierarchy—not that of Gen. Charles de Gaulle. There was no question but that Eddy, when he set up an OSS headquarters in Algiers, would cooperate with these Frenchmen, not with the handful of poorly organized Gaullists then in North Africa. Most obvious of these relationships were those with French intelligence (*Service de Renseignement*, or SR). The OSS quickly cooperated with Col. Louis Rivet, Col. Jean Chrétien (who had helped Murphy), Colonel Villeneuve, and Commandant Paul Paillole (who was in charge of counterintelligence). Thus the early operations involved agents who were enlisted by both the OSS and SR. The first agent was the controversial Frederic Brown, code-named TOMMY. Both name and code name would suggest someone American born and bred, while in fact the national origins of this cosmopolite were obscure—some considered him a Ukrainian Jew, while he himself claimed Canadian parentage and Luxembourg upbringing. He had run a radio shop in Algiers since 1938 and had developed radio communications for Robert Murphy and his vice consuls prior to the North African landings. His career has been described in considerable detail by Fabrizio Calvi—here we must limit ourselves to no more than passing notice of this fascinating OSS debut in Algiers.[6]

In the first months of 1943 the Algiers OSS office had difficulties in determining its true mission. One of the problems for the OSS was that the director of the Secret Intelligence Branch (SI) in these months, Arthur Roseborough, supported de Gaulle when the entire setup, especially after the Casablanca Conference in January 1943, was clearly Giraudist. In addition, those in the Research and Analysis Branch (R&A), such as H. Stuart Hughes, and those in Psychological Warfare, such as C. D. Jackson, tended to count themselves among American liberals who in large measure backed de Gaulle.[7]

Yet the infrastructure of the OSS still contained many of the contacts and personnel with whom Murphy and Eddy had worked in the pre-Torch days. Frederic Brown continued to be the sole agent for the OSS operating in France, and the radio networks continued, much improved, under Col. Peter S. Mero with installations at Cap Matifou.

An operation under Donald Downes to land agents in southern Spain had turned into a disaster. Efforts to develop an OSS program in Spain were hampered by the opposition of Ambassador Carleton Hayes. In spite of that, Gregory Thomas was able, in cooperation with a non-Gaullist Frenchman, the Vichy military attaché at Madrid, Colonel Malaise, to develop lines into France across the Pyrenees. Yet one of Thomas's best assistants, Frank Schoonmaker, ran afoul of the Spanish police and spent months in prison. Nevertheless, OSS circuits out of Spain, especially ME-DUSA, brought a great amount of intelligence to Algiers.[8]

While in the long run it must be admitted that Roseborough's position was correct, Eddy saw that for efficient cooperation with Rivet, Chrétien, and Paillole, Roseborough must go. He was replaced by Henry Hyde, who at age 28 had the advantages of a cosmopolite upbringing and perfect French. Through his family's friend, André Poniatowski, Giraud's *chef de cabinet*, Hyde obtained a written agreement from Giraud allowing him to recruit and use up to 35 Frenchmen whose status, so far as promotions and pensions were concerned, would remain as if they continued in the French Army. In exchange for this, Hyde agreed to develop purely military networks.[9]

Hyde got along well with Jacques de Guélis, who held the French desk for SOE and whose MASSINGHAM operation west of Algiers was also, under the direction of Dodds-Parker, rapidly expanding. Curiously, the British were confronted with a problem quite the reverse of that faced by the Americans. While British official policy favored de Gaulle, and while SOE had long cooperated with the Gaullist intelligence service, de Guélis worked very comfortably with the Giraudist administration and with the

Giraudist SR. Just as it had been clear to the Americans that Roseborough did not conform to overall policy, similarly the British, when de Gaulle's star began to ascend, knew that de Guélis would have to be replaced.

Even though de Gaulle had arrived in Algiers in June 1943, when the French Committee of National Liberation was formed, he had no control over the French North African army nor over SR, which operated under Giraud. Furthermore, as both SOE and the OSS had established working relationships with the Giraudists, these contacts could not be quickly altered. For example, when AFHQ made plans involving Corsica, the French SR, represented by Paul Colonna d'Istria, the OSS's Col. Robert Pflieger, and SOE's Jacques de Guélis, all worked together in developing contacts with the Corsican resistance without the Gaullist intelligence service, or de Gaulle himself, although present in Algiers, being consulted.[10]

The OSS and SOE cooperated in a number of ways. Carleton Coon, in a British uniform, participated in a Tunisian operation headed by SOE's Brooks Richards and later represented OSS in Corsica. Dodds-Parker was instrumental in getting Henry Hyde and his Penny Farthing agents first to England and then to France. Both services supported Col. Serge Obolonsky (OSS) in making arrangements for the Italian surrender in Sardinia. Both shared aircraft, but the OSS, with only three B-17s working with the Algiers post, could not equal the British contribution until well into 1944.

The cooperation between the two agencies did not mean that the OSS refrained from mounting separate operations or that SOE, with many agents already in southern France, had to share administration of its circuits with the Americans. In fact, a few American OSS agents operating in France and controlled from London already worked for SOE.[11]

With the decision to attack Sicily, the Mediterranean continued throughout 1943 to be the major theater of the European conflict. With Sicily occupied, Roosevelt and Churchill decided in August at Quebec to launch an invasion of Italy. They also confirmed Operation Overlord, the Normandy assault, and appended a resolution:

> Operations against southern France (to include the use of trained and equipped French forces) should be undertaken to establish a lodgement in the Toulon and Marseilles area to exploit northward in order to create a diversion in connection with Overlord. Air-nourished guerrilla operations in the southern Alps will, if possible, be initiated.

This resolution definitely affirmed that OSS/AFHQ would have a special mission in southern France, even though the commitments to Italy and the Balkans could in the long run be greater.[12]

The Allied landings in Italy in September opened up opportunities for Donovan, who could see great possibilities for the OSS with Eisenhower at AFHQ. Donovan had been at Quebec, where he had obtained approval for larger Balkan operations. He subsequently spent most of the remaining months of 1943 in Algiers, Italy, or Cairo. In mid-September he dealt with problems in Algiers, supervising a significant reorganization. The larger field of action was forcing Donovan to evolve from a cloak-and-dagger approach into operations more closely coordinated with specific military campaigns. The OSS, under G-2 and G-3 of AFHQ, became 2677 Headquarters Company under Col. Edward F. Glavin as commanding officer and a staff including Col. Thomas Early and Lt. Col. Edward Gamble. This terminated the first phase of the OSS in Algiers under Colonel Eddy, who later became Ambassador to Saudi Arabia.

The end of 1943, which saw the basic Overlord and Anvil operations confirmed at Teheran, also found OSS/SI in Algiers ending its relationship with Frederic Brown, who had been accused of being a double agent. The Brown case is discussed fully by Calvi.[13] This was also a period that marked the success of Henry Hyde's Penny Farthing network.

On the operations side, although hindered by a paucity of air transport, the Special Operations Branch (SO) was becoming involved in new activities. The OSS was assigning officers to the Jedburgh program, and of these three-man teams approximately one-third would come from the OSS. Another purely OSS program was under way—the Operational Groups, known as OGs. These were commando teams recruited from the Army, made up of 30 men, of whom two were commissioned officers. Trained in various parts of the United States, at Fort Bragg and at the Congressional Country Club near Washington, the OG units began to reach the field in late 1943. The first ones, destined to work out of Corsica for raids on the Italian coast, came under the command of Col. Russell Livermore. It is worth noting that as SOE began to have more operations in Italy, Colonel Dodds-Parker, commanding officer of MASSINGHAM, was devoting more of his attention to Italian matters and worked closely with Livermore. Under Livermore, Col. Serge Obolensky supervised the program planned for Italy, while Maj. Alfred T. Cox commanded the OGs destined to parachute into France. With Army acceptance of the OGs, Donovan was able to develop a purely OSS operation in coordination with military campaigns. In Italy some of the OG work along the Ligurian coast evolved into SI operations, but in France, as we shall see, it was strictly military.[14]

After the Teheran Conference, with its definite decisions to launch the Normandy and southern France invasions and to push the Italian campaign northward, the picture in the Mediterranean theater changed somewhat. In late December 1943 Eisenhower left Algiers to assume command of Supreme Headquarters Allied Expeditionary Force (SHAEF) in London, but before he left, he had a serious discussion with de Gaulle in which he virtually apologized for bypassing him. Clearly there would be more support for de Gaulle and Gaullist operations thereafter. This position was enhanced by a British commander, Gen. Sir Henry Maitland Wilson, becoming Supreme Allied Commander in the Mediterranean theater (SACMED). The Italian campaign continued, as did planning for Operation Anvil.

In December 1943 the OSS expanded its operations in Italy. A meeting on December 8 that included Colonel Glavin, Colonel Obolensky (returned to Algiers after contacts in Sardinia and Corsica), Lt. Comdr. Warwick Potter, Major Mero, Capt. Gerard de Piolenc, Capt. Max Corvo, and others started in motion the actions which would lead to the establishment of a base at Naples. Obolensky worked in Italy for a while before going to London as head of the OGs.[15]

In January 1944 Donovan spent some time in Algiers looking into the new relationships. In one meeting, which included Dodds-Parker, he conferred with the Gaullist services and Soustelle, who headed the Direction Générale des Services Spéciaux (DGSS). (Pflieger and Potter represented the OSS.) At another meeting Donovan met with Harold Macmillan and with members of the AFHQ staff—Chief of Staff (U.K.) Lt. Gen. Sir James Gammell, Deputy Chief of Staff (U.S.) Maj. Gen. Lowell W. Rooks, and others. By these meetings the high command confirmed three Mediterranean special operations missions: the eastern theater (Force 133), Italy (MARYLAND), and southern France (MASSINGHAM). Dodds-Parker and Glavin would coordinate SOE and OSS activity. With the recognition that French troops would participate in Anvil, Soustelle authorized a special section (Committee for Action in France) to work out liaison with SOE and the OSS. This function fell to Guillaume (Willy) Widmer, who actually took up residence at the Club des Pins, MASSINGHAM headquarters at Guyotsville, west of Algiers.[16]

The OSS in Algiers now had a definite mission—to plan for Operation Anvil. A planning staff, Force 163, under Brig. Gen. Garrison H. Davidson had been set up in Algiers, but while SOE and the OSS knew that the 7th Army would spearhead the attack, they were not sure of the place, the strength of the force, or even the date. Originally planned to coincide with the Normandy landings, Anvil had to be postponed because scheduled units and landing craft were tied up in Anzio. In spite of uncertainties and delays, the OSS continued to supply information to Force 163, and MASSINGHAM was well occupied because it had many agents, such as Francis Cammaerts, head of Circuit JOCKEY, already in the field. Indeed, MASSINGHAM, with good radio transmission facilities and more aircraft than the OSS, was an essential element in maintaining contact, even for the Gaullists, with the southern France Resistance.

An obstacle developed in regard to the Jedburghs and OGs at Algiers, which had been trained to go in by parachute behind the lines. Eisenhower, as Supreme Commander for all operations planned for France, controlled special operations. He feared that Jedburghs or OGs might give information on the proposed landings. He therefore ordered that Jedburghs should not be dropped earlier than May 20 or OGs earlier than May 28. These prohibitions meant that a large SO operation, which included several hundred commandos, had to be postponed. Between January and March 1944, some 14 OGs (over 400 men) and 13 Jedburgh teams, which included 11 OSS men, came to Algiers and waited for orders that would send them to France. Although trained and ready, none left for France before the Normandy landings in June.[17]

In the first half of 1944, two events occurred that had a great influence on OSS/Algiers. The first increased the OSS's capacity to obtain aircraft. In April, General de Gaulle had made a speech in which he stated that aid to the French Resistance had come much more from the British than from the Americans. Although Roosevelt had not changed his personal attitude regarding the Free French leader, the administration in general (e.g., Hull, Stimson, and Marshall) saw no alternative to cooperation with the Gaullists, who were certain to find support in France once it was liberated. Following a report from Eisenhower that affirmed de Gaulle's statement, the Joint Chiefs of Staff authorized the U.S. Army Air Force to make more planes and more flights of material available for special operations. In actual fact, even before de Gaulle's speech, the Air Force in February 1944 had ordered the 122d Liaison Squadron to be reorganized for work with the OSS, but units only started to operate out of Blida, the Algiers airport, in April. This move gave the OSS the use of seven B-25s, three B-17s, and eight B-24s, which were designated in June as the 885th Squadron. It should be noted that the 1,700 sorties flown from Algiers were supplemented by three special spectacular drops of material of which CADILLAC on July 14—Bastille Day—was the most spectacular. But it should also be noted that the 1,700 Allied air force sorties in southern France must be compared with the 11,632 for special operations in Yugoslavia, 2,652 in Italy, and 2,064 in Greece—figures that give some indications of where priorities lay.[18]

The other event concerned Anvil. After having been placed on the shelf while the Normandy landings and the liberation of Rome took place, Anvil was revived in late June and definitely authorized by the Combined Chiefs in early July. With the target date set for August 15, there were barely 6 weeks for intensive and detailed planning.[19]

The SI contingent working with Force 163, at first represented solely by Major Crosby in a liaison capacity, was expanded to include Lt. Comdr. Potter. When Gen. Alexander M. Patch's 7th Army planners took over from Force 163, whose headquarters were in Naples, the OSS group, designated as Strategic Services Section (SSS), G-2, expanded considerably under Col. Edward Gamble, Jr. General Patch and his G-2, Col. William W. Quinn, worked closely with the OSS. To quote the SSS report:

Patch was invited by Col. Glavin to see our installations. After his visit, which lasted for several hours, instead of the anticipated one hour, we found that a more intelligent and useful use of SSS was made. . . . [Patch's planning staff] took our raw material and kept a percentage of confirmed and unconfirmed material. Over a period of months it was found that over 60% of our material was confirmed by other sources.[20]

It has been estimated that between May 1943 and September 1944 the OSS made available to Allied headquarters more than 8,000 intelligence reports—with about half coming from the chains controlled from Spain over the Pyrenees, and about 2,000 from Henry Hyde's SI operation out of Algiers. Probably most of the material came from Hyde's most successful network, Penny Farthing.[21]

Thanks to the opening of OSS files, historians may examine many of the thousands of reports that reached the Army's G-2. In Entry 97 (the "Algiers" file) are 45 boxes for which NARA's catalogers (special thanks to Larry McDonald) have provided 57 pages of finding aids. In these files are many of the reports that came from France via Spain, with such delightfully geminated code names as AKAK, UPUP, HOHO, HIHI, and ZUZU. By May 1944, the five-man AKAK team was sending three voluminous pouches each week from Toulouse to Barcelona.[22] Some AKAK reports were extremely detailed—for example: one from the Toulon area, dated April 29, 1944, gives details of an Armenian company and precise descriptions of German artillery; another, dated May 1, 1944, provides exact information about Port St. Louis, of the Rhône, describing depth of water, width of waterways, and conjectures on minefields. When one considers the amount of information provided, and of course the reinforcement of air photographic surveys, G-2 was extremely well informed about conditions in France. A memorandum from G-2, AFHQ, dated October 30, 1944, is worth citing:

The intelligence for Operation DRAGOON was probably the fullest and most detailed of any provided by G-2, AFHQ in a series of combined operations. . . .

The material collected by G-2, AFHQ, came from a variety of sources but the very considerable contribution of O.S.S. merits special emphasis, not only on account of its intrinsic worth but because the results obtained provide a signal example of what can be done by an agency of this kind when it consents to work in closest cooperation with the Operational Headquarters which it is serving.

A rough estimate of the proportion of accepted ground intelligence supplied by the three Allied agencies shows that 50% was provided by O.S.S., 30% by the S.R., and 20% by I.S.L.D.[23]

It was a formidable task for the various G-2s to absorb all this information. In fact one occasionally finds grievances from the field—this one four days after the landings:

> We were amazed to learn that much of the information that we had furnished the Army during the planning stages had not reached the proper places.

The SSS report then explains that agents at considerable risk had obtained data regarding fords of the Durance River and that this data had gone to all 7th Army sections except to the combat divisions. As the Army had not kept a copy, it was necessary to get the information pouched from Algiers. "This caused a delay so great that when the information finally did arrive, it was too late to use it."[24]

The SO section of the OSS might have been as busy as SI except that a major concern, the sending into France of Jedburghs and OGs, was being held up by Eisenhower's order that they should not be despatched until late May. Furthermore, Eisenhower controlled all special operations for France and insisted that all such operations should support Overlord. In London, SOE and the OSS's SO had already been consolidated into a single section, Special Force Headquarters (SFHQ). Efforts were also being made to incorporate French special operations into this section. As D-day approached, SHAEF wished to cut off the major north-south routes that the Germans used. But not having embarked on any vast special operations to do this and unwilling to send in Jedburghs and OGs, SHAEF had to rely on existing means of communicating with the Resistance: coded messages to agents already in the field and BBC messages. This gave SFHQ, a joint SOE and OSS/SO operation, a key role. (Allen Dulles in Bern had some contacts, but we are here concerned with the OSS in North Africa.) Most of the operations missions in southern France at Normandy D-day had been sent in either by London or by MASSINGHAM. The OSS could boast that it had some 50 agents who were American citizens in France at this time—like Peter Ortiz, Virginia Hall, Ernest Floege, Victor Soskice, Henry Laussucq, Edwin Poitras, Elizabeth Reynolds, and Denis Johnson—but they had all been despatched from London and participated in what were essentially SOE missions.[25]

In anticipation of Operation Anvil, it made sense that AFHQ should follow the SHAEF pattern to incorporate SO and SOE into a single unit, which in a theoretical sense, under Colonel Dodds-Parker, it had been all along. This was accomplished in May 1944 by the establishment of the Special Project Operations Center (SPOC). In accordance with Allied policy, SPOC had two commanding officers, OSS Col. William Davis, Jr., then heading SO in Algiers, and Col. (later Sir) John Anstey, commanding officer of MASSINGHAM. Instead of moving SPOC into old buildings, a new establishment was rapidly constructed of tents, Quonset huts, and wooden structures. Administration, communications, and operations were accomplished at the new facility. Training areas, parachute rigging, and container loading were scattered, with some training at Chrea, Blida airport, and the Club des Pins at Guyotsville.

SPOC had four principal sections: French, Air Operations, Jedburgh/ OGs, and Intelligence, which were coupled with a signals unit that controlled the sending of messages to the field, to military headquarters (7th Army and AFHQ), and to SFHQ in London. Each section had both British and American chiefs, and while there were more SOE personnel than OSS, efforts were made to equalize the staff. At the command level, Davis and Anstey were each assisted by an officer, Major McKenney (OSS) and Major Hodgart (SOE). Later, when it was certain that Anvil would be launched and that the French would participate, Lt. Col. Jean Constans joined Widmer, already representing the French DGSS, as a member of SPOC. While theoretically at the Davis/Anstey level, Constans had closer relations with the French Country Section.

The OSS member of the French section was Capt. Gerard de Piolenc, of French origins, who had been with SO in the field for a year. He was outranked by SOE opposite number, Lt. Comdr. Brooks Richards, who had headed the MASSINGHAM French desk for 8 months. Among the OSS personnel in the French section were Captain Fontaine, Capt. Alan Stuyvesant, Lieutenant Bonnet, Lieutenant Brinkerhoff, and Lieutenant Geoffrey Jones, who, as an artillery officer and paratrooper, joined SPOC as a training officer shortly after it was established.[26] Richards and de Piolenc worked well together, and OSS-SOE rivalry was not a problem. The principal problems were shortages (personnel and aircraft), lack of preparation time, lack of clarity regarding relations with the military and the French, and questions over the use of Jedburghs and OGs. In July, Major McKenney commented that the staff was greatly inexperienced: The Americans "are all new and straight from Washington." The British, he thought, also lacked experience but not so much as the Americans. He felt that the Jedburghs were not happy: "as SPOC was understaffed there was no one to take care of them."[27] There was also a difficult French problem related to command of the Forces Françaises de l'Intérieur (FFI). While this was essentially a matter that needed solution at the military command level, it affected SPOC because SPOC controlled all communications with the FFI in France.

As OSS/SO had no exclusively OSS missions in France, the Americans at SPOC were mostly involved in training and in efforts to get the OGs and Jedburghs into action. Maj. Alfred Cox, who had worked under Colonel Livermore with the OG program, was assigned to SPOC. Because of the SHAEF restriction, no OG had been sent to France prior to the landings in Normandy. Furthermore, until July 15, SHAEF controlled special operations in all of France—only after that date could AFHQ carry out such operations without clearing with London. Thus, only two OGs went into France before that date, and neither was involved in Anvil planning. (OG EMILY was sent into the Lot Department, along with Jedburgh team QUININE, on June 9. This was to cut the north-south route known to be used by Germans and was in fact the route taken by the 2d Panzer Division ["Das Reich"] in going north to reinforce the German forces in Normandy. Both the OG and the Jed team arrived after the main body of the 2d Panzer had passed through the area.)[28]

The other OG, JUSTINE, along with EUCALYPTUS, a British mission with an OSS wireless operator (Lt. André Pecquet), was dropped onto the Vercors on June 29. These missions were to support a large Resistance contingent defying the Germans on this vast, lofty plateau southwest of Grenoble. The Resistance action had nothing to do with Anvil but had been sponsored by the Gaullist intelligence service and Soustelle's DGSS, with whom MASSINGHAM had been cooperating. As the Vercors was overrun by the Germans in late July, the missions accomplished nothing— indeed, they were fortunate to escape with their lives. Pecquet remained in the area and, when the American army neared Grenoble, served as liaison between Gen. Lucian Truscott's VI Corps and the FFI.[29]

The OG program constituted a purely OSS operation within SPOC, and after the despatch of EMILY and JUSTINE to the field, Major Cox still had 11 teams, some Italian-speaking and some French-speaking. But he was restrained from sending teams in until after July 15, when SACMED obtained authority for southern France from SHAEF. For the rest of July, partly because of the weather, he sent in only two groups, both to the Ardèche Department west of the Rhône, where they cooperated with the FFI until Lyon was liberated in early September. Cox himself later joined the OGs in the Ardèche, where altogether six of his teams operated. The remaining five groups went into southern France in the first 2 weeks of August just prior to the landings. They supplemented FFI units, but they were too few, and came in too late, to contribute a great deal of the Anvil campaign, although individual actions, in true Green Beret spirit, demonstrated courage and resourcefulness. In summarizing the OG accomplishment, Cox mentioned as least tangible but probably most important

> the tremendous lift given to the Maquis by the arrival of Allied troops far ahead of the Armies. Many French leaders have said that even if the men had not carried out a single tactical operation, their presence alone was of enormous value.

In cooperation with the FFI, the OGs in southern France took over 10,000 prisoners, caused almost 1,000 German casualties, and destroyed 32 bridges. Cox continued:

> All are in unanimous agreement that the teams should have been put into France much earlier than they were. Every day in training the

Macquis brought increased dividends in their combat effectiveness. After the debarkation from the South, the advance of the Army was so rapid that the sections sent in after D-Day barely had a chance to get started on operations before being over-run.[30]

Although the Jedburgh program was international, the OSS nevertheless played a considerable part in its organization and staffing. Twenty-five three-man teams went into France from North Africa, involving 73 individuals (two teams went in minus one person): 28 French, 23 British, 21 American, and 1 Canadian. The Jedburgh program suffered in the same way that the OGs did in having to clear with SHAEF, until July 15, the area and mission of the teams. Thus, three teams arrived right after Normandy D-day to help cut routes to the north, and four more went into the Anvil area at the end of June.[31] But throughout July no Jedburghs went to southern France, partly because Anvil's status was uncertain, partly because of the weather, and partly because of internal disputes as to where the Jeds would be most effective.[32] With the D-day for Anvil definitely set, SPOC doubled its efforts to despatch the teams, sending in 16 before August 20. These teams worked closely with the FFI, and an account of their activities and accomplishments would fill many more pages than are available here.[33]

SPOC of course was responsible for other missions besides OGs and Jedburghs, in particular a number of inter-Allied missions, French commandos, SOE circuits, and their resupply. Although the OSS members of SPOC, like de Piolenc and Jones, took part in training and briefing, few Americans (other than Jeds and OGs) from SO actually went into France. André Pecquet has been mentioned; another, Muthular d'Errecalde, was arrested by the Gestapo and put to death by the Germans. (His grave commemorates the only American among 26 members of the French Resistance buried in a lonely shrine known as the *Charnier* [Sepulcre] *de Signe*). Jones himself, promoted to captain, replaced d'Errecalde and was parachuted in to assist the 1st Airborne Task Force. Mario Volpe, later a judge in New Jersey, served with a British mission on the Italian border, as did Mario Morpurgo. Another mission, with Peter Dewey and three other OSS men (Mission ETOILE), went into southwestern France on August 11, but it was not related to the southern landings. A group of Marines, headed by Peter Ortiz and Capt. Francis Coolidge, jumped into France just south of Switzerland, but that mission also had little relationship to Anvil.[34]

After the Dragoon landings (the Anvil code name had been replaced), OSS personnel from both SI and SO played an important role in southern France. The SI group, making up the SSS that had been attached to the 7th Army's G-2 during the preparation period in Naples, landed on D-day. Led by Lt. Col. Edward Gamble, the unit of about 23 persons (first wave) was to remain at Army headquarters with representatives also at each of the three division headquarters. SI had found that if persons with language skills were attached at corps level, they tended to be used to translate and interrogate rather than to debrief and filter intelligence from the chains of agents already sent by Frank Schoonmaker and Henry Hyde into the field.

SSS provided both long-range and tactical intelligence. Ultimately the section had about 150 individuals working with Colonel Quinn, the 7th Army G-2. As the army progressed rapidly toward Grenoble and Lyon, many of Hyde's agents were overrun, but improvised arrangements continued to provide information. As an example, in the 2 months after D-day, the 3d Division unit had infiltrated 111 missions, handled 178 reports, and furnished the division with a total of 868 separate intelligence items (exclusive of vague or minor ones). Some idea of the unit's work can be obtained from excerpts from the SSS report now available:

> The chief accomplishment of this day's work [September 1, 1944] was the presentation of a complete defense plan of Lyon to the General [Dahlquist] commanding the 36th Div. The plans came from one of the last of our chains to be overrun. The team with the 36th [headed by Justin Greene] managed to get a courier into our people within the city and bring out the plans. . . . The General was very happy and called the captain of the team in to compliment him on the material. . . .
>
> [By September 4] all our important people behind the lines had joined us. There was only one radio left, and no other agents of great importance. . . .
>
> [September 7] General Donovan visited our unit for the second time, arriving late in the evening and discussing problems with Mr. Hyde and Col. Gamble.[35]

By the first week of September, the 7th Army had moved north beyond the range of supply from Algiers. Only one campaign remained in southern France, but of the 1st Airborne Task Force eastward toward Grasse, Nice, and the Italian border. Here the campaign would continue into 1945 with the SI contingent, now headed by Capt. Geoffrey Jones, handling agents who provided intelligence for Maj. Gen. Robert T. Frederick.[36] But Algiers was no longer headquarters for this operation as Colonel Glavin's base of operations had moved to Italy. AFHQ had left Algiers in July, establishing itself more conveniently as Caserta.

The relationship of SPOC to the 7th Army was somewhat different from that of SI because, for one thing, SPOC was an international body operating under General Maitland Wilson's Allied Force Headquarters. Wilson established a new section, G-5, to deal with Special Operations. So long as Force 163, the Planning Group for the 7th Army, remained in Algiers, it was not too difficult for SPOC to maintain contact with the planners, who kept SOE and the OSS abreast of high-level strategic thinking. Once General Patch decided to transfer his headquarters to Naples, where most of the Anvil units were training, the problem of liaison became acute. As the packing units and radio transmitters could not easily be moved, it was not feasible for SPOC, which in any case came under Wilson's overall Mediterranean command, to follow Patch to Italy. Nevertheless, a special unit, almost as large as SPOC itself, was organized for transfer to Naples, where it would be attached to 7th Army headquarters.

This was 4-SFU, Special Forces Unit No. 4, commanded by American Lt. Col. William G. Bartlett, with British Lt. Col. E.S.N. Head as deputy, assigned by AFHQ to the 7th Army on June 29 and later moved to Naples. The unit would operate under Patch's G-3 with liaison to G-2 and would "control Resistance groups in southern France in support of ANVIL," be a source for information about these groups, and be 7th Army's "channel for obtaining the assistance of Resistance groups." The unit was large, with 22 officers (10 American, 12 British) and 42 enlisted persons (12 American, 30 British) together with an all-British detachment—over 50 persons—for radio communications. 4-SFU would be provided with over 20 vehicles so that once landed, its teams would be mobile and independent of regular army support. It was planned that there would be officers at the various headquarters, Army, Corps, and Division, and teams to serve as interpreters and liaison or to organize sabotage missions behind the lines. The teams would have adequate mobile radios and would keep in touch with Algiers as well as with missions already in the field.

As the officers of 4-SFU were all French-speaking, they were in a position to assist the commanders, especially at the lower levels, in getting help not only from the FFI but from French civilians. In the field, 4-SFU operated much the same as the SSS unit. It was to land in three sections with the military landings and therefore on D-plus-1-day had only a third of its personnel ashore. The unit kept moving north, to Avignon, then to Lyon, while SPOC established a forward base at Avignon. With the rapidity of the campaign—Lyon was liberated in 2 weeks—4-SFU was hard pressed to keep ahead of the troops.[37]

On September 15, with the 7th Army far north of SPOC's basic jurisdiction, Gen. Jacob Devers absorbed the 7th Army and the French 1st Army into his 6th Army Group. Bartlett and Head offered to continue their services as the campaign moved toward the Vosges. Devers was unsympathetic to this offer and made it clear that he intended to run SO-type programs using Army Signal channels to SFHQ in London. Several operations, such as PROUST and SUSSEX, had not been part of the North African headquarters except for recruiting. Thus SPOC and 4-SFU were phased out and by October, having served their purpose, closed down.[38]

By the end of 1944, the main fronts lay beyond the reach of Algiers: Italy, the Rhine, and the Balkans engaged the major attention of the Allied Command and of the OSS. Donovan focused his energies toward the north and toward the future of an intelligence establishment.

NOTES

1. William L. Langer, *Our Vichy Gamble* (New York, 1947); Robert Murphy, *Diplomat Among Warriors* (New York, 1964); *War Report of the OSS*, intro. by Kermit Roosevelt, 6 vols. (U.S. Government Printing Office, available to the public in 1975), and edited by Anthony Cave Brown as *The Secret War Report of the OSS* (New York, 1976), which is the edition hereinafter cited. Arthur L. Funk, *The Politics of TORCH* (Lawrence, KS, 1974); Rygor Slowikowski, *In the Secret Service: The Lighting of the Torch*, ed. John Herman (London, 1988); Fabrizio Calvi, *OSS: La guerre secrète en France, 1942–1945: Les services spéciaux Americains, la Résistance et la Gestapo* (Paris, 1990); Anthony Cave Brown, *The Last Hero: Wild Bill Donovan* (New York, 1982). See also Stephen Ambrose and R. H. Immerman, *Ike's Spies* (New York, 1981); F. H. Hinsley et al., *British Intelligence in the Second World War*, vol. 2 (London, 1981), chap. 24.
2. Arthur L. Funk, "The United States and TORCH: Strategy and Intelligence," *Franco-British Studies* 7 (Spring 1989): 15–26, and discussion, "The roles of SOE and OSS in North Africa," pp. 45–50.
3. David A. Walker, "OSS and Operation Torch," *Journal of Contemporary History* 22 (Oct. 1987): 667–679. This is part of a doctoral dissertation in process at University of California at Davis.
4. OSS Algiers File, 45 boxes, Entry 97, Records of the Office of Strategic Services, Record Group 226, National Archives and Records Administration, Washington, DC (hereinafter cited as RG 226, NA); M.R.D. Foot, *SOE in France: An Account of the Work of the British Special Operations Executive in France, 1940–1944* (London, 1966), p. 32; Cave Brown, *The Last Hero*, pp. 320–323; Douglas Dodds-Parker, *Setting Europe Ablaze: Some Account of Ungentlemanly Warfare* (Windlesham, Surrey, 1983), pp. 118–135.
5. For example, Anthony Verrier, *Assassination in Algiers* (New York, 1990), a journalistic account that must be balanced by others. Claude Huan and Hervé Coutau-Bégarie, *Darlan* (Paris, 1989), chap. 21, discusses all the sources and arguments. For the assertion that he used a .22-caliber Colt Woodsman, see Cave Brown, *The Last Hero*, p. 472. The postmortem examination several times refers to the wound made by a 7.65 pistol. Peter Tompkins, in *The Murder of Admiral Darlan* (New York, 1965), set forth the facts as then known, including the use of a 7.65-caliber pistol (p. 221). He did not have available at that time Mario Faivre's *Nous avons tué Darlan* (Paris, 1972) nor the documentation available to Huan and Coutau-Bégarie.
6. *Secret War Report of the OSS*, pp. 363–369; Box 2, Entry 110, RG 226, NA; Calvi, *OSS: La guerre secrète*, pp. 55–60, 79–82, 154–179; Paul Paillole, *Services spéciaux* (Paris, 1975), pp. 403–478.
7. Barry M. Katz, *Foreign Intelligence: Research and Analysis in the Office of Strategic Services, 1942–1945* (Cambridge, MA, 1989), pp. 80–84, 166–169. R. Harris

Smith, *OSS: The Secret History of America's First Central Intelligence Agency* (Berkeley, 1972), pp. 69–71.

8. Ibid., chap. 3; Bradley Smith, *The Shadow Warriors: OSS and the Origins of the CIA* (New York, 1983), pp. 208–222; Cave Brown, *The Last Hero*, pp. 224–234, 345–348; Donald Downes, *The Scarlet Thread* (New York, 1953); Carleton Coon, *A North African Story* (Ipswich, CT, 1980); Carleton J. Hayes, *Wartime Mission in Spain* (New York, 1945), pp. 105–128; Jacques Soustelle, *Envers et contre tout*, vol. 2 (Paris, 1950), pp. 328–384; Langer, *Our Vichy Gamble*, pp. 297–300; Calvi, *OSS: La guerre secrète*, pp. 373–374n; Paillole, *Services spéciaux*, pp. 414–424.

9. The activities of Henry Hyde, and especially the circuit Penny Farthing, have been narrated in detail by Cave Brown in *The Last Hero*, chap. 20, pp. 316–340, and by Calvi in *OSS: La guerre secrète*, chap. 4, pp. 181–213, based on interviews and material provided by Mr. Hyde.

10. R. H. Smith, *OSS*, p. 176; Serge Obolensky, *One Man in His Time* (New York, 1958), pp. 368–371; Cave Brown, *The Last Hero*, pp. 468–472; Dodds-Parker, *Setting Europe Ablaze*, pp. 152–155; General Gambiez, *Libération de la Corse* (Paris, 1974).

11. All OSS/SI activities were strictly American, whereas most OSS/SO people worked with SOE. SOE controlled a number of circuits, which had been developed since the early days of the war. SOE also maintained most of the interallied missions.

12. U.S. Department of State, *Foreign Relations of the United States: The Conferences at Washington and Quebec, 1943* (Washington, DC, 1970), pp. 472–482.

13. B. Smith, *Shadow Warriors*, p. 228; R. H. Smith, *OSS*, p. 103; Cave Brown, *The Last Hero*, p. 503; Max Corvo, *The OSS in Italy, 1942–1945* (Westport, CT, 1990), p. 125; Calvi, *OSS: La guerre secrète*, pp. 157–179.

14. *OSS War Report*, pp. 110–113; Maj. Alfred Cox, "[OG] Operations in Southern France," Co. B, 2671st Special Reconnaissance Battalion, Sept. 20, 1944, Box 741, Entry 190, RG 226, NA (hereinafter cited as Cox Report); Dodds-Parker, *Setting Europe Ablaze*, p. 128; Obolensky, *One Man in His Time*, pp. 337–380; Corvo, *OSS in Italy*, p. 162.

15. Corvo, *OSS in Italy*, pp. 127–129.

16. Folder 144, Box 30, Entry 99, RG 226, NA; Sir Brooks Richards to author.

17. Cox Report; AFHQ History of Special Operations, Annex E, WO 204/2030B, Public Record Office, London; "OSS Aid to the French Resistance in World War II," assembled in 1945 by Col. J. F. French, which includes various reports found in Box 25, Entry 91; Box 1, Entry 101; Boxes 1–4, Entry 103; Box 56, Entry 154; and Box 741, Entry 190, RG 226, NA. On American air support, W. F. Craven and J. L. Cate, *The Army Air Forces in World War II*, vol. 3 (Chicago, 1951), pp. 499–506.

18. "Special Operations: AAF Aid to European Resistance Movements, 1943–1945," compiled by Maj. Harris G. Warren in 1947 for the U.S. Army Air Forces Air Historical Office, pp. 21–25, 231.

19. Alan F. Wilt, *The French Riviera Campaign of August 1944* (Carbondale, IN, 1981), pp. 20–24, 46–64.

20. Box 30, Entry 99, RG 226, NA.

21. Calvi, *OSS: La guerre secrète*, p. 381.

22. *Secret War Report of the OSS*, p. 480.
23. Memorandum by Col. H. B. Hitchens, G-2, AFHQ, Oct. 30, 1944: "O.S.S. Contribution to Intelligence Collated for Operation DRAGOON" (courtesy of Mr. Henry Hyde).
24. Report of Strategic Service Section (SSS) attached to 7th Army, Folder 145, Box 30, Entry 9, RG 226, NA.
25. Arthur L. Funk, "American Contacts with the Resistance in France, 1940–43" *Military Affairs* (Feb. 1970): 19–21.
26. *Secret War Report of the OSS*, pp. 359–361; Boxes 33, 34, 39, Entry 99, and Box 132, Entry 190, RG 226, NA. Interviews and correspondence with Sir Brooks Richards, Col. Jean Constans, and Geoffrey Jones. As training officer, Jones supervised not only the instruction of OSS and SOE personnel but also worked with Colonel Gambiez in the formation of several French *bataillons de choc*, comparable to the American OGs.
27. McKinney to Haskell, July 11, 1944, Folder 838, Box 139, Entry 190, RG 226, NA.
28. One of the Penny Farthing agents, "Jerome" Lescanne, had identified the Second Panzer in early June (Cave Brown, *The Last Hero*, p. 583; Calvi, *OSS: La guerre secrète*, pp. 293–328). OG reports in Box 741, Entry 190; Jedburgh reports, Box 25, Entry 19; Box 1, Entry 101; Boxes 1–4, Entry 103; Debriefing reports in Box 56, Entry 157, RG 226, NA.
29. JUSTINE Report; interview with André Pecquet (Paray).
30. Cox Report; also reports of OG's LOUISE, BETSY, RUTH, ALICE, NANCY, LEHIGH, HELEN, LAFAYETTE, WILLIAMS, PEG, PAT, all in Box 741, Entry 190, RG 226, NA.
31. Early June: Jeds QUININE, AMMONIA, BUGATTI; late June in Anvil area: CHLOROFORM, DODGE, VEGANIN, WILLYS.
32. Maj. J. Champion to Lt. Brinkerhoff, July 21, 1944, Folder 712, Box 132, Entry 190, RG 226, NA.
33. Jedburghs CHRYSLER, CINNAMON, CITROEN, COLLODION, EPHED-RINE, GRAHAM, JEREMY, MARK, MARTIN, MILES, MINARET, MON-OCLE, NOVOCAINE, PACKARD, SCEPTRE, JOHN. In these teams were 12 OSS agents, including Aaron Bank (PACKARD), later to be known as the "Father of the Green Berets."
34. On Jones: Folder 49, Box 3, Entry 110, RG 226, NA; on Volpe: Report of CONFESSIONAL mission (SOE Archives, Foreign and Commonwealth Office, London); on Morpurgo: Box 19, Entry 91, RG 226, NA; on Dewey: Folder 120, Box 97, Entry 190, RG 226, NA (also Cave Brown, *The Last Hero*, pp. 587–594); on Ortiz and Coolidge: Edward Hynoff, *The OSS in World War II* (2d ed., New York, 1986), pp. 313–316.
35. *Secret War Report of the OSS*, pp. 489–501; Cave Brown, *The Last Hero*, pp. 583–587, 594; Calvi, *OSS: La guerre secrète*, pp. 438–447.
36. Jones Report: 99/06 (FABTF)-0.3, Records of the Adjutant General's Office, 1917–   , RG 407, NA. For a journalistic account of Jones's activities, see R. H. Adleman and G. Walton, *The Champagne Campaign* (Boston, 1969), pp. 37–45, 52–59, 131–141, 193–198.
37. Folder 838, Box 13, Entry 190; Folder 67, Box 5, Entry 158, RG 226, NA.
38. Ibid; Folder 832, Box 139, Entry 139, RG 226, NA.

THE OSS AND THE ITALIAN CAMPAIGN

Max Corvo

In many ways the Italian campaign acted as the proving ground for the myriad ideas germinated by the various branches of the Office of Strategic Services (OSS). Because of the difficulty of the terrain and the constant manpower penury of the Allied armies, the campaign gave almost everyone an opportunity to experiment their ideas and theories, which ranged from intelligence to special operations to psychological warfare to political reporting. It called upon the panoply of OSS specialties assigned by charter or arrogated by the director and the various operators.

Of course, it did not hurt the experimental phase to have a man such as Bill Donovan as the director of the fledgling intelligence organization. An individual of broad vision, he encouraged experimentation as the mother of experience. Never one to create barriers, he listened, counseled, and then took action, no matter the consequences.

For the Italian section of the Secret Intelligence Branch (SI), the planning got under way in winter 1941 when David Bruce, then chief of the SI branch of the Coordinator of Information (COI), persuaded Earl Brennan, an old State Department hand, to take over the direction of the Italian-American section. Since they had known each other in Italy, when both had served there, Bruce gave Brennan the green light in creating his organization.

Bruce and Brennan worked to put their ideas together, and they produced a plan that they forwarded to Donovan. The plan contemplated a meeting by Bruce and Brennan in Italy with Crown Prince Humbert of Savoy in order to convince him to take Italy out of the war. So far as can be determined, no action was taken on the plan, perhaps because it was commonly known that Crown Prince Humbert had never been a tower of strength in his opposition to Mussolini.

Brennan and his office staff immediately enlisted Dale MacAdoo, who had been studying in Italy and had been recently expatriated. MacAdoo loved Italian culture, especially its literature. He spoke Italian fluently, but he did not have many ideas or drive.

In July of 1942 a broad program was initiated to establish contact with the Italian anti-Fascist organizations and the Italian-American labor groups in New York. As part of this program, a broad recruiting effort was undertaken on a nationwide basis, and a training system was set up for Italian SI agents with the help of the OSS schools.

An action plan was concurrently developed, which foresaw the early course of the war in the Mediterranean with the invasion of North Africa and the subsequent attack on Sicily and continental Italy as major factors in developing a winning strategy.

These programs were developed under the guidance of Max Corvo, who entered the OSS from the Army training center at Camp Lee, VA, where he had developed the preliminary intelligence plan that had been submitted through 3d Army headquarters in Baltimore to Washington, where it had found its way to Lt. Frank Ball, assistant to the special operations officer of COI, Col. Preston Goodfellow. It was decided to bring Corvo in under the joint sponsorship of the SI and SO branches to develop further Italian operations. In September he was transferred to COI.

Working Against Time

It became evident that U.S. intelligence was waging a war against time in order to keep up with events in North Africa, where the British 8th Army swept westward across Libya after the defeat of the Afrika Korps at El Alamein. As a result of carrying out several aggressive civilian recruiting trips across the nation, with the aid of Girolamo Valenti, editor of an anti-Fascist weekly newspaper in New York, SI did yeoman work in bringing into the organization viable agent personnel who received training in the OSS schools in Maryland and Virginia in special operations and intelligence collection.

The advent of the invasion of North Africa in November of 1942 put much pressure on the OSS to develop programs and dispatch its personnel to the field in connection with future Italian operations. During the North African invasion, the OSS had been praised for the work of a handful of individuals who operated under the direction of Col. William Eddy in North Africa to provide vital intelligence to our own and Allied armed forces in connection with the landings. The significance of the OSS contribution was never lost in the minds of Generals Eisenhower and Clark, who had tremendous respect for the potential of the fledgling Donovan organization.

Planning for the Future

The SI Italian section expanded its horizons with each passing month and played an important role in drawing up the overall plan of action for

Sicily long before the invasion ever took place. In the interim, it became plainly evident that the British were having little luck in landing infiltration agents in Sicily, and the OSS theater command at Allied Force Headquarters (AFHQ) sent repeated messages to Washington headquarters to dispatch personnel to North Africa.

In January 1943 Vincent Scamporino, a civilian, was dispatched to North Africa to head the Italian SI section as a member of Eddy's staff. Two officers, Lts. Frank Tarallo and Sebastian Passanisi, together with eight enlisted men who had been trained as agents and radio operators, were also included in the same travel orders, which were signed by General Donovan.

In the interim, the Washington SI staff was enlarged by a number of specialists in various fields. Contacts were expanded with the Italian-American anti-Fascist community so that the OSS could harness its efforts to our national objective. Mr. Luigi Antonini, president of ILGWU, Local 48, was a key contact, as was Augusto Bellanca of the CIO Amalgamated Clothing Workers Union. Contacts with the foremost Italian expatriate members of academia were maintained through Professor Giuseppe Borgese of the University of Chicago and Professors George LaPiana and Gaetano Salvemini of Harvard. Firm contacts were also established with Randolfo Pacciardi, who had commanded the Italian volunteer troops in the international brigade during the Spanish Civil War and who was free of any Communist taint, and with Don Luigi Sturzo, Italy's foremost expatriate.

During this period, Italian SI provided assistance in its recruitment program to the Special Operations division and to the Operational Groups then being created. This new unit was to be trained in commando work, and its members were selected along ethnic lines. Lt. Joseph Bonfiglio and a small Italian SI staff helped test the language capabilities of recruits from various Army camps.

Early Operations

It was not until May that Corvo was sent to AFHQ to head up the SI operations in Italy. By that time, Operation Torch was over, and the Axis had surrendered its considerable forces at Cape Bon. Sicily was sure to be the next Allied objective.

Clearly, in order for the OSS to have any operational freedom, it would have to break the apron strings that tied it to British Special Operations Executive (SOE) and Secret Intelligence Services (SIS), which controlled all of the operational transport systems in the theater. A meeting was set up by Colonel Eddy through Adm. Henry Kent Hewett for Corvo to discuss the impending operations with Adm. R. L. Connolly at Bizerte, Tunisia. Out of this meeting was born an agreement that would make available for OSS use a number of PT boats from U.S. Navy RON 15, commanded by Comdr. Stanley Barnes. This agreement remained in force until the end of the war.

The period before the Sicilian campaign was a most frustrating one for the OSS because planning for the Sicilian invasion (code-named Husky) was primarily in British hands and the OSS was not informed of its role in the impending operation.

The organization lacked an overseas document reproduction section. Consequently, we were dependent on the British SIS document section in Cairo, to which we dispatched one of our officers, hoping to speed the procurement of documents that would allow our agents to freely circulate in enemy terrain.

Lacking information from OSS headquarters or AFHQ, we prepared a combined operation with PT RON 15, which was originally calculated to land a team of agents at the northwest coast of Sardinia but, because of lack of documentation, was converted into a uniformed operation. The object of this landing was primarily to call the enemy's attention to Allied activity on the island and to keep him guessing as to our ultimate objective, the island of Sicily, with its population of 5 million and its strategic location at the center of the Mediterranean.

The Sardinia operation, code-named "Bathtub 1," was made up of Tony Camboni, Joseph Puleo, Vincent Pavia, and John DeMontis (four enlisted men) and one officer. The officer, Lt. Charles Taquay, was the radio operator. They were told that they were being sent to organize the resistance in order to aid a pending Allied landing.

On June 28, they rendezvoused with the PT squadron at Bone, Algeria, and late that evening the first OSS team was landed on Italy. The team was captured by Italian coastal troops, but its presence in Sardinia confused the enemy. After the Italian armistice was announced, it became a liaison team with the Italian authorities in Sardinia.

The Sicilian Invasion: Operation Husky

With little time for any preparation, SI was alerted by AFHQ to have a unit ready for the Sicilian invasion. As there were no other OSS branches ready with a pool of manpower, the total burden fell upon the shoulders of Italian SI. The mission was not spelled out, but the unit was attached to the G-2 (intellingence) section of Patton's 7th Army and was designated Experimental Detachment G-3, AFHQ.

The Sicilian campaign experience was varied and included tactical intelligence, line infiltration, counterintelligence work, psychological warfare, and providing intelligence for Allied Military Government (AMG).

One of the aims of the unit was to capture code books and collect intelligence for the coming Italian campaign, which we knew was the next step in the war because one of our groups was assigned to Clark's 5th Army in Morocco under the command of Donald Downes. SI did not neglect the opportunity to mount a Special Operations (SO)/Operational Group (OG) type of operation, which, with the assistance of PT RON 15 and the approval of G-2, 7th Army, captured the Lipari islands and turned their administration over to American Military Government Occupied Territory (AMGOT), brought back code books and captured some 50 prisoners of war who were considered worthy of being interrogated.

SI included the first Research and Analysis Branch (R&A) representative at its Palermo station in the person of Rudy Winnacker. Because there was a critical shortage of R&A personnel in the theater, we assigned a translator and interpreter team to him. The first counterintelligence (X-2) team also took to the field during this period, and SI worked out the arrangements with 7th Army G-2 counterintelligence to allow them freedom of action. Finally, Sicily served as the jump-off point for the next phase of the Italian campaign: the landing at Salerno.

Operation Husky: An Appraisal

1) Because very little information filtered down from higher headquarters to orient OSS policy, and Patton's 7th Army moved rapidly, the use of tactical intelligence gathered was valueless. Line penetration teams were often overrun before they could get back to our own lines.

2) A wealth of intelligence was gathered that was valuable later in preparation for the Salerno invasion, and the men who would later be active in gathering tactical and strategic intelligence gained a great deal of experience.

3) The OSS, which had been looked down upon as a poor relation, gained wide acceptance with the staff of the 7th Army and the various combat divisions in the field. This acceptance would later be an asset in other campaigns in the European theater.

4) The Italian SI section made many valuable political contacts on the island. Connecetions with men who were to play leading roles in the patriot movement and the governments that were formed after the armistice gave the OSS tremendous advantages in its political reporting and influence.

5) Husky gave Washington personnel the opportunity to visit the theater of operations and see, firsthand, what had been achieved.

6) Husky alerted Washington SO, OG, R&A, and the other branches of the need to rush available personnel to North Africa during the developing phases of the Mediterranean campaign.

7) It was determined that it would be better to use native personnel, rather than U.S. citizens who might have left Italy 5 years or a decade before, for certain intelligence operations.

The Interim Period

The awakening of Washington headquarters to the needs of the North African theater of operations became evident as more and more personnel arrived in Algiers. Many of those arriving were administrative personnel, others were branch representatives who were looking for opportunities to contribute to the organizational effort; a few were motivated by ambition to achieve personal success. As the table of organization of the Algiers headquarters grew, the situation became more difficult for Colonel Eddy, who was used to working with a small, intimate staff, to control.

Palermo served as the advance headquarters of the OSS while another OSS unit made up principally of Italian SI personnel was organized in Morocco, Mark Clark's headquarters, under the command of Donald Downes. This unit was to participate in Operation Avalanche, the code name for the Salerno landing.

The original plan was to have the 7th Army and 5th Army unite once Naples had been captured by the 5th Army. With the Sicilian campaign over, the Italian SI section turned its attention to continental Italy and to its participation in Operation Avalanche. It worked with the PT squadron that was now based in Palermo harbor to test the enemy shore defenses in the lower Tyrrhenian Sea and carried out several missions to attempt to contact Marshal Badoglio, who had succeeded Mussolini, in an effort to get Italy out of the war (the McGreggor Mission).

Orders were received from AFHQ through Colonel Eddy to prepare a commando-type mission to capture the island of Ventotene, off the Italian coast, and also approving a number of missions in conjunction with the Salerno landings. These missions were to be jointly undertaken with PT RON 15 and U.S. Navy force 80.4.

Ventotene was to be captured without infantry support, and only a platoon of paratroopers from the 509 Scout Co., 82d Airborne, were assigned to our mission. It became imperative that we arm a number of anti-Fascist civilians and our own SI GIs to undertake the task.

Because the attack on the island was to take place during a moonless night, it was our objective to use guile instead of force. On D-1, it was decided to avoid a firefight, if that was possible. The other missions were to go along with the task force 80.4 and were to be landed along the coast of Lucania. At the same time, a number of missions were prepared to land at Salerno and undertake tactical intelligence missions approved by G-2 5th Army.

On September 8 the Ventotene operation was carried out under cover of darkness by a unit under the command of Captain Tarallo. The enemy garrison, made up of communications and radar specialists, surrendered to our numerically inferior OSS forces without firing a shot, and the enemy's advance warning system was eliminated. A directional beacon was put up to guide the 82d Airborne to Rome. This parajump was later canceled.

At the same time, the OSS 5th Army contingent was on its way to Salerno as a part of the Avalanche task force, and they were later joined by a number of intelligence teams from Palermo. These 7th Army OSS teams cleared their missions with Col. Edwin B. Howard, G-2 5th Army, and immediately undertook their tactical missions, reporting back to 5th Army with their intelligence.

A Command Decision

By September 25 Donovan, who was at 5th Army HQ, directed that Lt. Col. Ellery Huntington take command of the 5th Army unit and all of the OSS personnel in the area. This, in fact, created two OSS units dealing with Italian operations.

By order of General Eisenhower, the 5th Army unit was then assigned the tactical mission while the Palermo station was assigned to strategic penetration of Italy, north of Rome. In order to carry out these orders, the Italian SI unit established a base at La Maddalena, Sardinia, and a strategic infiltration base at Brindisi.

The base at La Maddalena was later moved to Corsica, from which numerous operations were conducted against the islands off the Italian coast. Some of these operations were conducted in conjunction with the OGs that had set up their headquarters in Bastia under the command of Col. Russell Livermore.

The basic strategic infiltration of northern Italy was essentially conducted from Brindisi, where an airlift was made available by the British 334th Wing, which was later replaced by the U.S. 15th Bombardment Wing.

The Italian surrender, which was announced on September 9, while Avalanche was in progress, opened up new avenues of collaboration with the Italian Army general staff, which established its headquarters in Brindisi. The Italian intelligence organization (SIM) provided the OSS with personnel for missions to northern Italy and also made available a number of radio operators who were trained to use OSS procedures.

At the same time, the ORI (Organization for Italian Resistance), organized by attorney Raimondo Craveri, a proved and tried anti-Fascist, and composed of young professional elements and university students, provided key mission personnel for the strategic infiltration of northern Italy. Because of its close association with the CLNAI (Committee of National Liberation of Northern Italy), it became a key player in guiding intelligence and policy decisions of the north Italian Patriot Command. This made it possible for the OSS to have an input in both the liberal and conservative wings of the partisan movement.

While the assignment of tactical missions to the 5th Army OSS by General Eisenhower was on the record, the 5th Army operations found it difficult to honor the order. With the U.S. Army slugging its way north, Kesselring took advantage of every geographical feature to defend his ground, and the stalemate at Monte Cassino brought on Operation Shingle, the ill-fated Anzio landing, in which the OSS had a small detachment. In spite of the tactical surprise, neither the 5th Army nor the OSS took advantage of the opportunities presented by lack of German forces in the Rome area until it was too late and the Germans had closed the gap. As a consequence, the taking of Rome was delayed until June 4.

By August 1944 the constant changes in command of that unit had caused internal turmoil and loss of confidence. As a result, Col. Edward Glavin, the successor to Col. William Eddy, decided to merge all OSS units in Italy. The headquarters of the new unit was located at Siena and later in Florence, and Co. D. 2677th Regiment, as the unit was designated, was placed under the command of Capt. William Suhling. Suhling, who had been a member of the Medical Administration Corps (MAC), was an able administrator, and he reorganized the outfit along branch lines.

The Air Lift Corps was moved from Brindisi to the nearby Tuscan airfields, and a close rapport was established with the 15th Army Group's intelligence and operational sections so that the clandestine war could be better coordinated by the Anglo-American staff, which in many ways, was in competition.

These new staff procedures, in which operational briefs had to be filed, made it possible to control both personnel and supply drops throughout northern Italy by the OGs, SO, SI, SIS, and SOE. This reorganization also made it possible for AFHQ and the 15th Army Group to closely monitor partisan operations throughout northern Italy and to coordinate military movements in concert with orthodox operations by the 5th and 8th Armies and sometimes individual divisions.

SI gathered enough intelligence through its transmitters in northern Italy to produce the first daily intelligence bulletin, which was distributed to the operational army units, headquarters, and many of the agencies represented in the theater such as AMG, State, Justice, and the Office of Naval Intelligence. Eventually the daily bulletin was published as the Company D bulletin and included all intelligence collected from various sources.

By August almost all maritime operations, both subaqueous and surface, had come to a virtual end. As the Italian coasts in both the Adriatic and Tyrrhenian were occupied by the Allied northern penetration of the peninsula, both the British and U.S. secret services had to rely primarily on air resupply and penetration. The 15th Army Group Special Operations resupplied both the British and American organizations.

Coordinating the Guerrilla Movement

In late November 1944, the OSS and SOE finally managed to clear the way for a mission representing the CLNAI to come through Switzerland, via France to Italy, to meet with the Allied High Command at AFHQ and the 15th Army Group and work out procedures of political and military strategy. The mission included Alfredo Pizzoni, president of CLNAI; Ferruccio Parri, leader of the Action Party; Giancarlo Pajetta, representing the Communists; and Edward Sogno, representing the conservatives. As a result of the series of meetings at AFHQ, and with the Italian government, arrangements were made to finance the CLNAI activities in Fascist-occupied Italy, and the tactical controls of the widespread partisan forces were worked out. (The mission was also accompanied by Raimondo Craveri, who had been named as Italian SI representative in Switzerland.)

One of the outstanding achievements of the Italian anti-Fascist guerrilla movement was that, although it was made up of parties across the political spectrum, it had a central command that functioned much as a general staff. In fact, Gen. Raffaele Cadorna became the commanding general of the partisan forces after being parachuted by SOE into northern Italy on August 12, 1944.

Almost the entire intelligence staff of CLNAI was made up of Italian SI OSS agents who, working under the direction or Dr. Enzo Boeri, built up one of the most formidable intelligence organizations operating behind the German lines.

Winter Delays Victory

Allied plans to end the war in Italy before the onset of winter were delayed by the fact that the Allied troop ratio was insufficient to conduct offensive operations against a well-entrenched enemy who held the high ground in the Apennines. The delay provided the opportunity for the OSS and SOE to fully exercise all their guile in creating difficulties for the German troops at the rear of the front lines by coordinating the activities of the guerrilla forces.

The months of January and February of 1945 saw Allied aerial resupply reach its maximum point in preparation for the spring campaign, and the large cities of northern Italy were impatient for liberation. In order to better coordinate the clandestine movement in northern Italy, Lt. Emilio Daddario, assistant operations officer of SI Italy, was sent to Lugano, Switzerland, to help Allen Dulles to coordinate activities on the Italian frontier. Daddario established radio contact with Company D so his activities could better be coordinated with 15th Army Group plans.

To closely collaborate with other branches of the OSS, SI planned a series of joint operations with the Morale Operations Branch (MO), which was engaged in carrying out a psychological warfare program of disinformation among the German troops in Italy, and the reported results of this collaboration were excellent. A program of close collaboration between X-2 and SI was worked out with Jim Angleton, whose Counter Intelligence (CI) intelligence files benefited from the intelligence gleaned from our CLNAI sources and through a playback transmitter that had fallen into the hands of the Abwehr and which we had code-named MARIA GIOV-ANNA.*

A number of OG missions were parachuted into northern Italy at this time to help train the underground forces in the use of explosives and commando tactics. These missions were parachuted to both SI and SO pinpoints where reception committees awaited them. The OGs were under the command of Col. Russell Livermore with Capt. Albert Materazzi as their operations officer.

The Spring Offensive

Extensive preparations were made in connection with the projected spring offensive by both the 5th and 8th Armies. Meanwhile, Mark Clark had been promoted to commanding officer of the 15th Army Group, and Gen. Sir Harold Alexander had taken over the command of AFHQ. OSS headquarters had been moved from Algiers to Caserta in the summer of 1944, and the 15th Army Group was camped on the outskirts of Florence in order to be in close proximity to the front.

The Allied preparations included the activation of the "Rankin B" plan, which foresaw the placing of Allied officers in the proximity of the major cities of northern Italy so that, in the event of a German retreat, they could step in and take over the governance of the area and avoid the breakdown of law and order.

Preparations were also made to have an OSS unit led by "Mim" Daddario, who was stationed at Lugano, cross the frontier into Italy with orders to capture Mussolini and other leaders of the Fascist government and render assistance to the Committee of National Liberation in Milan.

In April, General Cadorna and Ferruccio Parri made another hasty trip to Caserta and Siena to work out the final details of the popular rising that was anticipated in northern Italy. Final details were discussed at OSS headquarters on how to handle the situation in northwestern Italy with the French and the situation on Italy's northeastern frontier with Tito.

On April 21, after a spirited attack by the 5th Army, the Poles, and the partisans, the city of Bologna fell, and the 8th Army broke through the Argenta gap entrapping large enemy forces in the movement and preventing sizeable German forces from crossing the Po River. All OSS teams and partisan forces immediately went into action, and the rising in northwestern Italy became an accomplished fact with patriot forces taking over Italy's industrial triangle, Genova, Turin, and Milan.

Daddario moved into Italy and captured Marshall Graziani and a number of outstanding Fascist personalities. Mussolini had already fallen into

---

*"Playback" as used here indicates a transmitter that has been captured by the enemy and is used to transmit disinformation in both directions.

the hands of a partisan formation and, together with his mistress and some of the ministers of the Salo government, had been summarily executed.

To all intents and purposes, the war in Italy came to an end with the fall of Milan and the takeover by the CLNAI. The surrender papers that were signed at Caserta on May 22 were an empty gesture ratifying what in fact had already taken place as a result of the massive rising engineered by the OSS and SOE officers in the field.

Appreciation

The Italian campaign taught the value of advanced planning and of studying options and contingencies to intelligence specialists who, for the first time, were engaged in the complex operations that the OSS was developing. Above all, it emphasized the need for coordination between the command structures in order to effectively and efficiently use intelligence. Another lesson learned was that improvisation is often necessary to exploit the opportunities offered when the antagonist lets down his guard.

The lengthy duration of the campaign provided enough time for the OSS to plan, organize, and coordinate the nationwide resistance movement throughout northern Italy. The various divisions of the OSS, from the single individual in the field to the policymakers in the White House, could play a role in the final phase of the Italian campaign.

The Italian theater of operations was unique in that an enemy country that was an absolute dictatorship should, midstream in a global war, produce the kind of liberation movement that the CLNAI eventually gave the nation, winning the respect of the Allied leaders for its integrity, its sacrifice, and its inspired leadership.

FAILURE OF A MISSION: Robert McDowell in Yugoslavia, 1944

Dušan Biber

Introduction

"I think our mission to Mihailovich was possibly not expedient since it served as a definite block with relations with Partisan army corps. And it probably decreased the amount of intelligence received from Tito's armies by about a half."
—Arthur Cox, Chief of the Office of Strategic Services (OSS) Yugoslav Section at Bari
Final report, June 23, 1945.[1]

This paper deals with the ill-fated OSS intelligence team, code-named RANGER, attached to Draža Mihailović's headquarters in the period August 26–November 1, 1944, led by Lt. Col. Robert McDowell. This intelligence operation had many political, international, and military implications involving the highest authorities on the Allied, Yugoslav, and German sides. Recently declassified OSS documents provide a great deal of important new information on this particular subject, and they can help us understand the historical background of the current civil war in Yugoslavia.

The reasons and circumstances that prompted the Allies to sever all links with Draža Mihailović and to recall their missions from Chetnik commands are already well known.[2] It is interesting to note that British Col. William Bailey and American Capt. Walter Mansfield, both accredited at the headquarters of Mihailović, considered it necessary, after the departure of Allied military missions, to leave behind at least one American and one British intelligence officer. Colonel Bailey, however, insisted that under no condition should the Americans send their own agent unless the British did likewise. If the Americans went ahead, Mihailović might try to play off

Americans against the British, which would harm the relations between the Allies and Marshal Tito.[3]

Gen. William Donovan, Director of the OSS, addressed a special memorandum to the U.S. Joint Chiefs of Staff (JCS) dated March 4, 1944. He informed them of the British request for the OSS officers to pull out of Mihailović's headquarters after having decided to recall their own missions. In the meantime, OSS in Cairo had recruited at least two groups of agents with a view to sending them to the territory under Mihailović's control. These groups were not only charged with maintaining contacts with Mihailović's forces but were also supposed to make sorties to central and southeastern Europe. The Cairo OSS therefore insisted that the Allies avoid publicly breaking relations with Mihailovič and that Great Britain and the United States retain their observers at his headquarters. General Donovan informed the JCS that the OSS intended to send its intelligence officer in uniform to Mihailović's headquarters and to go through with its plans to smuggle OSS intelligence teams to central and southeastern Europe through territory controlled by Mihailović's Chetniks.[4]

President Franklin Roosevelt agreed to Donovan's plan. In a letter dated March 22, 1944, Roosevelt recommended that the British be told that the Americans reserved the right to gather intelligence data in Yugoslavia independently of British control. On the other hand, American officers should explain to Mihailović that they had not arrived at his headquarters as liaison officers but exclusively as intelligence agents. For that reason, they were not going to meddle with political questions and would not permit political functions to be attributed to them. President Roosevelt, like the British officer Colonel Bailey, until recently stationed in Yugoslavia, believed that this detachment was "essential, lest these American officers be drawn into a position whereby, if the relations between Mihailovich and the British do not improve, he might try to play off, against the British, these American contacts."

Roosevelt backed OSS plans to smuggle intelligence teams to central and southeastern Europe, though not necessarily over the Chetnik territory. He believed that other possibilities should be sought out "without indicating a particular intention to make use of Mihailovích's facilities for sending teams into other regions."[5]

A March 1, 1944, OSS assessment of Mihailović's views was blunt:

> Mihailovich and his leaders have absolutely no confidence in the British, since they believe that the latter may have determined to disregard Mihailovich and back the Partisans. . . . At the present time the Chetniks are concentrating most of their strength in bitter civil war against Tito's forces in Herzegovina, east Bosnia, and further to the south. Mihailovich takes the position that this is by and large a racial conflict against the Croats. He insists that more than three

fourths are treacherous Croats, a large number of whom are Quisling Ustashi; that it was they who decimated the Serb population in 1941 and 1942, and are resolved to establish Croat supremacy regardless of the consequences; and that they were traitors who threw in their lot with the Partisans only when an Allied victory became a probability.[6]

General Donovan, in a letter dated March 31, 1944, informed Gen. Dwight Eisenhower about the withdrawal of the American mission from Mihailović's headquarters. He added, however, that "we have been authorized and intend placing at Mihailovich HQ intelligence officers for the purpose of infiltrating agents into Austria and Germany."[7]

Donovan reported to the JCS that British SIS in Cairo agreed to the OSS sending an intelligence officer to the Chetniks but that SIS headquarters in London and the British Foreign Office opposed the OSS plan. Prime Minister Winston Churchill sided with the Foreign Office and appealed to President Roosevelt.[8] On April 1, 1944, he sent a personal message to Roosevelt and pointed out the political aspect: "If at this very time, an American Mission arrives at Mihailovic's Headquarters, it will show throughout the Balkans a complete contrariety of action between Britain and the United States. The Russians will certainly throw all their weight on Tito's side, which we are backing to the full. Thus we shall get altogether out of step. I hope and trust this may be avoided."[9] On April 8, 1944, President Roosevelt revoked his endorsement of the American intelligence mission to Draža Mihailović's headquarters.[10]

Contrary to the decision of President Roosevelt, some high-ranking OSS officers still considered sending American agents to the Chetnik headquarters.[11] Maj. Linn Farish was mentioned on July 6, 1944, as a suitable candidate to lead such a mission.[12] On the same day, General Donovan agreed to the proposal that an OSS mission should, after all, be sent to Mihailović in spite of all known objections and doubts. Donovan made an arrangement with General Roderick to entrust this task to Lt. Col. Robert McDowell, who had hitherto been working in the Joint Intelligence Collection Agency, Middle East (JICAME).[13] On July 21, 1944, McDowell flew from Cairo to Caserta in the greatest secrecy.[14] Donovan did not particularly like the idea that the OSS might establish a contact with Chetniks through Konstantin Fotić, former Yugoslav Ambassador in Washington, DC.[15]

The McDowell team was set up in Cairo, and all preparations, including briefings, were supposed to be made outside Bari, Italy. Under no circumstances was the mission to be seen in Bari. Neither the Partisans nor the British, including the Yugoslav royal government in exile should be told anything. "If there are leaks to any of these we face the possibility of jeopardizing our work in Partisan areas, of running into the same blockade which hit us when the mission was proposed before, and of having the whole works royally ruined before it gets into operation."[16]

Robert Joyce, chief of the OSS Secret Intelligence operations in Bari, realized the importance of this decision. He, too, endeavored to keep all preparations for this mission in the greatest secrecy. There would be absolutely no discussions about it with the British. "The sending of a mission to Mihailovich represents a most important political act, a reversal in American policy, and, in a sense, a defiance of British policy in the Balkans," believed Joyce. He anticipated a possible strong, negative reaction of Marshal Tito and suggested that an independent American military mission should first be established with the Supreme Headquarters of the National Liberation Army and Partisan Detachments of Yugoslavia. "The mission to Tito is still the big show and we would do nothing at this point to prejudice its success."[17]

On August 22, 1944, American Ambassador and political adviser at Allied Force Headquarters (AFHQ) Robert D. Murphy and Joyce met in Rome to discuss these problems in detail. Joyce correctly assumed that the arrival of the McDowell mission "would probably be interpreted (and certainly made by Mihailovich to appear) that the United States was providing him with at least moral support in his struggle against the Partisans. In other words, there appeared to be in this sense a definite parting of the ways in British and American policy vis-à-vis Yugoslavia. Murphy admitted that this might be true."[18]

Air Crew Rescue Unit

According to the data gathered and published by Walter Roberts from August 9, 1944, until December 27, 1944, the Americans evacuated 432 American airmen from Chetnik territory and more than 2,000 Allied airmen from the territory under the control of Tito's Partisans.[19] As early as January 1944, the American Maj. Linn Farish and 2d Lt. Eli Popovich had initiated action for the rescue of American aircrews shot down over Yugoslavia. On two occasions, January 23 and March 15, 1944, they discussed this subject with Marshal Tito. "The Marshal fully agreed and issued orders to all units of the Yugoslav People's Army of National Liberation and Partisan Detachments that they were to rescue, by force of arms if necessary, American Airmen forced down over Yugoslavia," they wrote in their report.

The Americans planned and executed similar actions in Chetnik territory at a later date. On October 19, 1943, American 2d Lt. George Musulin parachuted in the vicinity of Mihailović's headquarters, where he subsequently acted as an interpreter. After the Allies had broken all contacts with the Chetniks, Musulin returned to Italy and repeatedly insisted that American representatives be sent to the headquarters of Mihailović with a view to organizing the rescue and evacuation of American airmen.[20]

This plan was enacted only after Ambassador Murphy and Joyce backed it. On July 13, 1944, Ambassador Murphy and American Gen. Ira Eaker met with the Supreme Allied Commander for the Mediterranean theater, British Gen. Henry Maitland Wilson. Brig. Fitzroy Maclean, head of the Anglo-American Allied Mission to Tito, agreed to send to both Marshal Tito and to General Mihailović two American technical teams responsible for the rescue and evacuation of airmen.[21] On July 14, 1944, General Eaker ordered the formation of a special unit, the Air Crew Rescue Unit (ACRU), as a part of the 15th Army Air Force.[22]

At the same time that OSS intelligence officer Nick A. Lalich flew into Chetnik headquarters, Mihailović sent a political mission to Bari aboard an American plane. The arrival of Adam Pribićević, Vladimir Belajčić, and Ivan Kovač caused British consternation. They were accompanied by the Chetnik major, Zvonimir Vučković, one of the principal Chetnik commanders. Such a political-military mission had not been authorized by Allied authorities.[23]

Reaction of Marshal Tito

American intelligence officers racked their brains over the question of whether or how to inform Marshal Tito of the proposed mission codenamed RANGER Unit that was due to leave for the headquarters of Draža Mihailović. During Tito's visit to AFHQ at Caserta, he was invited to lunch with Donovan on the island of Capri, near Naples. Brigadier Maclean was asked to acquaint Marshal Tito with the activities of ACRU. The official record of this conversation reported:

> This team would also continue to act as an intelligence unit. It was in no sense of the word a mission and its activities would be limited to rescue work and intelligence. The Marshal nodded and said it might not be pleasant with Mihailovich and that the names of the personnel had best be given him so his own troops might be advised to protect them in event of trouble (also that he might have full particulars without too much difficulty of course).[24]

Only later did the OSS receive more detailed information from a well-known American journalist of Serbian origin, Stojan Pribićević, who used the code name GAMMA in his reports: "General Donovan, according to Tito, assured the Marshal that no military help would be sent to Mihailovic. Tito told source that he had remarked to General Donovan that, while naturally he could not raise objections to this U.S. step, he thought it maladroit in the present situation."

Tito, as Pribićević wrote, in further discussion "said that even though the American motives for sending a Mission to Mihailovich may be the best-inspired and the most legitimate, they will not be believed: (a) at a time when neither the British nor the Russians have a mission with Mihailovich and when Tito is making a rapprochement with the Royal Government, from which Mihailovich has been dropped, the sending of an American Mission to Mihailovich will be interpreted by both the Partisans and Mihailovich as American last-minute political support of Mihailovich; (b) the public in the U.S. will also assume that the U.S. Government is playing a political game in Yugoslavia. Yet Tito did not seem particularly upset about the matter," considered the American intelligence officer.[25]

On August 29, 1944, on the island of Vis, American officers discussed with Tito the way to organize a secret American intelligence service in Yugoslavia and the manner in which they would cooperate with Yugoslav Partisans in this area. When the head of the mission, Col. Ellery Huntington, Jr., announced his intention to visit Serbia, Tito remarked sarcastically: "This will be an interesting place. Besides you are greatly concerned with Mihailovich since you have a Mission there."[26]

The next day, Colonel Huntington again cautioned his superiors: "It is evident that Marshal Tito is definitely more displeased at OSS liaison with Mihailovich than he ever indicated in his conversations at Caserta."[27]

We know from published British documents[28] that Marshal Tito asked the Supreme Allied Commander in the Mediterranean to convey to the American and British governments his protest against the arrival and activities of the American intelligence mission at the headquarters of Mihailović. At that point, Tito did not yet know that Churchill had, on September 1, 1944, strongly intervened with Roosevelt. "If we each back different sides," Churchill wrote to Roosevelt, "we lay the scene for a fine civil war." American relations with Mihailović bothered the Prime Minister. "General Donovan is running a strong Mihailović lobby, just . . . when many of the Cetniks are being rallied under Tito's National Army of Liberation."[29]

On September 16, Churchill informed Tito that upon his request Roosevelt was recalling the McDowell mission. Churchill complained that the Partisans were using Allied arms and equipment in the fight against Chetniks and that they were dragging their feet over the establishment of a common Yugoslav government.[30]

Harold Macmillan, the British Minister resident in the Mediterranean, informed Foreign Secretary Anthony Eden that Donovan had shown him a document initialed by Roosevelt: "O.K., F.D.R.," which endorsed the sending of the McDowell mission. Macmillan was making the point that there was no sense in reproaching Tito for using Allied arms against "his own countrymen" since the Chetniks collaborated with the Germans. Macmillan pointed out that at Naples Tito had not assumed any obligation to set up a government jointly with Šubašić.[31]

In existing literature, however, there is no mention of the protest Tito sent to the American mission on September 14, 1944, and Soviet backing of his move. Marshal Tito pointed out that the American policy was not in agreement with the positions advocated by Churchill in the House of Commons. Sending an American mission to Mihailović represented an interference in the internal affairs that might result in a civil war.[32]

Tasks and Activities of the McDowell Mission

We have touched upon earlier missions to Yugoslavia, and we have sketched the Allied diplomatic complications relating to the opposing forces in Yugoslavia. Let us now examine in some detail the tasks and activities facing McDowell's mission when it flew into Mihailović's headquarters in late August 1944.

While waiting to enter Yugoslavia, McDowell wrote on June 10 that Robert Joyce was "preparing recommendations to their Washington headquarters that an OSS intelligence mission be established to work with General Mihailovich and other Nationalist Serb leaders. It is expected that such a mission, through Nationalist channels, can establish contacts with groups in Bulgaria, Rumania, and Hungary other than those with which contacts may be established through Partisan channels."[33]

General Donovan informed Col. Edward J. F. Glavin on September 19, 1944, "I was under the impression that McDowell was to go into Austria; he told me that that was what plans called for." He added, "Apart from that, I desire very much to see that he enters Austria. Keep me up to date on him as you receive data from him."[34] Therefore, Col. Joseph Rodrigo of Secret Intelligence (SI) expected McDowell, after his evacuation from Yugoslavia, to be sent to Austria, since Donovan and McDowell had previously discussed this possibility.[35] Lt. Col. Lanning Macfarland was designated as the executive officer in the McDowell mission. Macfarland apparently knew Mihailović personally, and he could substitute for McDowell when the latter would be traveling through territory under Mihailović's control and in other countries. But since it looked as though the mission was cancelled, Macfarland was sent to Slovenia. His reports are still under lock and key.[36]

In the meantime, in Washington President Roosevelt on August 5, 1944, approved the McDowell mission. According to Donovan, Sir Alexander Cadogan, Gen. Henry Maitland Wilson, and the U.S. State Department had also agreed to this plan.[37]

As early as July 8, 1944, Robert Joyce made the suggestion, which was later accepted, that the head of the intelligence mission to the headquarters of Mihailović should have at least the rank of lieutenant colonel and should possibly speak French to be able to speak with Mihailović without an interpreter. An interpreter, a captain born in America, though of Serbian origin, should be attached to the mission. An additional interpreter with the rank of sergeant should also be assigned to the mission. At that time, Robert Joyce considered the Chetniks "a group which is playing and will play a vital role in the post-war organization of Yugoslavia."[38]

McDowell spoke French and German fluently. He was a professor of modern European history at the University of Wisconsin and an expert in Balkan questions. For the past year he had already been active in the joint intelligence collection agency (JICAME). Capt. John R. Milodragovich of SI was the second member of this intelligence team. He had been active in the territory under Chetnik control for the previous 2 months. He spoke Serbian very well and had a smattering of Spanish. Capt. Ellsworth R. Kramer, an SI officer, had been trained in propaganda and intelligence work. Sgt. Michael Rajachich also had served in the Chetnik territory for 2 months and had even studied at the Belgrade University. He spoke not only Serbian but also Slovene. The fifth member of the mission, Michael Devyak, spoke Serbian, had worked in SI, and was responsible for radio links.[39]

The McDowell mission was given the code name RANGER. According to the directives dated August 15, 1944, its task was to cooperate with the ACRU and collect data about the battle disposition of enemy and "nationalist" units, potential Chetnik collaboration with the occupying forces, armed encounters between Chetniks and Partisans, and successful Partisan attempts to win over Chetniks by force or by propaganda. The mission was also supposed to establish contacts with anti-Axis forces in Bulgaria and Hungary and to convey proposals for surrender to Allied forces.

The OSS directive to McDowell further stated: "You will inform General Mihailovich that your present mission is not of a political character and does not represent the Government of the United States except for the purposes of collecting and reporting strategic military and political information for use in the collective effort against the common enemy. You will make it entirely clear to General Mihailovich that you are not authorized to make any political commitment in the name of the United States."[40]

The OSS documents so far accessible do not provide an insight into the manner of establishing contact with the Chetnik headquarters of Draža Mihailović. Some information is available in the published collection of Chetnik documents. In an undated letter, evidently written in August 1944 from Italy, Živko Topalović informed Mihailović that McDowell was coming and advised: "All political questions must be tackled with him since it is only through Americans that it will be possible to effect a change in the Allied political direction."[41]

On August 22, 1944, a committee of experts with the Chetnik headquarters informed Mihailović about the conversations with Lieutenant Musulin, who, they stated, informed them that McDowell was a professor at California University (correctly the University of Wisconsin) and that he had direct access to President Roosevelt. The committee further reported that the Chetniks could expect deliveries of American arms and other materiel and that many people in the United States were turning away from Tito's movement and believed that the British policy was wrong.

Musulin, they said, showed particular interest in the possibility of seizing arms in German possession.[42]

On September 6, 1944, on the strength of reports from his own sources, but contrary to OSS directives, Mihailović informed his subordinate Chetnik commanders that McDowell was given "broad political authorization" and added "Jointly we have drawn up a detailed Allied military and political plan."[43] Jozo Tomasevich, a well-known American historian of Croatian origin, commented on Mihailović's report "as a clear reflection of wishful thinking, not of facts."[44]

The public proclamation of Draža Mihailović was also written in this vein and in this sense. The Partisan Lt. Gen. Koča Popović gave the leaflet with the Chetnik proclamation to the head of the American mission, Colonel Huntington. The leaflet introduced McDowell as "a personal representative of President Roosevelt" who was supposed to have brought personal messages from President Roosevelt and General Maitland Wilson offering "armed help" to the Chetniks.[45] Perhaps it was no coincidence that on the very day, September 14, 1944, when Koča Popović gave the Chetnik leaflet to Huntington, Marshal Tito sent his aforementioned sharp protest to the American mission.

The next day, OSS officer Joyce informed Colonel Huntington that McDowell had brought no messages from President Roosevelt or General Maitland Wilson to Mihailović nor any messages from any other high American officer or official:

McDowell's unit in no sense or form implied "political recognition" of Mihailovich or approval of his activities or policy.

McDowell was not authorized to promise supplies to Mihailovich nor was there any plan to assist him politically or materially.

"The unit sent to nationalist Serbia was in no way an 'American mission' but simply an intelligence [operation] to glean from a strategic area strategic information," advised Joyce, and he requested Colonel Huntington to issue an immediate and most resolute denial of all claims contained in the Chetnik leaflet.[46]

On October 10, 1944, Brig. Fitzroy Maclean informed the Permanent State Under Secretary at the Foreign Office, Sir Orme Sargent: "I gather that the documents recently captured by the First Corps contained evidence that [McDowell] has been going far beyond his instructions in promising Mihailovich Allied support against the Partisans."[47]

McDowell sent his first detailed reports by courier to his base in Bari. Between August 29 and September 2, 1944, he sent six reports regarding administrative problems, military and political events, Chetnik plans for military cooperation and mobilization, armed clashes between Chetniks and Partisans, and military operations.[48]

Mihailović notified McDowell that by September 1, 1944, he would complete mobilization throughout Yugoslavia. He told him that he had under arms 100,000 men and that half a million men had been already mobilized, though they were still unarmed. The Chetnik supreme commander announced that he intended to assume control over northern Serbia up to the Danube and Sava Rivers, but he left out Belgrade and the towns along the main railway lines. He also announced a concentration of his forces near Djerdap on the Danube and along the lower reaches of the Drina. Later, he would attack German garrisons along the railway lines south of Belgrade. Having protected his rear, he would commit all his available forces to attack two concentrations of Partisan units advancing toward Serbia.

"In discussing these plans with me he has limited himself strictly to a Yugoslav point of view, and has not mentioned any possible Allied reaction to his move, whether favorable or unfavorable," reported McDowell, adding:

> If the Parts were to withdraw their troops from Serbia and its borders, I believe there would be a considerable chance for an armistice in the Civil War in order to concentrate all Yugoslav troops against the Germans, the Parts in the West, the Nats in the east.

Mihailović told his American guest about his good relations with "Slovene nationalists." He hoped that he would be able to establish good relations also with the Croatian Domobrans, but only after the German withdrawal. However, he was worried about the attitude of the leader of the Croatian Peasant Party, Dr. Vlatko Maček.

"I feel that the General is convinced that he must follow Yugoslav line as a matter of practical policy, but that he would be perfectly happy to see the Croats go their own way so long as this did not harm Serb interests," reported McDowell.

From McDowell's reports, it is evident that the "Nationalists" hoped that the Bulgarians, too, would join the Yugoslav Federation and that they would reach an agreement about Macedonia. Bulgaria would be given access to the Aegean Sea. These plans provided for Greece to join the Balkan federation, while the Serbs after the war would incline even toward the U.S.S.R. if it would not impose communism on them. McDowell did not observe attempts by the Chetniks to play off the United States against Great Britain. They were even willing to forgive the British for having supported the Partisans if after the war they would not be subjected to Soviet control. They realized that in spite of everything, American political intervention in their favor was not probable, although they would have welcomed it. They expected, however, to receive postwar American loans for the reconstruction and economic development of Yugoslavia.

McDowell did not notice any special Chetnik interest in establishing an independent Serbia, though they stressed the Serbian character of Montenegro and Herzegovina. His interlocutors admitted that the concept of one single nation consisting of Serbs, Croats, and Slovenes had been impractical. McDowell reported:

> With regard to a boundary between Croatia and Serbia, they refuse the Drina of course, and refuse to recognize any reason for an autonomous Bosnia-Hercegovina. They recognize the difficulty caused by the ethnic islands and are willing to recognize the Bosnian Moslems as effectively a separate people who could be given autonomy. In general what they appear to have in mind is not exchange of population so much as a boundary that will leave approximately equal minorities on both sides. They strongly favor the expulsion of all German minorities and the encouragement of settlement in their place by Serbs from Croatia, in so far, that is, as Banat is concerned. There is some suggestion also that Hungarian and Rumanian minorities should be expelled.

Mihailović stressed that he had very good relations with the Albanian Col. Muharem Barjactar and that he had a representative with the Greek Gen. Napoleon Zervas. "I believe the General seriously believes his role is to rally all Balkan Nats to unified action to avoid Sovietization," claimed McDowell. He found that Mihailović was not suffering from a leadership complex and that he was not displaying political ambitions.

McDowell suggested that American special units should fly to Serbia and operate fully independently, taking over the Belgrade airfields. Other American officers and radio operators should be sent to Serbia and Belgrade to collect all the relevant information about the movements of German units and Gestapo activities. An American officer should also be sent to the "Slovene nationalists"—i.e., to the Slovene Domobranci, who were placed under German SS command—if necessary, via the headquarters of Draža Mihailović. The Chetnik leader expected to capture German arms after the withdrawal of Bulgarian troops from Serbia.[49]

The OSS, McDowell, and the Germans

The basic, although extremely meager, facts about McDowell's contact with the Germans are already known. McDowell, in the presence of Mihailović, met twice with the German go-between, Rudi Stärker. They first met early in September 1944 at Pranjani and later at the village of Draginje, near the town of Šabac. After the war, McDowell told Walter Roberts that "Stärker devoted himself mostly to the plea that the U.S. must save Europe from bolshevism through cooperation between Germany and the U.S."[50] McDowell sent exhaustive reports about these contacts to Robert

Joyce through an American military doctor. These reports, however, are not yet available.[51]

As early as September 4, 1944, McDowell sent his report about Stärker's proposals through radio communication links, but he did not mention Stärker's name nor did he describe the circumstances under which he had established contact with him. Jozo Tomasevich, in *War and Revolution in Yugoslavia*, gave the gist of this report. Stärker wanted the Allies to permit German troops to retreat to the Danube and Sava Rivers; the Germans would then fight only against the Russians. McDowell did, in fact, reject this proposal, but he was willing to continue negotiations.[52]

Stärker's proposals were immediately studied at AFHQ. On September 5, 1944, 1 day after the first meeting between McDowell and Stärker, detailed AFHQ instructions were sent to McDowell in case Germany would offer to surrender in the Balkans. The Allies, however, would accept only an unconditional surrender.

According to a more detailed report sent by McDowell on September 8, 1944, Rudi Stärker, during a lengthy discussion "showed hypnotic . . . conviction America will consign Germany and Europe to Communism." In this dispatch, McDowell did not mention the proposal that the United States and Germany should jointly combat bolshevism. "I believe German plan is to give maximum aid Nationalist forces eastern Europe before German capitulation and prepare for future German leadership Europe in anti-communist struggle," concluded McDowell.

Rudi Stärker then announced that Hermann Neubacher, the Auswärtiges Amt plenipotentiary for the southeast, would visit McDowell. Neubacher wanted to come immediately, but he had to postpone the visit because he was invited to Hitler's headquarters.[53]

As far as the German problem is concerned, a factual reconstruction and a historical analysis are still not possible because of incomplete documentation. However, partly declassified records of interrogations of German diplomats and military and intelligence officers conducted after the war by American counterintelligence officers do shed some light on this area. Hermann Neubacher, for instance, preserved the original notes that Rudi Stärker had written during the talks with McDowell. The notes included the following:

1. McDowell wants to speak to NEUBACHER and is even prepared to go to Belgrade for that purpose.
2. Nothing can be discussed which might be construed as contrary to the common interests of all the Allies.
3. He is authorized to discuss Balkan problems.
4. He is ready to talk over any other questions in order to refer them to his government.

5. He is also authorized to use an American plane attached to his mission to send the German participant abroad for further discussions. He is even authorized to send him to the U.S.
6. A special American plenipotentiary may also come over to participate in a very important conversation.
7. He considers NEUBACHER an experienced man and a German realist (praktischen Deutschen). He considers him therefore the man best suited to know how to act at a time when the war seems to be coming to an end.[54]

Neubacher cabled Hitler for agreement to his meeting with McDowell. At first, Joachim von Ribbentrop, the Foreign Minister of the Third Reich, had opposed this meeting, but he later changed his mind and even supported Neubacher's proposal and recommended it to Hitler. After the war, Neubacher told American interrogators that McDowell had intended to prevent the Soviet invasion of the Balkans, to oppose Tito, and to give assistance to the nationalist, i.e., Chetnik, forces. He advocated the view that the most reasonable solution would be for Mihailović to engage all his forces against Tito, since the Germans had to leave Serbia anyway.

Neubacher's interrogator noted:

> During the last stages of the battle for Serbia MCDOWELL advised Mihailovich to get as much equipment as possible from the Germans. MCDOWELL himself was unable to support the Chetniks with equipment after the TEHRAN conference. His very presence had nevertheless, according to Neubacher, been manna in the wilderness for the morale of all Serbian collaborationist groups (MIHAILOVICH, LJOTIC, and NEDIC).[55]

According to Dr. Wilhelm Höttl, Rudi Stärker visited Mihailović for the last time in March 1945, and the Chetnik commander complained that the Germans were not sending him sufficient supplies.[56]

The German security service (SD), at the close of the war, maintained two radio links with Mihailović in Yugoslavia. The first link was directly at the headquarters of Mihailović, while the other channel was kept open by the Germans through a transmitting and receiving station north of Sarajevo. "The link to D. M. was politically conditioned and primarily served the purpose of enabling him to make his supply requirements to the German Government."[57]

Dr. Wilhelm Höttl, when being interrogated about his former boss, Walter Schellenberg, stated:

> STAERKER had worked for years for NEUBACHER in the Balkans and had the closest connexions with British and American agencies. I assume that he also worked for them in intelligence. . . . His last activity was the establishment of contact with Drazha MIHAI-

LOVICH, and with British and American missions with him. He also set up contact with MIHAILOVICH for me, and I retained it by W/ T till German collapse. I last saw STAERKER at the end of March 1945 in Vienna, and arranged to meet him at the beginning of April in Switzerland, where he would set up contact for me with his American connexions. But I did not meet him, and so do not know whether he travelled before or after me.[58]

The American investigators, however, felt that Neubacher, during interrogation, did not reveal all the facts about his connections with McDowell. In fact, Neubacher was always very loquacious, but when he was interrogated about his contacts with McDowell, he became very circumspect and reticent, weighing every word he uttered.[59]

General Donovan was informed on September 18, 1944, about the second meeting between McDowell and Stärker. Neubacher had just returned from Hitler's headquarters and wanted "to talk also about German surrender." McDowell sent a report on this initiative as early as September 17, 1944. His retransmitted report was paraphrased as follows:

A. Neubacher wants to negotiate regarding total surrender by Germany, but alleges it is hard to find a liberal group within Germany competent to confer on same with the Allies or to undertake administrative tasks delegated by the Allies.

B. He is anxious to have the Allies prepare troops to be ready to occupy Germany when capitulation comes.

C. Hungary is on the brink of an internal explosion, Neubacher avers, and there is serious trouble of anarchy.

D. The Huns are keeping northern Yugoslavia only for the purpose of postponing the Hungarian explosion, which would set off trouble inside Germany.

E. Their chief aim is to forestall anarchy in surrounding regions which might spread into Germany.

F. At night on the road through Nis and Smederevo the Huns are sending troops from Greece to try to hold the East to West the Sava line, and the lines in Hungary marked by the rivers flowing south to the Danube.

G. All north Yugoslavia is being evacuated by the Gestapo.

McDowell had this to say concerning the above:

A. Thinks Neubacher honestly striving for unconditional surrender at once.

B. Is ignorant of the size of the group behind Neubacher.

C. Thinks Huns would allow Allied entry if Trieste—or Fiume-Belgrade line were held by armies other than Russian.

D. Thinks fear that the Allies would allow Germany to remain in chaos for some time is the sole obstacle to total surrender by Germany.

E. Recommends that State [Department] send a representative in.[60]

General Donovan was asked to advise the State Department about all these events. However, as early as September 18, McDowell received a firm and clear instruction:

In view of order to return, do not go to Belgrade nor take initiative in peace negotiations or any other activities but continue to furnish intelligence reports pending evacuation.[61]

Bradley F. Smith and Elena Agarossi have already mentioned this episode in *Operation Sunrise*. They added that an almost simultaneous suggestion was made by Glaise von Horstenau, the German commanding general in Croatia. The former Austrian officers would open the front line and would allow the Western Allies to break through unopposed. Thus, the American and British troops, and not the Russian troops, would occupy Austria.[62] It should be noted that the head of the Allied mission in Styria (Cuckold), American Maj. Franklin Lindsay, was about to be urgently transferred to the vicinity of Zagreb with a view to establishing personal contact with the German commander in the city.[63] McDowell, upon his return to Italy early in November 1944, proposed to his superiors "the possibility of securing the surrender of Germans in Yugoslavia through special Anglo-U.S. mission."[64]

At any rate, McDowell had not been sent on an errand blindfolded. The OSS, even before his departure for Mihailović's headquarters, had received reliable information in London that Mihailović was collaborating with the Germans and that he was trying to get German arms for the final showdown with Tito.[65] After the war, American counterintelligence officials secured evidence that Germany had provided the Chetniks with arms and medical supplies.[66] The task of Neubacher's office was, among other things, to get Mihailović's backing and thwart Communist elements in the Balkans.[67]

Robert McDowell, both in his radio dispatches as well as in his concluding report, insisted that "he saw no evidence of collaboration between Serb Nationalists and enemy."

Americans in the field appeared to support McDowell's views in their reports. Captain Milodragovich and Sergeant Rajachich went further and claimed that "Serb Nationalists were active in attacking enemy," while "Partisan forces avoided attacking Germans to concentrate and attack Mihailovich Serbs." They also claimed that "Serbian Nationalist movement has support of vast majority of people in Serbia proper, Herzegovina and southern Bosnia. These conclusions, based on personal observation, are entirely opposed to British intelligence reports on conditions in Serbia."[68] German radio broadcast McDowell's statement that there was no collaboration between Mihailović and the Germans, and all this was duly recorded by the British service monitoring radio broadcasts. Also attributed to McDowell by the German radio broadcast was the statement purporting that the United States would supply Mihailović on the basis of the Lend-Lease Act. OSS officers in Cairo did not know whether the reports were true or simply a British plant.[69] They did not consider that the German broadcast could be disinformation. Donovan requested that McDowell personally comment on this information. The OSS Director advised McDowell to take every precaution in his actions and statements lest they be used against him and the United States. McDowell denied making any such statements but admitted mentioning the economic aid on a nonpolitical basis.[70]

Recall and Evacuation of the McDowell Mission

On September 3, 1944, President Roosevelt, at Churchill's urging, decided to recall the American intelligence mission. At that time, General Donovan was not in the United States. In the memorandum of September 11, 1944, Donovan stressed again that there was an urgent need for independent American intelligence data "on the highly equivocal question of alleged Chetnik collaboration with the Germans." An intelligence OSS group had already left Mihailović's territory for Austria, and other groups were ready for departure. No further details were revealed.

Donovan also referred to the letter of Ambassador Murphy dated July 1, 1944, to the effect that "the lives of American airmen and the military advantage gained by their recovery overrides any objection the British might have on political grounds." When Brigadier Maclean went to Serbia, OSS headquarters interpreted it as going "into the Mihailovich area" and used it as evidence of "inconsistent action by the British," who had taken offense at the American decision to send intelligence officers to the headquarters of Mihailović.[71]

Donovan even assumed that Churchill had intervened with Roosevelt because political representatives of Mihailović had arrived in Italy in the company of American airmen. Only on September 13, 10 days later, did Donovan send to Bari Roosevelt's order to recall the mission.[72]

Even though Mihailović did try to make political capital of the arrival of the American mission, high-ranking OSS officers in Bari believed that President Roosevelt's recall decision was based on wrong or incomplete information. OSS Bari defended the Yugoslav operation. "McDowell has sent us intelligence reports of great value and the loss of this source of military, economic, and political intelligence at this particular time is very much to be regretted."[73]

McDowell answered on September 16, saying that he would obey the order for recall, though with the deepest regret, and he would advise Captain Kramer about the arrival of the plane. On September 20, Lt. Comdr. Edward Green gave encouragement to McDowell and asked about his movements at that moment. All the dispatches regarding this matter, however, are not yet accessible to researchers. McDowell, on September 29, reported on activities of the SS units, the Ustashi, and the Partisans and claimed that owing to incessant rains, evacuation by plane from eastern Bosnia was not possible. Captain Kramer was still delayed in eastern Serbia, and McDowell intended to break through in the direction of the Adriatic coast.[74]

There were numerous discussions of an eventual evacuation of Draža Mihailović. Late in October 1944, it was generally rumored in Dubrovnik that McDowell had refused to obey the order of evacuation, that the White House was sending him secret orders without intermediaries, and that the OSS had already brought Mihailović over to Italy.[75] However, as early as September 1944, the OSS unequivocally and firmly stated that it would assume no responsibility at all for the fate of Draža Mihailović. Even had higher American military or political authorities ordered the evacuation of Mihailović, British agreement would have been necessary.[76] "On this matter, we ought not to hold the bag nor should we let it appear that the U.S. stuck with Mihailović through to the finish," reasoned Robert Joyce.[77]

On October 26, 1944, McDowell sent the following message: "The General and the ACRU unit will go north today to come out themselves." He asked for American planes to land during daylight under protection of Allied fighters.[78] Maj. Charles Thayer, political adviser and later head of the American Mission in Belgrade, reported from Belgrade that the rumors about joint evacuation of Mihailović and McDowell had also reached Marshal Tito. He did everything in his power to prevent the spread of such rumors.[79]

Already, on October 9, the OSS base in Bari had suggested to McDowell to reach the first Partisan unit or Partisan landing strip and arrange this matter with Mihailović. McDowell again delayed his reply, but 2 days later he rejected this suggestion as very dangerous and impossible. In the end, McDowell was evacuated on November 1, 1944, almost 2 months after Roosevelt's decision to recall the mission. He took off in a plane from an airstrip hastily prepared by the Chetniks near Doboj.[80]

Robert McDowell's Final Report

Robert McDowell, on the very day when he received the order to evacuate (September 15, 1944), sent his political report (GB-1540):

1. Soviet entry into Serbia would be taken by the Nationalists and Mihailovich as proof that the Allies intend to allow Russian influence in Serbia after the War.

2. Delegates were sent by Mihailovich to the border to meet the Russians and to try to reach an understanding in case the latter enter Serbia.

3. There is nothing to show that Serbians are joining the Partisans.

4. The Nationalists are not working together with the Axis; only the Nationalists are attacked by the Partisans. The Partisans' principal enemy in Montenegro, according to another source in our GB-1543, are Chetniks.[81]

Hitherto, we have learned nothing about political reports or appraisals that McDowell wrote or sent in the next month and a half until his evacuation. After his return to Italy, McDowell, on November 7, 1944, hinted in a dispatch to General Donovan that within 5 days he would have his concluding report ready. In advance, he stressed the following basic conclusions: The actual leaders of Chetnik resistance in Serbia and Bosnia were local leaders rather than Mihailović himself, and they were much better armed and more disciplined than the Chetniks under the direct command of Mihailović. Though the Partisans would probably win a civil war, guerrilla warfare would continue at least for 2 years after the war unless the Allies occupied all of Yugoslavia. McDowell further warned:

> To entrust Yugoslav Government to Tito is to ensure civil war. The local leaders and masses among both Partisans and Nationalists will quickly agree and unite if the Allies will cease all support of the small communist group on one side and the small reactionary on the other.[82]

On his part, American Capt. Nick Lalich, in his report written upon his return to Italy, explained that he had been personally at the Mihailović's headquarters when the Chetnik commander decided to rename his subordinate Chetniks into Nationalists. He wanted to differentiate them from Chetnik organizations under Fascist control and command.

> Mihailovich objected to the Partisan plan to partition Serbia. He wants to remain as one unit and any other section populated by Serbs (as Lika) should form a separate unit within federated Yugoslavia. It would be an injustice, according to the General, for any large group of Serbs to be under Croatia.[83]

McDowell retired to his OSS villa on the island of Capri in the Bay of Naples. While he was writing his concluding report, the various rumors circulated in Caserta and Bari about his real or presumed activities at Mihailović's headquarters. It was said that McDowell had supported the struggle of "Nationalists," i.e., the struggle of Chetniks against the Partisans, and that he had discredited or at least underestimated the Partisan struggle against the Nazis. McDowell angrily requested all such rumors to be carefully recorded so that he could demand an official military inquiry at a later date.[84] The British Foreign Office was also interested in McDowell's concluding report. Harold Macmillan asked for at least a précis of this report. His representative in Bari, Philip Broad, stated that the report was needed for debate in the House of Commons. High-ranking OSS officers in Italy felt that political consultations of the American Ambassadors with the British and the Royal Yugoslav governments were urgently required:

> An airing of material from this report as American or in any way representing American policy or viewpoint might have very serious repercussions on our relations with the Tito regime and perhaps with the Russians as well.[85]

General Donovan therefore issued the order:

> The McDowell report will be forwarded to me directly here. All other copies will be held by Joyce as OSS property and disclosed to no one until so directed by me. As a matter of security and for McDowell's own protection from attack, he will deliver all copies to Joyce, retaining none for himself. I intend that this material will be made available to us only until after I have submitted it to the State Department and have obtained clearance from the Secretary of State.[86]

Jozo Tomasevich, in his book about the Chetniks, summed up the main recommendations in McDowell's concluding report as McDowell himself had revealed them to him during a conversation in 1968.[87] If we compare these recommendations with the proposals or requests made by Mihailović and the executive council of the Chetnik Central National Committee, dated September 18, 1944 (which were reported 3 days later through radio links by McDowell),[88] it is easy to establish a great similarity. In short, McDowell accepted the Chetnik requests in his concluding report in a somewhat changed form and presented them as his own recommendations.

Mihailović, in his first point, demanded that "the American Union take all the necessary steps to stop and prevent the continuation of civil war in Yugoslavia." The first proposal put forward by McDowell was for the Allies to order both Nationalist and Partisan leaders that "civil war and all acts of organized violence must cease immediately; that failure to comply will ensure withdrawal of Allied support—military, economic, and political—from that group."

As we know, as far back as early 1944, the Allies had stopped supplying Chetniks. McDowell was obviously suggesting stopping Allied aid to the Partisans.

Mihailović's second proposal provided for "the American Army to set up a command for Yugoslavia, while we agree to subordinate ourselves with all our forces to such a command." McDowell advanced the proposal that Allied missions be sent to all the provincial centers in Yugoslavia "charged with the duty of establishing temporary zones of local administration, recognizing temporarily in each area the local group now exercising the power of administration."

The third of Mihailović's proposals was formulated as follows:

> We ask for an immediate cessation of sending supplies of arms and ammunition to communists and for the stopping of propaganda which is unjustifiably favorable to them.

This idea is partially present in the first of McDowell's proposals.

The fourth of the Chetnik proposals stated: "We agree to the holding of a plebiscite among nationalist and communist forces throughout the country, when the newly established command of the American Army has introduced order. Thereafter a system is to be set up as the people will decide."

The third point of McDowell's recommendations presented this idea in the following manner:

> The undersigned recommends that a provisional National Government be set up on the following basis: One third of the members to be nominated by partisan authorities, one third by Nationalist authorities, and one third by the Allies from among Yugoslav personalities. The duties of this provisional government would be: (1) to accept the dissolution of the present Partisan and Nationalist armies and incorporate them in a Yugoslav Army which would be placed under Allied command for use against Germans; (2) set up the machinery for elections for a National Convention which would determine the future political organization of Yugoslavia. Failure of any group to carry out this program would insure withdrawal of Allied support from that group.[89]

Jozo Tomasevich remarked, "One can imagine the reaction to these recommendations among the British authorities and among the American authorities who supported British policy in Yugoslavia." He then made the following point, "In other words, the recommendations could hardly have been taken seriously."[90] We know now that these recommendations remained under seven seals even inside the American military intelligence apparatus.

Robert McDowell's final 39-page report, "Yugoslavia: An Examination of Yugoslav Nationalism," has recently been published.[91] There is no point in providing more elaboration on the final report beyond what I have just provided. An agreement about intelligence cooperation between the Allies and Yugoslav Partisans was reached only after the visit of SACMED Field Marshal Harold Alexander to Belgrade from February 22 to 24, 1945.[92] Nothing is yet known or published about the activities of Robert McDowell after his return from Yugoslavia. Was he ever sent to Austria or Slovenia as he had announced to Hermann Neubacher?[93]

NOTES

1. Arthur Cox: Report on Field Conditions, June 23, 1945, File 140, Box 28, Entry 99, Records of the Office of Strategic Services, Record Group 226, National Archives and Records Administration, Washington, DC (hereinafter cited as RG 226, NA).
2. F. H. Hinsley et al., *British Intelligence in the Second World War*, vol. 3, *Its Influence on Strategy and Operations*, part I (London, 1984), pp. 137–172; Jozo Tomasevich, *War and Revolution in Yugoslavia: The Chetniks* (Stanford, CA, 1975), pp. 359–372.
3. J. E. Toulmin to W. Donovan, Mar. 1, 1944, File 45, Box 6, Entry 116, RG 226, NA.
4. Memorandum, Donovan, Mar. 4, 1944, B 23007-14, Geographical Files 1942–1945, Box 736, Records of the U.S. Joint Chiefs of Staff, RG 218, NA.
5. F. D. Roosevelt to Donovan, Mar. 22, 1944, B 30912-13, ibid.
6. Mar. 1, 1944, B 23012-14, ibid.
7. Donovan to D. Eisenhower, Mar. 31, 1944, File 45, Box 6, Entry 116, RG 226, NA.
8. Memorandum, Donovan, Mar. 14, 1944, B 26030, U.S. Joint Chiefs of Staff, Geographical Files 1942–1945, Box 736, RG 218, NA.
9. Warren F. Kimball, ed., *Churchill & Roosevelt: The Complete Correspondence*, vol. 3 (Princeton, NJ, 1984), p. 80.
10. Ibid., p. 82; Walter Roberts, *Tito, Mihailovich and the Allies, 1941–1945* (New Brunswick, NJ, 1973), pp. 255–256; Tomasevich, *War and Revolution*, p. 376.
11. CASERTA-OSS-OP-1, G. E. Buxton to Algiers, Apr. 13, 1944; Intelligence Notes, Bari, SBS, May 4, 1944, File 1, Box 88, Entry 190, RG 226, NA.
12. CASERTA-OSS-OP-48, J. E. Green to Gamble, July 6, 1944, File 456, Box 120, Entry 190, RG 226, NA.
13. File 428, Box 120, Entry 190; CASERTA-OSS-R&C-2, Toulmin to Green, July 7, 1944, File Air, Box 76, Entry 121, RG 226, NA.
14. Toulmin to Green, July 21, 1944, File 360, Box 33, Entry 136, RG 226, NA.
15. Donovan to Toulmin and Green, July 19, 1944, File 233, Box 22, Entry 136, RG 226, NA.
16. BARI-SI-OP-18, SI Yugoslav Section, File 263, Box 19, Entry 154, RG 226, NA. See also S. B. Penrose to Green, July 11, 1944, File 360, Box 33, Entry 136, RG 226, NA.
17. BARI-SI-OP-20, SI Yugoslav Section, File 195, Box 14, Entry 154, RG 226, NA.
18. BARI-SI-OP-5, Political, R. P. Joyce to Toulmin, Aug. 25, 1944, File 176, Box 13, Entry 154, and BARI-SI-OP-20, SI Yugoslav Section, File 189, Box 14, Entry 154, RG 226, NA.
19. Roberts, *Tito, Mihailovich and the Allies*, p. 282.
20. Washington History Office, OP-23, M.D.T.O. 2677 Regiment, September 1944, File 106, Box 20, Entry 99, RG 226, NA.

21. Robert Joyce, Report for period 1 July–15 July inclusive, July 17, 1944, File 104, Box 20, Entry 99, RG 226, NA.

22. Independent American Military Mission to Marshal Tito, File 321, Box 23, Entry 154, RG 226, NA.

23. R. Joyce to Toulmin and Green, Aug. 15, 1944, File 174, Box 34, Entry 99, RG 226, NA.

24. BARI-SI-OP-PRO-1, Huntington Mission, File 289, Box 21, Entry 154; memorandum, E. C. Huntington, Aug. 11, 1944, File 176, Box 25, Entry 99, RG 226, NA.

25. YU-1550, Foreign Nationalities Branch, New York, File 23, Box 106, Entry 154, RG 226, NA.

26. BARI-SI-OP-PRO-1, Huntington Mission; memorandum, Huntington to Tito, Donovan, E. Glavin, Aug. 29, 1944, File 289, Box 21, Entry 154, RG 226, NA.

27. BARI-SI-OP-32, Independent American Military Mission to Marshal Tito; Huntington to Donovan, Aug. 31, 1944, File 321, Box 23, Entry 154, RG 226, NA.

28. Dušan Biber, ed., *Tito–Churchill, strogo tajno* (Zagreb, 1981), pp. 307–308, 313–316, 325.

29. Kimball, ed., *Churchill & Roosevelt*, vol. 3, p. 306.

30. Biber, ed., *Tito–Churchill*, pp. 314–315.

31. Ibid., p. 325.

32. Enclosure No. 3, despatch no. 783, Sept. 25, 1944, Box 44, Records of the Foreign Service Posts of the Department of State, RG 84, NA.

33. L 38843, RG 226, NA.

34. Donovan to Glavin, Sept. 19, 1944, File 295, Box 28, Entry 136, RG 226, NA.

35. Rodrigo to Green, Sept. 23, 1944, Files 391 and 219, Boxes 34 and 21, Entry 136, RG 226, NA.

36. Toulmin to Glavin, Aug. 20, 1944, File 219, Box 21, Entry 136, RG 226, NA.

37. Donovan to Glavin, Sept. 19, 1944, ibid.

38. BARI-SI-OP-20, Yugoslav Section, File 195, Box 14, Entry 154, RG 226, NA.

39. BARI-SI-OP-20, Yugoslav Section, Personnel, File 190, Box 14, Entry 154, RG 226, NA.

40. Washington History Office, OP-23, M.D.T.O., Yugoslavia, Independent American Military Mission to Marshal Tito, 1944–1945, Order by Lt. Comdr. Edward J. Green, Aug. 15, 1944, File 176, Box 35, Entry 99, RG 226, NA.

41. *Zbornik dokumenta i podataka o narodnooslobodilackom ratu naroda Jugoslavie*, XIV, 4, (Belgrade, 1985), p. 185.

42. Ibid., pp. 146–149.

43. Ibid., p. 397.

44. Tomasevich, *War and Revolution*, p. 380, n. 56.

45. CASERTA-OSS-OP-1, File 4, Box 88, Entry 190, RG 226, NA.

46. R. Joyce to Huntington, Sept. 15, 1944, File 216, Box 26, Entry 136, RG 226, NA.

47. Biber, ed., *Tito–Churchill*, p. 340.

48. BARI-SI-PRO-25, Ranger Team, McDowell's reports Nos. 1–6, Aug. 29–Sept. 2, 1944, File 314, Box 23, Entry 154, RG 226, NA.

49. Ibid.

50. Roberts, *Tito, Mihailovich and the Allies*, p. 279.

51. Washington History Office, OP-23, M.D.T.O., 2677 Regiment, September 1944, File 106, Box 20, Entry 99, RG 226, NA.

52. BARI-SI-PRO-32, Independent American Military Mission to Marshal Tito, November 1–15, 1944, File 325, Box 24, Entry 154, RG 226, NA. See also Tomasevich, *War and Revolution*, p. 383.

53. Ibid.

54. WASH-REG-INT-175, XX 10890, CI-IIR No. 36, Jan. 29, 1946, pp. 30–35, File 330, Box 60, Entry 109, RG 226, NA.

55. Ibid.

56. WASH-REG-INT-174, Situation Report Jugoslavia (1938–1945), Dr. Wilhelm Höttl, XX 10269, File 294, Box 52, Entry 109, RG 226, NA.

57. WASH-REG-INT-74, XX 7619, File 160, Box 28, Entry 109, RG 226, NA.

58. WASH-REG-INT-174, notes by Dr. Wilhelm Höttl on Schelenberg interrogation report, File 29, Box 51, Entry 109, RG 226, NA.

59. WASH-REG-INT-175, XX 10890, CI-IIR, No. 36, Jan. 29, 1946, pp. 10–11, 30–33, File 330, Box 60, Entry 109, RG 226, NA.

60. Green to Donovan, Sept. 18, 1944, File 353, Box 32, Entry 136, RG 226, NA.

61. BARI-SI-PRO-32, Independent American Military Mission to Marshal Tito, November 1–15, 1944, File 325, Box 24, Entry 154, RG 226, NA. See also Tomasevich, *War and Revolution*, p. 383.

62. Bradley F. Smith and Elena Agarossi, *Operation Sunrise: The Secret Surrender* (New York, 1979), pp. 55–56.

63. BARI-SI-OP-R&C-9, Suker to Huntington, Oct. 29, 1944, File 454, Box 40, Entry 136, RG 226, NA.

64. CASERTA-OSS-OP-4, McDowell to Donovan, Nov. 7, 1944, File 122, Box 97, Entry 190, RG 226, NA.

65. BARI-SI-PRO-1, London relay No. 18054, Aug. 23, 1944, File 289, Box 21, Entry 154; and File 233, Box 22, Entry 136, RG 226, NA.

66. WASH-REG-INT-175, CI-CIR/13, Jan. 31, 1946, p. 4, File 335, Box 60, Entry 109, RG 226, NA.

67. WASH-REG-INT-174, XX 10269, CIR, No. 3, June 21, 1945, pp. 9–10, File 170, Box 30, Entry 109, RG 226, NA.

68. BARI-SI-OP-R&C-6, Glavin and Joyce to Donovan, Dec. 2, 1944, File 424, Box 37, Entry 136, RG 226, NA.

69. BARI-SI-OP-R&C-6, Cairo to Caserta, No. 139, Oct. 11, 1944, File 422, Box 37, Entry 136, RG 226, NA.

70. Joyce and Glavin to McDowell, Oct. 21, 1944, File 447, Box 40; BARI-SI-OP-R&C-6, Joyce to Washington, No. 985, File 424, Box 37, Entry 136, RG 226, NA.

71. Donovan to Glavin, Sept. 19, 1944, File 219, Box 21, Entry 136, RG 226, NA.

72. Donovan to Green and Toulmin, Sept. 13, 1944, File 310, Box 30, Entry 136, RG 226, NA.

73. Green to Donovan, Sept. 15, 1944, File 340, Box 30, Entry 136, RG 226, NA.

74. BARI-SI-PRO-32, Independent American Military Mission to Marshal Tito, November 1–15, 1944, File 325, Entry 154, RG 226, NA. See also Tomasevich, *War and Revolution*, p. 383.

75. BARI-SI-OP-R&C-9, R. Deane to O. Suker, Oct. 28, 1944, File 447, Box 40, Entry 136, RG 226, NA.

76. Maddox to Joyce, Sept. 20, 1944, File 257, Box 25, Entry 136, RG 226, NA.
77. Joyce to Glavin and Maddox, Sept. 16, 1944, ibid.
78. BARI-SI-OP-R&C-9, McDowell to Caserta, No. 1169, Oct. 26, 1944, File 446, Box 40, Entry 136, RG 226, NA.
79. CASERTA-OSS-OP-4, Joyce and Glavin to Donovan, Nov. 7, 1944, File 122, Box 97, Entry 190, RG 226, NA.
80. BARI-SI-PRO-32, Independent American Military Mission to Marshal Tito, Nov. 1–15, 1944, File 325, Entry 154, RG 226, NA. See also Roberts, *Tito, Mihailovich and the Allies*, p. 279.
81. Joyce and Mitchel to Donovan, Sept. 16, 1944, File 295, Box 28, and File 353, Box 32, Entry 136, RG 226, NA.
82. CASERTA-OSS-OP-4, McDowell to Donovan, Nov. 7, 1944, File 122, Box 97, Entry 190, RG 226, NA.
83. CASERTA-OSS-OP-46, A-49464 (32230-100B, Jan. 10, 1945), File 340, Box 111, Entry 190, RG 226, NA.
84. CASERTA-OSS-OP-14, Maddox to Donovan, Nov. 23, 1944, File 122, Box 97, Entry 190, RG 226, NA.
85. CASERTA-OSS-OP-14, Glavin, Rodrigo, and Joyce to Donovan and Bruce, ibid.
86. Glavin and Joyce to McDowell, No. 320, Donovan's directive, Dec. 1, 1944, ibid.
87. Tomasevich, *War and Revolution*, pp. 383–384.
88. *Zbornik*, XIV, 4, pp. 303–306; BARI-SO-PRO-34, GB-1677, File 333, Box 25, Entry 154, RG 226, NA.
89. MEDTO-YUG (Mihailovich's Field Report, 1944), pp. 38–39, File 174, Box 34, Entry 99, RG 226, NA.
90. Tomasevich, *War and Revolution*, p. 384.
91. David Martin, *The Web of Disinformation* (New York, 1990), pp. 378–411.
92. Biber, ed., *Tito–Churchill*, pp. 475–476, 480–481.
93. WASH-REG-INT-175, XX 10890, CI-IIR, No. 36, Jan. 29, 1946, p. 32, File 330, Box 60, Entry 109, RG 226, NA.

ARTIFICE: James Angleton and X-2 Operations In Italy

Timothy J. Naftali

In the summer of 1943, as Allied forces reached Italian soil, U.S. Army counterintelligence warned GIs, "You are no longer in Kansas City, San Francisco, or Ada, Oklahoma, but in a European country where espionage has been second nature to the population for centuries."[1]

One soldier who did not need this warning was James J. Angleton, a 26-year-old second lieutenant in the Office of Strategic Services (OSS), whose code name was ARTIFICE. Not only had the young man spent the better part of his adolescence in Italy, but in the year since he had joined X-2, the counterespionage branch of the OSS, Angleton had picked up a precocious mastery of the discipline, earning the respect of his British mentors and his American superiors.

When Angleton first arrived in Italy, the administrative head of all OSS counterespionage in that country cabled the X-2 office in London: "Air much clearer."[2] Enthusiasm greeted Angleton's assignment to the field as it seemed to portend an improvement in the condition of X-2's local operations. In early October 1944, X-2's operational headquarters in London had received a series of signals from which Angleton's superiors concluded that the 17-man X-2 Rome unit needed a firm hand.[3] Unlike the military, which would not reach its next target city, Bologna, for another 5 months, Allied counterespionage was not in a holding pattern in Italy in the fall of 1944, and X-2's responsibilities were expanding.[4] The area under Allied occupation had still to be rid of German informants left behind by the Sicherheitsdienst and the Militarisches Amt when they fled north.[5] In addition, the counterespionage services bore the burden of identifying, catching, and interrogating the linecrossers that the German military was

Mr. Naftali is a National Security Fellow at the John M. Olin Institute For Strategic Studies, Center For International Affairs, Harvard University.
This paper is dedicated to the memory of Taylor J. Naftali-Saliba.

pushing across no man's land to collect order of battle information.[6] Amid the pressure for more and better information about German spies, the OSS's Italian counterespionage detachment had suffered a crisis of confidence and was losing the respect of other counterespionage services.[7] London wanted Angleton to turn the Rome unit around in 6 weeks so that X-2 could handle the enemy intelligence agents south of the Po Valley and then be able to do its part when it came time to liberate northern Italy.[8]

Nearly half a century later it may seem difficult to understand why the now legendary James Angleton inspired not only the trust of men many years his senior but was viewed as a source of wisdom by those around him. With a very few notable exceptions, the current image of James Angleton is that of a rigid, overrated, ideological menace.[9] Yet the operational files from his Italian posting, which are now in the National Archives, reveal a different man and leave little doubt as to why he was called to the field in 1944.

Angleton proved an adept field operative. The mission that was only supposed to take 6 weeks lasted 3 years. In the last year of the war, Angleton rose from chief of the X-2 unit in Rome to chief of all OSS counterespionage in Italy. By the age of 28, as bureaucratic initials and superiors were changing in Washington, he became chief of all secret activity, intelligence and counterintelligence, in Italy for the Strategic Services Unit (SSU), the successor of the OSS.[10] Although field promotions are not always dependable indicators of operational success, Angleton's rise to the top of all American secret activity in Italy paralleled a remarkable expansion of U.S. counterespionage capabilities in that strategically important country. By the end of 1946, Angleton, or those directly responsible to him, had amassed over 50 informants and had penetrated 7 foreign intelligence services, including Tito's OTSEK ZASCITA NARODA (OZNA), the French Service de Documentation Extérieure et de Contre-Espionage (SDECE), and the Italian Naval Intelligence Service, the Servizio Informazione Segreta (SIS).[11] Concurrently, through liaison channels, Angleton was receiving regular reports from various Italian intelligence services that included intercepts of foreign agent radio traffic and information about Soviet and Yugoslav intelligence ciphers.[12]

In this paper, we will review four representative operations to illustrate and evaluate Angleton's activities in Italy. As will be demonstrated, a general study of these operations delimits the contours of a consistent approach to counterespionage.* Also discernible in these operations is An-

---

*Counterespionage and counterintelligence are not synonymous. Counterespionage is a subset of counterintelligence. It refers solely to operations against or information about foreign spies; whereas counterintelligence includes information regarding all manner of foreign efforts to obtain national secrets—spy satellites, radio interception, etc.—and action designed to defeat those efforts. The terms were

gleton's understanding of the role of counterespionage in defending U.S. interests. A study of his Italian career therefore serves not only as a primer on what the OSS and the SSU achieved in counterespionage in Italy but also as an introduction to the world view. and professional skills of the man who would come to dominate American counterespionage for a generation.

Angleton's approach can be best understood as the implementation of what might be called "Total Counterespionage." The young Angleton was a political Realist.[13] He assumed that all governments have secrets that other governments want. The nature of a particular government influenced its capacity though not its desire to spy. When Angleton asked why a country spied, he did so not in search of moral justification but because countries often betray intentions in what they spy for.[14] The agnosticism of his view of the threat supported a broad view of the means necessary to protect U.S. interests. He believed that a counterespionage service had to have an insatiable appetite for information about foreign activities so as to be in a position to restrict, eliminate, or control the ways by which other states collected their intelligence.

The operations chosen represent the principal sources of counterespionage, as a form of information and as a type of activity, available to Angleton in the years 1944–46. The first involves Angleton's exploitation of UL-TRA-class intelligence. In other words, how he made best use of the fact that he could read many of the radio messages of his adversaries in the German Intelligence Services. The second is the SALTY case. SALTY, aka Capitano di Fregata Carlo Resio, was the pivot of Angleton's broad-based liaison with the Italian Naval Intelligence Service. The SALTY case illustrates how Angleton used cooperation with other services to expand his knowledge of foreign intelligence activities. The third is an example of a successful penetration operation that involved another Italian naval officer, whom we shall call SAILOR. And, finally, a second look will be taken at the notorious Vatican case, VESSEL or DUSTY, which was also a penetration operation but one that failed.

Before turning to these operations, it is useful to note that the end of the Second World War divided Angleton's career in Italy in two. Until August 1945, most of Angleton's operations were the extension of a program of military security.[15] As experts in the personnel and methods of the enemy, X-2 officers assisted the more numerous and larger units of the U.S. Army's Counterintelligence Corps in locating and neutralizing Ger-

occasionally confused during the Second World War because the U.S. Army did not make any distinction between the two functions, insisting instead on calling all activities directed against the German intelligence services, counterintelligence. "Outline of American Counter-Intelligence, Counter-Espionage & Security Activities, World War II," [1946], Wooden File, Box 2, Norman Holmes Pearson Collection, the Beinecke Rare Book and Manuscript Library, Yale University.

man and Italian Fascist agents. X-2 officers were in a position to direct aspects of the Army's security program because of their access to a more extensive archive of counterespionage information. In addition, X-2 case officers had received instruction in the arts of doubling and controlling enemy agents, skills that Army counterintelligence officers did not have. When the Army picked up an agent, an X-2 officer was called in to assess the agent's potential as a double agent. If the results of the review were affirmative, the X-2 branch assumed responsibility for the agent. Yet even in these double agent cases, security considerations predominated, and X-2 officers operated with the elimination of the foreign service as their goal.[16]

After the war, Angleton's concern became almost entirely "long-range counterespionage," in effect the surveillance of all foreign intelligence operations in Italy. The rationale for broad coverage was that the cessation of hostilities had brought the replacement of armies by intelligence services as the means by which countries challenged each other. This change in the international system blurred the traditional lines between positive intelligence and counterintelligence. With threats ill-defined, X-2's penetrations assumed added significance as sources of clues as to the intentions of other states.[17] Angleton noted the ease with which the intelligence services of the continental powers adjusted to peacetime. In September 1945 he wrote, "[a]s military commitments are gradually discharged, there is a sharp increase in the number of long-term espionage suspects which is accompanying the transitional phase to normalcy."[18] Angleton found that in the wake of the collapse of Italian power, the unsettled nature of Mediterranean politics invited intervention by secret services. In his reports to Washington, Angleton underlined that the governments of France, Italy, and Yugoslavia were deploying their secret services to maximize their territorial and political advantages before the stabilization of borders and regimes.[19]

Besides providing insight into the way in which states defined their interests, Angleton's adoption of broad counterespionage coverage in peacetime facilitated controls over the movements of likely foreign long-term agents.[20] On the strictly security side, Angleton's principal concern was that members of those long-range networks not be permitted to obtain American secrets either through penetration of an American facility in Italy or through the emigration of part of the network to the United States.

Linking these two periods of Angleton's field career was his talent for exploiting liaison and penetration for counterespionage purposes. Neither activity produced information in hermetically sealed compartments. The sources of counterespionage information available to Angleton interacted constantly to produce a better picture of the adversary. Some hitherto obscure reference in an intercepted message might begin to make some sense, for instance, when compared to an interrogation report gained from an Allied service. One always hoped for a snowball effect: a deciphered message might lead to penetration operations that brought the release of even more data.[21]

Angleton's most important source of counterespionage was the product of both liaison and penetration. Code-named ISOS or PAIR, this was a steady stream of deciphered German intelligence messages, mostly but not exclusively sent by members of the Abwehr, the German military intelligence service.[22] ISOS or PAIR belonged to the now famous ULTRA family of signals intelligence. These decrypts were a British triumph and came to Americans only as a consequence of the unprecedented Anglo-American collaboration that underwrote the Allied conduct of the Second World War.[23] When the advent of joint military operations in 1942 transformed the security of American field operations into a British concern, the British made the decision to share their best information with Washington.[24] In exchange for this material, the British required that the OSS imitate their own foreign counterespionage organization. In practice this meant establishing X-2, a self-contained unit with separate communications channels, whose management at all levels, from staff to line officer, was indoctrinated into ULTRA.[25] Recalling ULTRA four decades later, Angleton described it as "the superior source" that undergirded all counterespionage operations.[26]

Angleton's own London apprenticeship had exposed him to the conventional wisdom among Allied counterespionage chiefs that, at least in this war, signals intelligence was the basis of all serious counterespionage.[27] From late 1941, readable German intelligence messages were coming to the offices of British counterespionage in bales. By May 1944 the British were circulating 282 of these decrypted messages a day.[28] These decrypts created a sense of confidence among counterespionage officers who, perhaps for the first time in military history, believed that a complete understanding of the enemy's intelligence resources was within their grasp. Although sometimes incompletely deciphered and when fully deciphered often filled with code names instead of real names, these messages provided a bird's-eye view of the number of agents the enemy sent into the field and of the information that his networks were providing him.[29]

In Italy, Angleton made a distinctive contribution to the problem of managing this sensitive information. Like many Allied counterespionage officers, he understood that the success of Allied counterespionage depended on how well X-2 and its British sister services employed ULTRA information. Operationally, this meant striking a balance between the protection of this superior source with the requirement of exploiting it to catch spies. As chief of X-2 Rome, Angleton conceived and produced a series of special manuals for use by Army counterintelligence investigators that went a long way toward solving this problem. Between January and April 1945, Angleton developed the concept of the "Key," an easy-to-revise compendium of information about the various German and Fascist Italian intelligence services that could be shown to officers not indoctrinated into ULTRA.[30] The trick was to comb POW interrogations for corroboration of facts first learned from ULTRA. Once a detail had been found in a less sensitive place—a SECRET interrogation report instead of a TOP SECRET ULTRA decrypt—it could be disseminated more widely.[31]

The fact that ULTRA materials were the most important products of liaison in the war against Fascist agents did not negate the value of the other cooperative relationships formed by Angleton in the field. For intelligence as well as operational reasons, the counterespionage officer had an incentive to develop liaison channels.

Angleton recognized that the requirement of specific information about the real names, aliases, addresses, missions, modes of payment, and weaknesses of foreign agents placed demands that even the miraculous deciphered messages could not meet. German signals, of course, revealed only some of what had to be known about espionage activity by Mussolini's rump government. But even where it was a matter of detecting a German-trained and German-supplied agent, the intricate details required to track the agent down were less commonly the product of signals intelligence than of the interrogations of captured intelligence officers, agents, and subagents. As X-2 was only one cog in the Allied counterintelligence machine, Angleton had to rely on liaison channels for most of these interrogations. The ratio of his small number of interrogators to the number of suspects being processed at any given moment meant that only the most important cases became the direct responsibility of X-2. Accordingly, X-2 had to make its influence felt indirectly, through interrogation aids such as the "Keys," which guided Army interrogators, or through joint operations with other counterespionage services with the effect of maximizing the number of interrogation reports available to X-2.

Angleton's experience in Italy affirmed the principle that liaison is the most efficient way to expand the resources of a counterespionage service. Intelligence cooperation has the potential of opening archives to a service that it could not have created on its own without a massive investment of labor and capital, if at all. Liaison among counterespionage services has the added inducement that it is the only way for a foreign service to have systematic access to the myriad of banalities routinely collected by domestic institutions that often prove essential in determining the bona fides of a source. Hotel registration lists, airplane manifests, passport and visa information can all be used to detect suspicious activities by individuals or to test the biographical information of suspect agents with whom you have come into contact. The epitome of such liaison is the police file, which, when corrected for the political or cultural biases of the originating institution, can be the most important source of biographical, or "personality," information.[32]

Having learned the value of liaison as a desk officer in London, Angleton wasted no opportunity once in the field to broaden X-2 contacts with Allied and friendly services. Of particular importance to him were the underdeveloped links to the Italian services. Under certain circumstances a foreign service will decide to put its operational resources at a counterespionage officer's disposal. Until 1946 this was mandated for the Italian police and all Italian military intelligence services.[33] The challenge for X-2 was to provide the bases for a continuation of such collaboration past the life of the mandate.

Angleton's efforts at deepening liaison with the Italians built upon the accomplishments of others, especially those of his own father, Lt. Col. James Hugh Angleton. From late 1943 through half of 1944, the senior Angleton served as X-2's representative in discussions with Marshal Pietro Badoglio and leaders of the Italian military, including the army's intelligence service, the SIM.[34] Over the course of his brief career in X-2 (he had left Italy by the time his son landed in Caserta), Lt. Colonel Angleton drew upon the excellent contacts he had developed in the 1930s as the owner of National Cash Register's Italian subsidiary and as president of the American Chamber of Commerce for Italy.[35] Following the elder Angleton's lead, son Jim's predecessors as unit chief in Rome, Andrew Berding and Robinson O. Bellin, established a measure of collaboration with all five principal Italian intelligence services: the three Italian military services, the police of the Ministry of the Interior (the Pubblica Sicurezza) and the Royal Counterespionage Service, or the Carabinieri.[36]

Young Angleton considered his immediate predecessor, Bellin, overcautious in dealings with the Italians. Angleton's first important policy decision after arriving in late October 1944 was to overturn Bellin's recommendation that the Marine Unit, a maritime paramilitary arm of the OSS, suspend its operations in Italy. The source of the problem was that the unit had earlier recruited a number of Italian naval saboteurs. When one of these recruits was discovered to be a possible German agent, X-2 and the OSS Security Office in Caserta concluded that the OSS Marine Unit was insecure. So daunting was the task of checking the bona fides of the rest of the Italian group, because ULTRA apparently provided very little on the Italian services, it was thought best to close down the entire OSS marine detachment.[37]

Angleton understood these concerns but was willing to take a leap of faith in order to deepen X-2's relationship with the SIS. It was a calculated risk. The war had turned against the Germans, and only the most hardened Fascists would resist the call for assistance from the rejuvenated Italian military. Betrayals were still possible, but their cost had to be weighed against the potential rewards of liaison. The Italian Royal Navy had the key to dismantling the German intelligence and sabotage network north of Florence. ULTRA information showed that the Germans were planning to leave Italians behind in strategic centers with missions to report Allied military movements to headquarters in northern Italy and Austria.[38] Other information pointed to Prince Valerio Borghese, a former Italian naval officer, as possibly being responsible for setting up part of this organization.[39] Borghese, the chief of the naval sabotage unit, the Decima Flotilla MAS, had not surrendered with the rest of the Italian Royal Navy in September 1943. He and most of his men, who were famous for their underwater assaults against British shipping, had stayed in the north to serve Mussolini's Salo Republic. The SIS knew the biographies of Borghese's group and could predict which men might be vulnerable to an approach by an Allied field agent.[40]

Angleton's reversal of policy, implying U.S. confidence in the Italian Royal Navy, opened the door to wide-ranging joint operations with the SIS under Capitano di Vascello Agostino Calosi.[41] Italian Naval Intelligence was as eager to work with the OSS as Angleton was with them. In November 1944, Calosi's chief of intelligence, Capitano di Fregata Carlo Resio, approached Angleton with two offers of assistance.[42] First, he said he could provide four trained radio operators for future penetration operations in the north. Second, he urged that the OSS Marine Unit take over the Italian "GAMMA" frogman school at Taranto, which would soon be closed down. Resio suggested that with the equipment and the training staff from Taranto, the OSS could prepare its own naval sabotage group for operations in the Pacific.

By early January 1945, this liaison was producing counterespionage information in addition to operational opportunities. As he began providing reports based on SIS files, Resio earned the sobriquet SALTY.[43] The first batch of SALTY reports dealt primarily with two themes: one was the threat of Communist insurgency and Soviet support for same; the other, the existence of a Fascist residue that had to be wiped off the Italian slate.[44]

The SALTY reports brought criticism upon Angleton's head for having exceeded his brief. The references to Soviet activity embarrassed Washington, which, in February 1945, cleaved to a policy of not collecting counterintelligence on allies.[45] In its first assessment of Resio's information, X-2 headquarters lectured young Angleton on the possibility that this information was politically inspired. The SIS, they cautioned, had long been considered royalist and anti-Soviet: "[t]herefore, it seems possible that this information may well be in the nature of a propaganda plant."[46] Moreover, at a time when Washington was eager for information to confirm the governing assumption that the Germans planned to continue a twilight struggle from the mountains of Austria, Resio's information seemed at best premature. Washington was testy:

We would further like to know from you whether you feel that all of this information actually ties in with German activities, either in the present or along the lines of future operations. Without an explanatory tie-in and evaluation, much of this information seems to be rather meaningless.[47]

Angleton reacted to this upbraiding by never again forwarding to Washington any political intelligence received from SALTY.[48]

Plan IVY, which was the culmination of the wartime collaboration developed between X-2 and SIS by Angleton and Carlo Resio, did meet Washington's criteria. The plan involved the use of Italian naval resources to penetrate Borghese's XMAS network in the north. Resio introduced Angleton to IVY, a source in Florence who had worked in Borghese's XMAS.[49] IVY provided six radio sets.[50] For the period after the liberation of the north, he offered XMAS scouts who were to dress as U.S. enlisted men and be assigned to target teams being assembled for Genoa, La Spezia, Trieste, and Venice. These scouts were to assist X-2 in tracking down Borghese's stay-behind network.[51]

Plan IVY also involved Pubblica Sicurezza and partisan contacts. The object of using them together with Resio's assets was to extend X-2's coverage in the north. Angleton's plan was to work with the SIS, the Pubblica Sicurezza in Rome, and those branches of the OSS that had active informants among the partisans with a view to reestablishing contact with as many friendly assets in Fascist territory as possible. Once the liberation had begun, X-2 intended to send its few officers to the north to meet up with these contacts, who were expected to be able to facilitate the "raccolta" of enemy agents and archives.[52]

Despite the assistance of the Italian SIS, Plan IVY did not live up to its promise. The credit instead went to the British and Italian military intelligence for capturing the heart of Borghese's organization.[53] Plan IVY also incurred unexpected costs that would only have been warranted had there been more operational successes. Because IVY's network had not sufficiently coordinated its activity with the partisans in the north, some of its members were arrested and executed despite their work for the Allies.[54] One positive byproduct of IVY for X-2, however, was that Prince Borghese turned himself over to the OSS.[55] Until the Italian government forced his return for prosecution in the fall of 1945, he served as an X-2 source on the backgrounds of various members of the Italian military and diplomatic elite.[56]

After the war, Angleton intensified his cultivation of the Italian Royal Navy. This took many forms. He offered the use of X-2 as a postal service to Agostino Calosi, whose brother had been taken to the United States to advise the U.S. Navy on building torpedoes.[57] When someone in the Italian SIS requested a copy of an American trade journal that happened to have an article on welding ships, Angleton cabled Washington to have it dug out of the Library of Congress.[58] Another way of currying favor was to sponsor a hard-earned vacation for a friendly naval contact. In the summer of 1945, X-2 sent the head of B Section, the cryptographic service of the Italian Royal Navy, and his wife to the south of Italy.[59] This minor investment seems to have paid off. By 1946 Angleton could report that as part of an exclusive arrangement with Section B, he had received a partial reconstruction of a Yugoslav cipher table and was likely to see solutions to messages sent by the Soviets to their field agents.[60]

By 1946 Angleton had developed at least 10, and possibly as many as 14, informants in the SIS.[61] This network was as inexpensive as it was productive. Angleton reported in the fall of 1945 that he did not pay for anything that he received from the Italian Naval Intelligence Service. Simply by turning over some cigarettes or operational goods, he could gratify his opposite numbers without humiliating them. Angleton wrote in one of his general reports:

> A few such items represents the equivalent of month's pay to an Italian Intelligence officer. In practice, $500 worth of operational supplies has the operational value of $50,000 worth of Lire or more. This method of payment is generally in use by other intelligence services.[62]

Angleton's superiors echoed his pride in the liaison system of X-2 Italy. When taking stock of all liaison relationships in 1946, the leadership of X-2 deemed Angleton's liaison with the Italian intelligence community, including the SIS, the "most spectacularly productive" of any maintained by the organization.[63]

The SALTY case represented how liaison could be used to fill in gaps in ULTRA information. Another way was by means of penetration. Reading the enemy's mail, as typified by signals intelligence like ULTRA, was only one of the forms of penetration available to Angleton. In the handbook of an X-2 officer there were another four ways to penetrate a foreign service: first, by placing an agent within the foreign service; second, by exploiting captured agents; third, by capturing foreign intelligence documents; and, finally, by capitalizing on security lapses by enemy representatives in neutral (third) countries.[64]

Angleton's most productive penetration aside from ULTRA in the years 1944–46 involved an agent in place. As Angleton knew, the "agent in place," or mole, has distinct advantages as a means of penetration. This kind of operation can potentially combine the virtues of access to high-level information and operational flexibility. Signals intelligence has the former, but it is also a static penetration. The agent in place, on the contrary, can direct his activities in conformity with the shifting priorities of the counterespionage service. Like signals intelligence, the last three kinds of penetration—captured documents, interned enemy personnel, the fortuitous security breach—lack the dynamism of the agent in place. While excellent sources, they can provide only snapshots of the foreign service.

The double agent is the only form of penetration that can compete with the flexibility of the agent in place. But since, by definition, he or she is not an officer of the foreign service and operates only in the field, there is little chance of parlaying the agent's new loyalties into a high-level penetration.

Angleton expected that, like the other forms of penetration, the penetration agent could serve an important epistemological function. In practice, the responsibility of the X-2 officer to protect the integrity of the U.S. intelligence community meant checking the channels of information to headquarters to weed out deception or just bad intelligence. Angleton's term for this was "controlling information."[65] OSS field stations were beset with streams of information, of varying accuracy, from agents of uncertain credibility. Without a system of knowledge, a field officer found himself blindly picking and choosing among these details. There could be little certainty at the best of times for the analyst of current events, but for Angleton there was a way to reduce the possibility of error. If one could control another agent in the same office, or at least one likely to receive similar information, then the veracity of the first source's reports could be tested. The game of multiple penetration required patience and meticulousness—traits associated with Angleton's later hobbies of orchid-breeding and fly-fishing.

Angleton's prize agent in place realized the epistemological potential of his type. An SIS officer, he provided a check on the products of the important liaison with Italian naval intelligence. Angleton code-named him JK1/8, but for simplicity's sake, we shall refer to him as SAILOR.[66]

The passionate debate over the future of the monarchy in Italy, which followed the defeat of Nazi Germany and the Fascist puppet state in northern Italy, undermined the unity of the Italian Royal Navy. Many in the navy, which Angleton himself described as "the stronghold of Monarchism," opposed an Italian republic.[67] Angered by the militant monarchism of his superiors, a young republican in Carlo Resio's intelligence section took matters into his own hands and offered a confidential liaison to Angleton. From the summer of 1945, this officer supplied X-2 with information that cut across the grain of what was received from official Italian Royal Navy sources.

SAILOR represented the ideological agent. Apparently, he was not paid for his information.[68] Nor is there evidence that SAILOR intended this connection with Angleton to advance his own career in intelligence. On the contrary, 8 months into his work as a penetration agent, SAILOR mused about resigning from the navy to join his brother in South Africa.[69] SAILOR's reports betray an antimonarchist bias, reflecting a deep suspicion of his colleagues and concern for the future of the Italian republic.[70]

In the year for which there is evidence of his work for X-2, SAILOR strengthened Angleton's ability to monitor Italian efforts to rebuild an intelligence capability.[71] Notably, on three occasions, he revealed secret Italian intelligence activities and then maneuvered himself into a position from which he could act as X-2's eyes and ears.

As his first operational contribution, SAILOR disclosed contacts between the Italian and the Soviet intelligence services after the Italian Armistice. At the start of his work for Angleton, SAILOR had offered to turn over the files on his meetings with his Soviet counterpart in Istanbul, Akim Mihailov.[72] A few months later, this offer matured into a prospective penetration of the Soviet services. The Soviets attempted to reestablish contact with SAILOR in Rome in the fall of 1945. SAILOR informed X-2, which then monitored the relationship.[73]

The second major disclosure attributable to this penetration came when SAILOR warned the Americans that anti-Communist Albanians had approached the Italian Royal Navy for money and weapons to attempt the overthrow of Enver Hoxha's regime. Angleton's official contacts also reported this approach. Thus Angleton found himself being asked both by SAILOR and his liaison partners for guidance as to what the Italian response should be. In order to control this relationship between the SIS and the Albanian dissidents, Angleton risked disclosure of his own penetration by boldly recommending that SAILOR be the liaison between the two groups. SAILOR's superiors agreed, and for nearly a year, X-2 was able to monitor these discussions through SAILOR.[74]

Finally, SAILOR revealed an old secret to Angleton that he had learned while serving in the codes and ciphers section of Italian naval intelligence. He told the story of DURBAN, a mysterious source who had supplied British and French codes to the Italians in 1939 and 1940 through a cutout, or intermediary, known as Max Pradier. SAILOR recalled this case because in 1945 Max Pradier attempted to reestablish contact with the Italians, and SAILOR thought the United States might wish to participate.[75] When the Italians later decided to reactivate Pradier, SAILOR was well-positioned to report on the kinds of ciphers that Rome was requesting.[76]

These operational gifts aside, SAILOR's principal value lay in enabling James Angleton to master the important liaison with Resio (SALTY) and the rest of the SIS. SAILOR was in a position to reveal weaknesses in the service for Angleton to exploit. In January 1946, SAILOR told Angleton that the Italian Minister of the Navy had announced in a meeting with his chiefs of staff that the United States was "the only friend of CB-Land [Italy]."[77] As it was U.S. policy on the terms of a peace treaty with Italy that had occasioned this comment, Angleton reacted to this intelligence by requesting from Washington all speeches by U.S. Secretary of State James F. Byrnes and other significant U.S. foreign policymakers that highlighted the American predisposition to a soft peace. Intending to mount a serious campaign, Angleton asked to be forewarned by cable of any government speech seemingly favorable to Italy that he could use to convince the Italian intelligence services that "their loyal collaboration with our service works to better their dubious position at the peace table."[78] Thinking past the peace treaty, Angleton felt that this close liaison could be preserved if the Italians believed that the United States had done everything possible to limit reparations to be paid by Rome and to rescue the eastern province of Venezia Guilia, even if neither demand was met in the treaty.[79]

Additionally, SAILOR improved the value of the X-2/SIS liaison by providing a filter through which Angleton could assess the quality of the information he was receiving from the Italian Royal Navy. Intelligence from SAILOR confirmed that the elite of the SIS was actively supporting the Italian monarchy.[80] This put Angleton on his guard in dealings with his naval informants. While many factors may have contributed to this caution, SAILOR's reports no doubt influenced Angleton's growing suspicion of the quality of political intelligence from the Italian Royal Navy. By the fall of 1945, Angleton's reports to headquarters began to reflect the reserve that Washington had earlier shown, without much cause, toward SALTY. Lumping the SIS with all other Italian intelligence services in a criticism of the political biases of the Italian intelligence community, Angleton cautioned his desk chief in Washington:

> The services have used every event, incident to the Italian Revolution, as propaganda material to indicate Russia's subversive intentions of preventing the reestablishment of "law", "order", and democracy in Italy. At no time have the various items of intelligence (when submitted to the test) been proven to be other than consciously composed for the purposes of provocation.[81]

SAILOR was a successful operation. But not all of Angleton's attempts at penetration produced positive results. Whereas SAILOR could be considered a complete penetration by Angleton, the notorious VESSEL case illustrated the problems associated with an incomplete penetration. This case pushed Angleton to the limits of his ability to meet his own high standards of counterespionage, with severe consequences for U.S. intelligence.

The rough outlines of the VESSEL case are well known to students of the OSS.[82] In the fall of 1944, Col. Vincent Scamporino, the head of the Secret Intelligence Branch (SI) of the OSS in the Mediterranean, began to receive reports from a man who purported to be in touch with an information service in the Vatican. The reports drew the interest of policymakers in Washington, among whom was President Franklin D. Roosevelt, who took the reports to be reproductions of actual Vatican documents. When the documents turned out to be fabrications, the OSS suffered some humiliation.

What is less well known is that this humiliation might have been avoided had bureaucratic politics not prevented James Angleton from assuming control of this operation from the start. Shortly after Scamporino had bought his first Vatican reports, James Angleton began to receive nearly identical reports from his own cut-out, or intermediary, Fillippo Setaccioli, alias DUSTY.

The source of all of this Vatican information, both that received by Angleton through Setaccioli and what Scamporino was sending to Washington as VESSEL information, was a former journalist named Virgilio Scattolini, who directed the Social Center of Catholic Action in the Vatican.[83] Scattolini had sold bogus Vatican information to various newspaper wire services before the war and with the liberation of Rome sought to reestablish this lucrative trade.[84]

Shortly after his introduction to Setaccioli, Angleton learned that DUSTY was not Scattolini's sole middleman. When Angleton shared the first reports from Setaccioli with SI Italy, Scamporino revealed that his service had been receiving almost identical information from two other sources, one of which SI had code-named VESSEL.[85]

Two considerations rendered the Scattolini case a matter of the highest importance to Angleton. First, if, as then appeared likely, the Vatican material was genuine, it represented a leakage of secrets about U.S. activities at the Vatican.[86] Scattolini had boasted to Setaccioli of being able to report on Myron Taylor, the U.S. representative to the Holy See. Second, the fact that Setaccioli was not the only middleman complicated any attempt to control Scattolini and U.S. secrets.

Angleton believed that this case required at least limiting Scattolini's Vatican operation to one middleman, DUSTY, whom he believed he could control. Angleton had three good counterespionage reasons to want to restrict the information to one channel. The OSS could thus screen all of Scattolini's outgoing reports for information detrimental to Allied interests. With this channel under its control, X-2 would acquire the capability to uncover all of Scattolini's clients, most of whom were foreign intelligence officers in Rome. At some later date, X-2 could employ this channel to plant information on selected foreign intelligence services.[87]

Scamporino rejected Angleton's plan.[88] The risk inherent in shifting from the middleman VESSEL to Angleton's middleman, Setaccioli, made the plan seem inadvisable. The pressure on Scamporino not to fail was great. VESSEL's information gave the OSS the ear of President Roosevelt, who from January 1945 received reports that were entirely the raw intelligence "take" from this source in the Vatican.[89] The traditional rivalry with X-2—based on SI's ignorance of ULTRA and subsequent mistrust of X-2's aloofness—encouraged the conclusion, moreover, that Angleton's approach to handling the Vatican information was a veiled attempt to monopolize Scattolini.

As a consequence of Scamporino's decision to defer to DUSTY, from January 1945 until August 1945 the OSS paid two middlemen for the same information.[90] Had a doubling of OSS expenses on Vatican information been its only cost, this interbranch rivalry might have been excusable. The actual damage was much greater because the squabbling between SI and X-2 prevented the OSS from controlling Scattolini directly. The preclusion of an inside check on the quality of the VESSEL material rendered even more difficult the already challenging task of evaluating information from the Vatican. Since the departure of the German intelligence bureaucracy from Rome and the internment of Germany's diplomatic corps in the Italian capital, ULTRA could provide very little to challenge Scattolini's information. From the ease with which Scattolini's lies were accepted, one can conclude that the American intelligence community had few other sources on Vatican affairs.[91]

Angleton tried unsuccessfully to "control" the Vatican information. At the time that he had suggested putting all of the Vatican middlemen out of business save one, Angleton had also advocated direct contact with Scattolini.[92] Given Scattolini's Fascist past, Angleton was confident that the fabricator could be compelled to work for the U.S. government. Angleton never had the chance to test this proposition, however, because of SI's opposition to anything that might threaten the VESSEL operation. In the hope of overturning SI's veto, Angleton spent a good deal of time in February, March, and April 1945 fruitlessly arguing the case for turning Scattolini into a double agent. Finally, even fate conspired against Angleton. When it appeared that Gen. William J. Donovan, the Director of the OSS, might agree at least to let X-2 place an American penetration officer in the Vatican to watch over Scattolini, President Roosevelt's unexpected death caused Donovan to cancel his trip to Rome, and the whole plan fell flat.[93]

Fortunately for the U.S. government, Scattolini ultimately made a mistake that took the luster off his material. In mid-February, Scattolini, who apparently did not know the identities of all of his consumers, passed a report through VESSEL on a meeting between Myron Taylor and the Japanese representative at the Vatican, Harada Ken.[94] The State Department was astonished when it received this VESSEL report because Taylor had not reported this particular contact. When Taylor denied ever having met the Japanese representative, the VESSEL material finally fell under suspicion, and the OSS decided to curtail its distribution severely.[95] President Roosevelt, however, continued to receive VESSEL reports on the Far East, as did the other Washington consumers of this material.[96] For no apparent reason, it was thought that, though unreliable about European matters, VESSEL could be trusted when it came to Japan.

Neither Angleton nor X-2 bore direct responsibility for the fact that the President of the United States received a weekly diet of fabricated reports up to the closing down of SI's VESSEL operation in the summer of 1945. A counterintelligence service is ill-equipped to judge the merits of political intelligence. In short, X-2 could better evaluate the messenger than the message. Primarily at fault were analysts in the OSS Research and Analysis Branch in Washington, whose access to more political information put them in the best position to discredit this material.

While the course of the VESSEL case validated his operational approach, Angleton should not retrospectively escape personal responsibility in the Scattolini case. Despite his admonitions to Scamporino, he shared SI's trust in the basic veracity of what Scattolini was selling. Only he can be blamed for the decision to continue disseminating Scattolini's material after VESSEL, the OSS middleman, was fired in the summer of 1945. Thereafter Setaccioli was the sole source of these so-called "Vatican cables" to Angleton.[97] Instead of simply using them to detect foreign intelligence officers in Rome, Angleton held to the view that Scattolini's material was a valuable source of political intelligence. He gave the Vatican reports a high evaluation, shared them with the U.S. Embassy in Rome, and decided to leave Scattolini alone.[98] Why Angleton passed up his long-awaited chance to employ Scattolini as a U.S. agent, at least to bolster his confidence in the man's access to information, is unclear. As a result, a final reckoning for the Vatican material was delayed at least until 1946. Ultimately, a CIA postmortem on the case concluded that Scattolini's reports had contributed to "informing, misinforming and thoroughly confusing those individuals responsible for analyzing Vatican foreign policy during the period involved."[99]

The counterespionage officer who emerges from the four preceding X-2 operations is at odds with the fabled James Jesus Angleton of the Mole Hunt of the 1960s.[100] As evidenced by his treatment of information gained through liaison with SALTY and the other Italians, Angleton did not view World War II as a hiatus in the struggle against international communism.[101] In fact, at no time was the young second lieutenant transfixed by a single enemy, Communist or Fascist.[102] His instinctual reaction to DUSTY, it will be recalled, had been to control him in order to monitor all foreign intelligence activities in Italy.

Further evidence of Angleton's pragmatism was the healthy skepticism with which he treated his sources. Aware of the political context in which he was working, Angleton was sensitive to the twin needs of collecting from sources of all political persuasions and correcting for their political biases. In October 1945, with the benefit of information from SAILOR, he regretfully remarked that the doctrine of military necessity had led to an almost exclusive set of intelligence-producing liaison relationships with the Italian military services, which represented the monarchist right wing of the Italian political spectrum.[103] Since it was likely that Italy would become a republic with the center-left inheriting power, Angleton articulated his worry that X-2 faced being shut out of important Italian information.[104]

The success or failure of a counterespionage unit is not a simple determination. One ought to resist the tendency to award laurels to Angleton and X-2, for example, simply because the OSS and the rest of the U.S. government escaped serious Fascist penetration.[105] After all, the avoidance of penetration may be more the reflection of the weakness of the opponent's intelligence service, or more appropriately in wartime, it may likely be the consequence of one side's military prowess. Nevertheless, standards of competence can be set. If they are exceeded, then the service or the individual counterespionage officer can be said to have been truly exceptional.

In his use of ULTRA material and the other products of liaison and penetration operations, Angleton demonstrated a firm grasp of the principles of effective counterespionage. He knew both how to make use of the intelligence that he had and how to develop new sources. Throughout, his objective was to extend his coverage of foreign activities likely to affect U.S. interests. This implied an exacting definition of counterespionage, which obliged the field officer to monitor all foreign intelligence-gathering in strategic areas and to control every possible channel through which an adversary might acquire American secrets.

This sureness of touch also had its negative side. It nourished a self-confidence that occasionally led Angleton astray. The VESSEL debacle showed that Angleton could relax his principles if he became personally involved in a case. Once Scamporino and the rest of SI had lost their claim to the Vatican material, Angleton backed away from his previous bureaucratic position of stringent checks on Scattolini and ran the operation through the man whom he believed, Setaccioli (DUSTY). Perhaps, too, some arrogance contributed to his decision not to secure the coordination of the IVY plan with the partisans in the spring of 1945.

Angleton's mistakes in Italy, however, did not diminish his role as exemplar in the development of counterespionage as an American profession. As demonstrated through his operations with X-2 in Italy, Angleton's concept of total counterespionage discouraged the myopia that can lead intelligence services astray. His approach to counterespionage neither necessitated a principal enemy nor was biased politically to expect a greater threat from any particular country. Grounded in empirical evidence and historical memory, the world according to Angleton was flexible, open-ended. Though not looking for threats, Angleton as a young man was in a position to perceive them whenever and wherever they arose.

NOTES

1. Timothy J. Naftali, *X-2: An Appreciation*, OSS/Donovan Symposium, September 19–20, 1986. Counterintelligence Corps (CIC) Security Lecture, Summer 1943, Box 9, Entry 174, Records of the Office of Strategic Services, Record Group 226, National Archives and Records Administration, Washington, DC (hereinafter cited as RG 226, NA).
2. Maj. Graham Erdwurm to X-2 London, Oct. 24, 1944, Box 4, Entry 121, RG 226, NA.
3. In the fall of 1943, X-2 London received three ominous signals from the field. The Rome unit's monthly report for September betrayed a sense of having fallen behind events (CB-015 [Robinson O. Bellin], "Report of Activities, X-2 Italy, Month of September 1944," Box 207, Entry 108A, RG 226, NA). Though the Germans were sending fewer agents into Allied territory, the local X-2 authorities were describing them as "considerably more dangerous" and had warned Washington that each one therefore required more investigation to pin down. Meanwhile, British MI6 officers, who had three of their own counterespionage field units in Italy, were reporting low morale among their American counterparts (Norman Holmes Pearson, chief of X-2 London, to James R. Murphy, chief of X-2 [hereinafter, NHP and JRM] Oct. 23, 1944, Box 57, Entry 169, RG 226, NA). Finally, London received an urgent plea for help from the overall chief of X-2 in Italy, Maj. Graham Erdwurm, who believed that the working relationships necessary to conduct counterespionage in Italy were being lost because of weak management of the unit. (On Oct. 10 Erdwurm wrote: "It is imperative that BB008 [Angleton] be sent Rome as soon as practicable." Erdwurm to Murphy and the chief of X-2 London, Oct. 10, 1944, "Saint, Rome," Box 20, Entry 119, RG 226, NA.) The Rome representative of British counterespionage, it was argued, was increasingly reluctant to share his most secret sources (BB068 [Major Graham Erdwurm] to JJ001 [James R. Murphy] and Chief, X-2 London, Oct. 10, 1944, "Pair," Box 20, Entry 119, RG 226, NA). At the time of Angleton's arrival, the name of the X-2 field unit in Italy was SCI Z. It was derived from the term, Special Counterintelligence (SCI) unit, which X-2 employed for its French field teams. In October 1944, SCI Z had one substation, located in Florence.
4. Mark Clark's 5th Army went into hibernation in October 1944. The British 8th Army did continue its northern push through Christmas 1944. However it was behind the 5th Army and did not reach Bologna before the spring of 1945.
5. Sicherheitsdienst, or SD, was the intelligence arm of Heinrich Himmler's Reichssicherheitshauptamt (RSHA). Although the Militarisches Amt also belonged to the RSHA, it was composed of former members of the defunct military intelligence service, the Abwehr. As of October 1944, the Germans had three radio agents reporting from Allied-occupied territory. These agents, who were **not** under Allied control, regularly communicated with their German case officers from Florence, Leghorn, and Rome, respectively. British SCI, "German Espionage and Sabotage Activities in Italy, 1944," Box 23, Entry 119, RG 226, NA.

6. October and November 1944 brought the peak of German line-crossing activities in Italy. The Germans attempted "at least a hundred" of these crossings with a 50 percent success rate.

7. A still mysterious operational failure may have been responsible for the sudden drop in the self-confidence of this unit. According to Robinson O. Bellin, whom Angleton was to replace as head of the X-2 field unit (SCI Z), "a disaster" befell the unit in October 1944 because of a poorly planned operation designed to root out stay-behind agents in Rome. The scale of this disaster resists definition, yet it may very well explain the urgency with which Erdwurm sought Angleton's arrival. Responsibility for this plan is also not clear, for it was formulated in the confusing weeks during which Andrew Berding passed the leadership of the unit to Bellin. Bellin, whose career in X-2 was marked by careful investigative work and consistent preparation, denies that he planned this operation. Robinson O. Bellin, "Notes For Symposium," prepared for the OSS/Donovan Symposium, Washington, DC, September 1986.

8. NHP to JRM, Oct. 23, 1944, Box 57, Entry 119, RG 226, NA.

9. The thesis of Tom Mangold's recent book, *Cold Warrior, James Angleton: The CIA's Master Spy Hunter* (New York, 1991), is that James Angleton was an ideological cold warrior whose ability to differentiate between possible threats and probable threats deteriorated after he learned that his British colleague H.A.R. (Kim) Philby was a Soviet penetration agent. (*Cold Warrior*, pp. 63–70). Favorable reviews of this book reveal widespread agreement with the thrust of Mr. Mangold's argument. For example, see Tom Bower's review, "Lost in a wilderness of mirrors," *The Sunday Times*, June 23, 1991. Among works on Angleton, an important exception in tone and perspective is the chapter, "The Theorist," in Robin W. Winks's rich book on Elis in the U.S. intelligence community. See *Cloak and Gown: Scholars in the Secret War, 1939–1961* (New York, 1987), pp. 322–437.

10. November 1944: Angleton appointed head of SCI Z, X-2's Italian field unit headquartered in Rome (Box 4, Entry 121, RG 226, NA). April 1945: Angleton appointed head of X-2 Italy (Box 10, Entry 121, RG 226, NA). December 1945: Angleton appointed head of SSU Italy (Box 268, Entry 108A, RG 226, NA). November 1947: Angleton returns to Washington, where he becomes Special Assistant to Col. Donald H. Galloway, Assistant Director for Special Operations at the new CIA. See Winks, *Cloak and Gown*, p. 383. Regarding Galloway's position, see Arthur B. Darling, *The Central Intelligence Agency: An Instrument of Government to 1950* (University Park, PA, 1990), pp. 11, 270–271.

11. These were the emigré information service of the former Croat government, the information service of the democratic Croat emigration, the French SDECE, the chief intelligence service of the Georgian emigration, the Italian Naval Intelligence Service, the Italian Pubblica Sicurezza, and the Yugoslav OZNA. See Boxes 199–274, Entry 108A, RG 226, NA.

12. Regarding the regularity of reports from SIM and SIS, see Entry 108A, RG 226, NA; regarding the Soviet and Yugoslav ciphers, see Angleton's comments to NHP, in undated letter: James J. Angleton to NHP, Wooden File, Box 3, File: "XX," Norman Holmes Pearson Collection, the Beinecke Rare

Book and Manuscript Library, Yale University. Hereinafter James Jesus Angleton will be referred to as JJA.

13. Although there is no concise statement available of Angleton's political philosophy in this early period, his emphasis on the role of power in international affairs and his unwillingness to rank ideologies in terms of potential threat to the United States betray a Realist point of view. See Robert O. Keohane, "Realism, Neorealism and the Study of World Politics," in Keohane, ed., *Neorealism and its Critics* (New York, 1986), pp. 7–16, for a useful discussion of political realism.

14. In his seminal work on intelligence as an instrument of foreign policy making, *Strategic Intelligence for American World Policy*, Sherman Kent referred to the 1945 Gouzenko case in Canada as an example of the value of counterintelligence as a source bearing on foreign intentions (Princeton, NJ, 1949), pp. 216–217.

15. The difference between security and counterespionage lies in the use to which you put information about a foreign intelligence service. Security is a purely defensive activity that aims at the frustration of foreign intelligence activity. Security, in its strictest sense, connotes apprehending spies rather than seeking to penetrate the service that sent them. In the last months of the Italian campaign, X-2 could be said to have run a largely security operation. Angleton did not engage in any deception or doublecross operations. All information was collected for use in eliminating the enemy's intelligence networks. For a good discussion of the distinction between counterespionage and security, see Christopher Felix (James McCargar), *A Short Course in the Secret War*, rev. ed. (New York, 1988), pp. 126–127.

16. Naftali, *X-2: An Appreciation*. For a succinct description of X-2's various field responsibilities, see Office of Strategic Services, Planning Group, "Counter-Espionage Field Manual—Strategic Services, (Provisional)," Aug. 24, 1944, Box 2, Entry 176, RG 226, NA.

17. Angleton wrote: "In practice, a certain overlapping of X-2 [counterespionage] and SI [positive intelligence] functions exists, particularly in this turbulent period before the peace conference when most secret political activities of foreign powers are conducted through intelligence services' contacts and networks." JJA to the Director, SSU, Mar. 18, 1946, "Consolidated Progress Report for November, December 1945 and January 1946," Box 268, Entry 108A, RG 226, NA.

18. JJA to JRM, "Activity Report SCI/Z Units, 1–30 September 1945," Box 259, Entry 108A, RG 226, NA.

19. Ibid.

20. Ibid.

21. JJA, interview with the author, Sept. 16, 1986, Washington, DC.

22. BB068 [Maj. Graham Erdwurm] to JJ001 [James R. Murphy] and Chief, X-2 London, Oct. 10, 1944, "Pair," Box 20, Entry 119, RG 226, NA. For evidence of the use of the term ISOS, see F. H. Hinsley and C.A.G. Simkins, *British Intelligence in the Second World War*, vol. 4, *Security and Counter-Intelligence* (London, 1990), p. 183.

23. Naftali, *X-2: An Appreciation*.

24. [Undated], "X-2 Branch OSS," Box 80, Entry 99, RG 226, NA.

25. Naftali, *X-2: An Appreciation*. Since ULTRA was their source, the British added the proviso that they were to have veto power over the indoctrination of any American officer, most of whom would be trained in London. Interview with JRM, Nov. 16, 1983. An unfortunate side effect of X-2's exclusive access to ULTRA was the envy and suspicion of the other operational branches of the OSS, all of which were required for security purposes to share the names of agents and contacts with X-2, but none of which were told the reason for their sister branch's extreme secretiveness. The close cooperation with the British necessitated by the ULTRA link also served to widen the gulf between X-2 and the other branches.

26. James Angleton, interview, Dec. 15, 1983. Angleton argued that a successful counterespionage service required a superior source, either in the form of signals intelligence or another significant penetration.

27. Hinsley and Simkins, *British Intelligence in the Second World War*, 4: 180–183.

28. Ibid., p. 182. The British Government Code and Cypher School (GC and CS) issued 268,000 counterintelligence decrypts during World War II, of which 250,000 were deciphered German intelligence messages.

29. Ibid., p. 183; There are a few examples of ISOS/PAIR at the National Archives. Box 1, Entry 138, RG 226, holds some paraphrases of original decrypts pertaining to stay-behind networks in Europe.

30. A complete set of Angleton's Keys and their addenda are located in Boxes 10–13, Entry 174, RG 226, NA. Angleton introduced the concept to his superiors in Jan. 1945, Box 206, Entry 108A, RG 226, NA.

31. In July 1945 Angleton wrote: "Interrogations of captured G[erman] I[ntelligence] S[ervice] personalities to date have released much information which previously it was impossible to include in the KEYS." JJA to Major Erdwurm, July 3, 1945, "Application of GIS KEYS," Box 255, Entry 108A, RG 226, NA.

32. An excellent example of a personality file is the one that the Rome Police (JK4, also known as the PANSY group) turned over to Angleton on the socialite Barbara Hutton. JJA to JRM, "Barbara Hutton," Apr. 2, 1946, Box 270, Entry 108A, RG 226, NA.

33. See the "Instrument of Surrender of Italy, September 29, 1943," *Treaties And Other International Acts Series*, U.S. Department of State, Washington, DC, No. 1604. This document does not include any direct references to the Italian military intelligence services. It can be assumed that these services are subsumed in references to the Italian military. It may also be assumed that with the end of Allied military government in most of Italy in late 1945, the prohibitions on independent Italian military intelligence operations ceased.

34. Lt. Col. James H. Angleton to C.O., Hq., 2677th Regt., OSS (Prov.), Aug. 4, 1945, "Duty Assignment Completed as of 2400 hours, July 29, 1945," Box 120, Entry 174, RG 226, NA.

35. Ibid.

36. Andrew Berding and Robinson Bellin led the X-2 field unit successively from its establishment in Naples in January 1944. In making his October 1944 plea for Angleton's assignment to the field, Erdwurm had contrasted the weak liaisons then in place with what Berding had achieved (see note 11). Despite Erdwurm's outburst, Berding's successor, Bellin, was not without his own

achievements in liaison. As a consequence of the Cornacchia Abwehr case, Bellin established trust between X-2 and the Rome headquarters of the Pubblica Sicurezza, which led to a sharing of police archives and the use of police investigators by the perennially short-staffed X-2 field unit. See Bellin, "Notes for Symposium." There is reason to believe that Bellin's contacts in the Pubblica Sicurezza became the PANSY group that later undertook investigative duties for and provided police information to Angleton. Names of police officers on a PANSY document dated Dec. 28, 1944 (Box 106, Entry 174, RG 226, NA) are identical to those listed in an October 1944 document detailing a joint operation involving Bellin and the Pubblica Sicurezza. [Undated], Regia Questura Di Roma, Commissariato di P.S. di Castro Pretorio, "Arresto di Di Fede Giovacchino, agente del servizio di informazioni nemico," Box 261, Entry 174, RG 226, NA. There is textual evidence that this document was produced in October 1944.

37. Angleton described the affair in "Memo No. 139" to X-2 London, Dec. 1, 1944, Box 205, Entry 108A, RG 226, NA. Forty years later, Bellin said that he had not wanted to close down the Marine Unit: "I had learned that a member of the Decima Flottiglia MAS (motoscafi antisommergibili) had been detected passing information to the Germans. Very soon after I had read this report, I received a delegation consisting of two American naval officers from the OSS Marine Unit and an Italian naval officer. The Marine Unit wanted me to issue a security clearance, giving SCI's (X-2 field unit) benediction to use, [sic] by the MU, of the Decima FM. I declined respectfully, saying I had no objection to their use of the Italian group, but that I did not have enough information to grant a wholesale security clearance. Perhaps I was being over-cautious, but my intuition told me to be careful." Bellin, letter to the author, Jan. 10, 1987.

38. Hinsley and Simkins, *British Intelligence in the Second World War*, 4: 183.

39. CB015 [Robinson O. Bellin] to X-2 Washington and London, "Borghese," Oct. 19, 1944, Box 114, Entry 174, RG 226, NA.

40. See SALTY [Carlo Resio of the Italian Naval Intelligence Service] report on Capitano di Fregata, Junio Valerio Borghese. JJA to X-2 London, "Memo No. 429," Jan. 27, 1945, Box 207, Entry 108A, RG 226, NA.

41. Calosi is identified as the head of the Italian Naval Intelligence Service, SIS, in a memorandum prepared for the State Department by SSU, "Changes in Naval Intelligence Key Personnel, Italy," June 17, 1946, *CIA Research Reports: Europe, 1946–76*, Microform, University Publications of America, 1983, Roll 3.

42. Ibid. For biographical information about Resio, see "Report by Capt/Freg. Carlo Resio On His Activities From November 1939 To December 1944," Box 115, Entry 174, RG 226, NA. Before the Italian Armistice, Resio had headed Section D of the SIS, which was responsible for all naval intelligence-gathering abroad. In September 1943, fearing German capture, he ordered the destruction of all of the files of Section D and set up a clandestine SIS in Rome.

43. Angleton assigned maritime code names to all of his contacts in Italian Naval Intelligence. Aside from SALTY, Angleton received reports from BEACON, CORAL, and TAR. The code name for the Italian SIS itself was SAIL, Box

254, Entry 108A, RG 226, NA. Strong evidence that Resio was SALTY comes from the cover letter, BB090 [chief, Italian desk, X-2 London] to JJA, "Carlo Resio," Mar. 5, 1945, Box 115, Entry 174, RG 226, NA. Handwritten at the top of this document is "SALTY." SALTY's identity is also strongly suggested by the statement in a May 1945 report that "ARTIFICE [Angleton] will enter MILAN in company with PATERNI, MACAULEY, CALDERON, CER-UTTI, and SALTY." BB090 to SAINT DH001 [chief, X-2 Washington], "SCI/Z Activities," May 2, 1945, Box 20, Entry 109, RG 226, NA. This was just after Angleton and Resio had jointly prepared penetration operations in northern Italy.

44. See SCI Z [X-2 Rome] memos 419–420, 439 and 442–447, all dated Jan. 27, 1945, from "SALTY," Box 207, Entry 108A, RG 226, NA.

45. When X-2 Washington learned in February 1945 that one of Angleton's sources, DUSTY, was also passing information to the Soviets, it cabled Rome: "It is our understanding that present policy does not permit activities either with or against these persons, and in view of present political and diplomatic activities, it would seem particularly dangerous to undertake contact with such persons at this time." Box 248, Entry 108A, RG 226, NA.

46. X-2 Washington to JJA, Feb. 26, 1945, Box 248, Entry 108A, RG 226, NA.

47. Ibid.

48. Another explanation for the absence of subsequent political intelligence reports from Resio is that after February 1945 he confined himself to cooperation on operational matters with X-2 and left the sharing of intelligence to his subordinates. When X-2 Rome renamed its intelligence sources in the spring of 1945, Resio became JK1/1.

49. Confidential interview.

50. JJA to Lt. Col. P.G.S. Mero, Signal Section, OSS, Mar. 3, 1945, "Plan Ivy," Box 207, Entry 108A, RG 226, NA.

51. In February 1945 Resio provided X-2 with 21 radio operators. There was a shortage of radiomen across the branches of the OSS. After screening by X-2, these men were parceled out to the other branches, with only a few staying in counterespionage. These operators took part in the intelligence assault on northern Italy. JJA to X-2 London, Mar. 13, 1945, Box 252, Entry 108A, RG 226, NA.

52. Box 283, Entry 174, RG 226, NA.

53. Stato Maggiore Della R. Marina (Italian Royal Navy), "Organizzazione segreta della X M.A.S.," Aug. 11, 1945, Box 128, Entry 174, RG 226, NA. I wish to thank Dr. Leopoldo Nuti for translating this and other Italian documents for me.

54. Angleton wrote in July 1945: "We are afraid that IVY was somewhat responsible for the great success in shooting spies by the CLN [the partisans]." JJA to X-2 London, July 18, 1945, Box 256, Entry 108A, RG 226, NA.

55. X-2 contacted Borghese in Milan through one of its agents and brought him to Rome. He was transferred to CSDIC (Combined Services Interrogation Centre) after the British were informed. His arrest record had been falsified to prevent the Italian government from knowing he was in custody. It seems likely that Carlo Resio and the Italian Navy knew of his capture. Resio and Angleton jointly visited Milan soon after its liberation,

exactly at the time that Borghese's transfer was being negotiated by X-2. JJA to AC of S, G-2, CI, AFHQ, May 19, 1945, Box 254, Entry 108A, RG 226, NA. For evidence that Resio and Angleton went to Milan together see Italian Desk, X-2 London (BB090) to X-2 Washington, May 2, 1945, Box 122, Entry 174, RG 226, NA.

56. Ibid. JJA to Commander Titolo, Nov. 6, 1945, Box 260, Entry 108A, RG 226, NA. Angleton attempted to prevent Borghese's execution by the Italians because of X-2's "long term interest" in him. Although Angleton had to give him up to the Italians in late 1945, Borghese survived well into the 1970s.

57. JJA to JRM, Dec. 13, 1945, "Transmittal of Letter," Box 261, Entry 108A, RG 226, NA.

58. JJA to JRM, Jan. 19, 1946, "Publications Desired for Liaison," Box 262; JJA to JRM, Feb. 21, 1946, "Magazines," Box 266, Entry 108A, RG 226, NA.

59. [Undated], JJA to NHP, Wooden File, Box 3, File: "XX," Pearson Collection, Yale University. "Either with Rock (Raymond Rocca), or separately I am sending the latest crypt stuff. I believe that you will appreciate the effort put into this work by JK1/14. He is doing this solely for us." From internal evidence it appears the letter was written in early 1946, after Angleton returned from his November 1945 trip to Washington and before Pearson left X-2 in May 1946.

60. Ibid.

61. Angleton assigned the prefix JK1 to all cryptonyms for contacts in the SIS. See Entry 108A, RG 226, NA, for reports from JK1/1, JK1/2, JK1/3, JK1/4, JK1/5, JK1/6, JK1/7, JK1/8, JK1/11, JK1/14. The use of JK1/14 implies that there were 14 informants, although no reports from JK1/9, JK1/10, JK1/12, or JK1/13 have been found in this entry.

62. JJA, "Consolidated Progress Report for November, December 1945 and January 1946," Mar. 18, 1946, Box 268, Entry 108A, RG 226, NA.

63. "Status of Liaison Relations of SSU/X-2 To the Counter-Intelligence Branches of Foreign Special Services," [1946], Wooden File, Box 1, File: "IV Thoreau OK," Pearson Collection, Yale University.

64. X-2 London to X-2 Washington, "German and Japanese Penetration of OSS in ETO [European theater of operations]," July 7, 1945. William J. Donovan Collection, U.S. Army Military History Institute, Carlisle Barracks, PA.

65. JJA to Francis Kalnay, chief of X-2 Venice, Oct. 31, 1945, Box 260, Entry 108A, RG 226, NA. "Our present difficulty is mainly that of evaluating the various reports which have been produced by yourself, No. 5 SCI Unit and SIM/CS (Italian CE), and SCI Unit Z, Trieste. I feel that the time must come to carefully examine and control the Balkan information obtained in Italy during the past four months, and, therefore, we would appreciate your comments."

66. There are a few clues to the identity of JK1/8. The comparison of two documents regarding contacts between the Italian Navy and the Albanian resistance narrows down considerably the possible candidates. See documents JZX-7590, Apr. 8, 1946 (Box 270, Entry 108A, RG 226, NA), and JZX-7719, Apr. 9, 1946 (Box 271, Entry 108A, RG 226, NA), respectively. Further corroborative evidence can be found in the "CUBA" file (Box 261, Entry 174,

RG 226, NA), where a note from double agent CUBA to JK1/8 appears to confirm JK1/8's identity as the former SIS Istanbul station chief.

67. JJA comment on report, X-2 Italy to Washington, "Propaganda and Penetration of Left-Wing Parties vis-à-vis the Italian Royal Navy," Feb. 11, 1946, Box 265, Entry 108A, RG 226, NA.

68. JJA, "Consolidated Progress Report for November, December 1945 and January 1946," Mar. 18, 1946, Box 268, Entry 108A, RG 226, NA.

69. Capt. Henry R. Nigrelli, C.O., SCI Z Genoa, to JJA, Apr. 3, 1946, Box 143, Entry 174, RG 226, NA.

70. See two reports by JK1/8 pouched Oct. 7, 1946, by JJA to SSU Washington. One is entitled "SIS Contact with Monarchists," the other "SIS Activity in the Val D'Aosta." Box 248, Entry 108A, RG 226, NA.

71. As there is no postmortem on the JK1/8 case in the X-2 files at the National Archives, one must use his declassified reports as a guide to the length and substance of his career. From them, one can conclude that JK1/8 worked for X-2, at least, from August 1945 through October 1946 (an example of an early JK1/8 report is JJA to X-2 Washington, "Austro-Italian Economic Conference," Aug. 7, 1945, Box 257, Entry 108A, RG 226, NA; for October reports, see below). It appears that in January 1946, JK1/8 was moved from Rome to the SIS station in Genoa (X-2 Italy, "Albanian Resistance Group in Italy," Apr. 8, 1946, Box 270, Entry 108A, RG 226, NA). After 3 months there, he may have left the SIS. (In April 1946, CUBA, a joint SIS/X-2 agent, said to JK1/8 that he hoped "both Resio and I will come back into the service." Capt. Henry R. Nigrelli, chief, SCI Z Genoa to JJA, "CUBA," Apr. 25, 1946, Box 261, Entry 174, RG 226, NA.) There is reason to believe he returned to Italian naval intelligence after the republican victory in the referendum on the monarchy in June 1946. His October 1946 reports imply access to inside SIS sources, though conceivably he may have been running SIS contacts from the outside (JJA to SSU Washington, "SIS Contact with Monarchists," and "SIS Activity in the Val D'Aosta," both Oct. 7, 1946, Box 248, Entry 108A, RG 226, NA). The length of JK1/8's career is impossible to determine because the date of his last known reports coincides with the cutoff point for most of the operational material in the X-2 files.

72. Resio must have known that SAILOR had offered X-2 his records of contacts with Mihailov because at the time of the offer, SAILOR's files were still in Istanbul, and the only way for X-2 to obtain them was to ask the Italian naval attaché there, Comdr. Giuseppe Bestagno, to hand the documents to the X-2 chief in Istanbul, Joseph Toy Curtiss. It has to be assumed that Bestagno alerted his superiors to this request. The record clearly shows Bestagno disapproving of the order and dragging his feet for weeks on the excuse that he needed this time to "collect the necessary documents." Presumably he stalled because he wanted higher authorization. JJA to JRM, Oct. 31, 1945, Box 260, Entry 108A, RG 226, NA.

73. Ibid.

74. Apr. 8, 1946, "Albanian Resistance Group in Italy," Box 270, Entry 108A, RG 226, NA.

75. JJA to X-2 Washington, Aug. 19, 1945, Box 258, Entry 108A, RG 226, NA.

76. "Argomento: incontro con il Signor Max Pradier," Box 262, Entry 174, RG 226, NA. This report appears to be from August 1947. It is unclear whether SAILOR wrote this particular report.

77. Box 263, Entry 108A, RG 226, NA.

78. Ibid.

79. Ibid.

80. For example, see two reports by JK1/8 pouched Oct. 7, 1946, by JJA to SSU Washington. One is entitled "SIS Contact with Monarchists," the other "SIS Activity in the Val D'Aosta." Box 248, Entry 108A, RG 226, NA.

81. JJA to JRM, Nov. 6, 1945, "Report of Activities of the Italian Mission from 1–31 October 1945," Box 260, Entry 108A, RG 226, NA.

82. The standard account of the VESSEL case is in Anthony Cave Brown, *The Last Hero: Wild Bill Donovan* (New York, 1982), pp. 683–705. Cave Brown was the first to write an extended study of the case based on OSS documents. However, he did not see any of X-2's reports on the case. Unfortunately, as a result, he concluded that Scattolini was VESSEL and that DUSTY was a synonym for this source. Cave Brown also made no mention of Setaccioli. His account, therefore, leaves the counterespionage angle to the case unclear and Angleton's actions incomprehensible. The most authoritative discussion of all aspects of the VESSEL case was a 1982 BBC radio broadcast entitled "Little Boxes," written by Derek Robinson. (*Radio Times*, Apr. 10–16, 1982, pp. 17, 19). Robinson's script was based on the research of Father Robert A. Graham, S.J., an archivist at the Vatican, who had studied Scattolini for a decade. In the early 1970s Father Graham had demonstrated the falsity of the reports that Scattolini had sold to American newspapers before and during the war and linked the forger to two books on Vatican policy that appeared during the crucial Italian election of 1948: *Documenti Segreti della diplomazia vaticana. Il Vaticano e la Democrazia Italiana* (Lugano, 1948) and *Vaticano contro la pace mondiale* (Lugano, 1948). See Graham, "Virgilio Scattolini: The Prince of Vatican Misinformers, A Bibliographical Note," *The Catholic Historical Review*, Jan. 1974, pp. 719–721. Using the Freedom of Information Act, Father Graham later obtained documents regarding Scattolini's sales to the OSS and Angleton's role as controller of DUSTY. See Thomas O'Toole "U.S. Blessed with OSS Spy in Vatican," *The Washington Post*, Aug. 3, 1980. I am grateful to Father Graham for sharing his Scattolini file with me (hereinafter, Graham FOIA file).

83. X-2 Italy, "Plan DUSTY—Preliminary Report," Feb. 27, 1946, Graham FOIA file.

84. Setaccioli revealed himself to X-2 when he foolishly sent some of this Vatican material by mail. As all mail in Allied-occupied Italy was subject to censorship, this package ended up on the desk of James Angleton. Setaccioli was later picked up by Rome police officers working under X-2 supervision. X-2 Italy, "Plan DUSTY, Second Report," Mar. 23, 1946, Graham FOIA file.

85. Angleton and CB055, "Plan Dusty, Second Report," Mar. 23, 1946, Graham FOIA file.

86. JJA, "Vessel Traffic," report sent to General Magruder, Mar. 22, 1945, Graham FOIA file. Angleton wrote: "There is good evidence that Dusty's [Setaccioli's] information passed to us daily for redistribution to our unknowing clients is culled from actual Vatican documents."

87. Ibid.
88. Ibid.
89. CIA, "Memoranda For the President: Japanese Feelers," *Studies in Intelligence*, vol. 9, no. 3, Summer 1963 [declassified 1990].
90. JJA to Special Funds Officer, Sept. 5, 1945, Graham FOIA file.
91. "Plan Dusty," [undated], Graham FOIA file.
92. X-2 Italy report, "Plan DUSTY, Second Report," Mar. 23, 1946, Graham FOIA file.
93. Ibid.
94. Cave Brown, *The Last Hero*, pp. 699–701.
95. OSS Washington to OSS Caserta, Feb. 17, 1945, Box 228, Entry 134, RG 226, NA. General Magruder and Whitney Shepardson, head of SI, cabled: "[I]t is our impression that the current material is a mixture of the obvious, the unimportant if true, and plants. It has the earmarks of being concocted by a not too clever manufacturer of sales information. As a result, for the time being we are withholding the dissemination of most of this material."
96. CIA, "Memoranda For the President: Japanese Feelers."
97. In August 1945 Angleton wrote: "[T]hrough the use of our double agent 'DUSTY' [Setaccioli], we have gained information concerning the CG-LAND [Japanese] activities as revealed in Vatican cables." JJA to JRM in Washington, "CG-LANDERS Situation, Italy," Aug. 14, 1945, Box 258, Entry 108A, RG 226, NA.
98. See Box 1, Entry 174, RG 226, NA. This box contains cables from September 1945 through January 1946. The last cables in this collection coincide with the timing of an assessment of this material by SSU Washington. The analysts concluded that of the material submitted by Setaccioli in fall 1945, only 35 percent was partially or wholly true, whereas 16 percent had been "definitely proven false," and 49 percent could not be properly evaluated. This survey most likely brought an end to the dissemination for intelligence purposes of the Scattolini cables. U.S. counterespionage officers maintained relations with Setaccioli and Scattolini until September 1947 at least. "Plan Dusty," [undated], Graham FOIA file. I am grateful to Max Corvo for sharing a copy of this declassified document with me.
99. "Plan Dusty," [undated], Graham FOIA file. The same document added that this case "illustrated the danger of accepting at face value the product of an intelligence operation which had not been secured by adequate counter-espionage investigation."
100. Tom Mangold is the most recent writer on James Angleton to assume that once the Germans were defeated, Angleton immediately redirected his efforts against the Soviets. "When the wartime necessity for secrecy began to wane, only the enemy changed for Jim Angleton. Now the hammer and sickle replaced the crooked cross" (*Cold Warrior*, p. 43). Robin Winks had a more subtle view of Angleton's mindset. From interviews and the declassified X-2 records then available, Winks surmised that Angleton was "rather apolitical, mainly intent on his job and protecting counterintelligence." (*Cloak and Gown*, p. 434n).
101. On the tendency of some British intelligence officers to view World War II as a diversion from the contest with the Soviets, see Naftali, "The DSM and the Politics of Allied Counterespionage," paper delivered at the Eisenhower Lead-

ership Center, University of New Orleans, May 1990. According to the British official history of counterintelligence in World War II, as of the fall of 1939, most of the information collected by the counterespionage branch of MI6 and the domestic security branch, MI5, dealt with the Comintern. Hinsley and Simkins, *British Intelligence in the Second World War*, 4: 11.

102. Like many in X-2, Angleton believed the eventual collapse of the German intelligence services a foregone conclusion, and there is evidence that from early 1944, when he was still in London, he worked to build the data base necessary to monitor significant intelligence activities in Italy. BB008 [JJA] to CB001 [Andrew Berding], Feb. 28, 1944, "General," Box 145, Entry 174, RG 226, NA.

103. JJA to JRM, Nov. 6, 1945, "Report of Activities of the Italian Mission from 1–31 October 1945," Box 260, Entry 108A, RG 226, NA.

104. JJA to the Director, SSU, Mar. 18, 1946, "Consolidated Progress Report for November, December 1945 and January 1946," Box 268, Entry 108A, RG 226, NA.

105. There were no serious German or Japanese penetrations of the OSS. See two reports, X-2 London to X-2 Washington, "German and Japanese Penetration of OSS in ETO," July 7, 1945, and "Supplement to German and Japanese Penetration of OSS in ETO, dated 7 July 1945," both from the Donovan Collection, U.S. Army Military History Institute. Soviet penetration of the OSS remains a puzzle. As a good first attempt to resolve that issue, see Hayden B. Peake, *Soviet Espionage and the Office of Strategic Services (OSS): A Preliminary Assessment*, prepared for *The Conference on World War II & The Shaping of Modern America*, Rutgers, The State University of New Jersey, April 1986.

✦ The OSS in Western Europe

The third of four concurrent sessions addressed OSS operations in western Europe. A leading French journalist of intelligence and terrorism, Fabrizio Calvi, clarified the relationship between OSS operatives and the French Resistance movement during the German occupation. Calvi used OSS records during previous research in Washington and conducted numerous interviews with OSS veterans. The mention of Allen Dulles evokes the image and intrigue of the spymaster. Dulle's accomplishments were many. But former Department of State historian Neal Petersen studied message traffic between Switzerland and OSS headquarters in Washington and pointed out that Dulles was capable of error as well as success. The eminent British historian M.R.D. Foot examined the difficult question of whether OSS field personnel and their older cousins of the British Special Operations Executive cooperated with each other as they tramped the same areas of combat. Two special guests of this session were Gervase Cowell, British SOE Adviser, Foreign and Commonwealth Office of the British Government, and Christian Mauch of Tubingen University, Germany, who substituted for Professor Jurgen Heideking of the same institution. A spirited discussion took place during and after this session. OSS veteran and former Director of Central Intelligence Richard Helms chaired the session and introduced the speakers. Ambassador Helms also directed the commentary that followed.

THE OSS IN FRANCE

Fabrizio Calvi

Hundreds of Frenchmen worked with the Office of Strategic Services (OSS) to liberate their national territory. Their history and what became of them is something of which the French people are not yet aware. All of these figures, however, are an essential part of the history of the Liberation. There is no awareness of the extent to which the American networks of action and spying were involved with the preparation of the landings in North Africa, Normandy, and Provence or with the reconstruction of the German order of battle, not to mention the aid brought to the underground forces, and—for good reason—no details of the actions of the OSS in France are found in any history of the Resistance movement. Until the past few years, the main reason for this oversight was the unavailability of source documents. Since then, most of the OSS records in the National Archives of the United States have been opened to those who are attempting to find out the true story.

By going to Washington, DC, to examine these documents unearthed from the OSS Archives, our intention was, above all, to do justice to these forgotten underground networks and to bring our own contribution to the history of the Liberation. Our intention was to look at the facts in a new, radically different way and not to write a "revised history" of the Resistance movement. This new perspective led us to ask certain questions: What was the role of each person in the liberation of France? How effective would the underground networks in France have been without American assistance? In searching for the answers to these questions, we more or less had to describe the Resistance movement the same way the Americans did and not the way we saw it, understood it, or thought we understood it.

In our research at the Archives, a great surprise awaited us. On the battlefield as well as in the military staff, the relationships between the Americans and the French were beset by countless problems, conflicts, and rivalries. Did not several OSS leaders speak about the "French Gestapo" when referring to the methods used by the Gaullist secret organization in Paris, the BCRA? This particular expression was found in several of the documents consulted in Washington, DC. This mutual suspicion led the OSS to give financial support to the secret army of Henri Fresnay at the expense of de Gaulle's special envoy, Jean Moulin. It was difficult to dismantle it, even after General de Gaulle's victory over Giraud. This is why the OSS found its principal allies within the information service of the French Army, which in spite of the Armistice, still continued the struggle against the occupying forces, first in the free zone of France, then later from Allied-controlled Algeria or from Bern, where it maintained contact with Allen Dulles. Being the only Western service with perfect knowledge of Germany, the traditional enemy, the French Army information service only concerned itself with military affairs, and contrary to the Gaullists, was not concerned with the taking and administration of power. A history of the OSS in France, therefore, cannot disregard the substantial contributions of this information service, whose efforts long went unrecognized for unjust, petty political reasons.

In the course of our interviews in France, we also discovered that the wounds were still wide open and that the hatred, bitterness, and hostility were as pronounced as ever. We have already pointed out that barely any mention of the OSS is made in the official accounts of the French Resistance movement. The great Gaullist heads of war to whom we divulged our project often showed obvious surprise. "A history of the OSS in France— what a strange idea," said André Dewavrin, better known under his war name of Colonel Passy. He added, "The OSS did virtually nothing in France." As the founding myth of the Fifth Republic, the Resistance movement and its history leave no one indifferent, and even if some of our interviewees found it hard to hide their feelings of resentment toward an organization that had misgivings about the Gaullists (at least at the beginning), almost all of them agreed to answer our questions. This is when we realized that even the legendary figures of the French Resistance movement were unaware of the extent of the role played by the American secret services in France.

From the time of our first interviews, it became clear that several of the French OSS agents had the impression at the Liberation that they were considered traitors to their own country. Few received the honors and rewards in France that were their due. Whereas on the other side of the ocean, the U.S. Congress and President Harry S. Truman gave them the highest honors. From then on, our encounters with the French members of the OSS took on an aspect of unearthing the forgotten figures of official history. This is most likely the explanation for the more favorable welcome we received. Thanks to the National Archives and also to the help of OSS veterans, especially Henry Hyde and Geoffrey Jones, we were able to locate and interview about 200 Frenchmen who worked for or with the OSS.

Personal papers of these individuals helped us corroborate the OSS records. These eyewitness accounts also enabled us to give all due credit to the official archives. In addition, we were able to meet with agents of the Abwehr and the Gestapo who had been assigned to follow OSS field agents.

We voluntarily decided to limit the scope of our investigation for reasons of location and opportunity. Since the historian M.R.D. Foot had exhausted the networks of the British Special Operations Executive (SOE), with which about 100 OSS agents were affiliated, we did not think it necessary to deal extensively with this subject. Similarly, those interested in the major three-powered Allied operations involving OSS agents, such as the Jedburghs or Sussex can refer to Anthony Cave Brown's *The Last Hero*, William Casey's *Secret War Against Hitler*, the *OSS War Report*, or since I cannot treat in this presentation all the other networks that caught my attention, my *OSS: The Secret War in France*. Among these other networks are the first ever started by the OSS in France, under the leadership of Frederic Brown and Mission "Tomato," dismantled by the radio double agent DARTMOUTH, who is still alive and whom we interviewed. At this time I propose to present to you the two "chains" that interested me the most. These are the organization "Penny Farthing" and the network "Bruno," put in place by French secret services in Bern for the benefit of, among others, Allen Dulles.

Penny Farthing

Because he was born in France and completed part of his studies there, Henry Hyde, the Deputy Director of the Secret Intelligence Branch (SI) of the Algerian Division of the OSS, understood the French better than most Americans. He knew that in order to have a chance of recruiting agents, he had to become friends with the most influential people in Algeria. Thus, thanks to Col. André Poniatowski, head of Giraud's cabinet and a family friend, Hyde was able to recruit 30 Frenchmen who would be administratively taken into Giraud's army. This would effectively shelter them from any accusations of working for a foreign power. It was in this way that he was able to employ his first agent, Jean Alziary de Roquefort. Hyde quickly paired him with Mario Marret, a young anarchist who had already functioned as a radio operator for OSS agent Frederic Brown when the Allies landed in North Africa in November 1942.

After a few months and no action, Jean de Roquefort, known as "Jacques," and Mario Marret, known as "Toto," felt as if they would never leave on a mission. Their impatience was shared by their boss, Henry Hyde, who had recently been named head of SI in the Algerian capital. Hyde had two completely trained agents ready for action. Having attended the various OSS schools in North Africa, including the parachute training camp "Pine Club," the spy training school in Chrea, as well as the communications course offered at Maison-Carree, the two were now capable of completing the most far-reaching missions. Nevertheless, Hyde's Penny Farthing operation was in danger of never coming to fruition for lack of transportation.

From the time of his nomination, problems of logistics threatened the work of the young chief of the Algerian SI. The U.S. Air Force at first refused to accede to his requests, claiming that it did not even have enough aircraft to meet its own demands. In the summer of 1943, Henry Hyde informed William Donovan of the seriousness of the problem. The head of the OSS then recalled that he knew General Curtis of the Army Air Force staff in Tunis, who used to be the vice president of Eastman Kodak and whom Donovan knew well because he had represented that company at one time. Based upon Donovan's instructions, Hyde went to Tunis and told General Curtis that it was undignified of the American armed services to have to beg for methods of transportation from the British and the French and outlined the benefits that the U.S. Army Air Force would derive from the operation, such as installation of escape routes for the pilots and identification of targets. He made his case so well that in October 1943 the Algiers SI Branch of the OSS obtained the use of five or six B-17s that were based at the Blida airport near Algiers, at the foot of the Atlas Mountains.

Hyde could not wait for the U.S. Army Air Force to finally decide to supply him with planes. So in June 1943, accompanied by his two agents, he went to Great Britain to ask the British secret services to send his agents to France. This was a daring step that almost turned into a diplomatic incident. The affair had taken such an alarming turn that Sir Claude Dansey, Secret Intelligence Service (SIS) second-in-command, decided to personally take charge. He received Henry Hyde one Sunday afternoon in his office on 52 Broadway in London.

Hyde knew that Dansey was dying to know what he hoped to accomplish in France that the French and the English were not already doing. Dansey waited for Hyde's plea in order to make his decision. Without losing his equanimity, the latter outlined the instability of the British networks in France, all the while taking care to stress their importance, especially in regard to the American command. Then he brought up the Americans' need to have their own networks in light of an increase in their war effort.

"I am surprised," replied Claude Dansey, "that you are not aware of the proverb: a rotten apple can spoil the whole basket." "Nothing can prove that our apple is rotten, and no matter what, it has received instructions never to contact those fruits already in place."

Henry Hyde was not aware at that time that a top secret agreement bound the SIS and the OSS, to terms by which the Americans agreed not to launch "any independent unilateral operations in Europe from British soil." The OSS branch in London was only authorized to conduct joint operations, with one of the two British services operating in Europe, SOE or SIS. The head of SIS, Sir Stewart Menzies (the legendary "C"), who dreaded seeing his territory overrun by American secret agents, therefore saw in Penny Farthing a violation of a formal agreement. Henry Hyde was able to come up with arguments to calm British misgivings:

> "Penny Farthing" is the extension of an operation conceived by those in charge of the Mediterranean theater of operations. The OSS-SIS agreement therefore does not apply, because this is not an OSS-London operation, but an OSS-Algeria operation. We only want to use England as a launch pad, and only because OSS-Algeria suffers from a complete scarcity of methods of transportation. The only thing that concerns us is the possibility of an American disembarkation in the South of France. The American military staff wants to have its own sources of information, in addition to those of the British and of the French.

This last argument scored a bull's eye. Hyde's firm and polite tone was convincing, but so undoubtedly was the desire to make concessions to the all-powerful American allies. Three days later, Claude Dansey gave his decision: The Head of Services of His Very Gracious Majesty the Queen authorized Marret and Roquefort to parachute from the SOE plane.

After an initial attempt, which was aborted at the last minute, the reception committee put in place by SOE having apparently fallen into German hands, the two French agents were finally dropped by parachute not far from Lyon without anyone to wait for them (a blind drop) on August 17, 1943. In 1940 Lyon was not only close to Vichy in distance, but also still by opinion. But Lyon was also close to the demarcation line and the Swiss border. It also quickly became a turning point of the Resistance in the unoccupied zone. All the movements had their general staffs there. The editorship of the *Progrès de Lyon* (*Progress of Lyon*), which early on became dissident and would be scuttled after the German invasion of 1942, saw all of the Resistance leaders come and go. There were many resisters in Lyon, too many perhaps. "One could not go more than 10 meters," recalls the French official in charge of organizing the secret combatary, "without bumping into another clandestine comrade who had to be ignored. . . . I never understood why the Gestapo or the Vichy police was not able to make more arrests, simply by posting a man on the steps of the Comedie [Theater], for example, where probably one out of three clandestine meetings took place."

By November 11, 1942, when the city was occupied by the Germans, attacks and sabotages had multiplied. Repression had also increased, by reason of the installation in Lyon of the German information services and of the Gestapo, directed by Werner Knobb and SS Hauptsturmfuhrer Klaus Barbie.

At the time of the arrival of Jean de Roquefort and Mario Marret, the city was under the thumb of the collaborators. In January, Pierre Laval, the pro-German Premier of Vichy France, had installed a sympathizer of *Je suis partout* (*I am everywhere*) in the mayor's office. The militia men of Joseph Lecussan and of Francisque André, known as "Gueule-Tordue" ("Twisted Face"), followed suspects turned in by their fellow citizens and pursued Jews and resisters. The number of rebels at the STO increased, supplying the underground forces that were springing up in the nearby Alps. But at the same time that it was reinforcing itself, the Resistance suffered a severe setback: on June 21, 1943, Jean Moulin was captured in Caluire by Klaus Barbie's men.

Soon after his arrival, Jean de Roquefort began to appreciate the scope of the difficulties that awaited him. In his memoirs about the network, he conceded: "I quickly realized that the idea of a military information function such as had been required of me was too new, even though it was sympathetically received, for me to be able to ask for help in any direct way."[1]

In order to start a network of secret agents, he first had to recruit motivated young people and then had to train them. One man, Father Chaine, would greatly facilitate this task for him. Roquefort knew this Jesuit well, whose Conference Ampere he had attended in the course of his higher education. Undoubtedly, it was the memory of the spirit of mutual helpfulness that presided over the conference's activities that led him to believe that certain of his former fellow students would make acceptable secret agents, among them Jean Naville and Jacques Bonvalot. Jean de Roquefort had no illusions regarding the immediate operational capabilities of Naville and Bonvalot: "They left on this adventure without any military training, nor any training in clandestine activities and the strict discipline imposed by them," he subsequently noted.

> But they possessed some marvelous advantages. First of all, for both of them, a brilliant intelligence in the service of religious and patriotic faith, the one supporting the other intensely; secondly a team of comrades of equally exceptional integrity, all working together in the spirit of friendship. From the very founding of the organization, they made use of several comrades with such discretion, that at the time of the Liberation, even intimate friends had no idea that they had worked side by side for almost a year. They were able to define three types of activities and deploy their comrades among them to the best of their abilities and possibilities. First of all, those who could freely schedule their time and who had enough ability to be used in military intelligence-gathering activities; second, those with an equal amount of free time who were more suited to being liaison agents. They were well aware of the fact that the safeguarding of a network rests greatly

on the efforts of its liaison agents, who when arrested represent a significant danger to an organization of which they know many fixed points. Thirdly, there were those who were not totally free to leave their place of residence, but who could perform various services of locality research, transmission location, safe haven location, etc.[2]

On his side, Jean de Roquefort—thanks to his father-in-law, who was the doctor for the bordellos of Lyon—entered into contact with various unsavory characters whom he recruited without too much difficulty. These men had contacts in all of the whorehouses of the area. They got along best with the women when they were not supporting them.[3]

What better information agents than these women, whose business had more than doubled since the arrival of the Germans? Weren't they the first to be informed of the arrival of a new battalion, when they saw the arrival of the commanding officers assigned with scouting out the troops' new quarters? Weren't they in a perfect position to go through the pockets of their customers' uniforms?

Henry Hyde had explained to his agents that "by law, every German solider had to carry on his person the Feldbuch" (field book), a military identity document that gave his rank, his former unit postings, and his current posting. These documents provided absolute proof of the presence of a specific unit in a particular place. By recopying the military identifications of their customers, the prostitutes of the network would be able to reconstruct part of the German battle plan in the southeast of France.

This program had certain inherent problems: How would the military training of the OSS prostitutes be accomplished? They had to learn how to distinguish the different uniforms and recognize different honors and badges. The person in charge of falsifying papers for the organization, André Beau, printed tiny pamphlets for them that they could hold in the palms of their hands and that contained all the various German Army insignia.[4]

Pubescent students of Father Chaine's were given the responsibility of bringing the pamphlets to the prostitutes and teaching the women to use them to the best of their abilities. Regarding these little pamphlets, Jean de Roquefort pointed out:

> It is noteworthy that my team-mate (Mario Marrett) and I ourselves had to procure in France, with enormous difficulty, all of the pieces of information, in particular the make-up of the larger units and the tactical identification signs of the German units, and that our work would have been greatly accelerated and improved if the service would have been in a position to provide us with this information, prior to our departure from Algiers or London. Moreover, we later learned that the service, as soon as it had obtained the necessary information, edited it for the practical use of its agents. At the same time, not being

aware of this fact, we ourselves published a little brochure quite similar to that of the service, although unfortunately less complete. We faced enormous difficulties both in gathering the useful information and compiling it, as well as in clandestinely publishing it in great volume. Nonetheless, we succeeded, and subsequently all of the agents working on our various teams had this paper in their possession. It by itself made possible worthwhile work by agents who had no military training nor any personal knowledge of the German army.

These were valuable contributions to understanding the German order of battle in southern France. The military information gathered by the students of Bonvalot and Naville, as well as by the prostitutes of the group, flowed abundantly. Two radio operators, one of them Mario Marret, worked tirelessly. They were barely able to handle all of the traffic, not hesitating to increase the risks. On November 20, 1943, Henry Hyde had to call them to order with the following telegram: "DURING LONG BROADCASTS, I INSIST THAT YOU CHANGE YOUR FREQUENCY MORE OFTEN. DESPITE THE EXCELLENT INFORMATION YOU ARE PROVIDING US WITH, WE FEEL THAT YOU ARE BROAD-CASTING TOO OFTEN AND FOR TOO LONG PERIODS AT A TIME. I KNOW THAT YOU HAVE A WEALTH OF INFORMATION, NONETHELESS, PLEASE BE CAREFUL."[5]

The risks were incurred because there were too few radio operators and broadcasts were made almost always from the same locations.

"In the city and in the surrounding villages, we rather quickly obtained the use of 7 or 8 locations, which consisted of apartments or villas left to us by the parents of Lyon students," wrote Roquefort.

It is important to note that it was very difficult, in this comfortably middle class area . . . , to arrange for broadcast locations to be lent to us. People whose ready willingness and courage were beyond reproach and who, incidentally, gave us proof thereof, habitually shied away from the type of risks we were asking them to take there. This certainly stems in part from the fact that, once the German radio direction-finder located with certitude a broadcast coming from a given house, and even if all of the inhabitants had time to flee, the house was seized, ransacked and occupied until the end of hostilities. Of course, we assumed the responsibility of financially compensating for the damage done, but for the people concerned, it was less a question of money than a question of sentimental value. He who would willingly sacrifice his life was dismayed to see his family heritage and the antique furniture that was dear to him disappear. Additionally, this was a difficulty for us also. . . . We had several accidents of this type during radio broadcasts and the financial compensations we paid out greatly depleted our budget, even though they were for less than the damages actually sustained.[6]

Even though the OSS agents had the use of six or eight broadcast locations in almost a year, they never had the use of more than two locations at the same time. Most often, for lack of any other option, they had to "cool their heels" several days in a row in the same location.[7]

Mario Marret narrowly escaped being caught red-handed about 10 times. On April 11, 1944, he finally fell into a trap set for him by a double agent working for the Gestapo. It took Jean de Roquefort 6 days to communicate news of the Lyon arrests to the OSS general headquarters in Algiers. The message was transmitted by the radio station installed by Captain Lescanne in the southwest of France: Algiers received the news with the expected emotion. At the time of Mario Marret's arrest, the network had sent 226 messages pertaining to the enemy's battle plan and the movement of troops. The quality of information was such that the intelligence staff of the Allied Forces Headquarters (AFHQ) assigned it a very high source assessment ranking.[8]

The American military especially appreciated the telegram of February 3, 1944, announcing the imminent arrival of 18 German divisions in the south of France. They correctly inferred from it that this was only the beginning of important troop movements toward the coasts.

At the time, the Germans had a pressing need for fresh troops in Italy. Battle was raging around the monastery of Monte Cassino, and the German Wehrmacht was getting ready to launch a counteroffensive in Anzio, where the Allies had landed on January 21, 1944, in order to block Allied progress across the peninsula. The 18 German divisions indicated by Roquefort, came to replace troops suddenly transferred to Italy. The southeast of France would be the next important strategic site in the Mediterranean basin. In order to prepare for the disembarkation at Provence, the Algiers branch of the OSS had received orders to situate the greatest possible number of agents there. One of Henry Hyde's spies, "Ben," had also accomplished a mission there, which caught the attention of the American general staff. As for Roquefort, he had already sent certain of his agents on timely missions. The Lyon arrests gave Roquefort a pretext for redeploying his organization toward those regions chosen for an eventual landing in the south.

In the southwest of France, the Penny Farthing network was headed up by a former French Army officer, Capt. Jean Lescanne. Upon news of the Normandy landing, Lescanne assigned all of his men to observe the reorganization of the battle plan (of the order of battle) of the SS Das Reich division, which controlled the whole region. On the evening of June 9, Lescanne encoded a telegram: "NUMBER 67 DIVISION S.S. DAS REICH HAS LEFT REGION GARONNE IS HEADING NORTH VIA

NATIONAL ROUTES 20 AND 126 SINCE 7TH OF JUNE UNTIL MORNING OF 9TH."

"I hesitate a great deal to send such a message," confided Lescanne.

Think of it, I was charged with observing a division, it slipped between my fingers, and it was with 3 days delay that I announced this movement. I was thinking that this was not so great; finally, what convinced me to send it, was that I thought it would confirm the messages that the other information services were sure to have sent. In a manner of speaking, I felt that it was honest to send this message. I was without pride, I can honestly say.

I felt I was at the end of my strength. I was convinced that it was dangerous for me to continue, that I would take unadvised actions which would compromise the network and make my men take risks, so I made a decision which was very difficult for me: to rest for 48 hours. I knew that because of the extreme secrecy of my organization, my absence, no telegram would be sent, no matter what its importance. No matter what.

Once telegram number 67 was sent, Lescanne therefore left to rest for 2 days in Vire-sur-Lot, in the country house of a Fumel engineer. Upon his return, a great deal of work awaited him. His team had not been idle; Algiers had sent several telegrams that had to be deciphered. Rested and ready, Lescanne got to work.

"NUMBER 106 YOUR INFORMATION CONTINUES TO BE OF GREAT IMPORTANCE TRANSMIT AS SOON AS POSSIBLE ANY OTHER PLANS OF DIVISION S.S. DAS REICH WILL IT LEAVE ITS CURRENT LOCATION?"

The message was sent before telegram 67 reached Algiers. Lescanne could congratulate himself for having sent news of Das Reich's departure via national routes 20 and 126.

The OSS agent set about decoding a second message. After the first words, his heart started beating faster: "NUMBER 107 YOUR MESSAGE 67 THE BEST EVER RECEIVED HERE YOU DO YOUR COUNTRY GREAT SERVICE."

Lescanne was transported with delight: "Therefore, I was the first to announce the departure of Das Reich," he wrote, "and I didn't want to send the telegram! I am too close to my work to accurately judge the value of the information I transmit."

It actually is quite rare that a secret agent himself can appreciate the significance of the information he transmits. In this particular case, it is not certain that the head of the Penny Farthing network himself, Henry Hyde, was aware of the importance of the message his agent sent him. Perhaps it was as a matter of routine that Hyde sent it on to U.S. Army intelligence (G-2), which in turn disseminated it to the American general staff. Once the information was distributed among the military circuits, it was appreciated for its true value. The congratulations from Algiers were proof of this. What precisely was the importance of this message? It is difficult to say. It can be verified that it was distributed among the various Allied general staffs, however, because a few days later the British soldiers in turn sent their congratulations to the OSS agents.

That telegram alone justified the past activity of Jean de Roquefort's network. Until June 1944, the information sent to Algiers by the antenna of the Lyon OSS agents was not immediately useful to the Allied military forces. This does not mean to say that it was useless. Dealing essentially with the German order of battle in central and southern France, it often overlapped with data transmitted to the Allied secret services by other agents. Given the importance of cross-checking for the information services, the overlap was to be appreciated. But until telegram 67, the network had not sent any indispensable information to the Allies. Even so, Jean de Roquefort's organization belonged to the best OSS networks in France.

During this time in Lyon, Mario Marret was trying to save his own life. The Germans had no doubt as to Marret's importance: Investigators from Berlin were specially sent "to interrogate him, both regarding the sequential events of the Allied disembarkation in North Africa in which he participated, as well as regarding questions of radio technique."[9]

But for reasons unknown to him, instead of being remanded in the custody of the Gestapo torturers known for their cruelty, Marret passed into the hands of two noncommissioned Abwehr officers who had taken part in the arrest of April 11, 1944: Franz Oehler and Ako von Czernin.

"He knew so well how to take the upper hand, with his calm presence and unfailing lucidity," wrote Jean de Roquefort, "that it would not be wrong to say that he was the one who was in charge during all the interrogations, holding his own in regards to his interrogators. It is thus that he became the only detainee held at Fort Montluc who refused to sign his deposition because he couldn't speak German, the language into which his declarations had been translated. Although normally this sort of refusal would result in further torture, the Germans were inclined almost to accept it in good grace."[10]

Oehler and von Czernin wanted to believe that Mario Marret was an important OSS agent who benefited from connections all over town, but they needed concrete proof of this.[11]

In defiance, Mario Marret asked them to compose a message that he undertook to broadcast over the BBC airwaves. Getting the message on the air would show the officers that he was an agent with powerful Allied connections. Somewhat skeptical, the two officers accepted. Imagine their surprise when, around May 20, they heard the voice of the BBC announcer intone: "Here are fruits, flowers, leaves and branches."

From the depths of his prison cell, Marret succeeded in proposing a deal to the two officers, whom he saw almost every day: His life against theirs. Like many of their compatriots based in France, von Czernin and Oehler no longer believed in the victory of the Third Reich. Signs of impending defeat were growing on the horizon.

But the Abwehr agents required guarantees. As they wanted explicit agreement from Mario Marret's superiors, Roquefort mentioned the existence of Ako von Czernin and Franz Oehler to Henry Hyde. The chief of the OSS Secret Intelligence Branch in Algiers did not have the authority to guarantee immunity to the two Abwehr agents. He also needed his hierarchy's endorsement.

Henry Hyde gave his response without delay: The directors of the OSS accepted the deal, but not without having verified that the two men were not listed as war criminals.[12] The OSS Archives do not specify whether, as a rumor has it, the affair was brought to the attention of President Roosevelt by Donovan himself.[13]

All the same, it was impossible for us to verify whether, as claim certain survivors of the network, direct negotiations took place between OSS emissaries and German secret agents. There was talk of a ransom payment of such a high amount that the approval of an American congressional committee would have been required—not normal procedure, since the OSS at the time controlled substantial secret funds. Many unanswered questions remain today regarding these negotiations. If there was a ransom, to whom was it paid? At the end of the war, nothing in the lifestyles of Oehler and von Czernin gave any indication of sudden improvement.

At the time of Mario Marret's arrest, the OSS had established contacts first with heads of the Abwehr, and indirectly with heads of the Gestapo, in order to negotiate a separate peace with the Germans—an incredible story that would not be worth mentioning if some strange coincidences had not brought it close to the Marret case.

Four months before Mario Marret's arrest, during the night of January 8–9, 1944, an American airplane dropped by parachute above the town of Besse-en-Chandesse (Puy-de-Dôme region), a former cagoulard (member of a secret right-wing political society) Paul Dungler, assigned a noninsignificant mission organized by Giraud's general staff and by OSS heads, among them the chief of the Bern branch, Allen Dulles. As head of the Secret Intelligence division, Henry Hyde supplied the means of transportation. Paul Dungler was in charge of meeting with dissident officers of the Abwehr, who had already been contacted in France by one of his friends, Gabriel Jeantet, Marshal Pétain's deputy of missions. Dungler served as the liaison between the high officials of the Abwehr and the OSS. Soon after his arrival in France, Algiers sent him three radio operators who rejoined the villa in Nice, where the negotiations organized under the auspices of the Count Jean Couitas de Faucamberge took place.

Gabriel Jeantet's contacts—Hans Buccholz, local head of the Abwehr, and Fritz Unterberg, head of the Lyon branch of the Abwehr—were part of a group of conspirators who were on the verge of making an attempt upon the life of Adolf Hitler.[14]

The historian Jacques Delarue, who investigated the secret negotiations between the OSS, the Abwehr, and Vichy, pointed out that they were carried out with the approval of Pierre Laval; Otto Abetz, head of the Nazi Party's SD operations in France and close to both Laval and von Ribbentrop; and Foreign Minister von Ribbentrop, who supposedly informed Hitler of the possibility of a separate peace with the Americans. Several special German envoys were dispatched to a new negotiator, under the auspices of the magnate Jacques Lemaigre-Dubreuil, who had recently fled to Madrid, without success.

Given the current state of our knowledge, it is impossible to say whether the case of Mario Marret ever came up during these strange meetings. On his side, Mario Marret constantly had the impression that he could never have manipulated von Czernin and Oehler without outside intervention. Conversely, Henry Hyde believed the opposite and spoke of a simple coincidence. All the same, without the complicity of the two Germans, Marret would never have been able to save his own life and that of his secretary, who was arrested with him. On August 23, 1944, the two Abwehr agents, accompanied by Mario Marret and his secretary, crossed the German lines before going to the Allies.

Allen Dulles's French Friends

Of all the Frenchmen who worked for the Americans, the most misunderstood is without a doubt Col. Gaston Pourchot, who played a decisive role for the OSS, as reported by Allen Dulles's records filed at the National Archives. Pourchot was one of those heads of French military information services who, such as Commander Paillole, Colonel Rivet, or Colonel Villeneuve, had never agreed to lay down arms in 1940 and continued to fight a shadow war. A hero of World War I, Gaston Pourchot from 1928 to 1939 was deputy to the chief of the information services warpost of the Terre de Belfort army, spearhead of the French military information services in their information research on Germany.[15]

The German counterspy located Pourchot several times in the course of his innumerable missions in Germany and Central Europe. Accused of espionage, Pourchot was sentenced under various aliases and, due to nonappearance in court, to several years in prison by the tribunal of the empire of Leipzig. Since 1939, the surname, first name, ranking, and identifying marks of the French secret agent, could be found inscribed in the "Deutsches Fahndungsregister," the German listing of all those persons to be arrested immediately upon their entry into German territory.

At the beginning of 1939, when conflict already appeared inevitable, the heads of the French Army's information services had decided to send Gaston Pourchot to Bern to head up the Swiss bureau, a choice posting. As chief of the French information services in Bern, Pourchot felt compelled to make contact with his Allied counterparts posted there. Relations with the British mirrored the cordial misunderstandings that separated the politicians. By contrast, he got along well with the Polish, who would serve as intermediaries between the French and British information services. His relationships with the Americans were very warm and for good reason. The American military attaché, Gen. Barnwell Legge, shared Puorchot's hatred of the Germans without reserve. The two men had finished World War I in the same sector of the Somme if not in the same trench.

"Soon after my arrival in Bern as military attaché of the United States," wrote Legge to Pourchot, "we made contact. Since that time, you have steadfastly helped me by supplying me with valuable military information for me to transmit to the War Department. Since the United States entered the war, you have given me all of the information you had access to. Those who had knowledge of your work were well aware of just how delicate and difficult your position in Bern was."[16]

The simple fact of communicating confidential information to his American counterpart while the United States was not yet at war put Pourchot, as well as the service in general, in a delicate position. At worst, he could have risked being accused of treason, particularly since the first submissions started in June 1940, right after the French debacle. Two years later, with the entry into war of the Untied States, these communications amounted to choosing the Allied camp. This actually was the choice of the Vichy chiefs of military information services, with General Rivet at the head, in total opposition to the politics of Pétain. It was also the choice of Gaston Pourchot.

In Bern, Lieutenant Colonel Pourchot found himself faced with an increasingly delicate situation. Put on leave following the armistice of July 1940, he received hardly any more money from Vichy. His superior in Vichy, however, Colonel Rivet, had given him orders to continue the fight. For almost 2 years, Pourchot regularly sent him letters, cables, and coded telegrams. But after the dissolution of the French Army, Pourchot no longer received any kind of subsidy. The American military attaché, Barnwell Legge, came to his aid as can be seen in a letter written to him on December 18, 1942:

My dear comrade and colleague, during the past three years, we have worked together in total confidence and understanding. You liberally and loyally gave me your infallible assistance at a time when I needed it the most. Without your help, the directors would often have been poorly informed. Everyone concerned owes you a great deal. Given the present circumstances and the demobilization of your army, I realized that you are experiencing serious difficulties by continuing to work towards the common cause. It is with pleasure that I offer you all the financial assistance so that your valuable work can continue. I can guarantee you this assistance for at least five months and as soon as we begin on this basis, I will take steps to maintain this financial support. With the assurance of my great esteem, I am cordially yours, General Legge.

Pourchot accepted this tentative proposal, which would ensure the survival of his networks. Every month, Legge would disburse to him 45,000 French francs and engaged to honor all of the pecuniary interests of his French colleague.

After the French Army was dissolved and the information service heads went underground in November 1942, Pourchot had lost all contact with his superiors. He had tried communicating directly, using the radio transmitter of the naval attaché, Henri Ferran, with Algiers, where the heads of the information services were now to be found. But the Swiss had detected the broadcasts and put pressure on the French Ambassador to put an end to them.[17]

Pourchot was obliged to comply. General Legge again came to Pourchot's rescue by putting his means of communication at the Frenchman's disposal. Legge then sent the following message to the OSS bureau in Algiers:

To be transmitted to Colonel Rivet or Colonel de Winck (French information service): "Our transmissions have been intercepted, we temporarily cease but we continue to listen at 10 hours G.M.T. We show reception on 14114 kilocycles. Until we are better informed, we will communicate with you via the Americans, in our code. Our telegram will start with a group of four zeros. Signed 206." Please transmit immediately to American general headquarters. Urgent reply requested.

Legge had only attached one condition to the use of his radios by Pourchot: Washington, DC, was to receive a duplicate of all messages sent by Pourchot to Rivet's services in Algiers. Pourchot was aware he was taking a great risk and noted that his code book was a "thing to be put into the fire rather than lost."[18]

"I want Washington, D.C. and Algiers to be kept informed of what I am doing," Pourchot replied to Legge. "It is clear that I am not betraying my country. Also, I do not want Algiers to obtain my information from Washington, D.C."

The ground rules having been set, the work could now begin. The Americans had no complaints. Very quickly, Legge transmitted congratulations from Washington, DC, to Pourchot and showed him dozens of little notes from the general staff ordering him to keep informed by all means, and not at any price to sacrifice the source of this precious information.[19]

The Americans would need Pourchot's services and agents more than ever. Bern, in effect, was starting to become a strategic OSS base with the arrival of Allen Dulles.

Since June 1943, Gaston Pourchot fulfilled the functions of interallied information services head in Bern.[20] His situation nevertheless remained precarious. Being dependent on the Americans for financial and communications support, he was unable to establish a direct radio link to Algiers. In August 1943, thanks to the collaboration of French naval attaché Henri Ferran, Pourchot was finally able to do so. But the security of his communications remained his primary preoccupation, as evidenced by this note of Pourchot's:

> October [19]43. Admiral Bard, French Ambassador appointed by Vichy, was informed by me of my activity in the services of the Algiers information services and of the presence of my hidden radio transmitter in the Consulate's offices. Not only did he fail to raise any objections, but he adroitly evaded several objections from federal political departments, demanding that an end be put to the activities of that post. The Swiss authorities are actually isolating our embassy within a separate electric sector and as soon as my broadcasts start, they cut the current. Radio traffic continues in a form of hide-and-seek (changing schedules, changes of quartz, shadings of overtones, etc.).[21]

Since the total occupation of France in November 1942 and the escape of its heads of state to Algeria, Gaston Pourchot had the impression of being relegated to diplomatic limbo. His position remained strange: military adjunct attaché of an officially dissolved army—that of Pétain—he only continued to occupy his offices because Vichy had, so to speak, "forgotten" to recall him and because no one came forth to denounce this singular omission. Furthermore, being a diplomat posted in a Vichy embassy, he was a man of Giraud's army secret services. He was even present in full uniform at the burial of one of his agents, who died in Switzerland after having been seriously wounded by the Germans as he crossed the border.

In the French Embassy in Bern, Pourchot's delicate position forced him to be even more discreet. He was unable to voice his opinions, unlike most of the diplomatic personnel, who boycotted the new embassy adviser, Jean Jardin, who was very close to Pierre Laval and whose Cabinet he had directed.[22]

Pourchot was soon faced with a dilemma. On November 16, 1943, he sent a coded telegram to Algiers:

The Commissariat of Algiers for Foreign Affairs has invited those of its agents in Switzerland who would like to join together [a number of them had already secretly done so several months before] to finally break all ties with Vichy.

Most of them (advisers, secretaries, consuls) have decided to resign in about 15 days, the amount of time necessary to finish consultations. I am wondering what my attitude should be at that moment.

If I stay, I can continue my activities, but my comrades and I will be judged severely by people with whom we have official relations, both professional and personal. The output of the post will certainly decline, at least at first.

If I leave, this output will diminish considerably, since I will see myself assigned, as will my collaborators, to a fixed place of residence by the Swiss authorities.

In all good conscience, I see the solution of staying in places the most difficult for us, as well as the best advised if the post's activities should be continued in the general interest.

I await your orders.

Signed: Pourchot.

The reply arrived 6 days later.

Algiers, November 22nd.

Reply to your telegrams 110 and 111:

Colonel Rivet and I understand how difficult staying at the embassy would be when others were leaving, for you and your collaborators. Given that by staying at your post you can continue to serve as you have done until now, you must stay. The general commander in chief and your service chief here are covering you.

I will let you judge what is the most opportune time to inform the local Allied representatives whom you are in contact with of this decision, and the reasons which govern it.

Signed: Villeneuve.[23]

The death of the Vichy Ambassador in Switzerland, Adm. François Bard, on April 1, 1944, could have put the delicate position of Lieutenant Colonel Pourchot in jeopardy again, had his replacement, Jean Jardin, named interim chargé d'affaires at the embassy, so desired. During the course of his initial contact with the latter on April 10, 1944, Pourchot decided to put all of his cards on the table. Was the head of the Bern information services right to take Jardin into his confidence? The answer can be found in a report written by Pourchot after the war:

[Jardin] told me he appreciated my honesty, because he was totally informed and added that he would do everything possible to help me. I answered that I wanted these promises to be turned into action.

On April 19, 1944, Jardin received a letter by special courier that was personally signed by Laval, urging him to have all activity of Commander Pourchot's services in Switzerland stopped, to dissolve his services, to seal off the offices they occupied in the Consulates, and to make the personnel working there return to France.

M. Jardin gave me this letter, written in such a peremptory tone, to read, asked me my opinion, and at my request without hesitating a single instant, wrote back: "that there once was an information service operating out of the Embassy and the Consulates, but that this service disappeared a long time ago and that the activity of the accused members of the military is purely ceremonial." I personally checked with the Embassy's mail service that this reply had indeed been sent.[24]

Of all of Pourchot's agents, a young 18-year-old man named Albert Meyer, recruited in September 1940, would prove to be the best one. Despite his inexperience in matters of espionage, Albert Meyer quickly recruited dozens of informers on his various expeditions. He based a solid network within the Association of Enlisted and Voluntary Combatants of the War of 1914–18, which was presided over by his father until his death in June 1940. The religious order of the Marianists, by which he had been educated in Belfort, provided him with lodging, alibis, protection, and information. His many cousins rounded out his initial organization. Chance encounters took care of the rest. Very quickly, Meyer could count on the collaboration of dozens of informers who regularly sent him messages and correspondence to a post office box in the Belfort region, where accessory employees intercepted all of the letters addressed to one or another of his various false names. This was an ingenious system, which also served him well during his travels and kept him from having to carry compromising evidence on his person.

Lieutenant Colonel Pourchot had many opportunities to observe that Albert Meyer worked "as efficiently as the most well-trained of technicians . . . recruiting and instructing with complete authority a magnificent network of information agents skilled in evasion and action." Pourchot was impressed by his young agent's "prodigious output," which enabled him to

> provide the commanding forces with military, economic and political documentation of crucial importance, due to its abundance, richness and precision. Identifying among others more than 300 divisions of the Axis.[25]

Taking care of his own mail distribution, he has secretly crossed the borders of Alsace, Belgium and Switzerland more than 200 times, always under very dangerous and sometimes exhausting conditions, due to his night crossings over mountains and through the snow.

Pourchot felt that Albert Meyer was "since 1941, far and away the best of the 250 agents of the French information services posed in Switzerland."[26]

Meyer returned to Switzerland nearly every month. Once he reached Bern, he would give his report to his superior. Gaston Pourchot could then begin his slow and meticulous reconstruction of the battle plan of an army always on the move. The commanding officer never questioned his subordinate about the composition of his networks located behind enemy lines.

In Gaston Pourchot's office, there was a large map of Europe on which, month by month, he made note of upsets in the battle plans of the German divisions. Details of the various regiments were also noted in a notebook, regularly kept up to date with the help of, among others, Albert Meyer.[27]

At the end of August 1943, Pourchot entrusted Meyer with a most delicate task, the idea for which occurred to him in the course of a conversation with Allen Dulles and General Legge. These two men had asked Pourchot questions about the possibility of an Allied landing in the west of France that were too precise not to awaken his attention.

They wanted to know whether the head of the French information services in Bern was familiar with the German battle plan in his region and whether he could obtain more precise information on the coastal defense or on the morale of the civilian population. Dulles had also contacted one of Pourchot's colleagues, the French naval attaché, Corvette Captain Ferran, with whom he had become acquainted at the beginning of 1943.

"What would be the best place to land in the West or the North of France?" asked the American. "In Spring of 1942," replied Henri Ferran, "Admiral Darlan asked my services to prepare a study of the feasibility of an Allied landing in France. We concluded that the landing could only take place in one spot: the bay of the Seine, because of the radius of action of the airborne cover. Incidentally, you should have that study. I remember that it was transmitted to the Americans and not to the Germans."[28]

Gaston Pourchot took Allen Dulles's concerns very seriously. Despite the solid network of information he controlled in that region, he decided to send Albert Meyer, his best agent, there with precise instructions. This was no general mission concerning the German battle plan in France, but a more elaborate operation, based exclusively in Brittany and Normandy. Meyer understood that he was entering a sensitive area.

At his home in Belfort, Meyer had received a summons from the obligatory work service, notifying him of an order to present himself to the construction site of the German engineering firm Todt in the port of La

Pallice, next to La Rochelle. The happenstance was too good to be true. What better way to experience firsthand the importance of work done by the firm of Todt within the framework of construction of the Atlantic Wall? He also hoped to learn everything there was to know about the German submarine base at La Pallice.

The summons from the firm of Todt had arrived at his family's home in Belfort. At the time, the German services did not have access to any centralized files. If they had, the executives of the engineering firm would not have taken the trouble of summoning a man wanted by the Gestapo. For the first time, Albert Meyer was to carry out a mission under his real name, with authentic identity papers and a legal passport. Since the Todt construction sites were not closely supervised, it would be easy to disappear once his observations were complete. For several days, he led the monotonous life of a construction worker at La Pallice. He was always watchful, however. Once his investigation was complete, he reported his first impressions:

> Some time ago, the Germans conducted testing of new mines in La Pallice, the characteristic of which is sound-wave attraction. The study of these mines was then continued in the Arcachon basin, after which the research engineers left to do more research in Norway, with the intention of returning to the region. It consisted of a normal mine, inside of which was to be found an adapted sound recording device of the type used in cinematography. The tests were conducted at various depth levels and at points more or less far removed from the coast.
>
> La Pallice: Until recently, the Germans used minesweepers to locate British mines. Since the passage at La Pallice is very narrow (300 meters wide) and the mines exploded in 5 seconds, it often happened that the minesweepers became the victims of their own detonation devices. To solve this problem, the Germans are currently using an ordinary airplane equipped with a round disk under the fuselage. The disk acts as an electromagnet, detonating the mines from a distance. The results obtained are good and identical to those obtained by the minesweepers.

Meyer made reference to the iron gates that the Germans placed over the town exits every night in order to isolate it from the rest of the world. Once he left La Pallice, he would draw them to their exact dimension.

> At the submarine base, modifications have been made to the submarines concerning their defensive weapons against aircraft. On the 30th of September, there were 13 submarines there, the usual number of based there, 6 large tankers used to provision the coast with fuel oil, and beached submarines which were being repaired. Since the crane of La Pallice was blown up (sabotage), a 300-ton crane was specially

brought from Bordeaux to take out the warships. But during the most recent bombardment of La Pallice, the new crane was also destroyed, such that the tankers, which were about to be repaired, could not be put back in the water. The Germans are actively building something which will slide them out to the sea.

He also observed how much the shortages of fuel oil, lubricants, and other petroleum products affected the Germans:

At the submarine base, the Germans are currently using a type of wooden filter covered with a fine screen to collect the grease and fuel oil which floats in the section of the port reserved (for their use). It is this very poor quality oil, containing up to 70% fuel oil, that the French bargemen are using. The proportion of the oil used by the fishermen is the following: 50 liters of more than mediocre-quality oil for 8,000 liters of fuel oil.

In a few weeks, Meyer reconstructed the German battle plan in Britanny, and he had enough agents in the area to accomplish his monthly updates. He still had to organize the last part of his expedition, which touched upon one of the most sensitive zones of the region. Pourchot had in effect asked him to take his explorations as far as Upper Normandy in order to check out the coastal defenses of what would—although Pourchot did not know it yet—become the beaches of the Allied landing of June 6, 1944.

Since riding around on a bicycle was too risky, in order to work effectively, Meyer had to take the train. From Paris, he had made sure to send false passes from the German engineering firm Todt to the address of his Langrune hideout. Armed with the precious blue piece of paper, he would make a perfectly acceptable STO worker. He only had to melt into the crowd to observe the coastal defenses at his leisure.

In the mornings, he was up at 6 o'clock, like the other workers of the region whom he met at the counter of the local bistro for his first meal of the day. Like everyone else, once he had swallowed the hot water colored with coffee, he had to down a glass of calvados in one swallow. Once this test was passed, he followed the workers in their silent procession to the closest train station and went with them in the little local train that took him to the Normandy coast, its cows, . . . and its blockhouses.

One week later, the secret agent handed in his report to Gaston Pourchot. The head of the French information services would use it to write a long letter to the attention of the American secret services, synthesizing the German battle plan in France, a letter that was much appreciated by the heads of the general staff (JIC), as is borne out by a letter from Legge to Pourchot, February 3, 1944: "My dear colleague and comrade, Mr. Dulles asked me to tell you that he just received from Washington, DC, a great praise for the telegram summing up the Wehrmacht's situation as of

Prior to the Allied landing in Normandy, the OSS received information on German battle plans and coastal defenses. (26-G-2343)

January 1st. He would like this praise to be communicated to you since you supplied this information."

Thanks to the networks implanted by Meyer throughout France, Pourchot was now sure of regularly receiving information that allowed him to update his knowledge of the enemy's manpower and positions. Little by little, the territory overseen by the information services grew. Pourchot now had the means to achieve what would without a doubt be the greatest coup of his career as master spy: provide the Allied general staff, via OSS channels, with the complete, detailed battle plan of all the German troops stationed on French soil 15 days before the Normandy landing.

To our knowledge, no history of the Second World War mentions this fact, albeit crucial to the Allied forces. A letter from General Legge to Pourchot dated June 19, 1944, attests to its veracity: "My dear colleague and comrade, I have the great pleasure of informing you that Washington, DC has observed that your reports summarizing the situation in France, completely and accurately correspond to the divisions seen at the battle-front. The telegram also mentioned that this information was of crucial importance."[29]

On July 3, 1944, the OSS representative in Bern, Allen Dulles, sent a letter to the American military attaché, General Legge:

Top secret.
A cable from London confirms that S.H.A.E.F. would like to send a trained observer to Belfort or to Mulhouse in order to have radio reports on military movements by road or train, and would like your assessment of the possibility of putting this plan into action from Switzerland, either by sending radio equipment to people already there, or by sending a person there for the express purpose of doing this work. I think P. [Pourchot] would probably be the best person to carry this out and give us his advice. Of course, it is with pleasure that I will cover all expenses and I suppose that we could parachute in the equipment."

Before leaving Bern, Albert Meyer was given a brief summary. Everything happened too fast, explained Pourchot; the French Army pushed the Wehrmacht to the gates of Besançon so quickly that the logistic services could not keep up. De Lattre could not launch a sanctioned attack against Belfort. He preferred waiting for the means necessary for victory, even if it entailed giving the Germans time to reorganize. The only sure way not to lose the advantage gained was to maintain a solid network of spies behind enemy lines, in order to evaluate the state of the forces and the reorganization of the 19th German Army. For the time being, not much was known about the enemy troops grouped within this 19th Army, said to be thrown together from here and there. More precise information was needed. This was Albert Meyer's new mission, baptized "Stuka."

The young agent was put at the disposal of the operational information service (SRO) of the 1st Army; he had to report only to his boss, Gaston Pourchot, to Commanding Officer Simoneau, in charge of the SRO, and to his superior, General Carolet, head of the Second Office of the general staff of de Lattre. He had free rein to spy on the military apparatus put in place by the Germans. He had to know everything, for any detail could be the decisive one, down to the location of the most insignificant battery, nestled in the smallest of hamlets, its caliber, the number of the company assigned to protect it, the infantry elements, and the number of Panzers stationed in the neighboring countryside. If, until the month of August 1944, the German military occupation had been rather diffuse, the recent presence of German soldiers in certain villages of Trouée changed everything. The enemy was prepared to use the smallest nook and cranny in order to defend the gateways in Alsace. The lives of thousands of French soldiers, not to mention the entire outcome of the battle, depended on information to be obtained by Albert Meyer.

The Germans had requisitioned all able-bodied inhabitants of Belfort and assigned them to work details of embankment in order to consolidate the defenses of the town, which was declared to be in a state of siege. The men now walked down the streets of Belfort with shovels and pickaxes, completely surrounded by armed soldiers. Meyer was left with only the women. Soon after his return to Belfort, Meyer had recruited five young girls, to whom he gave advice on how to best gather information. He taught them to recognize the different insignias, grades, and coats of arms of the German Army and how to determine their location from the signal boards. Then he assigned each one to a different sector, where she was to recruit willing informers. Thanks to a mail network, he arranged to have the information dispatched to Pourchot on a regular basis.

The network functioned at full capacity from September 25 onward. Not a single town in the region escaped the coverage of the information agents. Thanks to their regular informers, they methodically reconstructed the German battle plan, village by village, carefully noting the names of the companies and artillery batteries, without omitting the caliber of the guns. The women were even more to be congratulated since at first the German troops were constantly on the move. It was not military tactics that dictated the movements, but rather an incredible disorder. Surprised by the Allied offensive and by the retreat of its troops, the general staff of the Wehrmacht tried as best as it could to reshuffle the units it could and to create new ones. Things calmed down by the beginning of October, when all of the troops had taken to their quarters. The work of Albert Meyer's network was thus made easier, but it only became more dangerous.

Meyer was arrested on November 11, 1944, on a tip from a double agent. News of Albert Meyer's arrest quickly reached the SRO of the 1st Army and caused some consternation among the general staff of General Lattre de Tassigny. The final offensive against Belfort was subject to some scheduling modifications: The SRO had neither the time nor the means to implant a new network behind German lines, and the 1st Army wanted to benefit from the advantage gained thanks to the information of its agent. The attack began on November 15. Several days before the liberation of Belfort, Meyer would be taken prisoner in Germany. He escaped when he took advantage of a bombardment and lived in the depths of a forest for several months before being liberated by the American troops.

History has not done justice to Gaston Pourchot, who finished out his life as a simple colonel, whereas Albert Meyer was made a general, following his campaigns in Indochina and Algeria. Like the other Frenchmen who labored alongside the OSS, Jean de Roquefort, Mario Marret, and their Penny Farthing companions believed that they did not get the recognition that was due. One can imagine their bitterness and their sadness when they learned that certain of the torturers of the OSS networks, such as the radio double agent DARTMOUTH, who was responsible for the arrests of dozens of agents, were retrieved, among others, by the French secret services, thus escaping punishment for their crimes.

NOTES

1. Jean de Roquefort's memoirs, May 1948, private archives.
2. Jean de Roquefort memoirs.
3. Interviews with Mario Marret and the other survivors of the Penny Farthing network, 1987–90.
4. Jean de Roquefort memoirs.
5. Telegrams of Ravina, File 134, Box 16, Entry 136, Records of the Office of Strategic Services, Record Group 226, National Archives and Records Administration, Washington, DC (hereinafter cited as RG 226, NA).
6. Jean de Roquefort memoirs.
7. The radio sites of the Penny Farthing network were also listed in the OSS Archives under the heading of "Chaine Durrants," (Durrants station). There were 10 of them.

Ravina	September 15, 1943–December 3, 1943
Alpina	December 16, 1943–December 31, 1943
Carthage	January 23, 1944–July 18, 1944
Hastings	March 25, 1944–August 16, 1944
Shilling	June 24, 1944–July 28, 1944
Sixpence	June 13, 1944–August 30, 1944
Millen	July 24, 1944–August 30, 1944
Hallicrafter	August 18, 1944–August 29, l944
Mallory	August 21, 1944–August 25, 1944
Simpson	August 22, 1944–August 23, 1944

8. Henry Hyde, memoirs concerning the activities of the various SI networks in Algiers, prior to May 14, l944, 49 pages. File 575, Box 33, Entry 97, RG 226, NA.
9. Jean de Roquefort, report dated May 1948, op. cit.
10. Ibid.
11. Interview with Ako von Czernin, Jan. 18, 1988.
12. According to Henry Hyde, the investigation was conducted by Whitney Shepardson, the head of the OSS Secret Intelligence Branch in Washington, DC.
13. At the end of the war, Donovan said to Hyde: "I went to see the boss and spoke to him about it, and he seemed interested." Nonetheless, Roosevelt was not in favor of contacts with enemy secret services. He had forbidden Allen Dulles to pursue his interviews with the Abwehr conspirators who dreamed of a separate peace. And for good reason: Roosevelt was a staunch supporter of unconditional surrender.
14. Following one aborted attempt, the conspirators succeeded in planting a bomb in Hitler's general headquarters on July 20, 1944, but Hitler escaped the assassination attempt. The head of the Bern OSS division, Allen Dulles, was undoubtedly the person most familiar with the affair, having practically followed it as it happened, thanks to his personal contacts with one of the conspirators, Hans Bernd Gisevius, an agent of the Abwehr. (Subsequently, the conspirators would be replaced by the two men who supervised Mario Marret's arrest.) On this subject, see *To the Bitter End* by Allen Dulles, as well as a report by Allen Dulles dated February 1945, File 2004, Box 117, Entry 148, RG 226, NA.

15. Biography of Col. Gaston Pourchot, edited by General Meyer, in reference to the files of General Rivet (private archives). To our knowledge, the role played by Commander Pourchot is referenced in four works: *Le Temps des Verités (The Time of Truth)* and *La Service de Renseignements 1871–1944 (The Information Service, 1871–1944)* by Henri Navarre; *Services Spéciaux 1935–1945 (Special Services, 1935–1945)* by Paul Paillole; and *Une Eminence Grise (A Gray Eminence)* by Pierre Assouline. In Belfort, Pourchot operated with Captain Serot, who was the head of the information services of the Belfort Air Force, and who would be assassinated along with Count Bernadotte in Jerusalem on September 17, 1948.

16. Letter from Brig. Gen. Bromwell Legge to Lt. Col. Gaston Pourchot, Jan. 4, 1945 (private archives).

17. According to Henri Ferran, the broadcasts from the French diplomatic quarters had been detected by the Germans due to some two-way, direction-finding cars (a special device used to locate radio transmitters) they had in Switzerland.

18. Interview with Col. Gaston Pourchot in Belfort, Oct. 23, 1987.

19. Gaston Pourchot would be decorated in October of 1946 with the Legion of Merit, one of the highest American decorations. The accompanying letter, signed by President Truman, thanked him for having delivered to the Americans information of the greatest importance between 1940 and 1945.

20. A telegram from General de Winck, chief of the general staff of the Head Command, dated July 7, 1943, to General Legge attests to this nomination (private archives).

21. Gaston Pourchot, notes on the Jardin affair (private archives).

22. See Pierre Assouline, *Une Eminence Grise.*

23. Colonel Villeneuve was the head of the information services in Algiers and was assisted by Commanding Officers Rendu and Simoneau.

24. Gaston Pourchot, notes on the Jardin affair (private archives).

25. This figure looks enormous. There were never 300 divisions of the Axis in France. Actually, Pourchot is also including the divisions that passed through France.

26. See the report concerning the activity of and honors bestowed upon Albert Meyer of Belfort by the Army General Staff's Special Services in Switzerland, signed by Lt. Col. Gaston Pourchot on December 16, 1945, at the French Embassy in Bern (private archives).

27. Interviews with Gaston Pourchot and Albert Meyer, 1987–90.

28. Interview with Henri Ferran, Nov. 18, 1987.

29. Correspondence between Legge and Pourchot (private archives).

FROM HITLER'S DOORSTEP:
Allen Dulles and the Penetration of Nazi Germany

Neal H. Petersen

Introduction

For 32 months during the Second World War, the Office of Strategic Services (OSS) mission in Bern, Switzerland, was an American observation post on Hitler's doorstep. It transmitted thousands of messages to Washington, many of which bore evidence of the personal involvement of Allen W. Dulles, the mission chief. Throughout, the principal target was the principal enemy—Nazi Germany. Secret information provided to OSS Bern by an official in the German Foreign Ministry and by members of the internal opposition to Hitler constituted one of the great intelligence breakthroughs of the war.

OSS Bern resembled a Central Intelligence Agency in itself, its operations ranging from gathering order of battle information to running espionage networks to orchestrating unconventional military operations. Dulles ventured far beyond the domain of intelligence to offer his own views on grand strategy and psychological warfare. The reports from Bern, found largely in the cable files of the OSS operational records, offer an exceptional source for the study of the OSS, Allen Dulles, intelligence tradecraft, Nazi Germany, and the course of the war in Europe.

Background of a Spymaster

Hours before the Germans sealed the French border in November 1942, Allen Dulles arrived in Switzerland, eminently qualified to conduct intelligence operations focusing on Germany. His grandfather and uncle had been Secretaries of State. As a fledgling U.S. diplomat in World War I, Dulles was posted to Vienna and then Bern, where his duties included the collection of intelligence on Germany, Austria-Hungary, and the Balkans. This on-the-job training familiarized him with European politics and taught him the craft of intelligence. He established U.S. and European contacts that would serve him well 25 years later.

At the Paris Peace Conference, Dulles served as an adviser on the Central European settlements. He and his brother, Foster, had influence beyond that afforded by their official positions since the Secretary of State, Robert Lansing, was their uncle. Allen served with numerous future foreign service luminaries including Leland Harrison, Hugh Wilson, Joseph Grew, and Adolph Berle. The Dulles brothers, supportive of Wilsonian principles, left Paris partially dissatisfied with the conference results, particularly the stern provisions with respect to Germany.

After the Peace Conference, Dulles helped to reopen the U.S. mission in Berlin and witnessed the anarchy of 1920. In 1926, he left a promising career in the Foreign Service to practice law with his brother at Sullivan and Cromwell in New York. From 1926 to 1941, he interacted with East Coast financial leaders and established powerful international business connections, some of them in Germany. He also served as a prominent member of the Council on Foreign Relations and as an occasional State Department adviser on disarmament, in which capacity he traveled to Germany and Switzerland. In 1933 he met Hitler as part of a U.S. delegation.

As international lawyers, the Dulles brothers arranged loans for Weimar Germany, motivated in part by the belief that Germany's economic health was essential for international stability. Allen reacted vigorously to the rise of Hitler and, over the objections of Foster, convinced Sullivan and Cromwell to close its Berlin office in 1935. Allen became a leader of the interventionist movement in the United States, promoting the theme that U.S. self-interest was best served by assisting the democracies of Western Europe in resisting Nazi revisionism.

In 1941 Dulles joined William Donovan's emerging intelligence organization as head of its New York office, which was located in the same building as British Security Coordination. His principal activity was the gathering of information on Germany and the exploitation of German emigres. Toward the end of 1942, he was assigned command of the OSS mission in Bern. He arrived as an experienced diplomat and man of the world. His power base rested less upon the President or General Donovan than on dozens of friends and connections in the State Department, the Eastern establishment, and international commerce. German affairs had figured importantly in his career. Dulles undertook his Swiss assignment with broad understanding and sympathy for the German nation, as well as feelings of revulsion for its leadership.[1]

OSS Bern and Wartime Switzerland

Surrounded by Axis-controlled territory, wartime Switzerland was a center of intelligence activities, offering the Allies an unsurpassed vantage point of Nazi Germany. When Allen Dulles appeared on the scene in

November 1942, the diplomatic, military, and intelligence components of the American legation were already operating networks into adjacent countries, including Germany. The Dulles system, involving scores of sources and intermediaries with code numbers and names, was an extension of this previous practice.[2]

By early 1944, the Bern OSS mission consisted of 5 actual OSS officers and 12 cipher and translation clerks. There were more than 100 subagents and other paid informants reporting on Germany and other areas.[3] The intelligence operation utilized the services of State Department employees, private American citizens trapped in Switzerland by the war, downed airmen, and foreign nationals. Dulles's top aide was Gero von Gaevernitz, a naturalized American whose father had been an important professor and liberal political figure in Germany before the war. Other key operatives were Frederick Stalder, a Swiss; Royall Tyler, an American who had served as a League of Nations official; Frederick Loofbourow of Standard Oil; and former members of French intelligence. Dulles relied heavily as well on Gerald Mayer, the legation's representative of the Office of War Information (OWI), and worked closely with military attaché Brig. Gen. Barnwell Legge and members of his staff. OSS representatives at Geneva, Zurich, Basel, and Lugano reported to Dulles at Bern.

Dulles bore the title of Special Assistant to the Minister, Leland Harrison, and represented himself as a personal envoy of President Roosevelt. Operating in a relatively open fashion, he utilized his great personal charm and active social life to develop contacts. This is not to say that Dulles was inattentive to business. The documentary record of his service at Bern indicates extraordinary energy and competence.

The OSS in Bern operated espionage nets into all adjacent countries but relied primarily on indirect penetration. This was particularly true with regard to Germany, where foreign agents introduced from Switzerland, or anywhere else, into a hostile population stood almost no chance of survival. Most of the "sources" identified in Bern OSS reports resided in or visited Switzerland. They included political and cultural exiles, refugees, emigre lawyers and doctors, socialists and trade unionists, and above all, diplomats and intelligence officers of Allied, neutral, satellite, and enemy nations stationed in Switzerland. The Vichy French and Polish legations were intelligence bonanzas. International business and religious connections survived amazingly in wartime conditions; travelers regularly supplied reports on conditions in Germany. The OSS went to great lengths to respect Swiss neutrality and maintained satisfactory ties with Swiss intelligence, which improved as the outcome of the war became apparent.

Dulles cooperated extensively with the British Secret Intelligence Service and Special Operations Executive in Switzerland. U.S. and British intelligence often shared sources and exchanged information. Friction and the withholding of information also existed in the relationship, however. The

British sometimes concealed their contacts and resented interference by the Americans, whom they tended to regard as dangerous amateurs. They frequently disparaged OSS sources and information. For his part, Dulles objected to excessive British caution and inadequate support for resistance movements. He was less than forthright in 1943 when he wrote in response to news of British criticism of his security procedures: "Broadway's [British intelligence in London] comments for my guidance are always welcome."[4]

Initial Operations, 1942–43

From the moment of his arrival, Germany was Dulles's principal concern. However, opportunities for espionage within the Reich were initially limited, and OSS Bern devoted much of its effort to more promising avenues in Italy, France, and Eastern Europe for much of 1943. At the same time, Dulles addressed the psychological aspects of the war against Germany and offered Washington unsolicited advice on grand strategy.

The Dulles Policy toward Germany

The role of intelligence under Dulles at Bern must be considered in connection with his political agenda. His top priority was fulfillment of the complementary objectives of Nazi defeat and the emergence of a democratic and pro-Western Germany. He repeatedly emphasized the strength of left-wing sentiment in Germany and the danger that even the German generals might opt for the "eastern solution"—an accommodation with the Soviet Union.

In January 1943, 2 months after Dulles's arrival in Switzerland, President Roosevelt and Prime Minister Churchill promulgated the doctrine of unconditional surrender at the Casablanca Conference. Dulles initially extolled this approach as sound psychological warfare but soon spoke out against any interpretation that could be viewed by the German people as meaning dismemberment, poverty, humiliation, and Soviet domination.[5] From the beginning, Dulles saw the war as an East-West battle for the hearts and minds of Germans. This theme permeated Dulles's reports throughout the war. He insisted that the war be fought with concurrent regard for postwar settlements and that the probability of future rivalry with the Soviet Union should be taken into account. This put him at odds with basic Presidential policy.

The German Target in 1943

Dulles soon began reporting heavily on matters within the Reich. Among the German sources that Dulles developed were lawyers Eduard Waetjen and Max Doerner, former Chancellor Josef Wirth, Baron Michael Goden, Wilhelm Hoegner (a German Socialist emigre), trade unionist George Richter, Friedreich Hack (formerly of Krupp), and Evert Smits of Fokker. Intelligence transmitted by OSS Bern in 1943 included the views of the Swiss psychiatrist Carl Jung on Hitler's psychological state, German industrialist Walter Bovari's information on German arms production, and details of the German V-1 and V-2 programs at Peenemunde. A Professor Braun was said to be the driving force. Other typical reports provided the impressions of a Swiss traveler to Cologne and the views of Prince Maximilian Hohenlohe, a Sudeten German aristocrat living in Spain who had access to both Himmler and Allen Dulles and crossed international borders at will.[6] Following the war, Soviet propaganda sought to establish that Dulles's contact with Hohenlohe in 1943 constituted an effort to negotiate a separate peace with Himmler.[7] German industrialist Eduard Schulte supplied OSS Bern with valuable information on the German economy, as well as early warning of the Holocaust.[8]

Order of Battle and Industrial Production

Most OSS Bern reports concerned military subjects: enemy formations, troop movements, military production, and bombing targets and results. This nuts-and-bolts military and industrial intelligence originated with information received from indigenous patriots across Europe and brought to Switzerland by resistance or OSS couriers. A portion of the take related to the German homeland. The raw data was usually processed in Geneva prior to transmittal by a Dulles assistant or by a former French intelligence officer working closely with OSS Bern. Dulles sometimes added a comment or a caveat. This type of information took a long time to reach London or Washington and was not closely keyed to day-to-day wartime developments. The value lay in quantity and detail. The Bern information was used to confirm and supplement ULTRA intercepts. Bombing result reports and suggestions for targets were valued highly. The U.S. military initially discounted reports from Bern, but ratings from Washington improved as the war progressed.

Dulles Radiotelephone Transmissions

To report the wide range of classified and unclassified information he was receiving, and to disseminate his own opinions, Dulles established a scrambler-equipped radiotelephone link with New York. Transmitting in the evening on some 300 occasions from 1943 to 1945, he presented far-reaching analysis of current aspects of the war. Dulles referred to these reports as "flashes." This commentary, which dealt with Germany above all, received extensive distribution in Washington and was often sent to the White House in the last year of the conflict.[9]

Psychological Warfare

From the date of his arrival, Dulles concerned himself with various tactical aspects of psychological warfare, as well as with espionage and grand strategy. He sent a barrage of suggestions to Washington outlining themes for undercutting German morale and separating the Nazi leadership from the people. Proposed dirty tricks included the distribution in Germany of bogus ration cards and train tickets and measures to undermine the value of German currency.[10] Dulles also collaborated with Gerald Mayer, the Bern representative of the Office of War Information, in producing printed propaganda and disinformation locally for distribution in German-controlled areas. The OSS and OWI produced a spurious German newspaper and other propaganda mailings.

Fritz Kolbe ("GEORGE WOOD")

On August 21, 1943, Dulles reported the establishment of contact with Fritz Kolbe, code-named "GEORGE WOOD," a mid-level official in the German Foreign Ministry who had come to Switzerland to offer his services to Allied intelligence.[11] A committed anti-Nazi, this walk-in arranged for official duties to take him to Switzerland and first approached the British, who turned him away as a likely plant. Kolbe then contacted Dulles through intermediaries and, returning to Berlin, became one of the most important agents of the war. From 1943 to 1945, he smuggled the texts or summaries of some 1,600 documents to Bern.[12]

An assistant to Karl Ritter who was responsible for liaison between the Foreign Ministry and the military, Kolbe had access to an incredible array of documents that were exchanged between the two entities. The papers that he presented to the Americans in August 1943 included warnings that the Germans had penetrated U.S. communications from Cairo, information on conditions in Germany, bombing results and targets, and indications of German espionage and machinations in Iberia and Africa.[13] In October, Dulles transmitted numerous additional GEORGE WOOD reports on subjects including an impending submarine attack on an Allied convoy near the Azores, German-Italian relations, German activities respecting Turkey, and Nazi spying on the Allies in Portugal.[14]

Establishing Kolbe's Bona Fides

British experts in London, including Claude Dansey and Kim Philby, were skeptical of the Kolbe material. The source also seemed to be too good to be true in Washington, where it was subject to an evaluation over the course of many months. In addition, the Allies feared that even if Kolbe were genuine, he posed a threat to a far more important source— ULTRA. Bern's communications security was suspect, and should the Germans thus become aware of their own security problem, they might undertake a shakedown that could uncover the compromise of ENIGMA transmissions. Dulles staked his reputation on the validity of the WOOD traffic,[15] and the accumulation of evidence vindicated him.

Once Kolbe's good faith was established, the information he provided was circulated widely, probably too widely for the agent's safety. Additional

As part of its efforts to undermine the Nazi regime, OSS propaganda linked Hitler's policies with death. The bottom row of counterfeit stamps express this idea. (Record Group 226)

major consignments arrived in Bern in December 1943 and April 1944, swamping coding capabilities. OSS Bern cabled the WOOD traffic to Washington with the designation "KAPPA." At OSS headquarters, the take was reorganized by subject as the "Boston Series." The White House received this material on a regular basis, although there is no evidence that it was seen by the President or acted upon.[16] The WOOD traffic shed light on German policy, plans, activities, and problems around the world. It was particularly helpful on the Reich's relations with neutral Turkey and its difficulties with its satellites. The WOOD traffic contributed to the unmasking of CICERO, the German spy in the household of the British Ambassador in Turkey.[17] Dulles described the material received in April 1944 as the deathbed contortions of Nazi diplomacy—Berlin trying in vain to retain influence over wavering satellites and neutral neighbors.[18]

The WOOD Traffic in the Latter Stages of the War

The Nazi crackdown after the failed attempt on Hitler's life in July 1944 compelled Kolbe to suspend operations only briefly; the flow of material resumed in August. After Allied armies reached the Swiss border in September 1944, OSS Bern was able to transmit the actual microfilm received from Kolbe to Paris for processing and distribution. In 1945 "GEORGE WOOD" transmitted copious amounts of information on the war in East Asia as reported by German diplomats and attachés in Japanese-controlled areas. Ongoing themes were the danger perceived by the Germans of a separate peace between Japan and the Soviet Union and Japanese efforts to promote a separate peace between the Soviet Union and Germany, which Tokyo thought would permit Germany to concentrate its forces in the West and hence draw Allied attention away from the Pacific.[19]

Kolbe remained in place until the last month of the war, reporting on the disintegration of the government in Berlin and providing information on the relocation of agencies and their records. By early April 1945, the Foreign Ministry had virtually ceased to function, and Kolbe faced the prospect of being drafted. Only then did he seek well-deserved refuge in Switzerland.[20]

The German Resistance[21]

In large measure, Dulles established his credibility in Washington by reporting on the emergence of the German military opposition to Hitler, which culminated in the July 20, 1944, attempt on the Fuehrer's life.[22] He first reported on the internal opposition, or lack thereof, in January 1943, and at that early date set forth the theory often to be repeated that opponents to Hitler might well be inclined to favor the Soviet Union after the war.[23] The doctrine of unconditional surrender followed a few days later, and became inseparable from Bern's reporting on the resistance.

In September 1943 Dulles asserted that there was no opposition in Germany aside from uncoordinated nuclei with which contacts were being sought: Protestant and Catholic Church circles, labor elements, Communists, special departments of the government, and the army. He stated that any change of government would come from the top, and that influential circles were divided between the Eastern and Western solution.[24] In November of the same year, Dulles began answering a series of questions on the opposition posed to him by OSS headquarters. His replies appeared in cables slugged "Bakus." He stated that Gestapo terror had thus far prevented the emergence of organized opposition.[25] During the same period, he had another meeting with Prince Hohenlohe, who contended that some German leadership elements might be receptive to the replacement of Hitler. Himmler, he said, favored an accommodation with the West.[26]

Emergence of "Breakers"

On January 27, 1944, Dulles first described a coalescing of opposition elements that he called "Breakers."[27] He said that the group was composed of various intellectuals from certain military and government circles, which maintained foreign contacts and communications through the Abwehr,

German military intelligence, headed by Admiral Canaris. Dulles added: "I quite understand that you may doubt the foregoing statement but I am convinced of its accuracy after examining the situation for a period of many months."[28] In fact, Dulles's main contact with the group was Hans Bernd Gisevius, an Abwehr officer serving under cover as German Vice Consul in Zurich. This stern and physically imposing individual also had a Gestapo background and was distrusted by the British. Dulles supported his writing of an ongoing history of the German resistance, which was published after the war.[29]

Also on January 27, Dulles reported the view of Eduard Waetjen that Breakers had three tendencies: those who wanted to see Hitler take the blame for the collapse, revolutionaries who favored the Eastern solution, and those with a Western orientation. What, Dulles asked Washington, would you be interested in achieving via Breakers? What offers could we make to the resistance movement? On February 4, Dulles cited the Socialist leader Leuschner, General Oster of the Abwehr, and Goerdeler, the former mayor of Leipzig, as potential opposition figures. He emphasized that Breakers was essentially a center-left movement.[30] The people of Europe had moved to the left, he said. They did not want communism, but they wanted a new social order. The West was losing an opportunity in not dealing with opposition elements. "Our policy," he said, "seems to have been predicated upon the idea that a military victory plus unconditional surrender was all that was needed." Soon thereafter, Dulles reported that Canaris and the Abwehr were about to be absorbed by Himmler and the Sicherheitsdienst (SD), the Nazi Party security service, threatening OSS contacts.[31]

In March 1944 Donovan proposed that a questionnaire be submitted to members of the German resistance. Dulles responded sharply, inferring that Donovan had not been paying attention. Dulles submitted the answers that he thought the Germans would give, based, he said, not on idle theorizing but on "innumerable reports and extended consultations with individuals qualified to discuss such topics, who have come from Germany." Dulles then said in effect, that there was no point in discussing a deal because nothing had been done to qualify the Allies' stated determination for an unconditional surrender, and most Germans felt that the Allies intended to ruin Germany economically as well as militarily.[32]

On April 6, 1944, Dulles reported a long conversation with Gisevius and Waetjen, who had just returned from Germany. They said that General Beck and others were thinking about a coup and sought Western help. Dulles replied that no action would be taken without Soviet knowledge. The following day, Dulles cabled that according to his sources, Breakers was gaining strength and was ready to try to oust Hitler if the West was willing to negotiate. Generals Rundstedt and Falkenhausen were said to be ready to receive Allied paratroop drops in strategic areas. Dulles repeated to Donovan on May 13 that the Breakers group was actually willing to help Western forces enter the Reich if they were permitted to maintain the Eastern front.[33]

The Failed Putsch of July 20, 1944

From July 12 to 15, 1944, Dulles transmitted a number of messages giving clear indication that an internal move against Hitler was about to occur. The success of the Normandy invasion and Soviet victories had given the Breakers group new vigor. He reported that Gisevius had returned to Germany to participate and that Adam von Trott zu Solz, Goerdeler, Helldorf (Chief of Police in Berlin), and Generals Beck and Fromm were among the conspirators. Dulles expressed doubt as to the intestinal fortitude of the military leaders involved but emphasized that the moral consequence of a display of bravery by the Germans in setting their own affairs in order would be of great value to Germany's postwar status in Europe. He now described the Breakers group as wanting as much of Germany as possible to come under Western control and called for a Presidential announcement disclaiming any desire for the complete annihilation of the German people.[34]

Dulles received no immediate firm information on the July 20 attempt on Hitler's life. On July 22, he cabled that "Breakers are breaking," and that the outcome rested with certain army reserve units. He urged that if an opposition survived, President Roosevelt issue some statement and that Nazi strongholds be bombed and rebel-held territory spared. In fact, the bomb planted by Count von Stauffenberg failed to kill Hitler. The conspirators in Berlin hesitated, and most were quickly killed or arrested. Gisevius went into hiding, escaping to Switzerland 6 months later with the help of OSS-produced documentation. Dulles reported the failure of the putsch in his radiotelephone transmission on the evening of July 22; he lamented that the next such attempt would probably be made by elements favoring accommodation with the Soviets.[35]

Aftermath of July 20

In the aftermath of July 20, Dulles recommended that the British be provided with Breakers information but was apprehensive in light of their distrust of Gisevius and others involved. He advised against providing the Russians with complete documentation. Dulles stressed to Washington that he had not instigated the coup or encouraged the Breakers group, which had acted on its own. He transmitted extensive after-action reports detailing the roles of various German notables, suggested methods for psychological warfare exploitation of the events of July 20, and reported the survival of opposition elements despite the ongoing purge.[36]

Dulles expressed concern about Soviet sponsorship of a Free Germany Committee. He endorsed the Western policy of letting the Germans fight it out among themselves but said that he saw no indication that the Russians were following the same procedure.[37] The flow from Bern of information on German bombing targets, secret weapons, order of battle, production, and civilian morale continued.

Latter Stages of the War, 1944–45

External Penetration of the Reich

During the summer of 1944, OSS headquarters began planning for massive penetration of Germany and Austria by agents inserted from abroad. Donovan and Dulles corresponded on the subject in a series of cables labeled "Gerplan." Dulles emphasized the difficulties involved in operations from Switzerland in light of controls on both sides of the border. He felt that penetration operations would compromise other successful forms of espionage. He also noted that the doctrine of unconditional surrender ensured that Allied agents would receive no help from the indigenous population. He did hold out some hope for penetration via his German labor contacts and especially from other areas such as Alsace.[38]

Soon after Allied forces reached the French-Swiss border in September 1944, Dulles left his post, met with General Donovan in France, and then flew to the United States for consultations in Washington and New York. After his return to Bern in October, he focused increasingly on liaison with advancing units and the setting up of camps on the French side of the frontier to assist in the penetration of Germany by Allied agents. As part of the overall Allied effort in the last months of the war to insert agents, primarily left-wing German exiles, into the Reich by parachute drop and overland, Gerhard Van Arkel of the OSS Labor Branch arrived to take charge of such operations based in Switzerland.[39]

Thereafter, Dulles considered or suggested various devices for penetration or disruption in Germany, including promotion of a railroad strike. He even advanced the suggestion of Noel Field, his liaison with the German left in Switzerland, that the OSS establish relations with CALPO, the Paris branch of the Soviet-sponsored Free Germany Committee, in order to enlist the services of German Communists as penetration agents.[40] Late in the war, OSS Bern finally achieved a degree of penetration of Austria, primarily via the resistance representative Fritz Molden.[41] Dulles remained convinced of the superior utility of his indirect penetration methods. He urged that disaffected German diplomats, officers, and intelligence operatives not be encouraged to defect because they were of more potential value in place.[42]

The Battle of the Bulge

The Dulles organization was no more successful in anticipating the Ardennes offensive than were military intelligence and ULTRA. Dulles's assessments of the state of the war in late 1944 shared the unwarranted optimism present in other appraisals and contributed to the Germans' achievement of surprise. For example, on November 23, he had cited evidence that Germany was going through a particularly serious and possibly fatal crisis due to military reverses.[43]

In his after-action analysis, Dulles stressed the political side of German motives for launching the attack. The Nazi hierarchy hoped to induce the Allies to consider peace offers. Dulles said that the Ardennes offensive showed that the fatalistic resignation of the German people did not affect military operations. Germany was fighting like a cornered beast that saw no possible alternative. He also told Donovan that the Ardennes intelligence failure was partially attributable to the presence of too many senior OSS officials in the United States rather than in Europe, where they would be more useful.[44]

German Peace Feelers and Contacts

In early December 1944, Dulles had reported signals from Neurath, the German consul general in Lugano, to the effect that SS Generals Harster and Wolff, and possibly Himmler himself, sought to achieve some sort of understanding with the West. In addition, Dulles pursued indirect or secret lines to Generals Rundstedt, Westphal, Blaskowitz, and Kesselring via Neurath and Gaevernitz channels. There were indications that the generals might consider opening the western front to the Allies under the proper circumstances. Dulles asked in vain for permission to tell non–war criminal German officers that if they helped to bring an end to the war, it would be taken into consideration. On March 1 he reported that General Eisenhower had been informed of these contacts through General Sibert, 12th Army Group G-2.[45]

In February 1945 OSS Bern began to receive a separate series of indirect German soundings, these from Himmler and Kaltenbrunner through their henchman Wilhelm Höttl and the Austrian industrialist Fritz Weston. The thrust of this initiative, which persisted until the end of the war, was that Himmler and Kaltenbrunner were anxious to eliminate warmongers like Bormann and come to terms with the West. Dulles told Washington that naturally persons of the Himmler-Kaltenbrunner type could gain no immunity, but they might be used to further dissension within the enemy ruling circle.[46]

Among other German elements seeking a last-minute deal was a conservative Catholic faction in Bavaria centered on the Nazi General Von Epp. Dulles asked Washington if any encouragement should be given to such rascals in order to weaken the German home front and detach Bavaria from Berlin's control, or whether men like Von Epp were beyond the pale.[47] On April 5, 1945, Dulles reported efforts by Walter Schellenberg, head of SD intelligence, to establish contact with the Western Allies through the

Swiss. General Masson, head of Swiss intelligence, indicated that Schellenberg's idea was to open the Western front while holding the Eastern front. Dulles told Masson that the Western front was already opened up without Schellenberg's help.[48]

Planning for Postwar Germany

Dulles began planning for postwar Germany soon after his arrival in 1942, compiling lists of "useful Germans" who could serve in a reconstructed democratic nation. He encouraged Eduard Schulte and others to develop plans for economic reconstruction; presented analyses of the likely postwar German political situation, in which he foresaw the emergence of two groups based on the social democrats and Christian center; and addressed details of occupation policy.[49]

Dulles was the driving force behind the organization of an OSS postwar mission in Germany ("the German Unit"), which he ultimately headed and for which he unsuccessfully sought extensive administrative independence. He urged the preparation of a strike force, including his top advisers on Germany, to enter the country immediately upon victory. He visualized securing important German intelligence documents in Russian-occupied Berlin. Late in the war, Dulles proposed that agents be sent into Germany for activation only after the end of hostilities and discussed with OSS officials Henry Hyde and Hugh Wilson the development of means for the penetration of Germany from France after the war. He also suggested that occupation zones be drawn with the postwar East-West rivalry and operational intelligence requirements taken into consideration.[50]

Dulles recognized the importance of securing German scientific and technical expertise after hostilities and urged that individuals possessing specialized skills and knowledge be allowed to seek refuge in Switzerland. This approach sometimes ran afoul of the Allies' Safe Haven program designed to prevent the Nazis from exporting and hiding items of value in neutral countries. Dulles and other Allied operatives, including Moe Berg, reported from Switzerland on German atomic energy and missile programs with a view toward assessing their wartime threat and obtaining personnel and equipment at the war's end.[51] On April 30, 1945, Dulles reported that Professor Messerschmidt was prepared to come over with jet aircraft plans. Immediate action was deemed necessary to prevent the French from obtaining this windfall.[52]

In February 1945 Dulles warned that the Soviets would come to Germany with an occupation regime of German sympathizers already organized. He urged that the United States should seek a joint occupation government for the entire country and secretly groom pro-Western individuals for positions of influence. He also suggested that anti-Nazi, pro-Western Germans in Switzerland could organize a committee on their own. "While I recognize importance of taking no action which would give Russians any just ground for complaint," he cabled to Donovan, "I feel . . . that unless we can show some interest . . . there is grave danger that anti-Nazi elements . . . will find no practical alternative except to throw in with Russians." Subsequently, he reported an upsurge of activity in the German colony, including organization of a Democratic Germany group and publication of an anti-Nazi, pro-Western newspaper.[53]

The National Redoubt

From 1944 onward, Dulles reported German plans for making a last stand in an Alpine redoubt. The German Army in Italy, unless Dulles could arrange its surrender, would presumably be the backbone of this final defense. On January 15, 1945, Dulles reported that the Nazis would make a last stand in the Bavarian and Austrian Alps in the hope that the Anglo-Saxons and Russians would clash soon after linking up. He judged the national redoubt concept to be in line with the Wagnerian complex of the whole National Socialist movement. Until virtually the end of the war, he persisted in the belief that the national redoubt would come into existence despite acknowledged lack of evidence of material preparations and his occasional doubts. He also discussed the possibility of guerrilla warfare by die-hard Nazi elements after the end of organized resistance.[54] Allied military intelligence, press, and the public also anticipated a Nazi last stand in the Alps. In fact, the Alpine redoubt never materialized. It was part fantasy born of the unreality of Hitler's last days and part an outright German deception operation. Dulles's reporting probably contributed to a result totally contrary to what he would have wished. Concerned by the threat of an Alpine concentration of German forces, the western armies hesitated slightly in their drive into central Germany and thereby permitted the Red Army to penetrate deeper into the Reich.

The Secret Surrender

The best known success of Allen Dulles in World War II was his negotiation of the surrender of the German Army in Italy (Operation Sunrise). It was a direct outgrowth of earlier indirect contacts with German military and SS leaders. Those involved included Dulles's assistant Gero Gaevernitz, Swiss intelligence officers, Swiss and Italian intermediaries, Field Marshal Alexander's headquarters at Caserta, future NATO commander Gen. Lyman Lemnitzer, a Czech radio operator secreted in German headquarters, and the most unlikely participant in a conspiracy to surrender, SS Gen. Karl Wolff. Dulles accurately recounted this story of high adventure in *The Secret Surrender* (1966). Although the surrender was not achieved until the last days of the war, partially because of indecision in Washington and London, many lives were saved. The episode precipitated an ugly exchange of correspondence between President Roosevelt and the suspicious Stalin that presaged the outbreak of the cold war.[55] In the last days of the war, Dulles hoped to obtain the additional separate surrender of German forces in Austria.[56]

Conclusion

Contrary to his expectations, Dulles remained in Switzerland for 2 months after V-E Day. In addition to wrapping up lingering aspects of Sunrise, he engaged in contacts with the Japanese that might have assumed great importance had not the atomic bomb intervened. Only in July 1945 did he assume command of the OSS mission in Germany. He achieved some success over the next several months in securing German intelligence assets but was frustrated by the postwar administrative chaos of U.S. intelligence. After the dismemberment of the OSS in September 1945, he returned to his law practice in New York. In the immediate postwar period, he extended personal assistance to certain of his German wartime contacts. He published *Germany's Underground* in 1947 in an effort to promote the moral basis for Germany's return to the Western community of nations.

Evaluation of Dulles Operations Targeting Germany

A definitive evaluation of the intelligence on Germany provided by OSS Bern awaits detailed research by many experts. The admixture of intelligence and policy, fact and opinion, and secret and open information in the Dulles reporting make a firm judgment difficult. So also do the matters of timeliness, duplication of and by other sources, and Dulles's lack of modesty in taking credit. Students and practitioners of modern intelligence methodology should be uneasy in regard to Dulles's old-fashioned excessive reliance on instinct, impressions, and personal relationships.[57]

This much is certain. The Dulles material, some of which, such as the WOOD traffic and Breakers, was of first-rate importance, was not properly employed in the policy formulation process in Washington. It often received wide and high-level OSS and interagency distribution but not systematic analysis or integration with information from other sources. From early July 1944 forward, General Donovan sent many of the Dulles reports to President Roosevelt verbatim, but, aside from the case of Sunrise, there is scant record of White House reaction. Nor was Dulles's input discussed by FDR and Churchill. One searches in vain for a single instance in which the riches of Bern's intelligence on Germany made a difference on the high policy level.[58]

The principal contribution of Allen Dulles in Bern may lie in the indirect impact of his widely read reports, which reflected the belief that war is properly the instrument of ongoing policy and accurately forecast the postwar threat posed by Stalinist Russia. His foresight and reservoir of contacts across the political spectrum assisted the West in persevering in the first difficult years of the cold war, with the result that Germany and other European nations ultimately escaped from under the cloud of totalitarianism. However one assesses the importance of the OSS mission in Bern, there is no denying that it constituted a unique and fascinating episode in intelligence history.

NOTES

1. The Allen Dulles Papers at Princeton University constitute the most important source on his career prior to World War II. This material contains extensive information on his early life, education, diplomatic service, and law career with Sullivan and Cromwell. Letters and other personal papers document Dulles's accumulation of friends and contacts. State Department records at the National Archives (Record Groups 59 and 84) contain some documents pertaining to his service from 1916 to 1926 and as an adviser in the 1930s. Regarding the Dulles family, see Eleanor Lansing Dulles, *Chances of a Lifetime: A Memoir* (Englewood Cliffs, NJ, 1980). Leonard Mosley's *Dulles: A Biography of Eleanor, Allen, and John Foster Dulles and Their Family Network* (New York, 1978) is an important source but should be used with caution. *A Law Unto Itself: The Untold Story of the Law Firm of Sullivan and Cromwell* by Nancy Lisagor and Frank Lipsius (New York, 1988) is revealing on the role of the Dulles brothers.

2. The primary source for the history of the OSS mission in Bern is Record Group (RG) 226, the operational records of the Office of Strategic Services at the National Archives and Records Administration, Washington, DC (hereinafter cited as NA). Some 25 boxes in Entry 134, Cable Files, are particularly important. Bern "Field Files" (mission files) in Entries 125 and 190, RG 226, NA, include material on OSS administrative operations and Dulles correspondence with persons residing in Switzerland, as well as intelligence reports. Documentation on Bern operations in the larger OSS context is included in consolidated Washington Director's Office microfilm records, RG 226, National Archives Microfilm Publication M1642. Reports of the OSS Research and Analysis Branch based on messages from Bern are interfiled in Entries 8–52, RG 226. Records of the U.S. Legation in Bern and the Consulates at Bern, Geneva, Zurich, and Lugano are located in RG 84 (State Department Post Files). State Department decimal files (RG 59) contain OSS Bern material, especially under 103.918 and 740.00119 European War. War Department correspondence with the Military Attaché office in Switzerland for the late 1930s and early 1940s are in Entry 57, Records of the Army Staff, RG 319.

   Dulles provided a general description of his Bern experience in *The Secret Surrender* (New York, 1966), chap. 2. Important overviews of the Dulles operation in secondary sources include treatments in Bradley F. Smith, *The Shadow Warriors: OSS and the Origins of the CIA* (New York, 1983); R. Harris Smith, *OSS: The Secret History of America's First Central Intelligence Agency* (Berkeley, 1972); and Anthony Cave Brown, *The Last Hero: Wild Bill Donovan* (New York, 1982). Cave Brown also presents significant information on OSS Bern in *Bodyguard of Lies* (New York, 1975) and *"C": The Secret Life of Sir Stewart Menzies, Spymaster to Winston Churchill* (New York, 1987). Cave Brown provides extensive and important, but not uniformly accurate, coverage based in part on his exclusive access to OSS Office Director's records made available to him years ago by General Donovan's law office. This vital collection finally became open to the general public in 1990–91 in the Donovan Papers at the U.S. Army Military History Institute, Carlisle Barracks, PA, and at the National Archives on microfilm in Entry 180 (A3304), RG 226. Other published sources include Jozef Garlinski, *The Swiss Corridor: Espionage Networks in Switzerland during World War II* (London, 1981) and Jon Kimche, *Spying for Peace: General Guisan and Swiss Neutrality* (London, 1961). Mary Bancroft, an American in Switzerland during the war, recalled her association with Dulles at Bern in *Autobiography of a Spy* (New York, 1983).

3. Tel. 2612–2617 from Bern, Mar. 28, 1944, Box 342, Entry 134, RG 226, NA.

4. Information on the interaction of Dulles and OSS Bern with British intelligence is presented in Cave Brown, *The Last Hero*; Anthony Read and David Fisher, *Colonel Z: The Secret Life of a Master of Spies* (New York, 1985), which treats the career of Sir Claude Dansey; and *My Silent War* (New York, 1968) by Kim Philby, the Soviet spy in British intelligence. Each, especially Philby, should be used with caution. Numerous Dulles cable reports in Entry 134, RG 226, confirm that he had difficulties with "our cousins" on a range of matters.

5. Tel. 723, Jan. 31, 1943, Box 171; and tel. 967, Feb. 11, 1943, Box 307, Entry 134, RG 226, NA.

6. Tel. 41–43, Feb. 3, 1943, and tel. 44–45, Feb. 5, 1943, Box 171; tel. 188–189, Feb. 27, 1943, and tel. 1051, Feb. 15, 1943, Box 307; tel. 2181, Apr. 7, 1943, Box 171; and tel. 1257–1261, Dec. 9, 1943, Box 274; all are Entry 134, RG 226, NA.

OSS Bern reported on the V-1 and V-2 programs throughout the war, contributing to overall Allied intelligence that made possible the bombing of production centers and launch sites and reducing the effect of surprise. Messages on this subject include tel. 338–342, June 24, 1943, Box 307; tel. 703–705, Sept. 9, 1943, Box 340; tel. 5752, Sept. 15, 1943, Box 340; tel. 1692–1693, Jan. 10, 1944, Box 274; tel. 2435–2439, Mar. 14, 1944, Box 191; tel. 3918–3920, June 28, 1944, Box 192; tel. 3991–3997, July 6, 1944 (CIA/FOIA); and tel. 8787, Apr. 7, 1945, Box 232. All except 3991–3997, which was received from the Central Intelligence Agency under the Freedom of Information Act, are in Entry 134, RG 226, NA.

7. Moscow, *New Times*, July 1960; Bob Edwards and Kenneth Dunne, *Study of a Master Spy* (London, 1961).

8. Schulte's role is described by Walter Laqueur and Richard Breitman, *Breaking the Silence* (New York, 1986). OSS Bern received numerous other accounts of the extermination of the Jews from the International Red Cross and Jewish organizations in Switzerland and, for example, from the Geneva office of the Ecumenical World Council of Churches on May 19, 1943 (Box 5, Entry 125, RG 226, NA). Walter Laqueur discusses the extensive knowledge of the situation possessed by U.S. intelligence in Switzerland in *The Terrible Secret* (London, 1980) and "Hitler's Holocaust: Who Knew What, When & How?" *Encounter* 55 (July 1980). But with a few exceptions, such as tel. 1597, Mar. 10, 1943, on the shooting of Jews in Germany (Box 171, Entry 134, RG 226, NA), Dulles chose not to emphasize the Holocaust in his reports to Washington. He was neither ignorant nor insensitive; the mother of his top aide, Gaevernitz, was Jewish. Perhaps Dulles believed that in view of German and European

anti-Semitism, the denunciation of the Holocaust would be counterproductive for purposes of Western psychological warfare. Perhaps he feared that the flight of new refugees to Switzerland would interfere with his espionage activities. Whatever his reasoning, his reticence on this subject is controversial, to say the least.

9. The texts of the Dulles radiotelephone transmissions ("flashes") are found in Boxes 169 and 273, Entry 134; Boxes 591 and 613, Entry 88; and Box 1, Entry 160, RG 226, NA.

10. For example, tel. 5688, Dec. 6, 1943, and tel. 528, Jan. 23, 1943, Box 171; tel. 333–334, June 23, 1943, and tel. 3894, June 30, 1943, Box 307, Entry 134, RG 226, NA.

11. Tel. 164–166, Aug. 21, 1943, Box 339, Entry 134, RG 226, NA.

12. The WOOD/Kolbe reports are interfiled in Bern cable files, Entry 134, RG 226, NA. Separate collections of Bern cables based on WOOD information exist in Entries 121 and 138. Kolbe's exploits are described in "The Spy the Nazis Missed," by Edward P. Morgan in *True* (July 1950), reprinted in Allen W. Dulles, ed., *Great True Spy Stories* (New York, 1968). Cave Brown provided detailed coverage of the GEORGE WOOD operation in *The Last Hero*. Kolbe's motivation is treated in Mother Mary Alice Gallin, *The Ethical and Religious Factors in the German Resistance to Hitler* (Washington, DC, 1955).

13. Tel. 651–652, Aug. 25, 1943, Box 273, and tel. 654–657, Aug. 26, 1943, Box 339, Entry 134, RG 226, NA.

14. Tel. 840, Oct. 8, 1943; tel. 852–853, Oct. 11, 1943; and tel. 880–887, Oct. 16, 1943, Box 273, Entry 134, RG 226, NA.

15. Tel. 1477–1479, Dec. 29, 1943, Box 274, Entry 134, RG 226, NA.

16. The White House set of the Boston Series is not present at the Franklin D. Roosevelt Library because it was returned to the OSS. A set exists in Box 79B, the William J. Donovan Papers at the U.S. Army Military History Institute, Carlisle Barracks, PA. A separate series of "Special OSS Reports" in Box 86 covering the period 1943–45 is based in large part on GEORGE WOOD material.

17. On Jan. 1, 1944, Dulles noted on the basis of information supplied by Kolbe that reports from the German Ambassador in Turkey were based on documents which "seemingly, were taken from the Zulu [British] Embassy through a source designated as Cicero" (tel. 1503–1505 [CIA/FOIA]).

18. Tel. 2787–2792, Apr. 12, 1944, Box 307, Entry 134, RG 226, NA.

19. Tel. 4335–4336, Aug. 19, 1944, and tel. 4551–4554, Aug. 19, 1944, Box 231, Entry 134; tel. 969, Nov. 19, 1944, and tel. 8399, Apr. 7, 1945, Box 7, Entry 90, RG 226, NA.

20. Tel. 8099, Apr. 4, 1945, and tel. 8179, Apr. 5, 1945, Box 7, Entry 90, RG 226, NA.

21. The best study on the internal opposition to Hitler is Peter Hoffmann, *The History of the German Resistance* (Cambridge, MA, 1977). Other important sources include Allen W. Dulles, *Germany's Underground* (New York, 1947); Hans Bernd Gisevius, *To the Bitter End* (London, 1948); Fabian von Schlabrendorff, *They Almost Killed Hitler*, edited by Gero von Gaevernitz (New York, 1947); and Hans von Herwarth von Bittenfeld, *Against Two Evils* (New York, 1981). The Allen Dulles Papers at Princeton contain rich material on the

subject. Regarding German intelligence, including the Abwehr, see David Kahn, *Hitler's Spies: German Military Intelligence in World War II* (New York, 1978). OSS Bern was not, of course, the only source of information on groups in opposition to Hitler, which made their views known to U.S. and British authorities through various channels before and during World War II, as described by Hoffmann. Efforts by dissident Germans to contact the Allies in Switzerland and elsewhere during 1944 are documented in U.S. Department of State, *Foreign Relations of the United States (FRUS), 1944,* vol. 1, *General* (Washington, DC, 1966), pp. 484–579.

22. Interview with Ray S. Cline, Jan. 13, 1989.

23. Tel. 314, Jan. 14, 1943, Box 307, Entry 134, RG 226, NA.

24. Tel. 763–767, Sept. 21, 1943, Box 273, Entry 134, RG 226, NA.

25. Flash (radiotelephone transmission), Nov. 13, 1943, Box 169, Entry 134, RG 226, NA.

26. Tel. 1023–1028, Nov. 9, 1943, Box 341, Entry 134, RG 226, NA.

27. "Breakers" was used henceforth to identify cables dealing with the main German resistance. Messages thus designated are interfiled chronologically in the Bern cable collections, Entry 134, RG 226, NA. Discrete groupings of some Breakers material also exist in Entries 99 and 138.

28. Tel. 1888–1889, Jan. 27, 1944, Box 274, Entry 134, RG 226, NA. The OSS cables from Bern fail to clarify the relationship between Canaris and the Allies, which is obscured by a thicket of indirect contacts and hearsay. Canaris was assigned the OSS code number 659, but such numbers were often used to identify individuals who were not agents or friendly informants.

29. Gisevius, *To the Bitter End.*

30. Tel. 1890–1893, Jan. 27, 1944, Box 2, Entry 138; tel. 1965–1966, Feb. 4, 1944, Box 228, Entry 134; and flash, Feb. 19, 1944, Box 273, Entry 134, RG 226, NA.

31. Tel. 2173–2175, Feb. 24, 1944, Box 274, Entry 134, RG 226, NA.

32. Tel. 2659–2667, Mar. 31, 1944, Box 191, Entry 134, RG 226, NA.

33. Tel. 2714–2716, Apr. 6, 1944, Box 307; tel. 2718–2722, Apr. 7, 1944, Box 228; and tel. 3423–3431, May 13, 1944, Box 228, Entry 134, RG 226, NA. OSS R&A summaries L39970, July 18, and L39971, July 22, based on Bern reports, were transmitted to the White House, State Department, and Joint Chiefs of Staff (JCS); the texts are printed in Hoffmann, pp. 749–753.

34. Tel. 4085, July 12, 1944, Box 228; tel. 4110–4114, July 13, 1944, Box 228; flash, July 13, 1944, Box 273; and tel. 4111–4112, July 15, 1944, Box 228, Entry 134, RG 226, NA.

35. Tel. 847–848, July 21, 1944, Box 276; flash, July 21, 1944, Box 273; tel. 4199–4202, July 22, 1944, Box 228; and flash, July 22, 1944, Box 273, Entry 134, RG 226, NA. In tel. 4443–4446, Aug. 11, 1944, Box 231, Entry 134, RG 226, NA, Dulles reported that a courier had seen Gisevius in Berlin. Purportedly, Beck and Goerdeler had favored an accommodation with the West, while von Stauffenberg had inclined toward the Eastern solution. Dulles asked that this message be shown to President Roosevelt and General Marshall. A 45-page account of the putsch and its background based on information provided by Gisevius after his escape in January 1945 is in Box 14, Entry 99, RG 226. Dulles's initial cables based on new information from Gisevius include tel.

4039, Jan. 24, 1945, Box 7, Entry 90; and tel. 4077, Jan. 25, 1945, Box 2, Entry 138, RG 226, NA.

36. Tel. 851–855, July 23, 1944, Box 228; tel. 860–861, July 24, 1944, Box 228; flash, July 24, 1944, Box 273; tel. 4222–4224, July 25, 1944, Box 228; tel. 866–867, July 26, 1944, Box 228; tel. 4361, Aug. 5, 1944, Box 231; tel. 4673, Aug. 25, 1944, Box 231; and tel. 4699, Sept. 3, 1944, Box 191, Entry 134, RG 226, NA. Despite Dulles's misgivings, some Breakers material reached the Soviets via the State Department in accordance with agreements reached at the Moscow Conference of 1943. See, for example, Riddleberger memorandum to Warren, May 22, 1944 (*FRUS, 1944*, vol. 1, p. 515). The USSR may well have also received additional information from Kim Philby in London, who had access to Breakers cables.

37. Tel. 4270–4272, July 28, 1944, Box 191; and tel. 4305–4307, Aug. 1, 1944, Box 228, Entry 134, RG 226, NA.

38. Tel. 4396–4400, Aug. 9, 1944, Box 231; tel. 4401–4406, Aug. 9, 1944, Box 231; and tel. 4411–4415, Aug. 9, 1944, Box 231, Entry 134, RG 226, NA.

39. Material on OSS Bern's liaison with the advancing Allied forces in France and Germany in the latter stages of the war is located in Entry 99, RG 226, as well as in the cable files of Entry 134. Direct penetration operations are described in Joseph E. Persico, *Piercing the Reich: The Penetration of Nazi Germany by American Secret Agents during World War II* (New York, 1979), and William J. Casey, *The Secret War Against Hitler* (Washington, DC, 1988). An especially interesting report by agent "Philip Keller" of his trip from Switzerland to Munich and back in March 1945 is in Box 7, Entry 125, RG 226. On October 7, 1944, while in New York, Dulles transmitted two papers to Donovan that accurately forecast the situation in Europe and Germany after the war (Washington Director's Office microfilm, M1642, roll 81).

40. Tel. 1407, Nov. 29, 1944, Box 193; tel. 1487, Nov. 30, 1944, Box 278; and tel. 4107, Jan. 20, 1945, Box 278, Entry 134, RG 226, NA. The curious career of Noel Field and some information on his wartime relationship with Dulles is presented by Flora Lewis in *Red Pawn: The Story of Noel Field* (Garden City, NY, 1965).

41. Tel. 3037, Jan. 24, 1945, Box 7, Entry 90, RG 226, NA. Fritz Molden describes his role and the Austrian resistance in *Fires in the Night: The Sacrifices and Significance of the Austrian Resistance, 1938–1945* (Boulder, CO, 1989). The direct penetration of Austria is detailed by Persico in *Piercing the Reich*.

42. Tel. 1937, Dec. 9, 1944, Box 278, Entry 134, RG 226, NA.

43. Flash, Nov. 23, 1944, Box 273, Entry 134, RG 226, NA.

44. Flash, Dec. 21, 1944, Box 273, Entry 134; tel. 2319, Dec. 22, 1944, Box 7, Entry 90; and flash, Dec. 26, 1944, Box 273, Entry 134, RG 226, NA. Charles B. MacDonald, *A Time for Trumpets: The Untold Story of the Battle of the Bulge* (New York, 1985) incorporates recent information on intelligence aspects of the Ardennes offensive.

45. Tel. 1757, Dec. 5, 1944, Box 277, Entry 134; tel. 2769, Jan. 19, 1945, Box 7, Entry 90; tel. 360, Feb. 9, 1945, Box 60, Entry 139; tel. 5839, Feb. 23, 1945, Box 7, Entry 90; and tel. 6149, Mar. 1, 1945, Box 7, Entry 90, RG 226, NA. A collection of cables on contacts with German generals in the West and Italy is included in Box 19, Entry 121, RG 226, NA. U.S. policy was governed by a

memorandum from President Roosevelt to General Donovan of Dec. 18, 1944, that ruled out any guarantees to Germans seeking accommodations outside of a general unconditional surrender (Washington Office Director's microfilm, M1642, roll 81).

46. Tel. 6097, Feb. 28, 1945, Box 228, Entry 134; tel. 6209, Mar. 2, 1945, Box 6, Entry 190; tel. 6909, Mar. 14, 1945, Box 7, Entry 90; tel. 7037, Mar. 15, 1945, Box 7, Entry 90; tel. 7589, Mar. 24, 1945, Box 7, Entry 90; tel. 8619, Apr. 13, 1945, Box 2, Entry 110; tel. 9099, Apr. 21, 1945, Box 193, Entry 134; and tel. 9519, Apr. 29, 1945, Box 7, Entry 90, RG 226, NA. Self-serving personal accounts by individuals involved in contacts on the German side include *The Labyrinth: Memoirs of Walter Schellenberg* (New York, 1956), and Wilhelm Höttl, *The Secret Front: The Story of Nazi Political Espionage* (New York, 1954).

47. Tel. 7569, Mar. 23, 1945, Box 6, Entry 190; and tel. 8759, Apr. 7, 1945, Box 7, Entry 90, RG 226, NA.

48. Tel. 8139, Apr. 5, 1945, Box 2, Entry 110, RG 226, NA.

49. Tel. 946–947, Oct. 29, 1943, Box 273; tel. 971–974, Nov. 3, 1943, Box 341; flash, Feb. 14, 1944, Box 273; tel. 2054–2056, Feb. 15, 1944, Box 170; tel. 2057–2061, Feb. 15, 1944, Box 170; tel. 3800–3806, June 12, 1944, Box 192; and tel. 4498–5000, Aug. 16, 1944, Box 231, Entry 134, RG 226, NA.

50. Tel. 1162–1168, Nov. 29, 1943, Box 341, Entry 134; tel. 2188, Feb. 24, 1944, Box 275, Entry 134; tel. 1607, Dec. 2, 1944, Box 277, Entry 134; tel. 2129, Dec. 14, 1944, Box 7, Entry 90; tel. 3047, Jan. 6, 1945, Box 192, Entry 134; tel. 3289, Jan. 12, 1945, Box 7, Entry 90; tel. 5377, Jan. 30, 1945, Box 6, Entry 90; tel. 6447, Feb. 13, 1945, Box 162, Entry 134; tel. 6847, Feb. 19, 1945, Box 278, Entry 134; and tel. 9857, May 8, 1945, Box 232, Entry 134, RG 226, NA. Documentation on Germany in Washington Director's Office microfilm, M1642, roll 81, presents an overview of OSS postwar planning.

51. Tel. 747, Nov. 15, 1944, Box 277, Entry 134; tel. 1849, Dec. 2, 1944, Box 7, Entry 90; tel. 2207, Dec. 16, 1944, Box 193, Entry 134; tel. 2369, Dec. 23, 1944, Box 7, Entry 90; tel. 2487, Dec. 26, 1944, Box 193, Entry 134; tel. 2677, Dec. 27, 1944, Box 277, Entry 134; tel. 2909, Jan. 2, 1945, Box 7, Entry 90; and tel. 3317, Jan. 12, 1945, Box 92, Entry 134, RG 226, NA. Regarding the exploits of Moe Berg, see Louis Kaufman, Barbara Fitzgerald, and Tom Sewell, *Moe Berg: Athlete, Scholar, Spy* (Boston, 1974). The Bern cables in Entry 134, RG 226, confirm the presence of Berg in Switzerland on intelligence matters in 1945.

52. Tel. 9569, Apr. 30, 1945, Box 7, Entry 90, RG 226, NA.

53. Tel. 4909, Feb. 5, 1945, Box 7, Entry 90; tel. 5527, Feb. 19, 1945, Box 228, Entry 134; and tel. 8567, Apr. 12, 1945, Box 2, Entry 110, RG 226, NA.

54. Dulles reports on the national redoubt issue include tel. 6761, Oct. 29, 1943, Box 273, Entry 134; tel. 4471–4473, Aug. 12, 1944, Box 191, Entry 134; flash, Jan. 18, 1945, Box 1, Entry 160; flash, Jan. 22, 1945, Box 1, Entry 160; flash, Feb. 13, 1945, Box 1, Entry 160; flash, Mar. 3, 1945, Box 1, Entry 160; flash, Mar. 16, 1945, Box 1, Entry 160; flash, Mar. 27, 1945, Box 1, Entry 160; tel. 8349, Apr. 6, 1945, Box 7, Entry 90; and flash, Apr. 18, 1945, Box 1, Entry 160, RG 226, NA. The question of the Allied intelligence failure is treated in Rodney G. Minott, *The Fortress That Never Was: The Myth of Hitler's Bavarian Stronghold* (New York, 1964), and Persico, *Piercing the Reich.*

55. Material on Operation Sunrise is located in Entries 90, 110, 139, and 165, RG 226, in addition to cables interfiled chronologically in Entry 134. The records amplify and support Dulles's *Secret Surrender* and *Operation Sunrise: The Secret Surrender* by Bradley F. Smith and Elena Agarossi (New York, 1979), a secondary account. The heads-of-government-level acrimony precipitated by the Dulles-Wolff negotiations is treated in *FRUS, 1945*, vol. 3, *European Advisory Commission; Austria; Germany* (Washington, DC, 1968), pp. 717–783, passim, and by Herbert Feis in *Churchill, Roosevelt, Stalin: The War They Waged and the Peace They Sought* (Princeton, NJ, 1957). Some observers attach great importance to this episode as undermining the Grand Alliance; further research on the subject is necessary. However, it is likely that the basic differences between East and West, and the depths of Stalin's ambition and suspicion, were such as to exceed Allen Dulles's power to add or detract.

56. Tel. 9769, May 3, 1945, Box 6, Entry 134, RG 226, NA.

57. Difficulties in analyzing the substantive value of the intelligence provided by OSS Bern are compounded by the continued classification of hundreds of messages. It appears that the primary basis for withholding documents in the declassification process was the protection of the identities of foreign sources. Documents withheld can be requested under the Freedom of Information Act.

58. Copies of Dulles/OSS Bern material sent by OSS to the White House, State Department, and Joint Chiefs of Staff are located in Entry 162, and in Donovan Office Files microfilm, A3304, Entry 180, RG 226, NA. Copies of some OSS cables sent from Bern via State Department channels and receiving internal State Department distribution are in RG 59, especially under file number 103.918. Copies of OSS cables in the Franklin D. Roosevelt Library, Hyde Park, NY, include many Dulles reports that were sent to President Roosevelt by General Donovan. In addition, the Map Room Files contain a large collection of OSS cable-based reports with a large Bern component, transmitted by Gen. John Magruder, OSS Deputy Director for Intelligence.

THE OSS AND SOE:
An Equal Partnership?

M.R.D. Foot

An old and sound Special Operations Executive (SOE) rule laid down that one should always deal with the man at the top, not with underlings. Let us therefore start with one British senior commander addressing another on how to handle Americans. Gen. Sir Harold Alexander, chief of land forces under Gen. Dwight Eisenhower in Tunisia, wrote to Brooke, the chief of the imperial general staff, on April 3, 1943:

"We must tread very warily—if they think we are sneering at them— and God forbid that—or that we are being superior, they will take it very badly, as they are a proud people. We must take the line that we are comrades and brothers in arms, and our only wish is for them to share the horrors of war (and the handicaps) and reap the fruits of victory together."[1] This was the line that SOE tried to follow in its dealings with the OSS— not always with success.

When we recall from what different social contexts the two services arose, it is a marvel that they could work together at all. English society was still closed and formal, even more class-ridden than American; more hostile to self-made, self-advertising men; still aware, particularly in the officer class, of the importance of the monarch; and fully aware that on the empire, which then covered a quarter of the globe's land surface, the sun never set. Publicity, like advertisement, was regarded as not quite decent. There were still some subjects one did not discuss in the presence of ladies, children, servants, natives; there were questions that, everyone was brought up to believe, were better left unasked. It was an ideal society, in fact, in which to run a secret service.

The United States by contrast provided a wide open society, aggressively republican, full of enthusiasm for those who had come up from nowhere, and profoundly anti-imperial—hostile to the British empire, at any rate. Though this was practically a pre-televisual age, the newspapers and sound broadcasters were already revered enough to amount to an extra estate of the realm, and the idea that anything ought to be kept secret for long did not readily enter most American minds. Of all the allied wartime capitals, Washington was by far the leakiest, and a Chicago newspaper almost gave the secret of "MAGIC" away to the Japanese, who did not believe what it said.[2]

Moreover, isolationist feeling had been very strong in the United States until the summer of 1940, and pockets of it remained thereafter in spite of SOE's efforts to persuade the American news media that the anti-Nazi side was a more constitutional line to follow in the European war than the neutral side.[3] SOE undertook this task before a great campaign in Whitehall had torn from it its political warfare wing, which became a separate Political Warfare Executive. It was this that gave William ("Little Bill") Stephenson his real claim to world importance, for he was at the bottom of it.

Partnership between SOE and the OSS was at first very uneven, with the scales tilted heavily in SOE's favor from the simple fact that SOE had had 2 years' head start. It had been founded in July 1940, while the United States of America was still profoundly neutral, by the amalgam of three small departments, of which the oldest dated back to the spring of 1938. One was the sabotage branch of SIS, the Secret Intelligence Service, one was the research branch of War Office intelligence, and one was the propaganda branch of the Foreign Office. Stephenson was in charge of all that it did west of the Atlantic, as of the work of all other British secret services there; his responsibilities east of it are fictional.

We have General Donovan's word for it, after all, that "Bill Stephenson taught us all we ever knew about foreign intelligence";[4] but intelligence gathering was seldom SOE's primary task. In passing, it is worth noting that there were a few areas, such as Czechoslovakia and Denmark, in which it suited SIS to have SOE collect intelligence. But SOE's normal objectives were those of the Special Operations Branch (SO) rather than the Secret Intelligence Branch (SI) of the OSS.

Long before the OSS had been founded, General (still then Colonel) Donovan had visited England as well as several other countries in Europe in the winter of 1940–41. He made friends both with the new head of SIS and with Brig. Sir Colin Gubbins, the linchpin of SOE, who was from November 1940 in charge of its operations and training. Donovan had been told a great deal that the English would normally have kept from a visiting foreigner, partly because of his own gifts for inspiring trust and partly because of an instruction from Churchill that he was to be treated generously.[5] The friendships he then formed did the OSS no harm at all, and when the body was formally set up in the summer of 1942, it was taken for granted on both sides of the Atlantic that OSS-SOE cooperation would be close.

In the earliest stages of this cooperation, there were endless little demarcation disputes about who was to act where and with whom. A suspicious-minded staff officer in SOE observed that it was difficult to play straight with the OSS because the OSS, having been told it was not to attempt SO work in a particular area, would allot several SI staff to the area, and then switch them to SO work behind SOE's back.[6] This may only have been a touch of that paranoia which so often affected secret staff officers; alternatively, it may have been an example of the OSS's being more nimble-hooved than SOE.

The most important of these demarcation disputes dealt with preparations for Operation Gymnast, renamed Torch: the invasion of northwestern Africa, which was planned from Norfolk House in St. James's Square. (Many of the English officers who worked in or visited Norfolk House knew that the Americans' great bugbear George III had been born on the site, but none of us was tactless enough to mention it.) Bickham Sweet-Escott has recounted the trouble: that exactly what role which service was to play was negotiated separately in London and in Washington; that Washington's conclusions were sent to London in a cipher message, marked "most secret and personal decipher yourself" to an individual who paid a trifle too much importance to absolute secrecy and simply put the message in his own pocket; and that when London's version of the arrangements, more favorable to SOE, was sent to Washington, Donovan thought he had been double-crossed. "I was never quite clear," Sweet-Escott wrote, "whether they suspected our integrity or doubted our competence. Whichever it was it did not help us."[7] From this contretemps resulted the quite separate SOE and OSS organizations in northwestern Africa, which cooperated but remained apart in the Mediterranean theater of war.

In that first winter of Anglo-American occupation of Algiers, Eisenhower sent for the local SOE and OSS leaders, Douglas Dodds-Parker and William Eddy, and talked to them in the presence of both Donovan and Gubbins. Clasping his hands together as he sat at his desk, he told them they must work together as closely as his fingers were intertwined; everyone nodded agreement. Donovan buttonholed Dodds-Parker as the meeting broke up and reminded him that, all the same, Eddy would now and again have to go off and perform by himself so that Donovan could keep up a run of interesting telegrams to show his President. Dodds-Parker was in no position to complain.[8]

On June 16, 1943, Sir Charles Hambro, then executive head (CD) of SOE, explained at one of his weekly meetings that the OSS was under constant pressure in Washington, part political and part prestige-hunting, to set up its own organizations and to produce its own results, whatever any agreement drawn up formally between the OSS and SOE might say. He stressed that SOE's senior staff must be aware of this and take care not to resent it, while not surrendering control where it was due to them.[9]

SOE made it a general rule to keep few of its own secrets from the OSS. Several times over, senior staff officers inquired at council meetings whether they had authority to tell the OSS SOE's inmost secrets; the answer was always yes.[10] One important exception lay in Latin America, where SOE had taken quite extensive precautions against the Nazi- and Japanese-inspired fifth column activity. Perhaps on a hint from Stephenson about how upset J. Edgar Hoover of the FBI would be if he heard any whisper of this, Hambro ordered that none of SOE's arrangements in this field— though they were currently "suspended"—were to be reported to the Americans at all.[11] SOE even had a codeword, "Rocket," to be prefixed to telegrams of which the content was not to be passed to the OSS [12]—a useful marker when riffling through a newly opened archive. In May 1943 Hambro laid down that all of SOE's sabotage reports were to go to the OSS to help to make the United States chiefs of staff sabotage-minded.[13]

Like many other branches of the British war machine, SOE was happy to use the enormous productive capacities of the United States when they became available. For example, the Americans readily undertook to supply time pencil fuses in large quantities on a formula (derived by Gubbins from the Poles in 1939) supplied by SOE. This particular scheme at once ran into difficulties, about quality control: the Americans did not seem to bother about it at all, and it was some time before SOE was at all satisfied with the end product. On August 10, 1943, council ruled that the OSS could draw on any SOE stores depot in the British Isles just as SOE could as part of the preparation for a joint effort into northwestern Europe.[14]

Regarding the infiltration of France, Belgium, and Holland, it was generally agreed that the OSS and SOE should work as one body—not in any sense as rivals. Donovan emphasized on July 26, 1943, at a meeting with (among others) David Bruce, Stephenson, R. H. Barry, and A. R. Boyle in London, that he was all for an integrated OSS-SOE team to work in France.[15] Eric T. Mockler-Ferryman, in charge of SOE's operations into northwestern Europe, had not worked under Eisenhower in the combined Allied Force Headquarters that had run Torch for nothing. Mockler-Ferryman ran his London Group, as far as he could, as an interallied team. He used to have a routine meeting every Thursday for heads of departments under him, who were encouraged to bring their OSS deputies with them, even when he decided that the meetings had been getting too full.[16] When he was away, Joe Haskell, his own OSS deputy, took charge of the meeting. These OSS deputies had appeared in SOE's western European country sections in early August 1943 after spells at SOE's training schools to give them some idea of what the agents they were going to control could do.

Sweet-Escott wrote with feeling of SOE's attempts to indicate to the OSS what the pitfalls of attempts at underground work were likely to be, only to find that the OSS insisted on making its own mistakes, in its own way, irrespective of anything SOE might say.[17] As time passed, the OSS grew more and more competent; a balance point can even be shown at which the OSS was recognizably no longer the weaker partner in the alliance.

Gubbin's deputy, H. N. Sporborg, remarked at one of CD's weekly meetings, on December 1, 1943, that "OSS had now definitely established themselves and we must resist the temptation to continue to treat them as an inexperienced younger brother."[18] Thereafter the OSS moved on from strength to strength, and SOE began to lag behind. By the end of the war there was no doubt that it was SOE that was the weaker partner.

Early in 1943, the OSS went on record that they did not think they could offer any substantial help in France or the low countries,[19] but they soon changed their minds. The Jedburgh teams provide the best example of the OSS and SOE working together in an equal partnership. Many survivors can testify to the warmth and strength of the Anglo-Franco-American, or Anglo-Dutch-American, friendships that were formed in a Jedburgh context. Nearly 300 agents, about a third each American and British, took part in Jedburgh operations; their casualty rates were comparatively low, and the miracles they helped to work on the ground were many.

The temptation is irresistible: there is one name to add to the Yale men in secret service listed in Robin Winks's splendid *Cloak and Gown*.[20] No doubt he left out Arie Dirk Bestebeurtje because he only stayed a year at Yale as part of his Grand Tour (his father was then managing director of Unilever), instead of staying to take a degree. Bestebeurtje jumped at Nijmegen with the 82d Airborne Division in Operation Market Garden, did well, and jumped again into the northeastern Holland in April 1945, this time breaking both his ankles. His English colleague Robert Harcourt just got him into safe Dutch hands before he was himself taken prisoner. Both survived.[21]

A more general point needs to be made about the Jedburghs: Gallant and important though their work was, it all depended on what had been done already. They normally went into areas where resistance had already been brought well beyond the seedling stage to that of vigorous young growth. Their task was to bring it to maturity. The most difficult and most dangerous stages were already past. Necessarily, more of this early work had been done by SOE than by the OSS.

In conclusion, let one example illustrate how the OSS overtook SOE in the competent handling of operations in northwestern Europe: the German case. SOE was at pains to explain to the OSS that bitter experience had made it clear that actual operations into Germany were all but impossible. The local populace were too unfriendly, and the Gestapo on its home stamping-ground was far too strong. Even with G.W.R. Templer to direct it, X section had hardly a success to report.[22] The best they could manage was a series of deception plots by wireless intended to discredit prominent Nazis.[23] This did not seem good enough to the OSS, and David Bruce, aided by a young lieutenant, junior grade, USN, called William J. Casey— who was heard of again later—set out to do better. They did; Casey claimed about 40 successful drops into Germany.[24] Though the agents

Casey sent worked for SI, not for SO, they used as one of their tools an SOE invention, as improved by American ingenuity. This was the S-phone, conceived by one of SOE's founding fathers, Tommy Davies, in 1940, which as SOE developed it, was somewhat cumbrous.[25] With it, agents could conduct secure telephone conversations with nearby aircraft. "Joan Eleanor," the American version of the device, could be carried in a pocket.[26] She can stand for the triumph of manufacturing technique over earnest enterprise. As SOE reported to the chiefs of staff in October 1943, "It is not in the nature of our work to be able to guarantee success."[27] It can be claimed, both for SOE and for the OSS, that they did what they could.

NOTES

1. Quoted by Sir David Fraser from the Alanbrooke papers in John Keegan, ed., *Churchill's Generals* (London, 1991), p. 114.
2. Ronald Lewin, *The American Magic* (New York, 1982), pp. 113–117.
3. M.R.D. Foot, *SOE: An Outline History*, 2d ed. (London, 1990), pp. 247–248.
4. H. Montgomery Hyde, *The Quiet Canadian* (London, 1962), p. vi.
5. Cp Martin Gilbert, *Finest Hour* (London, 1983), p. 638.
6. Unpublished SOE archive, Dec. 16, 1942.
7. Bickham Sweet-Escott, *Baker Street Irregular* (London, 1965), pp. 139–140.
8. (Sir) Douglas Dodds-Parker, *Setting Europe Ablaze: Some Account of Ungentlemanly Warfare* (Windlesham, Surrey, 1983), p. 117; private information.
9. Unpublished SOE archive.
10. E.g., Apr. 21, 1944, on special printing techniques; and Nov. 14, 1944, any signals technique (unpublished SOE archive).
11. CD's weekly meetings, Feb. 10, 1943, unpublished SOE archive.
12. Ibid., Mar. 8, 1943.
13. Ibid., May 10, 1943.
14. Unpublished SOE archive.
15. Ibid.
16. Nov. 6, 1943, ibid.
17. Sweet-Escott, *Baker Street Irregular*, pp. 126–153.
18. Unpublished SOE archive.
19. CD's weekly meetings, Jan. 13, 1943, ibid.
20. London 1987.
21. Unpublished SOE archive.
22. John Cloake, *Templer Tiger of Malaya* (London, 1985), p. 143.
23. Private information.
24. William Casey, *The Secret War Against Hitler* (Washington, DC, 1988), pp. 194–216.
25. Pierre Lorain and David Kahn, *Secret Warfare* (London, 1984), pp. 96–99.
26. Casey, *The Secret War Against Hitler*, pp. 186–187.
27. SOE council minutes, Oct. 12, 1943, unpublished SOE archive.

↤ The OSS in Asia

Elizabeth McIntosh was an OSS Morale Operations officer in Asia. After the war, she published an account of her experiences. McIntosh presided over the fourth concurrent session, "The OSS in Asia," and introduced the speakers. Professor Carolle Carter of Menlo College introduced the audience to a special American mission sent in 1944 to the Chinese Communist headquarters at Yenan. Carter's presentation integrated the findings of OSS records research with personal interviews she had conducted. James Ward, a veteran of Detachment 101 and extensive jungle warfare experience in Burma, argued persuasively the military value of organizing native forces and operating in guerrilla warfare fashion. Professor E. Bruce Reynolds has opened the door toward a better understanding of the forces of war, colonialism, and nationalism at work in Thailand during the war. His research draws upon foreign language expertise and extensive research in Asian and United States repositories. Diplomatic historian Michael Schaller of the University of Arizona provided comments on the three papers and suggested some areas for future research. From the papers and discussion at the session, there was a feeling that additional research is needed before a more complete synthesis of the intelligence war in Asia is realized.

MISSION TO YENAN:
The OSS and
the Dixie Mission

Carolle J. Carter

The Dixie Mission was an American detached military unit stationed in Yenan, Shensi Province, China, from July 1944 to April 1947 to function as liaison with the Chinese Communists and to gather information. Its men came from many units including the 14th Air Force, the Office of War Information (OWI), G-2 (Army intelligence), and the Office of Strategic Services (OSS). Members of the mission reported to Dixie's commanding officer, but they were also expected to report to their parent units.[1] This paper explains the origins of this unique contact with the Chinese Communists and why the Chinese Communists chose to cooperate. Some of the activities the OSS undertook within the framework of the Dixie Mission are described. The paper examines where Dixie fit into the organizational framework of China-Burma-India theater intelligence and how the OSS planned to expand it. It will assess whether Dixie affected the OSS's China operations and how it could have played a more important role in the overall war effort. The old spelling of names and places is used deliberately to retain the atmosphere in which the Dixie Mission existed.

The idea of stationing an American group in Yenan developed in stages. It began when two OSS men journeyed from India to Tibet in 1942 to assure the 10-year-old Dalai Lama of U.S. friendship and explore a possible military route between India and China through the Tibetan mountains. The two OSS men were Ilia Tolstoy, grandson of the great Russian novelist, and Brooke Dolan, a skilled adventurer and Far Eastern explorer. It took them 3 months to travel from New Delhi to Lhasa, the capital of Tibet. The Dalai Lama received them as formal ambassadors from President Franklin D. Roosevelt[2] and asked them for a powerful radio transmitter so he could communicate with the most remote parts of his country.[3]

Tolstoy and Dolan left Lhasa in March 1943. Five months later they arrived in Chungking. The photographic record of their journey appeared in the August 1946 issue of *National Geographic* magazine. In their report to the OSS, they stated that they had not broached the subject of a trans-Tibet road with the Dalai Lama because it could take 2 years to build and would require very advanced technology to construct.[4] However, a supply line could be established from India to China through Tibet using pack animals and possibly Tibetan traders. Up to 1,000 tons could be moved over this route the first year, which would greatly assist OSS operations in China.[5] OSS Director William Donovan approved Tolstoy's suggestion, noting that the proposal offered an alternative to flying "the Hump," should that method of supply be threatened.[6]

At the time Tolstoy and Dolan were making their trip, John Davies, a Foreign Service officer attached to Lt. Gen. Joseph W. Stilwell, sent Stilwell a lengthy memorandum stating why he believed the United States should send an observer group to Yenan.[7] In subsequent memorandums he re-marked that no American observer had visited the Chinese Communist areas since Marine Capt. Evans Carlson had gone in 1939.[8] It seemed reasonable to Davies that the United States should witness firsthand what was going on in the Communist-controlled parts of the country as well as in the parts dominated by Chiang Kai-shek to increase our understanding of both the situation in China as it related to the war and the country's domestic political relationships. To accomplish these ends, Davies recommended that military and political personnel be dispatched to Yenan. He believed the Communists would welcome them.[9]

Davies discussed his proposal at great length with a number of inter-ested people, including Capt. Joseph E. Spencer and Lt. Charles Stelle of the OSS. Spencer knew the idea would interest a new bomber group being formed because of the tasks involved: potential pilot rescues, weather re-ports, and the collection of ground data from north China and southern Manchuria.[10] Both Stelle and Spencer wanted Donovan to be made aware of Davies' plan because the Sino-American Cooperative Organization (SACO), the secret service created in 1943 under the joint direction of Vice Adm. Milton E. (Mary) Miles and Gen. Tai Li, chief of Chiang Kai-shek's combined secret police and intelligence organization, had stalemated the OSS in China.[11] Donovan and Dr. William Langer of the Research and Analysis Branch (R&A) had already conferred in Chungking with Maj. Gen. Claire L. Chennault, Commander of the 14th Air Force, which badly needed a widespread tactical intelligence service to pinpoint enemy tar-gets.[12]

Originally, Chiang Kai-shek refused to allow an observer group to be stationed in Yenan. His resistance to the idea collapsed in June 1944, after FDR sent Vice President Henry A. Wallace to persuade him, and by early August the Dixie Mission was in place. Col. David D. Barrett, who would serve as the unit's first commanding officer, chose his staff from men he knew and from highly recommended candidates. Five of the original 18 were OSS, the most senior of whom was Stelle. How the results of this undertaking would be communicated back to OSS-China Headquarters were left to Stelle's discretion.[13] As time went on the original 18 men left the unit and new ones were assigned. The mission, which Spencer had originally called Palisades, after his home town, was officially called the United States Army Observer Group, Yenan, from July 22, 1944, to April 11, 1946. From April 13, 1946, until the last man left in March 1947, it was called the Yenan Liaison Group. As long as it existed it followed the guidelines issued by theater G-2 Col. Joseph K. Dickey to Barrett.[14] It was ordered to get information on enemy order of battle and to learn the strength, composition, disposition, equipment, training, and combat efficiency of the Communist forces.[15]

In spite of its OSS origins, Dixie was a G-2 operation as far as theater headquarters in Chungking was concerned. Dickey was enthusiastic about it[16] and favorably inclined toward the OSS.[17] The OSS's rival in the China theater, however, Naval Group, China, did not look favorably on the operation. Vice Admiral Miles, the head of the Naval Group, was hoping to "provoke the Reds" at the very time Stilwell was trying to get them and the Nationalists to "bury the hatchet."[18] No member of Naval Group, China, nor anyone associated with SACO was ever stationed with the mission,[19] which may explain why Miles was so completely against its existence. He accused Barrett of misrepresenting the purpose of the observer group to the Nationalist government, and he alleged that the men assigned to it were blindly sympathetic to the Communists. The Communists, he said, actively supported the Japanese, and vice versa.[20] Ironically, Miles himself did little against the Japanese, although he did a lot for Tai Li, who did nothing whatever for the United States.[21]

After the China-Burma-India theater was split and Gen. Albert C. Wedemeyer replaced Stilwell as commander of the China theater in October 1944, Miles' power began to decline.[22] Wedemeyer ordered him not to permit any SACO-American military operations in Communist areas[23] and made both the OSS and the Naval Group responsible to the theater commander. Henceforth, Col. Richard P. Heppner, Strategic Services chief in China, was invited to attend weekly meetings of the committee Wedemeyer formed to devise theater policy.[24] This pleased Donovan, who sent a memorandum to the White House the following April reviewing the past difficulties the OSS had encountered in China. He suggested that, "Now is the time to make OSS in China directly responsible to the U.S. Commanding General and to service him and his subordinates, as well as General MacArthur and Admiral Nimitz." Wedemeyer was not opposed to the OSS being in his theater, and to Heppner's surprise he agreed to let the Special Operations Branch (SO) as well as the Secret Intelligence Branch (SI) operate there. He told Heppner he would probably let the OSS take over the Dixie Mission but that he was extremely concerned about the type of personnel being sent to Yenan. He hoped to avoid types subject to political influence and likely to dabble in [political] movements.[25]

Thus, for the first time the OSS gained authorization to organize resistance activities, conduct intelligence and sabotage, and equip and direct special commando groups in support of the Chinese armies.[26]

The OSS men attached to the Dixie Mission engaged in a variety of activities. They supplied Dixie with its radio lifeline. Capt. Paul Domke, the signal communications officer, and Sgt. Tony Remineh brought the radio and generators with them on the first plane to Yenan, and by the time Sgt. Walter Gress arrived on the second plane, they had already decided to operate it out of one of the adobe-type houses on the hill in back of the caves that housed the mission.[27] The Communists provided the electricity, a one-lung (one-cylinder) diesel engine. Remineh, a longtime amateur radio operator, thought the setup very primitive, noting that he had better gear in his home,[28] but soon regular communication took place with Chungking, 1,000 miles away. The transmission between Yenan and Chungking, usually very good, was all in Morse code at first, as they did not have sophisticated voice radio equipment. Later, the lighter radio transreceiver type of equipment developed for the OSS was sent up,[29] but at first everything was improvised. Remineh thought it strange that, on what was supposed to be an important mission, he was not given a generator. In general, he considered his job with the mission nothing more than his ham radio experience in action, especially when he had to go out in the field and operate or repair equipment with nothing but his hands and wits. His skills were first put to use the very day the mission arrived in Yenan, when the receiver burned out and had to be repaired during the very transmission that was to notify Chungking of their safe arrival. Using what was available, however, he soon taught some of the Chinese guerrillas how to use the hand-generated Signal Corps equipment that they were given in small quantities, just enough for training.

In addition to maintaining regular communications with Chungking and occasional contact with Kunming, the Yenan radio, code-named YEN-SIG, received data from American Navy personnel stationed in the Gobi Desert. The Navy was in the desert to read the weather as it flowed from Siberia toward Guam, and Remineh received their information on a certain frequency at a particular time. The radiomen also tried to determine whether there was radio traffic between Moscow and the Yenan Communists, a difficult assignment given Dixie's poor equipment. Remineh scanned the band regularly, but to no avail. He did determine that the Communists had more than one installation, including one just 10 miles from Yenan. Once, when his generator went out, the only way he could keep his 8 a.m. schedule was to get on a Mongolian pony and ride 10 miles to use the Communist station.

Remineh prepared special machine codes for men heading behind the Japanese lines. At various times he used both simple and complex transpositions.[30] He usually forwarded encoded messages that came in from the field to the relay station in Chungking, where theater headquarters translated them. Messages for individual OSS members were handed to the person for whom they were intended, however, and the recipient did his own decoding.[31] The real "hot stuff" was not sent over the air but in letters or written reports that were sometimes hand carried by the sightseers or journalists who frequently visited Yenan. From the security standpoint, it was wise not to use the radio for really important news, since Yenan transmissions could be picked up as far away as San Francisco.[32]

Besides establishing the radio net, the men of the Dixie Mission also built the Communists a war room and a photography laboratory and also participated in some of the world's best pheasant hunting.[33] The OSS members of the mission demonstrated the use of explosives to the Communists, traveled with the Communists behind the Japanese lines on inspection tours, and organized the Chinese for fighting in places where they could be moved around in small airplanes.[34]

In July 1945 John Colling, an OSS agent attached to the mission, made a film, "Mission to Yenan," about the daily life of the Yenan Group and the demonstrations OSS was giving the Communists. He sent the completed film to OSS headquarters in Chungking. It arrived at the time Wedemeyer was directing the Americans in Yenan to distance themselves from the Chinese Communists, not to supply them with arms, ammunition, or supplies, and not to make any commitments to them.[35] Heppner got Ambassador Patrick Hurley to approve the movie script, which was fairly enthusiastic about what was going on in Yenan and not objectionable from a factual point of view. The film did not go into the larger political issues, nor did it compare the fighting effectiveness of the Nationalists and the Communists.[36]

A few months after Dixie arrived, the OSS set up a microfilm laboratory and began training Chinese to film captured documents, newspapers, and magazines. Two copies were made of everything, and the microfilm was then sent to Chungking for transmission to Washington. This meant building a photography laboratory to process microfilm. The OSS planned to build additional laboratories at Fouping and elsewhere.[37]

After the war, many of those who had participated in intelligence gathering and had seen multiple agencies, including the OSS, operating at cross purposes with each other analyzed the weakness of the system. Some concluded that during World War II anyone with a bright idea and access to someone on top could build himself a little empire. In wartime, it was easy to get money and, if one knew the ropes, people. Little thought was given to combining military efficiency, and money was spent loosely in hopes of *improving* military efficiency. In part, this was because the public did not care about saving $10 billion if doing so would mean losing a battle. Furthermore, if money was saved, the budget would probably be cut.[38] The OSS was a conglomeration of people who honestly wanted to contribute to the war effort but sometimes did not know how. John Davies described the organization as a "pungent collection of thugs, post debutantes, millionaires, professors, corporation lawyers, professional military, and misfits, all operating under high tension and in whispers." Davies found them a diverting contrast to Cordell Hull's stupefying State Department.[39] Whatever and whoever they were, they fit into Donovan's formula for using brains. Donovan himself often behaved irresponsibly. An example was when he and Carl Eifler, the man who had originally convinced Stilwell that the OSS could make a major contribution to the war in his theater, went joyriding in a Piper Cub over Japanese-held territory in Burma. The two men had a combined weight of over 400 pounds, and they flew a plane that was never designed to carry more than 250 pounds. Afterward, Donovan told John Coughlin, Carl Eifler's executive officer who later served as OSS chief in China, that he made the flight, which violated all rules of security, so Eifler would not think he was a coward.[40]

Wedemeyer recognized Donovan's freewheeling ways and the tendency of OSS people to act independently. He also knew that many military and intelligence professionals were jealous of Donovan because he had the ear of the President. He admired Donovan, "a civilian soldier, a very courageous World War I Congressional Medal of Honor winner, and a very nice Irishman, too," and he allowed the OSS to remain in the China theater when he took over with the understanding that they would not act in harum-scarum fashion. Donovan went to China to reassure Wedemeyer on this very point.[41]

There was a great deal of rivalry within Dixie.[42] The traditional military intelligence agencies tended to specialize and were suspicious of the OSS, which saw itself not as competing with other agencies but as better prepared than the others to do certain kinds of jobs.[43] To some extent the mission mirrored the duplication of effort that stemmed from interagency competition, and there was some backbiting among the men. Shortly after the mission was established, Colonel Dickey went to Yenan for a brief visit to straighten some of these things out, afterward reporting to Stilwell that his headquarters was maintaining very close contact with the Yenan Observer Group.[44] Yet there was less discord and inefficiency in the Dixie Mission than there was in many other intelligence operations in the China theater, which may make the mission appear to have been more viable than it actually was.[45] The basic reason there *was* a mission was that Davies had talked with Spencer and Stelle, who were interested in setting it up, not only because it could aid the war effort, but because it would provide a "tremendous opportunity for OSS to come out nicely."[46] Once in place, reports from the mission seemed to validate their enthusiasm, viz. the comment that Col. David D. Barrett added to Maj. Ray Cromley's July 30 report on Yenan as the major order of battle China base of operations: "In my opinion the possibilities of an Order of Battle Office in Yenan are limited only by the amount of trained personnel which can be assigned to it."[47] Stelle and Colling's report to Col. R. B. Hall and Lt. Col. Ray Peers on August 7, 1944, stating it "will be possible to secure thorough cooperation from the Chinese Communists for OSS operations . . . [including] an independent communications and agent net . . . and provid[ing] Chinese personnel for training in our methods," also echoes this optimism.[48]

Sometimes members expressed ambivalence toward their roles in the group. Such was the case when Stelle, in an October 27, 1944, memorandum to Spencer, wrote:

> My assignment had been that of 'target analyst', presumably representing the 14th Air Force. . . . G-2 at Chungking had originally asked the 14th to send either Barnett or Schultheis on the Dixie trip. Either because of the indispensability of Bob and Fred at Kunming, which is the reason the 14th gave or because the 14th didn't want to incur the onus of taking part in a mission to the Communists and didn't like participating in something run by AMMISCA [American Military Mission to China], which are the reasons theater suspected, the 14th was slow to name anybody and finally suggested somebody who was unacceptable to Dickey.
>
> Colonel Dickey decided to send me . . . and because of my AGFRTS[49] connection chose to regard me as the 14th representative. The detachment from AGFRTS to the mission was cleared with Col. Smith, then CO AGFRTS, but not with 14th HQ. The 14th, which is habitually disgruntled with theater, didn't like the idea of being represented in spite of itself. . . . Nevertheless the 14th was naturally eager to get the results of the Mission.
>
> My actual position has been something like this. G-2 and Colonel Barrett have considered me to be a representative of the 14th specializing in target work. The 14th states that it has no representative in Yenan . . . [but] considers me the officer most nearly connected with it and whenever it is annoyed at the delays occasioned by the channeling of intelligence through G-2—and given the predisposition of the 14th to be annoyed with theater and the limitations staff at G-2 this will probably be fairly frequently—the 14th will to a certain degree be inclined to hold me responsible.

Part of the problem, Stelle complained, was that G-2 did a poor job of distributing the reports and intelligence the OSS provided.[50] In fact, G-2 frequently received information from the OSS that conflicted with what Combat Intelligence provided, and Dickey's people usually dumped the

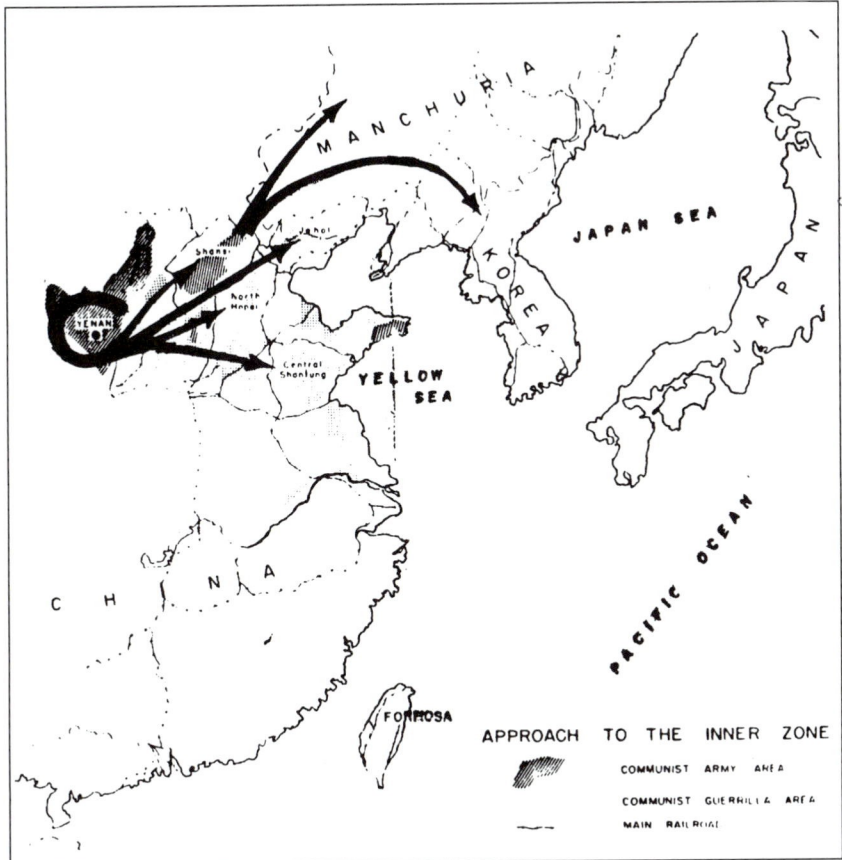

Figure 1: Comprehensive Plan—Approach to the Inner Zone
(Map cropped for presentation)

OSS messages in the wastebasket. Dickey did note that messages from different persons in the field who had contact with the Communists but not with each other tended to be similar.[51]

Many people in OSS-China thought Dixie could be the core of a fairly large organization servicing North China. Figure 1 shows the comprehensive plan that Dr. Charles B. Fahs, and Maj. Joseph Spencer, then R&A Chief for China, and Maj. Philip K. Crowe, the SI Chief for China and India-Burma, Lt. (sg) Guy Martin, and Lt. Thomas J. Davis, Heppner's aide, drew up for General Donovan in late 1944 and early 1945, which they hoped he would present to theater headquarters.[52]

The plan recommended that the OSS establish a major intelligence organization in North China based at the Communist capital of Yenan. Figure 2 illustrates how they expected the OSS to operate through four main forward bases in the 8th Route Army or guerrilla areas in Shansi,

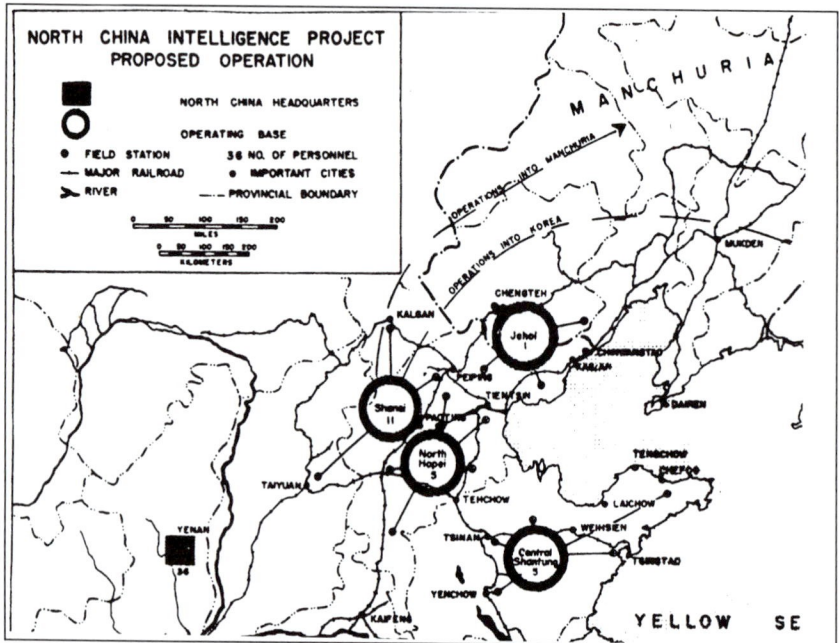

Figure 2: North China Intelligence Project Proposed Operation
(Map cropped for presentation)

Hopei, Shantung, and Jehol, with 17 advanced teams and a large number of native agents. The OSS justified this expansion by pointing out that the north was the most important area in China for strategic intelligence on Japan. Also, little was known about Manchuria and Korea, and neither the United States nor Britain were utilizing guerrilla capabilities in those places.

The plan envisioned maximum utilization of the Communists, who were regarded as a significant possible source of information on the Japanese war effort. In fact, such an undertaking would have depended on Chinese estimates of the size and stability of the territories they controlled. Smaller guerrilla areas owing allegiance to Yenan were in South China, in Fukien, around Canton, and on Hainan Island. In North China itself, the OSS would have systematically reported military and economic movements on each of the main rail, water, and air lines of communication leading to possible scenes of U.S. military action; on the production and shipment of the principal strategic commodities that Japan obtained from the area (coal, iron ore, pig iron, salt, bauxite); on fortifications, particularly in such key defense zones as Hangchow Bay and the Shantung Peninsula; on Japanese order of battle; on Japanese and puppet political moves; and on collections of Japanese documents and printed materials. The plan also proposed organizing an operating base in the Shansi-Hopei area for the development of long-range penetration into Manchuria and Korea for intelligence purposes and stated how many tons of supplies would be needed. Fifty-eight Americans would have been required to implement this plan. Available personnel could have organized a headquarters within 2 or 3 weeks after full OSS and theater approval and, with full Washington support, some, if not all of the operating bases could be under way within 90 days, with the project fully operational within 6 months. The authors believed their project was politically practical, that it would compete neither with Miles's organization nor with AGFRTS, since North China was the area where Tai Li's organization was least effective. Of all the arrangements Chiang might approve, a program strictly based on intelligence seemed least objectionable, as it would involve neither major supply of military equipment nor instruction in demolition.

The project would have been an integrated SI-R&A operation, with major support by Communications and Services. It was to be headquartered at Yenan because liaison with the Border Region Government and the 8th and New 4th Armies was needed, and because Yenan was within easy flying distance of Chengtu. It was expected that, with full support from Washington, it would be possible to initiate the project effectively within a few days of its approval, with the basic program operating effectively within 6 months.[53] The final plan envisioned the number of OSS personnel stationed in North China (SI, SO, and Communications) to increase from 24 in June 1945 to 145 by November of that year, including an OSS medical officer who would be stationed at Yenan. He would be responsible for the collection of medical intelligence in addition to medical duties.[54]

This project was submitted to theater headquarters, where it was held in suspense pending a policy decision by Wedemeyer.[55] In June the OSS asked theater to authorize more personnel in Dixie so it could carry out its planned expansion of the radio net,[56] but instead Wedemeyer suggested that the OSS make a further study with a view to curtailing activities not of the utmost importance.[57] Personnel had already been ordered not to discuss politics with anyone, including Americans; not to give arms, ammunition, commitments, or promises to the Communists except with specific approval and for specific missions; and in the event of a conflict between Communist and Nationalist columns, Americans were to be withdrawn from the Communist column.[58]

All these OSS activities and planning sessions took place against the backdrop of deteriorating relations with the Chinese Communists, who by this time knew that cooperation was not going to win them recognition at the war's end. Gen. Chu Teh's request to Donovan in January 1945 that the U.S. Army loan the Chinese Communist Party $20 million to be used to strengthen subversive activities among puppet troops was ignored.[59] Brooke Dolan noted in June that "when the honeymoon was on, 8th Route

Army leaders in Central Hopei informed me that it was their intention to blow the enemy railroad communications sky high at the time of an Allied landing on the coast of China. I do not know whether this intention has survived the general letdown in enthusiasm on the part of 8th Route Army leadership." Dolan believed that, given the green light, demolition teams of the Dixie Mission could effect important damage and destruction to enemy railroad communications and other installations in North China.[60]

In summary, some OSS planners saw the American operations in Yenan as the possible centerpiece for what some might call an OSS empire. Dixie, however, was not a major concern for OSS R&A people outside of China for a number of reasons. First, matters dealing with the Japanese were more important to the greater war effort, and very few OSS people even heard of Dixie until after the war. Second, the timing of the Dixie Mission itself was wrong because it was established too late to significantly influence the outcome of the war. If it had been created earlier, Stilwell would have had more influence, the mission would have had more credibility and more notoriety, and it could have been used to validate the consular reports of Oliver Edmund Clubb, the U.S. Consul General in Peking at the time relations with China were broken off, in 1950. Then, it might have been very beneficial to the war effort and increased our understanding of the Chinese situation.[61]

Further, as the Yenan Group was constituted under the 1945 directive from theater headquarters, the OSS was supposed to have a large share in the supply, function, and activities of the group. But the OSS reputation with the Yenan Group was not good, partly because some men, like Cromley, were difficult to get along with, and partly because OSS operations in the Communist areas apart from the Yenan Observer Group often had severely embarrassed the Dixie Mission. For example, OSS teams with Chinese civilians were sometimes dropped into the Communist areas without prior clearance or even notifying the mission commander.[62]

Stelle's vision of what the mission might have become may also have worked against its being an OSS success story. Stelle thought Dixie could prove that the Communists were outstripping the Kuomintang in waging the war. Instead, Stelle, a visionary with regard to China, wound up frustrated. The men should have been reporting more about the Communists and their plans. Indeed, the OSS in general should have been looking more closely at the relationship between the Communists and the Russians, figuring out how to see the camps and other things that the Communists were not letting the mission visit.[63]

What if OSS arms and supplies had actually reached the Yenan armies? Their postwar oratory notwithstanding, in the spring of 1945, Hurley, Wedemeyer, and Chennault all had words of praise for the Communists. Even Curtis LeMay, commander of the 20th Bomber Group, exchanged gifts with Mao and later remembered that "everything was smooth as silk in our mutual relations."

The OSS certainly had as much or better justification as any other agency in China for establishing close operational contacts with the Chinese in Yenan. After all, Donovan's men had been charged with gathering intelligence from any and all sources. If the OSS had been able to use the Dixie Mission to maximum advantage, not only might our relations with China have been changed, but also our position vis-à-vis Moscow. FDR's willingness to compromise on Stalin's political demands at the Yalta Conference of February 1945 was partially based on his belief that we needed the Russians to fight a massive Japanese army in Manchuria. OSS infiltration of that area, with the willing cooperation of Mao and his followers, would have revealed that the enemy force had been steadily depleted to meet Japan's strategic needs in the Pacific. Such knowledge would have made Russian assistance in the Asian war considerably less attractive.[64]

In the long run, while it was not allowed to grow the way the OSS had hoped it would, the Dixie Mission continued to perform a variety of functions even after its original purpose of helping to defeat Japan had been achieved. The Communists treated it with an imperceptible but increasingly evident coolness as their hopes for tangible political rewards in return for the cooperation and goodwill shown the mission faded. They noticed the mission's lack of a proper military bearing and were aware of its internal discord,[65] yet they also knew that the Dixie Mission was an exception to the theater prohibition on dealing with the Communists[66] and originally they had sought to capitalize on this. SACO never missed an opportunity to demean and vilify Donovan's officers for "working with the Communists," and since many of those involved with the mission wrote reports advocating more extensive dealings with the Communists, the Miles/Tai Li propaganda mill was well fueled.[67] Even as relations chilled, the Communists remained unfailingly polite, though they became more and more discouraged by American unwillingness to see the part they expected to play in China's future. As a result, while the United States chose not to reward the Communists for their contributions to the war effort by helping them get political recognition, evaluations and reevaluations of the American role in China during World War II would polarize American political thinking for years to come.

NOTES

Documentation available in the National Archives can be found in the following record groups and microfilm:

Record Groups: 59, General Records of the Department of State; 165, Records of the War Department and Special Staffs; 226, Office of Strategic Services.

Microfilm: Yenan Observer Group, Dixie. 4 vols. Office of the Chief of Military History, Department of the Army.

Copies of documents not otherwise cited were provided to the author by Col. Wilbur J. Peterkin, formerly of the Dixie Mission, now deceased. They, and the typescripts of the interviews, are in the possession of the author and are cited as the Carolle Carter Collection (CC).

1. Interview with F. MacCracken Fisher, Aug. 1978. Carolle Carter Collection (CC).
2. R. Harris Smith, *OSS: The Secret History of America's First Central Intelligence Agency* (Berkeley, 1972), p. 254.
3. Although the OSS could provide a transmitter easily enough, the State Department preferred they did not because of concern over how the Chinese might react. U.S. Department of State, *Foreign Relations of the United States, (FRUS), 1944,* vol. 6, *China* (Washington, DC, 1967), pp. 624–625.
4. Report: "Route From India to China Traversed by Capt. Tolstoy and Lt. Dolan. Motor Road Possibilities," July 25, 1943, CC.
5. Memorandum from Tolstoy to Edward G. Buxton, Jan. 20, 1944, CC.
6. Gen. William Donovan to James Dunn, Apr. 14, 1944, 893, 24/1711, General Records of the Department of State, Record Group 59, National Archives and Records Administration, Washington, DC (hereinafter cited as RG 59, NA).
7. David D. Barrett, *Dixie Mission: U.S. Army Observer Group in Yenan, 1944* (Berkeley, 1970), pp. 22–23.
8. John Paton Davies Jr., *Dragon by the Tail* (New York, 1972), p. 196.
9. Memorandum from John Davies to State Dept., Jan. 15, 1944, CC.
10. Memorandum from Capt. J. E. Spencer to Dr. William Langer and Burton Fahs, June 4, 1944, Records of the Office of Strategic Services, Record Group 226 (RG 226), NA.
11. Memorandum from Spencer to Langer and Fahs, June 4, 1944, CC.
12. Corey Ford, *Donovan of OSS* (Boston, 1970), p. 168.
13. Memorandum to Langer, attention Fahs, from Spencer, Subject: Palisades-Dixie, Aug. 1, 1944, Entry 53, RG 226, NA.
14. Col. Henry M. Spengler, "American Liaison Groups," *Military Review* 27 (1947): 61.
15. Other responsibilities of the mission included utilization and expansion of Communist intelligence agencies in enemy and occupied territory; getting complete lists of Communist officials; locating enemy air fields and air defense in North China; target intelligence; bomb damage assessment; weather; economic intelligence; learning the operation of the Communist forces and the enemy; operations; evaluation of present contribution of Communists to the war effort and the extent of areas under Communist control (with maps); the most effective means of assisting the Communists to increase the value of their war effort; naval intelligence; learning the order of battle of the Communist

forces; and evaluating the potential contribution of the Communists to the war effort. Barrett, *Dixie Mission,* pp. 26–27.

16. Interview with Dr. Alfred Burden, Aug. 1977, CC.

17. Memorandum to Langer, Attention Fahs, from Spencer, Subject: Palisades-Dixie, Aug. 1, 1944, Entry 53, RG 226, NA.

18. Michael Schaller, *U.S. Crusade in China, 1938–1945* (New York, 1979), pp. 240–242.

19. Interview with S. Herbert Hitch, Oct. 1989, CC.

20. Vice Adm. Milton E. Miles, USN, *A Different Kind of War: The Little-Known Story of the Combined Guerrilla Forces Created in China by the U.S. Navy and the Chinese During World War II* (Garden City, NY, 1967), pp. 343–344.

21. Sterling Seagrave, *The Soong Dynasty* (New York, 1985), p. 397.

22. Schaller, *U.S. Crusade in China,* pp. 240–242.

23. Ibid., pp. 246–247.

24. Memorandum to Donovan from Col. Richard Heppner, Apr. 20, 1945, CC.

25. Ford, *Donovan of OSS,* p. 270.

26. Memorandum to Donovan from Heppner, Apr. 20, 1945, RG 226, NA.

27. Interview with Paul C. Domke, Dec. 1977, CC.

28. Interview with Anton Remineh, Aug. 1978, CC.

29. Domke interview, Dec. 1977.

30. Remineh interview, Aug. 1978.

31. Interview with Jack Klein, Aug. 1977, CC.

32. Remineh interview, Aug. 1978.

33. Interview with Clifford F. Young, Aug. 1977, CC.

34. Memorandum to Lt. Col. Peterkin from Capt. E. J. Brown, China theater, Mar. 27, 1945, RG 226, NA; report from Capt. Charles Stelle to Col. Richard Heppner, Apr. 12, 1945, and interviews with Arnold Dadian and Col. Wilfred Smith, Washington, DC, July, 1979, CC.

35. Memorandum from General A. C. Wedemeyer to CO, Yenan Observer Group, July 28, 1945, CC.

36. Memorandum of Aug. 12, 1945, from Louis Hector to Col. William P. Davis for Col. Heppner, CC.

37. Memorandum to Peterkin from Brown, Mar. 27, 1945; report from Stelle to Heppner, Apr. 12, 1945; and Dadian interview, July 1979, CC.

38. Charles F. Romanus and Riley Sunderland, *United States Army in World War II, China-Burma-India Theater: Time Runs Out in CBI* (Washington, 1954), p. 158.

39. Davies, *Dragon by the Tail,* p. 287. Others found them not always professional, given to playing games. For instance, the group that was connected with Chennault's 14th Air Force headquarters in Kweilin and operated under the cover of AGFRTS received a substantial shipment of materiel from the OSS office in Kunming. Stenciled on the outside of the crate was "AGFRTS (OSS)," Wilfred Smith interview, July, 1979, CC.

40. Interview with Col. John C. Coughlin (ret.), Feb. 1979, CC.

41. Interview with Gen. Albert C. Wedemeyer, Aug. 1978, CC.

42. Fisher interview, Aug. 1978, CC.

43. Each branch within the organization had its specialty: R&A collected and assessed documents, X-2 dealt with counterintelligence and tried to catch spies

trying to find out who was being sent in to spy on their country, and Morale Operations tried to disturb the enemy's confidence using propaganda. They once came up with something to spray on Japanese officers that would make them smell bad so they would lose face. Memorandum to Peterkin from Brown, Mar. 27, 1945; report from Stelle to Heppner, Apr. 12, 1945; and Dadian interview, July 1979, CC.

44. Col. David D. Barrett to Col. Joseph K. Dickey, Aug. 27, 1944, CC. Dickey and Barrett exchanged letters over reports that Ray Cromley had tried to send directly to Washington without going through Barrett or G-2 headquarters. "Cromley seems to take a lot upon himself in these reports," Dickey wrote, especially in recommending people for decorations and promotions (including himself). Cromley had the audacity to request that all sorts of equipment, a radio operator, and a stenographer named La Donna Anderson be sent to help him. "I must have her here," he wrote, "she knows the ropes." Barrett described Cromley as a troublemaker, an officer who did not understand the principles of command, childish in his desire to build up an OSS "cell." He was not the only member of the mission Barrett criticized. The colonel saw Colling as a "very low-powered officer but at least willing to work to the best of his limited abilities, unlike Stelle, who had plenty of ability but was lazy." The problem with Cromley was resolved when Coughlin transferred him to G-2. After praising his order of battle work and reminding him that he was not the head of a mission, nor did he have any personnel assigned to him, Coughlin reminded Cromley that he would be responsible to Dickey and Barrett simultaneously, since he was still attached to the Dixie Mission, and that all communications were to be channeled through the head of the mission. Lt. Col. Jos. K. Dickey to Col. David D. Barrett, Aug. 19, 1944; report by Maj. Ray Cromley, Subject: Personnel Needed for China Order of Battle Work, July 31, 1944; Memorandum to Gen. Jos. W. Stilwell from Col. Jos. K. Dickey, Subject: G-2 Summary of Items of Interest, Sept. 5, 1944; Col. David D. Barrett to Col. Joseph K. Dickey, Aug. 27, 1944; Memorandum to Cromley from Col. John G. Coughlin, Subject: Change of Unit, Sept. 12, 1944, CC.
45. Wilfred Smith interview, July 1979.
46. Memorandums to Langer and Fahs from Spencer, July 4 and July 8, 1944, RG 226, NA.
47. Memorandum to Commanding General, Forward Echelon, Chungking, from Cromley. Subject: "Yenan as the Major Order of Battle China Base of Operations," July 30, 1944, CC.
48. USAOS to the Commanding General Forward Echelon, Aug. 6, 1944, CC.
49. AGFRTS was the "abbreviation" used for the Air-Ground Resources Technical Staff, OSS's cover group created in April 1944 to conduct intelligence for the 14th Air Force. R. H. Smith, OSS, pp. 260–261.
50. Memorandum from Stelle to Spencer, Subject: Interim Report on Mission to Yenan, Oct. 27, 1944, RG 226, NA.
51. Burden interview, Aug. 1979.
52. Letter to Spencer from Stelle, Dec. 8, 1944, and letter to Stelle from Spencer, Dec. 28, 1944, RG 226, NA.
53. Draft proposal for a major OSS secret intelligence operation in North China and from North China into Manchuria and Korea prepared by Lt. Guy Mar-

tin, Dr. Charles B. Fahs, Maj. Phillip K. Crowe, Lt. Thomas J. Davis, Jan. 5, 1945, Entry 148, RG 226, NA.

54. Memorandum to Asst. Chief of Staff, G-5 from Lt. Col. Harry W. Little, Subject: "Personnel for Observer Group," June 6, 1945, Entry 148, RG 226, NA.

55. Memorandum for the files signed Lt. Col. Willis H. Bird, Subject: North China-SO and SI Projects, Feb. 26, 1945, CC.

56. Letter from Peterkin to Dickey, June 4, 1945, CC.

57. Memorandum to commanding general, attention Assistant Chief of Staff, G-5, from Col. William P. Davis, July 31, 1945, CC.

58. Memorandum to Heppner from Col. Paul Helliwell, June 8, 1945, CC.

59. Translation of letter to Donovan from Chu Teh, CG, 18th Group Army, Jan. 25, 1945, CC.

60. Memorandum from Capt. Brooke Dolan to Lt. Col. Harry W. Little, Executive Officer, Deputy SSO, June 16, 1945, RG 226, NA.

61. Confidential source, Former Foreign Affairs Specialist, R&A Branch OSS and State Dept., 1991, CC.

62. Memorandum to Chief, Research and Intelligence Service, China, from 1st Lt. Leonard C. Meeker, subject: Yenan, Oct. 23, 1945, RG 226, NA.

63. Confidential source, Former Foreign Affairs Specialist, R&A Branch OSS and State Dept., 1991, CC.

64. R. H. Smith, *OSS*, p. 274.

65. Letter for signature to Commanding General Army Air Force, China theater, from Dickey, concerning supply of Yenan Observer Group, Dec. 6, 1945, CC.

66. Young interview, Aug. 1977.

67. R. H. Smith, *OSS*, p. 265.

THE ACTIVITIES OF DETACHMENT 101 OF THE OSS

James R. Ward

Detachment 101 of the Office of Strategic Services (OSS) was the first unit in U.S. military history created specifically for the purpose of conducting unconventional warfare operations behind enemy lines. It was formed on April 14, 1942, to perform espionage, sabotage, guerrilla warfare, propaganda, and escape and evasion operations in support of U.S. military objectives in China. The strategic situation developing in the Far East at the beginning of World War II seemed to indicate that unconventional warfare operations could be very useful in China or Burma.

The war in the Far East began in 1931, when Japan invaded and annexed Manchuria. In 1937 the Japanese Navy gained command of the sea approaches to China by controlling the coastline, and the Japanese Army occupied China's key port cities. Chiang Kai-shek's Nationalist government fled from the Japanese invaders to Chungking, deep in the interior of China. Having lost his ports and access to the sea, Chiang needed a supply route to the rest of the world, so he ordered a road built from Kunming, China, to Lashio in Burma. The 681-mile road was built by tens of thousands of Chinese laborers in a year and a half and was opened to traffic in mid-1939. Supplies for Chiang's government and troops were shipped by sea to Rangoon, by rail to Lashio, and then by road to Kunming. It was called the Burma Road, and it was Nationalist China's main source of supply from the outside world for 2½ years—from mid-1939 to early 1942.

When the Japanese attacked Pearl Harbor on December 7, 1941, their strategic objective was to knock out the U.S. Navy so that it could not interfere with Japan's plans to conquer Asia. From bases in French Indochina and Thailand, the Japanese knifed down the Malay Peninsula to defeat the British in Singapore, took the Philippines away from the Americans, and captured the oil-rich Dutch East Indies. They did this with bewildering speed.

Japanese aircraft first bombed Rangoon, Burma, on December 23, 1941. Three weeks later, two Japanese Army divisions invaded southern Burma from Thailand. It was obvious to President Roosevelt and his top military advisers that the Japanese would soon cut the Burma Road. The need to keep China in the war became a major strategic objective of the United States. Chiang Kai-shek had 346 divisions, totaling almost 4 million men, which were poorly supplied, inadequately trained, and badly led, but they tied down a large number of Japanese divisions. Despite other priorities, the United States would do what it could to supply Nationalist China and keep it in the war.

In January 1942, while the Japanese were moving into Burma, Gen. George Marshall appointed Maj. Gen. Joseph Stilwell to be commander of all U.S. forces in the China-Burma-India theater as well as Chief of Staff of Allied Forces in China under Gen. Chiang Kai-shek. Stilwell had spent 13 years of his army career in China and spoke fluent Mandarin.

General Stilwell faced many problems. He was about to get his third star, but he had no American ground combat forces under his command, and there was no likelihood that he would get any American units for at least another year. The U.S. Pacific Fleet was badly damaged at Pearl Harbor, the Japanese Navy had complete command of the western Pacific, and the Japanese Army was in the process of conquering and occupying all of the Far Eastern countries rimming the Pacific Ocean. Also, the European and Pacific theaters had higher priorities than the China-Burma-India theater. The only ground forces General Stilwell would have under his command for the next year or two were Chinese, but the Japanese were moving fast to close the Burma Road, the only supply line Stilwell had for those Chinese troops.

So in those dark days of late January 1942, when General Stilwell received a staff study proposing that a small detachment of American officers and men be sent to his command to conduct intelligence and unconventional warfare operations behind Japanese lines in China or Burma, he accepted it. The study had been sent to General Stilwell by Col. Preston Goodfellow of the Office of Coordinator of Information, later the OSS.

General Stilwell welcomed the proposal that Detachment 101 be created, but he refused to accept the army officer initially proposed as commander of Detachment 101. Stilwell said the unit would need a leader who would not be deterred by the difficulty of the mission. When Colonel Goodfellow asked General Stilwell to recommend someone, Stilwell proposed Carl Eifler, who had previously served as a lieutenant in a reserve unit Stilwell once commanded. Eifler had been called to active duty and was serving as an infantry captain in Hawaii. In mid-February 1942, even before General Stilwell arrived in China to take over his new command, Captain Eifler was recruited as the first member and commanding officer of Detachment 101.

Eifler was a good choice. His first task was to cut through the red tape and bureaucratic delays that had to be cleared for the original contingent of Detachment 101 to be selected, recruited, trained, equipped, and transported halfway around the world to the China-Burma-India theater. Eifler needed to find good men with a variety of military skills at a time when America's military forces were expanding faster than ever before, when everyone with any military skills whatsoever was in great demand. Detachment 101 needed men with knowledge of the languages and cultures of the Far East and skills in logistics, military science and tactics, engineering, communications, medicine, photography, explosives, parachuting, and flying airplanes.

Eifler was given authority to pick anyone he wanted for his new unit. First, he selected Capt. John Coughlin, a West Point graduate, to be his deputy. Coughlin, in turn, recruited Capt. William R. Peers. Within a few months these three men selected, recruited, trained, and equipped the original contingent of Detachment 101 personnel.

It took the Japanese slightly more than 3 months to capture all of Burma, a country about the size of Texas. The Japanese had excellent intelligence on the strong and weak points of the British defenses in Burma. They bypassed the strong points and broke through the weak points with quick thrusts. The Japanese Army was effective in the use of jungle warfare tactics. They used deep penetration strike forces to set up roadblocks and ambush the British troops behind their own lines. The British forces were roadbound. They became demoralized and incapable of stopping the Japanese.

Months before the war began, Japan had recruited and exfiltrated 30 young Burmese, mostly students from Rangoon University, who were very eager to rid the country of British colonialism. When these young men returned, they led the Japanese Armed Forces into Burma, conducted subversive tactics among the Burmese people, and provided the Japanese with intelligence. The effectiveness of these "Thirty Comrades" on behalf of the Japanese later made it very difficult for OSS agents to operate in territory occupied by ethnic Burmese.

When Rangoon fell on March 8, 1942, the Burma Road was closed. Two more Japanese divisions were landed in Rangoon. General Stilwell flew into Burma to command the two Chinese divisions that had been committed in support of the British. The Chinese forces were no more effective in stopping the Japanese than the British forces had been, but the better trained of the two Chinese divisions performed reasonably well before it ran out of supplies, proving Stilwell's contention that the Chinese could fight well if properly trained, led, and equipped. By May 5 all of Burma was in Japanese hands except the tiny British outpost of Fort Hertz at Putao close to the northern tip of Burma where the frontiers of Tibet, India, and China almost converge.

General Stilwell refused to fly to safety. He walked out of Burma to India, where he announced to the world that he had taken a hell of a beating and was humiliated by it, but that he wanted to return and retake Burma.

While Stilwell was in Burma retreating with his Chinese divisions, Detachment 101 was being formed. It was activated in mid-April 1942. Less than 3 months later, Eifler, Coughlin, Peers, and the first group of 21 members of Detachment 101 were at the China-Burma-India headquarters in New Delhi, India. When Stilwell arrived, he met with all the officers and men of Detachment 101. He urged them to set up a base in northern India and begin operations into Burma as soon as possible. He said he wanted the officers and men of Detachment 101 to learn to survive and live in the jungles, and to consider themselves as pioneers in blazing the way back into Burma. Stilwell wanted information, and he also wanted sabotage operations aimed at reducing the effectiveness of the Japanese air base in Myitkyina. Japanese aircraft flying out of the Myitkyina air base were shooting down our planes flying with supplies for China over "the Hump"—the Himalayan mountain range between Burma and China. Stilwell ordered Detachment 101 to blow up road and railroad bridges leading to Myitkyina from the south. He said he wanted "to hear lots of booms coming out of Burma." In addition, he asked Detachment 101 to maintain liaison with the British so that the colonial government would have no complaint about Detachment 101's activities.

The remainder of 1942 was devoted to setting up Detachment 101's base and training camps at Nazira in northern Assam; establishing communications with Washington; recruiting and training Burmese nationals to serve as intelligence agents, radio operators, and saboteurs; and devising and making lightweight portable radios that could transmit messages over mountains from positions in Burma 500 miles away. The British were cooperative in making available potential agents found among the Burmese nationals in the Indian Army. Other potential agents were found in refugee camps.

It was obvious from the beginning that Caucasian Americans could not pass themselves off as natives of Burma. Detachment 101 did not drop operational groups (OGs) of Americans by parachute for reconnaissance, sabotage, or other specific operational purposes deep behind enemy lines in Burma as the OSS did in Europe. Later in the war, Detachment 101 did deploy American OG units on reconnaissance operations along the Arakan Coast of Burma in support of British 14th Army operations. Detachment 101's Maritime Unit was also used in coastal reconnaissance operations searching for potential agent and troop landing areas as well as probing for underwater minefields and Japanese beach defenses. For the most part, however, the military mission in Burma entailed training, deploying, and supporting native agents in intelligence collection operations and organizing, supporting, and leading native guerrilla forces in combat to maximize the potential military effectiveness of these native forces against the Japanese.

The sign at the entrance to Detachment 101's base camp in northern Assam stated that it was "The U.S. Army Experimental Station." That was an excellent cover name because it was sufficiently innocuous to lead some of the local people to conclude that it was a research facility for the study of tropical diseases, a fact that deterred the curious from prying into what was going on at the base camp. It was also an appropriate name because much of what Detachment 101 did initially was experimental. Lessons were learned through trial and error and on-the-job training. A great deal was learned about surviving and fighting in the jungles from natives, especially the Kachin hill tribesmen, some of whom came from such remote and primitive mountainous areas that they had never seen a wheel until they first saw them on airplanes.

At the end of 1942, when Detachment 101 attempted its first infiltration operation, there were six Japanese divisions scattered throughout Burma. The mission of the first infiltration unit, known as A Group, an eight-man team composed of Burmese natives and two Burma-domiciled Englishmen, was to attack and sabotage the roads and railroad used for bringing supplies from the south into Myitkyina, where the Japanese 18th Division headquarters was based, and where the airfield was being used to attack planes flying supplies over the Hump to China. Detachment 101 had not yet acquired an air drop capability, so the initial plan called for A Group to infiltrate overland from Fort Hertz, where British officers commanded a battalion of mountain tribesmen which was called the Northern Kachin Levies. It soon became apparent that the terrain was so formidable and dangerous and the distance to the target area—250 miles—was so far that they could not complete the mission and return to Fort Hertz before the monsoon began in May. They decided to abort the overland mission and infiltrate by parachute. A deal was made with the Air Transport Command (ATC), which was losing pilots and planes on the Hump run. The ATC would furnish the planes, parachutes, and parachute instructor personnel, and 101 would develop an air crew rescue program and help train air crews in jungle survival skills.

With the help of the ATC, A Group was parachuted into the Kaukkwee Valley, where they established a base camp. They sent their first message to 101 headquarters in India, and then headed over the mountains to the railroad. On the first night after reaching the railroad, they split into 2 teams and blew the railroad in 30 places using variable time delay fuses. On the second night one of the teams blew up a railroad bridge, dropping two spans of the bridge into a river.

At the same time in January 1943, an American major was leading a team down from Fort Hertz to Ngumla in the center of the triangle formed by the Irrawaddy River north of Myitkyina to establish an intelligence base and train guerrilla forces to conduct sabotage and harassment operations. Detachment 101 was finally in business.

These early operations were relatively insignificant as compared with what Detachment 101 was to accomplish later, but they were the beginning. A great deal was learned from those early missions about infiltration techniques into Burma and supporting men in the field by air.

By the end of 1943, Detachment 101 had six intelligence bases that were staffed by Americans operating in northern Burma. Each of these bases ran intelligence collection operations and had Kachin guerrilla forces that were able to defend the approaches to the bases and conduct sabotage and harassment operations. In addition, even deeper behind Japanese lines, 101 had agent/radio operator teams scatttered along the main transportation arteries leading to northern Burma. All of these communicated by radio with the main base in Nazira, India.

In late 1943, a 40-foot speedboat arrived to facilitate sea infiltration operations along the Burma coast. While planning other uses for this boat, Colonel Eifler was informed that an American B-24 had been shot down and crash-landed in the Bay of Bengal west of Rangoon. Eifler immediately led the crew of his new boat 450 miles deep into enemy waters in a successful rescue of the B-24's nine-man crew. Shortly after this, Eifler was badly injured during a sea infiltration operation in which he brought two rubber rafts from the beach where the agents were infiltrated back to the launch boat waiting 600 yards out at sea.

When General Donovan visited 101 headquarters in December 1943, he placed Colonel Peers in command of Detachment 101, put Colonel Coughlin in charge of OSS strategic operations in the China-Burma-India theater, and transferred Colonel Eifler back to the United States to brief authorities in Washington and for reassignment to other duties.

Detachment 101 continued to expand slowly but steadily until the beginning of 1944, when General Stilwell told Colonel Peers he wanted Detachment 101 to expand its guerrilla forces rapidly to 3,000 men. Stilwell wanted 101 to assist the Merrill's Marauders and the Chinese troops in their drive down the Hukawng Valley. He said that if the guerrillas were really effective, 101 would be authorized to expand its guerrilla forces to 10,000 men. General Stilwell then provided Detachment 101 with eight additional officers, some arms and ammunition, and six aircraft from the Troop Carrier Command for air supply purposes. More of everything, including personnel, was also ordered from OSS headquarters in the United States. During 1944 and early 1945 Detachment 101 greatly expanded its guerrilla force to a peak of about 10,800 in March 1945.

Detachment 101 was fortunate. Its members had more than a year to build an intelligence base before they were required to conduct guerrilla warfare. That was a tremendous advantage, because with this intelligence base they always knew more about the enemy than the enemy did about them. When Detachment 101 did commit its guerrilla units, it was initially in support of conventional military forces, the Merrill's Marauders, the Mars Task Force, and the Chinese and British troops. Detachment 101 provided them with intelligence, at times scouted for them on the march, patrolled their flanks, and occasionally served to screen their movements so that the Japanese would think that only a guerrilla force was on the move in their area. Guerrillas generally controlled the jungles on the flanks and to the front of these conventional forces so that the Japanese were confined to the main north and south corridors—the roads, the railroad, and the Irrawaddy River—where conventional forces and the 10th Air Force could attack them. Detachment 101 harassed the Japanese supply lines and rear bases, thereby forcing them to devote more of their combat forces to cover their flanks and rear.

The war in northern Burma was fought in three phases. The first phase began in November 1943 and ended in late August 1944 with the capture of Myitkyina and the securing of flights over the Hump to China from disruption by the Japanese Air Force. The second phase ended with the capture of Lashio, Maymyo, and Mandalay in March 1945. The third phase ended in July 1945 with all of the old Burma Road from Rangoon to Lashio and Kunming back under Allied control. During the first two phases, Detachment 101 played an important role both as a supplier of intelligence and as a guerrilla force in support of American and Allied conventional military forces. During the third phase, however, Detachment 101 was assigned the conventional military mission of clearing the enemy from an area of about 10,000 square miles in the Shan States in order to secure the Burma Road. For its success in accomplishing that mission, Detachment 101 was awarded the Presidential Distinguished Unit Citation.

Although it won the Presidential Citation for its success in completing a conventional military mission, Detachment 101 had been created to perform unconventional tasks such as espionage, sabotage, guerrilla warfare, propaganda, and escape and evasion missions.

In the performance of its espionage task, Detachment 101 provided 75 percent of all the intelligence from which the 10th Air Force chose its targets and 85 percent of all the intelligence received by General Stilwell's Northern Combat Area Command. In addition to a number of American-staffed intelligence bases established in Burma, Detachment 101 infiltrated 162 native agent/radio teams into Burma by air, by sea, or overland.

Detachment 101 sabotage agents and guerrillas demolished 57 bridges, derailed 9 trains, destroyed or captured 272 trucks or other vehicles, and destroyed 15,000 tons of Japanese supplies. These sabotage operations also had the effect of forcing the Japanese to deploy additional troops to protect their rear echelon bases and lines of communication.

Using conventional military missions, guerrilla warfare, sabotage, and espionage, Detachment 101 won many successes in Burma. (226-FPK-45-352)

Detachment 101's greatest effectiveness was in the field of guerrilla warfare. The unit's members pioneered the use of air and radio communications to support and coordinate guerrilla warfare activities. They recruited, organized, trained, equipped, and led over 10,800 guerrillas in effective support of conventional military operations. Detachment 101's guerrilla forces killed 5,428 members of the Japanese Army, wounded an estimated 10,000, and captured 78 Japanese prisoners. Their own losses were 27 Americans, 338 native guerrillas, and 40 espionage agents killed.

Reports on the success of the escape and evasion operations vary from a total of 232 to 425 Allied airmen rescued. The Detachment built trails and cache sites along the Hump run, and the higher figure may include those who parachuted to the ground and used these trails and cache sites to escape. It may also include airmen who were brought to safety by Kachins who were influenced to help by 101, but were not directly under the control of Detachment 101 personnel. The lower figure, 232, was taken from the Northern Combat Area Command's historical account of the northern and central Burma campaigns and does not include those who may have been rescued during the last four months of the war in Burma.

The success of the propaganda and psychological warfare efforts was difficult to measure. It is impossible to judge how effective Detachment 101's efforts were in demoralizing the Japanese Army in Burma. The members knew from intelligence reports that Allied military victories had a very demoralizing effect upon the Japanese Army, but the unit was not successful in persuading individual Japanese soldiers to surrender through its propaganda. It was also difficult to determine the value of propaganda in helping to win the loyalty of the Kachins, and even some of the Shans. It was even more difficult to evaluate the impact of propaganda on the Burmese people, but when the "Thirty Comrades," the Burmese nationalists who aided the Japanese entry into Burma, decided to switch their allegiance to the Allies because they were disillusioned with Japan's empty promises of independence, Detachment 101 helped them to do so. A Detachment 101 agent called "Mac" led a representative of Gen. Aung San, a man named Thakin Pe Tint, to a secret airstrip built by the OSS specifically for the purpose of exfiltrating him. He was flown to British 14th Army headquarters, where General Slim made arrangements for the Burma National Army to switch sides on March 26, 1945. But that was more of a secret political coup engineered by the British with Detachment 101's help than a propaganda achievement.

Detachment 101 was fortunate for many reasons. Its members had time to experiment, to learn through trial and error, and to build an intelligence base before having to undertake guerrilla warfare activities. By early 1944, they had built a very efficient support organization, without which they would not have been able to support by air the guerrilla force they had created.

Detachment 101 was also lucky that the people living in the areas they first had to infiltrate were Kachins and that the American and Irish missionaries who worked with them had won their loyalties to the extent that they did. The unit had none of the political problems that would have plagued it if the members had to operate in countries such as China or Vietnam. The Kachins were not by nature inclined to engage in conventional assault and defensive combat, but they were outstandingly effective in the use of guerrilla tactics in mountainous jungle terrain to surprise, deceive, and confuse the Japanese.

Detachment 101 made mistakes, but also learned a great deal from these mistakes and tried not to repeat them. Unfortunately, the Detachment was instructed to keep no records while behind enemy lines because of a fear at OSS headquarters that such records might be used by the Japanese to justify torture in the event Detachment 101 members were captured. As a result, they wrote no after-action reports covering each guerrilla warfare operation. Such reports would have been invaluable in recording for historical purposes the lessons they learned through trial and error.

Detachment 101's contribution to the Allied war effort in Burma was very valuable but cost very little. Only about 120 Americans served in the field at any one time directing and supporting a guerrilla force that grew to over 10,000 natives. Detachment 101's casualty rate was exceptionally low for the number of men fielded and the damage inflicted on the enemy.

The veterans of Detachment 101 are unanimously proud of their unit's accomplishments, and they all concur that much of its success was attributable to the leadership provided by Colonels Eifler and Peers. Although very different in personality and temperament, they were both men of extraordinary integrity, courage, and dedication to the successful accomplishment of Detachment 101's mission. Each seemed to be the right person at the right time in command of Detachment 101. It was reassuring to the men in the jungles in close proximity to the enemy to know that when they needed it they could count on the timely delivery of an emergency ammunition drop, a piece of vital intelligence, an air strike, or medical support and evacuation. Eifler and Peers made Detachment 101 a well-integrated, efficient team that responded effectively to the demands of the theater commander.

Although OSS Detachment 101 clearly functioned under and responded to the military chain of command in the China-Burma-India theater, its OSS support structure provided it with vitally needed flexibility that it would not have had if it were fully integrated into and totally dependent on the U.S. military support structure that existed at that time. Detachment 101 was able to draw much of what it needed from the military support structure but was also able to rely on its OSS resources when the military was not able to support it as swiftly as requirements demanded.

The Office of Strategic Services contributed to the overall Allied war effort in World War II by providing useful tactical and strategic intelligence and by promoting and supporting the resistance potential of the people in enemy-occupied territory in the entire spectrum of unconventional warfare. It is probable, however, that the greatest contribution of the OSS in the long run was to prove for the historical record that the United States needed a centralized intelligence agency and that the armed forces of the United States have much to gain by developing and retaining a permanent unconventional warfare capability such as exists today in the United States Special Operations Command.

THE OPENING WEDGE:
The OSS in Thailand

E. Bruce Reynolds

Thailand served as a staging area and supply base for Japan's southern armies during World War II. No major battles were fought on Thai territory, and when the war ended, Allied ground action against Japanese forces there—which in any case would have been carried out by British troops—was, at best, still months away. Nonetheless, the Office of Strategic Services (OSS) developed an extensive operation in Thailand during the last year of the war and attached a significance to it which far exceeded that country's strategic importance to the American war effort. This anomaly is explained in part by the fact that the OSS had to scramble for a meaningful role in the war against Japan and in part by the increasingly political nature of the Thailand operation.

As the only independent state in a region that before the war had been dominated by America's European allies, Thailand offered special opportunities for the OSS. Gen. William Donovan's expansive organization had failed to gain significant access to the decisive Pacific theaters, had seen its operations in China hobbled by poor relations with Chiang Kai-shek's government, and found its freedom to operate in the former European colonies in Southeast Asia limited. In the latter instance, not only did the British seek to check-rein the OSS because of suspicions that it was promoting an anticolonial political agenda, but most Americans, including OSS officers, considered European colonial rule anachronistic and wished to avoid direct involvement in its restoration. Under these circumstances it is not surprising that the ambitious leaders of the OSS sought to carve a niche for their agency by taking full advantage of Thailand's independent status and its leaders' eagerness to escape the onus of alliance with Japan. Although it became increasingly apparent that the Thailand operation would contribute little to the defeat of Japan, the OSS succeeded in expanding it in the closing months of the war. This was possible largely because the State Department shared the OSS view that the operation might serve as the opening wedge for postwar American economic and political influence in Southeast Asia.

Ironically, this American vision of Thailand as a potential foothold strikingly resembled the Japanese view of that country in the early 1930s, when they were the ambitious outsiders seeking greater access to a resource-rich region. Faced with trade restrictions imposed by the western colonial powers in the wake of the Great Depression, the Japanese then saw Thailand as an outlet for exports and a source of rice, tin, and rubber. Later in the decade, as world war loomed on the horizon, the Japanese also came to view Thailand as an essential launching pad for land assaults on the adjacent British colonies of Malaya and Burma.

Thai leaders had taken advantage of Japanese interest in promoting bilateral relations by playing them off against the Europeans to escape the last vestiges of extraterritoriality in 1937 and to extract "lost territories" from French Indochina in 1941 after Germany had defeated France. However, Japan's military sweep into the region in December 1941 shattered the balance of power, and the ambitious Thai leader, Field Marshal Phibun (Pibul) Songkhram,[1] allied his nation with the invaders in hopes of maximizing Thai autonomy and gaining advantage in the event of a Japanese victory.

The Americans, who had little material stake in Thailand, had distrusted Phibun for some time and essentially had written the country off. However, the Thai Minister to the United States, Seni Pramot (Pramoj), cast his lot with the Allies and on December 12, 1941, called upon his countrymen to resist the Japanese in a speech broadcast by an American shortwave radio station. Seni's stance, and the fact that his staff and several dozen Thai students also refused repatriation and volunteered to support the American war effort, made a strong impression in the dark early days of the war in the Pacific.[2]

Accordingly, when the Thai government sought favor with the Japanese by declaring war on the United States and Britain on January 25, 1942, the Americans chose to disregard the action.[3] The British, however, humiliated by their battlefield disasters in Malaya and angry with the Thai government for its support of the Japanese offensive, responded in kind. These divergent reactions set the stage for subsequent Anglo-American quarrels over Thai policy and eventually would provide a new opportunity for the Thai to play one rival power off against another.

The newly established OSS, eager to develop special operations, soon entered into negotiations with Seni and his "Free Thai" followers. These talks bore fruit in August 1942, when the Joint Psychological Warfare Committee sanctioned operations by a Free Thai military corps. This group would operate under OSS auspices but would be funded by the release of frozen Thai government assets in the United States and led by the Thai military attaché, Lt. Col. Khap Khunchon (Kharb Kunjara).[4] As plans called for the infiltration of Thai agents into their homeland from China, a 21-man contingent, shepherded by Capt. (later Lt. Col.) Nicol Smith, who had previously carried out an OSS intelligence mission in Vichy France, embarked for the Far East in March 1943, ultimately reaching Chungking in the late summer.[5]

Initial hopes were high. The German defeat at Stalingrad in early 1943 had awakened Thai politicians to the fact that Axis military fortunes were waning and that Thailand faced a difficult future as an ally of Japan. Premier Phibun responded by initiating surreptitious military contacts with Chinese forces in Yunnan Province, but his political enemies, who could claim to have disapproved of the alliance with Japan, were better positioned and had become active, too. Early in the war Phibun's chief civilian rival, Pridi Phanomyong (sometimes referred to by his title, Luang Pradit Manutham, and in OSS literature by the code name RUTH), had been elevated to a prestigious but previously politically impotent position as one of the regents for the young Thai king. Pridi, whom both the British and Americans considered anti-Japanese, hoped that he and at least two other key political figures could slip out of the country to establish a government-in-exile. An emissary charged with laying groundwork for this scheme reached China in the spring of 1943, and two more arrived in Chungking in September 1943, shortly after Smith's OSS party.[6]

Despite these promising signs that an anti-Japanese underground existed in Thailand, Smith and his men soon were swept off course by the complex political currents that swirled through wartime China. Tai Li, the head of Chiang Kai-shek's secret police, threw all manner of roadblocks in the path of Smith's men, particularly after December 1943, when General Donovan relieved Tai's American naval ally, Capt. Milton Miles, from command of OSS-China and told Tai in no uncertain terms that the OSS intended to operate in China whether the Chinese cooperated or not.[7] Due in large measure to Chinese obstructionism, it was June 1944 before any of Smith's agents managed to cross the Thai border. Two were killed by Thai policemen—who apparently were after their valuables—and six more were arrested and incarcerated in the jail of the Criminal Investigations Division (CID) in Bangkok.[8]

The CID lockup also housed 10 British-trained Thai agents who had parachuted into Thailand or landed by submarine in the first half of 1944.[9] The Japanese knew about the parachutists and had interrogated them under Thai supervision but had not demanded custody. The commander of the Japanese garrison force, Lt. Gen. Nakamura Aketo, was dealing gingerly with the Thai, as he considered the maintenance of good relations essential to maintaining order and the flow of supplies to the Burma front.[10]

Although all of the agents had carried radio sets, none had been able to make contact before being arrested, and the Allies would not hear from any of them until after the fall of the Phibun government at the end of July 1944. This change of regime became possible because Phibun's domestic political standing had declined in step with the diminishing fortunes of the Axis and because he had alienated the Japanese by obvious attempts to distance himself from them. Pridi and his allies goaded Phibun into submitting his resignation by parlaying the domestic discontent into National Assembly votes against two government measures. Although Phibun expected to be recalled to office, as had been the case after previous resignations, Pridi had other plans. When his timid fellow regent refused to cross Phibun and resigned, Pridi had the assembly declare him sole regent, then selected a new prime minister, Khuang Aphaiwong, who was charged with maintaining a facade of friendly cooperation with the Japanese. With support from the navy, the police, and the Japanese occupation force—which wished to avoid disorder—Pridi deterred army loyalists from staging a coup to restore Phibun. With men of his own choosing in power, Pridi abandoned his previous plan to leave the country but intensified efforts to establish channels of communication with the Allies.

On August 18, 1944, one of the imprisoned Thai agents of British Force 136 (the code name for the Asian branch of the Special Operations Executive [SOE]) made radio contact with his base in India. With help from Pridi's men he had tried earlier, but he had not been heard because the British had quit monitoring his frequencies. However, a message he had been permitted to send out overland to China had alerted Force 136 to his signals.[11]

Although the Thai police commander, Gen. Adun Adundetcharat (codenamed BETTY by the OSS), had apparently facilitated this contact and had played a key role in bringing about the change of government, Pridi did not trust Adun because he had formerly been a close ally of Phibun. Consequently, Pridi requested additional Force 136 men who could operate under his direct control and whose presence would not be known to the Japanese. The British successfully airdropped two Thai agents on the night of September 6, 1944.[12]

As the American-trained Free Thai still languished incommunicado in Adun's jail, the OSS authorities had begun to despair that their China-based operation would produce any results.[13] The OSS unit at the South East Asia Command (SEAC) Headquarters of Admiral Lord Louis Mountbatten in Kandy, Ceylon, now also had a Free Thai contingent but its initial attempt to infiltrate two of these agents into southern Thailand via a British submarine had just failed.[14] The officers of this unit, Detachment 404, believed that the British were systematically limiting OSS operations in Malaya and the Netherlands East Indies, and they now feared being shut out of Thailand, too.[15]

The fact that the British had contributed to the development of the OSS had, ironically, deepened the natural professional rivalry between the two nations' intelligence agencies, as the Americans were eager to show their independence and to outshine their mentors.[16] In Asia the rivalry was further intensified by American suspicions that SEAC was part of a clever British strategy to gain American support for the reestablishment of the European colonial order. John Davies, a highly regarded Foreign Service officer attached to the headquarters of the Anglophobic American commander in China, Gen. Joseph Stilwell, had spelled out this view at the time of SEAC's inception in late 1943. He argued that while British military weakness made an embarrassing American presence in colonial India necessary, the British hoped, through the new command, to "consolidate us with themselves for 'efficient' cooperation and then, by dominating the integrated partnership, bring us into line with their policy and action."[17] The officers of Detachment 404 had similar opinions and agreed with Davies that U.S. agencies had to protect America's image as the champion of self-determination by remaining aloof from British efforts to reassert colonial control. Accordingly, they saw sinister motives behind all British efforts to tighten coordination of Allied secret operations in the theater and resisted these as best they could.[18]

Suspicions of British intentions in Southeast Asia ran deep in Washington, too. Several months earlier, on January 26, 1944, OSS representatives had apprised ranking State Department officers of their concern that British intelligence activities in Thailand seemed "more political than military in intent" and emphasized London's reluctance to clarify that nation's policy toward Thailand. In response, Assistant Secretary of State Adolf A. Berle suggested that "it was to American national interest to help establish strong nations on the western shore of the Pacific and that a strong Thailand would be to our national advantage." Berle added that the American side "should not be hesitant or diffident in such a way as to let the British take the lead."[19]

Subsequent State Department efforts to get a British pledge to respect Thailand's postwar sovereignty accomplished nothing, and Davies reported that British officials in India were talking about incorporating Thailand into the British Empire.[20] A State Department memorandum to the President prior to the September 1944 Quebec Conference warned that the British seemed oblivious to the rise of nationalist sentiment throughout Southeast Asia and suggested that any British effort to restore the prewar colonial order would produce negative results.[21]

President Franklin D. Roosevelt, however, despite his persistent, if not always consistent, complaints about European colonialism, would not raise the issue of Southeast Asia at the Quebec Conference. As neither he nor British Prime Minister Winston Churchill wished to face this divisive issue head-on, the unresolved inter-Allied differences on the subject intensified suspicions on each side about the other's intentions. The fact that intra-bureaucratic disagreements on the colonial issue festered in both Washington and London only made matters worse.[22]

Southeast Asia's low priority status in the overall anti-Axis war scheme also adversely affected Anglo-American relations in the SEAC theater. At a time when their comrades were sweeping forward elsewhere, frustrated Americans tended to attribute the lack of action there to British timidity. Although even Stilwell had viewed Mountbatten's appointment as signaling a more aggressive British approach, disillusionment soon set in as critical supplies were directed elsewhere, and the Allies bickered over whether the main SEAC effort should be aimed at opening a supply line to the China theater, as the Americans wanted, or at the recapture of Singapore, the main British interest.[23]

It was in this thick atmosphere of distrust that Detachment 404 chief Col. Richard P. Heppner seized an opportunity presented by General Stilwell's presence in Kandy as substitute for his absent superior, Lord Mountbatten. Heppner easily convinced Stilwell, who bunked at the OSS billet, to authorize the dropping of two Free Thai agents from an American aircraft, an operation that, contrary to all agreements, they concealed from the British. The agents were instructed to establish contact with Pridi and lay the groundwork for the introduction of an American OSS officer to discuss "the development of intelligence, sabotage, and guerrilla operations."[24]

Appropriately dubbed "Hotfoot," the operation was so hastily conceived that the two Thai agents, who had just returned from the abortive submarine operation, received only simulated parachute training. Bad weather held up the mission for 3 days, but it was launched on the night of September 8, 1944. As the pilots were also inexperienced, the two men parachuted in the vicinity of Phrae in north central Thailand from the unusual height of 5,500 feet. Consequently they were separated and were unable to find each other or their equipment in the dense jungle. The Thai police arrested one of them, but the other eluded capture and managed to meet Pridi. This contact led to the jailed OSS agents' being given access to their equipment and on October 5, 1944, nearly 7 weeks after Force 136 had established communications, Smith's men in Szemao, China, received their initial signal from one of their comrades in Bangkok.[25]

Although this seemed to open the door for the OSS, matters did not proceed smoothly. As the early reports from Bangkok contained little useful information, Detachment 404 intelligence officer Dr. Dillon Ripley became suspicious. In a November 17 message he suggested to General Donovan that Pridi might be favoring the British over the Americans or, alternatively, that the Japanese might have authorized Pridi's contacts because they had recognized their coming defeat and were permitting the Thai to cut their own deal. Also, in a monthly report at the end of November, Ripley wrote pessimistically about the quality of the remaining Thai agents and expressed doubts about how to proceed. He indicated that a project was being planned to send agents, who would remain independent of Pridi, into eastern Thailand.[26]

An OSS decision to ignore Pridi's request that arrangements be made for the reception of any new missions and to proceed with two previously planned infiltration efforts also reflected Detachment 404's distrust. Only at the last minute, "as a matter of courtesy," did the OSS advise Pridi of a personnel drop aimed at establishing a base near Doi Angka, a mountain 35 miles southwest of Chiang Mai, on the night of November 1. Although the plane spent a noisy half hour looking for the landing zone, three Thai agents were dropped 15 miles off target, and police promptly arrested them.[27] A parallel submarine operation ended in similar fashion. Three men were deposited on an island (Ko Kadan) off the Andaman Sea coast of southern Thailand, but fishermen spotted them and reported their presence to the authorities, leading to their capture.[28]

In the wake of these failures, strong objections to plans for two additional missions, which were not to be coordinated with Pridi, were voiced from within OSS ranks. On December 21, 1944, John Holladay, a former medical missionary who worked closely with the Free Thai agents, criticized his superiors in Detachment 404 for their "defeatist" attitude in a letter to Lt. Col. H. L. Berno, then the OSS representative to the intelligence coordination organization (P Division) at Mountbatten's headquarters. Holladay repeated a previous injunction that "we must have faith in the Free Thai, and we must prove ourselves faithful to them if we expect to accomplish anything worthwhile." He stated that he would have no part in any future operation unless he felt it was well planned and had a good chance of success. Moreover, the Thai with whom Holladay worked made it known that they would refuse to undertake any mission without his approval.[29]

Although Holladay risked being sacked for insubordination, his letter was well timed. Developments in Bangkok had already begun to change attitudes at Detachment 404 headquarters. On December 14, Pridi, responding to a query from General Donovan, had indicated his willingness to supply military intelligence and receive an American military representative. A memorandum written by John Wester, an OSS officer with long prewar business experience in Thailand, attributed this new responsiveness to the fact that, despite their arrest, members of the party landed by submarine had managed to deliver a message to Pridi from one of the agents he had sent out of Thailand. Wester believed that this message from Sanguan Tularak—who was strongly pro-American and anti-British—had "firmly cemented" relations with Pridi and had given Detachment 404 agents the "inside track and first call on intelligence."[30]

Wester meant that men from Detachment 404 were not only favored over their Force 136 rivals but also over the agents from Smith's OSS-

China group, whom Pridi distrusted because they remained under Adun's wing. A corollary of Detachment 404's new view of Pridi was the adoption of his negative attitude toward Smith's men. This, coupled with broader concerns about security in Tai Li's bailiwick, led to the consolidation of Thai operations under Detachment 404 and the transfer of Smith's unit to Ceylon in early February 1945.[31]

Meanwhile, the American political agenda in regard to Thailand had begun to take shape. In early August 1944, immediately after the change of government in Bangkok, OSS Special Operations chief Lt. Col. Carl O. Hoffman had begun to lobby for the stockpiling of supplies for a 20,000-man resistance force in Thailand. As a timely cable reporting Stilwell's interest in supporting resistance groups in Thailand and Indochina lent weight to his argument, the OSS decided to establish an overall regional stockpile of equipment for 50,000 guerrillas in India. Hoffman then proceeded, apparently on his own initiative, to advise Seni that the OSS intended to provide necessary arms to the Thai underground. When Hoffman informed the Asian detachment commanders of this in mid-September, he cited the necessity "to keep our sphere of influence in Thailand" as the reason for his action.[32]

At the end of the same month, Army Specialist Dwight Bulkley, the son of a prewar missionary to Thailand and an OSS political analyst, had submitted a memorandum entitled "The Importance of Thailand's Political Future." He cited Thailand as a "singular example of an Asiatic nation with stable, capable, and streamlined government" in arguing that its "post-war status will be the example to the rest of Asia, and will determine to a large extent whether we have the hope and confidence of Asiatics in post-war problems, or whether the dominant attitude is of disillusionment and resentment." He also noted Thailand's strategic importance, particularly in terms of air traffic, strongly implying that Bangkok's Don Muang airfield should not fall under British control. Bulkley suggested that the Americans could win Thai cooperation by guaranteeing the nation's political sovereignty, establishing "most favorable" liaison with Thai leaders, and assuring them that the United States was not ignoring the "intrigues" of the British and Chinese. In a similar vein, in an October 9, 1944, letter to Donovan, Bulkley's commanding officer, Colonel Heppner, wrote of America's "great post-war stake" in Southeast Asia and referred to a "tug of war now going on in Thailand and Indo-China with our Allies."[33]

In late December, Don Garden, an OSS staffer in Washington who had worked in Thailand as a journalist some years previously, laid out ambitious goals for the proposed OSS mission to Bangkok. While he said that preparing the Thai Army to fight the Japanese should be the mission's first priority, he added that the OSS also should seek "to win the friendship of the Thai people, as a possible island of American goodwill in a future uncertain Orient" and "attempt to preserve the integrity and sovereignty of Thailand against British encroachments." He suggested that in order to achieve these goals it might be necessary to keep the mission secret, not only from the British but, for the sake of deniability, from American military and civilian authorities as well. After all, he argued, the OSS had been "created to do things the established elements could not do."[34]

Although the OSS did not take up Garden's proposal for an "off the books" adventure, the Thailand desk officer in the State Department, Kenneth Perry Landon, a former missionary, scholar, and ex-OSS employee, and his immediate superior, Abbott Low Moffat, agreed with Garden's estimate of Thailand's postwar importance. A State Department policy paper of January 10, 1945, emphasized that Thailand—"the only market in Southeast Asia not complicated by colonial relationships"—could be an important postwar outlet for American goods and a source for rubber and tin. The document stressed the importance of protecting and capitalizing on America's anti-imperialist image in securing access to the Thai market, warning that the nation would suffer a "severe loss of prestige throughout Asia" if Thailand "should lose prewar Thai territory or have its sovereignty impaired by the victors."[35]

Accordingly, shortly before the departure of the OSS mission to Bangkok, OSS headquarters advised that the participants might give Pridi "their own well-founded American opinions" that:

American interest in postwar independence of Thailand is realistic since as a non-colonial power our best interest is served by keeping the people of the world free and it would be contrary to policy and damaging to our friendships and prestige if we allowed Thailand as a result of this war for freedom to have its freedom impaired.[36]

The OSS party, which included Wester and Richard Greenlee, in the prewar days a member of Donovan's New York law firm, set out—ironically via two Royal Air Force (RAF) seaplanes—on January 25, 1945. A Thai Customs Department launch picked them up and ferried them from the landing point in the Gulf of Thailand to the capital, where they were sheltered at the residence of one of Pridi's men.

Pridi, now keenly aware of the problematic British attitude and deeply concerned about how Thailand might escape the onus of the alliance with Japan, unveiled a war plan. It called for a Thai uprising against the Japanese coordinated with an invasion from the Gulf of Thailand by two American divisions. He also emphasized his continuing differences with Adun, convincing his visitors that he should be dealt with as the sole leader of the resistance.[37]

Leaving Wester behind, Greenlee slipped out for a seaplane pickup in the gulf on February 4 and flew back to brief his superiors. Pridi's war plan did not impress Lt. Gen. D. L. Sultan, now commander of American forces in the India-Burma theater, but the new head of Detachment 404,

Col. John Coughlin, a career Army officer educated at West Point and a veteran of OSS-China, decided to send Greenlee to Washington, where it was hoped his enthusiasm for the Thai operation would have a positive impact.[38]

General Donovan submitted the Thai war plan to the Joint Chiefs of Staff, although it was clear from the beginning that it was a nonstarter. As an alternative, he suggested that the OSS supply and train the Thai underground—as Hoffman had already promised to do—a proposal that garnered strong and invaluable endorsement from the State Department. A supporting memorandum from State praised the Free Thai, criticized British policy, and advocated the continuation and expansion of OSS activities as the best means to encourage Thai opposition to the Japanese and "give substantial support to the political objectives of this Government with respect to Thailand."[39]

Colonel Coughlin encountered firm resistance, however, when he sought General Sultan's support for the project. On April 20, 1945, Donovan aide Charles Cheston advised Coughlin that the Pentagon had lost interest in SEAC military operations and Sultan was under pressure "to confine his theater to a zone of communications." Cheston suggested emphasizing the potential for penetrating Japan through Thai channels in an effort to convince the military authorities that the Thailand operation deserved support.[40]

Meanwhile, Detachment 404 intelligence officer, Lt. Cmdr. Edmond Taylor, suggested that the OSS might scale back its ambitions in Thailand and attempt to accomplish American political goals by maintaining agents there to keep an eye on the British and gather evidence of the Free Thai contribution to the Allied cause. He expressed hope that, even in the absence of military backing, such political support might induce the Thai to continue to feed intelligence to the OSS. His new colleague, Lt. Col. Waller (Wally) Booth, a recent transfer from Europe, favored a more aggressive approach, however. Booth called for new efforts to convince American commanders of Thailand's strategic importance and of the necessity to support intelligence activities with special operations.[41]

Ultimately General Donovan did gain Joint Chiefs of Staff support for arming the Thai underground. He advised Coughlin in mid-May that the Operations and Plans Division had recognized the validity of Booth's argument, and subsequent "for American eyes only" orders from Sultan's headquarters authorized a supply and training program for the Thai underground at a level commensurate with available resources. As such operations were "designed to enhance United States influence in Thailand and to strengthen American efforts to establish Thai independence," the document stressed the need to maintain their "distinct American character."[42]

Meanwhile, Greenlee, accompanied by Capt. Howard Palmer, who had spent his childhood in Thailand as the son of a missionary educator, had returned to Bangkok by seaplane on the night of March 31. The two scored a major success by extracting a promise from Adun that he would cooperate fully with Pridi, but soon after their arrival, Wester's nerves gave way, and his uncontrolled behavior greatly imperiled the group's security. After many anxious days awaiting the dispatch of an RAF seaplane, Palmer managed to escort a heavily drugged Wester and a Flying Tiger pilot, Lt. W. D. McGarry, who had been a POW for over 3 years, out of the country on April 21. Palmer returned to rejoin Greenlee on May 23 and stayed on alone when Greenlee departed on June 30.[43]

In mid-May, just before Palmer's return, Pridi suddenly radioed his desire to stage an early Free Thai uprising against the Japanese. Ostensibly this came in response to a "crisis" created by new Japanese demands for loans to cover their military expenditures in Thailand, but in fact it resulted from Pridi's anxiety over the failure of his efforts to establish a government-in-exile or to gain some sort of recognition from the new United Nations organization. The timing of the proposal was no doubt influenced by an expanding Japanese military presence and an April warning from Coughlin stating that time was growing short and it might be best for the Thai to seize the initiative before it was too late. As they believed an uprising would be crushed and were in no position to render much assistance, the Allies, very much to their credit, instructed Pridi to wait. This was a most fortunate outcome from the Thai perspective, as it permitted them to take credit for the initiative but spared them its bloody consequences.[44]

By this time the OSS had taken steps to establish a nationwide intelligence network in Thailand. Radio-equipped Free Thai agents were sent out from Bangkok, and on May 12 Holladay and a Free Thai companion parachuted into northeastern Thailand to set up an intelligence base near Sakon Nakhon.[45] Three Americans were dropped for intelligence and guerrilla training purposes near Petchaburi, southwest of Bangkok, on the night of May 26,[46] but a Japanese fighter shot down a British Liberator carrying a subsequent mission over central Thailand 2 days later. An OSS enlisted man, Edward Napieralski, and four British crew members died, but nine survived the crash and were rescued by Thai police. Five of them, accompanied by a shot-down American flier and an escaped Australian POW, were picked up by a C-47 cargo plane at the remote Royal Thai Air Force field at Phukhieo in northern Thailand on June 14; the others were placed in the Bangkok internment camp for safekeeping.[47]

By June 1945, with Joint Chiefs of Staff endorsement of its program, the OSS had begun receiving much greater support from the American military, including the services of a dozen C-47s. Late in the month it mounted its first significant supply drops (a total of nearly 75 tons) for the underground, and an American guerrilla trainer and a Thai radioman were successfully parachuted near Kanchanaburi, west of Bangkok near the Burmese border, on the night of June 25.[48]

It must be emphasized that the OSS did not view the guerrilla training program as an end in itself but as a means to other ends. The training teams were briefed to consider good will their first priority, followed by intelligence, "with preparations for future operations the number three priority."[49] The OSS plan envisioned that 214 Americans and 56 Free Thai would train 12 guerrilla battalions of 500 men each. Although the OSS believed that Force 136 had more ambitious goals, it considered this an adequate effort. A memorandum to the Operations and Plans Division of the Joint Chiefs explained that:

> we wish to avoid giving the Thais, who have enormous respect and good will towards America, the impression that we are a mere tail to the British kite. We feel that even a limited program, if it is well and expeditiously carried out, with no political strings attached, we will be able to retain and increase the good will of Thailand toward America in this politically critical area.[50]

Although it appears that Force 136's program was, in fact, comparable to that of the OSS, both agencies had stepped up their activities to the point at which they could not escape the notice of the Japanese, creating a dilemma for General Nakamura. His unit had been upgraded to a field force (39th Army), he had begun preparations to defend against an anticipated Allied attack, and he felt confident that his troops could crush any anti-Japanese uprising. However, a clash with the Thai would disrupt the flow of vital supplies, tie down many soldiers, and knock the props from under a Japanese propaganda strategy, which since 1943 had increasingly stressed Asian liberation.[51]

The desire to maintain good relations with the Thai as long as possible had deterred the Japanese from fully investigating suspicious OSS and Force 136 radio emissions from the vicinity or premises of Thai government buildings in Bangkok; but the supply drops, including a showy, mid-day, Office of War Information (OWI)-engineered release of medical supplies over the center of Bangkok on June 18,[52] could not be ignored. The Japanese lodged formal complaints, and Pridi, who feared a military takeover patterned on Japan's early March 1945 move against the French in Indochina, requested a temporary halt to the supply drops on June 30. Also, as a security measure, the Bangkok headquarters of the OSS shifted from the former residence of a deceased regent to its third location, Suan Kulap (Rose Garden) Palace, once Phibun's official residence.[53]

The dropping of guerrilla trainers and supplies resumed during the full moon in late July. Two Americans and a Thai parachuted into the Klong Pai area on July 21; two parties, totaling seven Americans and two

Thai, were dropped near Rayong on July 24 and 26; three Americans and a Thai parachuted near Phrae on July 27; three Americans were dropped to reinforce the Kanchanaburi camp on July 27; and American C-47s delivered nearly 100 tons of supplies.[54]

In the meantime, the Japanese had complained to the Thai about newly constructed airfields they had spotted near a Force 136 guerrilla training center in the vicinity of Sakon Nakhon. On one hand they demanded a joint inspection of that area and others, including Phukhieo; on the other they laid plans for a pincer assault on the Sakon Nakhon fields by troops from Bangkok and French Indochina. Forewarned, the OSS and Force 136 men in the affected areas withdrew before the inspection, which took place from July 24 to 27. Pridi feared that the airfields would be used as a pretext for a Japanese takeover, but by revealing their concerns the Japanese were actually attempting to avert a major confrontation. They had not yet launched the planned attack on the airfields when the war came to its abrupt end in mid-August 1945.[55]

As the war contributions of the OSS figured to weigh heavily in the decision on whether the organization would survive as a peacetime intelligence agency, its officers had become increasingly anxious to score a major success in Thailand in the final months of the war. Taylor lamented in a memorandum of June 7 that despite a "remarkable achievement" in establishing an intelligence network in Thailand, "there has not yet been one single report of outstanding value." As the American military no longer had much interest in local intelligence from Thailand, he suggested aiming for some "closely guarded secret of the Japanese army which would be put to immediate use in other theaters." This, he argued, should be top priority, ahead of "political and economic intelligence of interest to State," with lowest priority going to "tactical reports of value to British air, ground and sea operations." Similarly, in a mid-July memo to General Donovan, Lt. Col. A. D. Hutcheson complained that a great chance was being lost since "in no place do we have the unique contact with the enemy which we have in Thailand."[56]

In an effort to improve the productivity of the Bangkok station, a Detachment 404 intelligence specialist, Lloyd George, flew into Thailand in mid-July in the company of Smith, who had just returned from a political briefing in Washington, and Maj. Alexander Griswold. Griswold remained at the port of entry, the Phukhieo airfield, while the Royal Thai Air Force delivered George and Smith to Bangkok, where they joined Palmer at Suan Kulap Palace.[57]

Although the abrupt end to the war left the OSS without its much-desired intelligence coup, the agency still wanted maximum publicity for its activities in Thailand. High hopes were pinned on Smith, a writer of adventure travelogues before the war, who was promoted and dispatched home on August 19.[58] Ten days later Smith's opinion that the Thai had pulled the "biggest double cross in history" on the Japanese appeared in a front page story in the *New York Times*. The same paper featured a lengthy article on the OSS Thailand operation on September 9. Within a matter of months, Smith and collaborator Blake Clark, an OSS staffer in Washington, had produced a book on the Thailand operation, *Into Siam, Underground Kingdom*, aimed at the popular market. Also, the well-known journalist Edgar Snow wrote of the venture in the *Saturday Evening Post*, and Stewart Alsop and Thomas Braden, devoted a chapter of their book, *Sub Rosa—The OSS and American Espionage*, to it.[59]

Although these publicity efforts were part of a broader campaign to win public support for the preservation of the OSS,[60] there were other considerations, too. As the officers of Detachment 404 and their State Department allies were still convinced that the British intended to punish and subjugate Thailand, they wished to publicize the efforts of the Free Thai underground as a means of strengthening Thailand's negotiating position. This, they believed, would further enhance the image of the United States in Bangkok.[61]

These suspicions and desires ultimately led Colonel Coughlin to violate instructions by intervening directly in early September negotiations between Lord Mountbatten's headquarters and a group of Thai representatives. Convinced that the British were attempting an end run to impose unacceptable postwar controls on Thailand's economy, the Detachment 404 commander first urged the Thai to delay signing a proposed agreement, then dispatched urgent telegrams to Washington asking for high-level American intervention.[62]

Washington did intervene, and Anglo-American bickering over a British-Thai peace settlement continued for several months. The Americans actually took a more adamant line against the softened, but still demanding, British terms than did most Thai leaders,[63] an oddity that shows the remarkable extent to which the officers of Detachment 404 and the State Department's Division of Southeast Asian Affairs had come to see themselves as guardians of that country's interests. Their zeal was doubtless intensified by the fact that it was only in regard to independent Thailand that these anticolonialists were able to exert real influence on the Truman administration's Southeast Asian policy. Despite the correctness of their view that the old order could not be restored in the region, they had been left behind the curve in a convergence of American and British policies. The new prevailing wisdom in Washington was reflected in an OSS appraisal sent to the President at the beginning of May 1945 that emphasized the threat of Soviet expansionism in China and warned that the United States:

> should avoid any policy that might weaken the position of Britain, France or the Netherlands in Southern Asia or the Western Pacific. It

is altogether likely that these powers will themselves reform their colonial systems; and it would be entirely in our interest to have them
strengthen and stabilize their empires through such reforms. . . .
None of the European powers has a strong position in the Far East.
The least we can do is to avoid any action that may weaken it further;
our interest in developing a balance to Russia should lead us in the
opposite direction.[64]

Although overly optimistic about the viability of reformed colonial empires, this report was certainly on target in recognizing the weakness of
the European position. Consequently, while the American "pro-Thai"
stance did score political points in Bangkok, the struggle to modify the
British demands had much less significance than the anticolonialists imag-
ined. It is clear in retrospect that any lingering British hopes of dominating
Thailand were unrealistic and doomed to failure.[65]

In the wake of the Japanese surrender, in addition to the priority business
of rescuing 296 American POWs from Thailand[66] and keeping an eye on
the British, the OSS took up the task of gathering political intelligence. It
now seemed expedient to assess the situation in Thailand from a broader
perspective, one which took into account views other than those of Pridi's
faction. The OSS men, who were taken aback by the absence of Thai
hostility toward the defeated Japanese and a general Thai lack of interest
in prosecuting domestic war criminals, did seek out and report a variety
of views, even to the point of interviewing Phibun. However, despite picking up old allegations of past communist connections and less-than-dem-
ocratic tendencies on the part of his followers, they continued to view Pridi
as the man best qualified to lead postwar Thailand.[67]

The OSS contingent at Suan Kulap Palace ballooned to nearly 30 officers
and men in early September, and as victors they were treated to lavish
Thai hospitality. Although their numbers rapidly dwindled with the formal
demise of the OSS in the fall of 1945, the station remained operative into
1946 as an adjunct to the American legation. Bulkley, the OSS political
analyst, assumed a similar role under State Department auspices, Maj.
James (Jim) Thompson became a military adviser, and the legation employed radiomen from the OSS group.[68]

This was only the beginning of the involvement of former OSS officers
in Thai-American affairs after the war. Thompson and the officer responsible for closing out the former OSS station, Lt. Comdr. Alexander
MacDonald, returned to Bangkok as private businessmen after leaving
military service. They were joined by Wester and Lt. Col. Willis Bird, a
veteran of OSS-China. Colonel Hoffman, who had played a key role in
Washington, became the honorary Thai Consul General in New York
(1945–50); General Donovan himself registered as an agent for the Thai

goverment; and Palmer, who joined Donovan's law firm, would handle matters related to Thailand.[69]

In evaluating the achievements of the OSS operation in Thailand, it must be noted that some of these have been exaggerated, particularly the number of Allied pilots rescued. The OSS internal history claimed that "numerous downed American aviators had been saved from Japanese hands," while some subsequent accounts have upped the tally into the hundreds.[70] In fact, while the OSS did facilitate the evacuation of several hundred American POWs (only some of whom were airmen) from Thailand before the formal Japanese surrender on September 2, 1945, the number of Allied personnel exfiltrated before V-J Day amounted to two American fliers who had been interned in Bangkok, two Britons and three Americans from the May 29, 1945, OSS flight that was shot down by a Japanese fighter, and one escaped Australian POW. Eight escaped POWs, including two sailors from the U.S.S. *Houston*, were sheltered at the OSS guerrilla training camp near Petchaburi prior to the end of the war.[71]

Also, the Smith and Clark book, through the omission of certain details and a less-than-clear chronology, gives the impression that the OSS guerrilla training effort had advanced further than was the case,[72] and while Alsop and Braden claimed that by July 1945 there were "dozens" of Americans operating in Thailand,[73] no more than 23 were on the ground at any one time during that month. In fact, the guerrilla training program, which in any event was limited in scope and designed primarily to promote good will and to encourage Thai intelligence cooperation, was just gearing up when the war ended.

As suggested earlier, the OSS records make clear that the military intelligence gathered in Thailand had relatively little value to the United States. While in part this was because the Americans had no plans for significant involvement in Southeast Asian military operations, much of what was obtained was duplicated or surpassed by data derived from MAGIC intercepts of Japanese communications, materials that were not available to the OSS. Although as late as 1943 the OSS had considered Thailand an intelligence black hole, those with access to MAGIC had ample information on conditions there from Japanese diplomatic traffic. Later, they also had translations of Japanese Army signals.[74]

Accordingly, there is little question that the OSS Thailand operation made its real mark in the political realm. Three months after the end of the war, a visiting State Department official reported that all Americans were being "treated royally" in Bangkok because of resentment toward the British,[75] and Brig. Gen. Thomas Timberman, Mountbatten's American deputy, noted after being wined and dined in the Thai capital in January 1946 that the Thai had not forgotten American intervention on their behalf and "certainly show gratitude."[76] The favor subsequently shown to various former OSS officers by members of the Thai elite further testifies to the success of the operation in generating good will. The high-level welcome, including a royal audience, given to participants in an OSS veterans reunion in Bangkok in late 1987 suggests that the agency's "pro-Thai" stance is still remembered.

Moreover, the OSS goal of increased American influence in Thailand was achieved, although the U.S. government did not fully focus its attention on Southeast Asia until it discerned a Chinese Communist threat to the region's security in the late 1940s. Again, parallels with the Japanese precedent are striking. In the immediate postwar years the Americans, like the Japanese in the early 1930s, made modest gains in pursuit of largely economic goals. In the 1950s and 1960s, however, the relationship intensified as Thailand assumed a role similar to that it had played in Japanese strategy in World War II—as a support base for war operations, this time by the Americans in Indochina.

Ironically, the direct personal influence of the OSS veterans who had involved themselves in American-Thai relations had been greatly reduced before the bilateral partnership reached full flower. Pridi and his allies, the Thai with whom the OSS men had close personal links, were ousted from power by a military coup in November 1947, and it was Phibun, a man they had despised as a Japanese collaborator, whom the Americans embraced at the height of the cold war. Nonetheless, the OSS operation had focused unprecedented American attention on Thailand and had made the Thai aware of the advantages of American patronage. Consequently, as suggested by the Eisenhower administration's highly symbolic dispatch of General Donovan to Bangkok as Ambassador in 1953, it is accurate to say that the OSS Thailand operation did indeed serve as the opening wedge in the development of the cold war alliance between the two nations.

NOTES

1. Thai names are rendered according to the romanization system of the Royal Thai Institute. If a divergent form of romanization of the person's name is commonly used, it appears in parentheses on the first reference. Thai individuals are subsequently referred to by given name, not surname, according to the Thai practice.

2. See, for example, Remer to Donovan, Dec. 31, 1941, roll 60, Donovan Microfilms, U.S. Army Military History Institute, Carlisle Barracks, PA (hereinafter cited as USAMHI).

3. See two Berle to Hull memorandums dated Jan. 28, 1942, Adolf A. Berle Papers, Box 58, Franklin D. Roosevelt Library, Hyde Park, NY.

4. See documents concerning the decision of the Joint Psychological Warfare Committee on the Free Thai proposal on roll 34, Donovan Microfilms, USAMHI. A contemporary account of the origins of the American Free Thai movement by a participant is Nai Samret, "That Thailand May be Free," *Asia and the Americas* 45: 94–95.

5. Nicol Smith and Blake Clark, *Into Siam, Underground Kingdom* (Indianapolis, IN, 1946), pp. 13–68.

6. Phibun's efforts to contact the Chinese are described in a memorial volume for one of the officers involved. This has been translated and issued on microfilm by the Library of Congress under the title "The Biography of General Luang Haansonkram." The standard Thai language source on Pridi's activities is *X-O Group* by Nai Chantana, originally published in 1946 and reissued in Bangkok in 1964. A number of OSS documents on the arrival of Pridi's men in China are found in Box 52, Entry 99, Records of the Office of Strategic Services, Record Group 226, National Archives and Records Administration, Washington, DC (hereinafter cited as RG 226, NA).

7. Donovan's confrontation with Tai Li has been described in numerous works, including Edmond Taylor's *Awakening from History* (Boston, 1969), pp. 346–347. On the impact of this clash and others on Chinese-American cooperation, see Miles to Chief of Information Branch Central Planning Staff, May 17, 1946, Box 3, Milton E. Miles Papers, Hoover Institution, Stanford, CA.

8. Smith and Clark, *Into Siam, Underground Kingdom*, pp. 69–169. A Thai account of the death of the two OSS agents is Thammanun Ruangsin, *Khamphiphaksakhadi Seri Thai chak Amerika* [The Judgment Concerning the Free Thai from America] (Bangkok, 1979).

9. On these British Force 136 operations, see Charles Cruikshank, *SOE in the Far East* (Oxford, 1983), pp. 105–107; Andrew Gilchrist, *Bangkok Top Secret* (London, 1970), pp. 45–49; and Puey Ungphakorn's account of his mission in Direk Jayanama, *Siam and World War II*, trans. Jane G. Keyes (Bangkok, 1978), pp. 138–139.

10. See the author's "General Nakamura Aketo—Khaki-clad Diplomat in Wartime Thailand," in Chaiwat Khamchoo and E. Bruce Reynolds, eds., *Thai-Japanese Relations in Historical Perspective* (Bangkok, 1988), pp. 161–202. It appears that the Japanese were unaware of the arrival of the OSS agents.

11. Gilchrist, *Bangkok Top Secret*, pp. 55–61; and Cruikshank, *SOE in the Far East*, pp. 107–108.

12. Gilchrist, *Bangkok Top Secret*, pp. 61–82, 213–221; Cruikshank, *SOE in the Far East*, p. 107; and Judith A. Stowe, *Siam becomes Thailand* (Honolulu, 1991), p. 298.

13. Smith and Clark, *Into Siam, Underground Kingdom*, p. 178.

14. According to the "OSS/SEAC Monthly Report for October 1944," File 306, Box 48, Entry 99, RG 226, NA, it "failed due to the somewhat arbitrary cancelling of the submarine's operation orders and the general faulty mechanical behavior of the submarine itself."

15. On this point, see Richard Aldrich's excellent article, "Imperial Rivalry: British and American Intelligence in Asia, 1942–46," *Intelligence and National Security* 3: 21–28; and Taylor, *Awakening from History*, p. 352.

16. Bureaucratic rivals were quick to criticize OSS-British connections. For example, Col. Richard Park, Jr., of military intelligence wrote in a 1945 memorandum attacking the OSS that "the British are believed to know everything about OSS and exercise quite a good deal of control over the OSS." A copy of the report is found in Box 15, President's Secretary's File, Harry S. Truman Library, Independence, MO.

17. "Anglo-American Cooperation in East Asia," Nov. 15, 1943, File 355, Box 573, Entry 190, RG 226, NA.

18. "OSS/SEAC Monthly Report" for June and September 1944, Files 302 and 305, Box 47, and the report for October in File 306, Box 48, Entry 99, RG 226, NA.

19. State Memorandum of the Jan. 26, 1944, meeting, roll 131, Donovan Microfilms, USAMHI.

20. U.S. Department of State, *The Foreign Relations of the United States* (*FRUS*), *1944*, vol. 5, *The Near East, South Asia, The Far East* (Washington, DC, 1965), pp. 1312–1319. The British unwillingness to make a clear commitment on Thai sovereignty was a result of Prime Minister Winston Churchill's desire that the Kra Isthmus be ceded to British Malaya for security reasons and a general desire on the part of many British officials to punish the Thai for their collaboration with the Japanese. British statements regarding Thailand are reported in Davies' "Policy Conflicts and the United Nations," File 184, Box 15, Joseph W. Stilwell Papers, Hoover Institution.

21. *FRUS: The Conference at Quebec, 1944* (Washington, DC, 1972), pp. 261–265.

22. These issues are discussed in great depth in Christopher Thorne's masterful *Allies of a Kind* (New York, 1978), especially pp. 209–224, 339–351, 455–469. See also Aldrich, "Imperial Rivalry," pp. 6–8.

23. Thorne, *Allies of a Kind*, pp. 332–339, 450–455, and Edmond Taylor, *Richer By Asia* (Boston, 1964), pp. 27–41.

24. Interview of Heppner by Robert Warner, File 518, Box 52, Entry 110; Scofield to Operations Committee, Sept. 14, 1944, File 708, Box 45, Entry 148, RG 226, NA; and Taylor, *Awakening from History*, pp. 352–353.

25. "Story of BUTTON," File 2558, Box 149, and "Greenlee's Diary," File 2069, Box 114, Entry 154; Weaver to Scofield, Sept. 18, 1944, and "Report on Operation Hotfoot I," File 708, Box 45, Entry 148; "Report of Interview With Ken," File 520, Box 52, Entry 110, RG 226, NA; and Smith and Clark, *Into Siam, Underground Kingdom*, p. 180. Some Detachment 404 documents date the first contact on October 9 because the first message from one of its agents was transmitted on that day.

26. Ripley to Donovan, Nov. 17, 1944, File 2327, Box 133, Entry 154; and "Monthly Report of SI Branch," Nov. 30, 1944, File 307, Box 47, Entry 99, RG 226, NA.

27. "Materials for ARISTOC," Sept. 7, 1944, File 705, Box 45, Entry 148; message of Oct. 30, 1944, File 2599, Box 153; and Williams to Scofield, Nov. 15, 1944, and "ARISTOC—Report of Escorting Officer," Dec. 4, 1944, File 2484, Box 141, Entry 154, RG 226, NA.

28. Smith to Berno, Dec. 15, 1944, File 2318, Box 133; and "Greenlee's Diary," File 2069, Box 114, Entry 154, RG 226, NA.

29. Holladay to Berno, Dec. 18, 1944, File 2328, Box 133, and Callahan to Burstein, n.d., File 2570, Box 150, Entry 154, RG 226, NA. Holladay also noted that while Force 136 was making good use of its Thailand experts, "not a single person who knows Thailand has even an influential position as a consultant" in Detachment 404.

30. "OSS/SEAC Set-up in Thailand"/"Evaluation of Reports and Intelligence from OSS/China," n.d., File 2289, Box 131, Entry 154, RG 226, NA. This view was

iterated in a memorandum by Ripley and Taylor, "The Thai Group from China," n.d., in File 2094, Box 116, Entry 154, RG 226, NA.

31. Ibid.; Coughlin to Peers, Feb. 10, 1945; Coughlin to Donovan, Feb. 16, 1945; Coughlin to Peers, Feb. 23, 1945; and Coughlin to Wilkinson, Mar. 7, 1945, all in File 228, Box 20, Entry 110, RG 226, NA.

32. Hoffman to Fisher, Aug. 7, 1944, roll 131, and a series of documents on the subject on roll 130, Donovan Microfilms, USAMHI; and Hoffman to Coughlin, Heppner, and Peers, Sept. 14, 1944, File 2318, Box 133, Entry 154, RG 226, NA.

33. "The Importance of Thailand's Political Future," 892.00/9-3044, General Records of the Department of State, RG 59, NA; and Heppner to Donovan, Oct. 9, 1944, roll 130, Donovan Microfilms, USAMHI.

34. "Possibility of Introducing a Military Mission Into Thailand," Dec. 21, 1944, File 2712, Box 160, Entry 154, RG 226, NA. An attached letter from Lilly to Ripley (dated Dec. 30) said of Garden's plan: "This is a brainchild of Don's from which something useful with perhaps local adaptations may be extracted. Do not take it as a directive from us, but a slant which you might develop if it seems expedient."

35. "Postwar Status of Thailand," 892.00/1-1045, RG 59, NA.

36. Lilly to Taylor, Jan. 19, 1945, File 2338, Box 133, Entry 154, RG 226, NA.

37. "Operation SIREN" and "Greenlee's Diary," File 2069, Box 114, Entry 154, RG 226, NA.

38. Coughlin to Peers, Feb. 10, 1945, File 228, Box 20, Entry 110, RG 226, NA.

39. "Aid to the Thai Resistance Against the Japanese," Donovan to JCS, Mar. 26, 1945, File 315, Box 49, Entry 99, RG 226, NA; and "American Policy with Respect to Thailand," Mar. 26, 1945, *FRUS, 1943*, vol. 6, *The American Republics* (Washington, DC, 1965), pp. 1260–1262.

40. Wilkinson to Greenlee, Apr. 17, 1945, File 2070, Box 114; and Coughlin to Thai Committee, Apr. 18, 1945, and Cheston to Coughlin, Apr. 20, 1945, File 2650, Box 156, RG 226, NA.

41. Memos by Taylor and Booth dated Apr. 24 and 25, 1945, File 2092, Box 115, Entry 154, RG 226, NA.

42. Donovan/Thai Committee to Coughlin, May 15, 1945, File 2654, Box 157, and "Instructions for Thailand Operations," May 16, 1945, File 2341, Box 134, Entry 154, RG 226, NA.

43. "Diary Report of SIREN III-D," File 520, Box 52, Entry 110; "Operation SIREN," File 2069, Box 114; and messages from Greenlee to Coughlin of Apr. 12, 14, and 15, File 2070, Box 114, Entry 154, RG 226, NA. The exfiltration of McGarry was a calculated effort to please his former commander, Gen. Claire Chennault, who had rendered important assistance to the OSS in China (Smith and Clark, *Into Siam, Underground Kingdom*, pp. 190–191). McGarry was not "in a crude jungle stockade," as Corey Ford asserts in *Donovan of OSS* (Boston, 1970), p. 264. After his plane was shot down during a raid on Chiang Mai in March 1942, he was brought to Bangkok and imprisoned at CID headquarters. In May 1943 he was transferred to the civilian internment camp, then at the University of Moral and Political Sciences. A record of McGarry's debriefing on Apr. 23, 1945, is found in File 2323, Box 133, Entry 154, RG 226, NA.

44. *FRUS, 1945*, vol. 6, *The British Commonwealth; The Far East* (Washington, DC, 1969), pp. 1268–1271; Coughlin to Wilkinson, Apr. 17, 1945, File 2650, Box 156; Greenlee to Coughlin, May 20, 1945, File 2069, Box 114; and "Capabilities of the Siamese Resistance Movement," May 29, 1945, File 2335, Box 134, Entry 154, RG 226, NA; Cruikshank, *SOE in the Far East*, p. 117; Gilchrist, *Bangkok Top Secret*, pp. 195–197; and Direk, *Siam and World War II*, pp. 104–105.

45. The mission report is in File 2643, Box 156, Entry 154, RG 226, NA.

46. The mission report is in File 2609, Box 155, Entry 154, RG 226, NA.

' 47. "Operation SIREN," File 2069, Box 114; Coughlin to "P" Division, June 19, 1945, File 2600, Box 153; and "Report of DIAGRAM Operation," File 2681, Box 158, Entry 154, RG 226, NA.

48. Coughlin to Doering, July 12, 1945, File 228, Box 20, and "Thailand Operations," File 330, Box 31, Entry 110; and the mission report on the Kanchanaburi operation in File 2545, Box 148, Entry 154, RG 226, NA.

49. Coughlin to Hutcheson, June 29, 1945, File 2297, Box 131, Entry 154, RG 226, NA.

50. "Background of Thailand Operations for OPD," n.d., File 315, Box 49, Entry 99, RG 226, NA.

51. The summary of the Japanese situation is based on various sources, but particularly Nakamura Aketo, *Hotoke no shireikan* [The Buddha's Commander] (Tokyo, 1958), and Zenkoku kenyûkai renaikai [The National Alliance of Kempei Associations], *Nihon Kempei seishi* [The True History of the Japanese Kempei] (Tokyo, 1976). For further details, see the author's "General Nakamura Aketo," pp. 161–202.

52. See memo by Thompson, File 2320, Box 133, Entry 154, RG 226, NA. Pridi had specifically requested the airdrop of medicine on the parade ground. See Coughlin to Ryan, June 1, 1945, roll 130, Donovan Microfilms, USAMHI.

53. Kandy to Washington/New Delhi/Kunming, June 30, 1945, File 315, and "Thailand," Box 314, Box 49, Entry 99, RG 226, NA. The OSS contingent had first been sheltered at the residence of Chuan Bunnak.

54. "Monthly Report, Operations Office," July 31, 1945, File 2593, Box 152, and mission reports in File 2313, Box 133; File 2578, Box 150; and File 2635, Box 155, Entry 154, RG 226, NA.

55. "Probable Japanese Reaction to Internal Development in and Allied Actions Affecting Thailand," July 27, 1945, File 2329, Box 133, Entry 154, RG 226, NA, is a very perceptive analysis of the Japanese situation; Smith and Clark, *Into Siam, Underground Kingdom*, 296-301; Bôeichô bôei kenshûjo senshishitsu [Self-Defense Agency Defense Research Office War History Room], *Shittan-Mingo sakusen* [The Sittang-Mingo Operations] (Tokyo, 1969), pp. 692–693; and MAGIC Far East Summary, Army Supplement, July 24, 1945, Records of the National Security Agency/Central Security Service, RG 457, NA.

56. Taylor Memo, June 7, 1945, and Hutcheson to Donovan, July 17, 1945, File 2324, Box 133, Entry 154, RG 226, NA.

57. Smith and Clark, *Into Siam, Underground Kingdom*, pp. 203–223.

58. Coughlin to Donovan, Aug. 18, 1945, and "Chief of Mission Report," Aug. 1945, File 228, Box 20, Entry 110, RG 226, NA.

59. Snow, "Secrets from Siam," *Saturday Evening Post*, vol. 218 (Jan. 12, 1946), and Stewart J. Alsop and Thomas Braden, *Sub Rosa—The OSS and American Espi-*

onage (New York, 1946). Snow's article is particularly riddled with errors of fact.

60. Bradley F. Smith, *The Shadow Warriors: OSS and the Origins of the CIA* (New York, 1983), pp. 405–407.

61. Coughlin to Donovan, Aug. 18, 1945, File 228, Box 20, Entry 110, RG 226, NA.

62. A series of messages relating to Coughlin's intervention are contained in File 802, Box 66, Entry 136, RG 226, NA. See also Aldrich, "Imperial Rivalry," pp. 40–41, and Judy Stowe, "Relations Between Thailand and Britain, September 1945," in D. K. Bassett and V. K. King, eds., *Britain and South-East Asia* (Hull, U.K., 1986), pp. 48–64.

63. Ripley and Taylor were aware that this odd situation was developing immediately upon arrival in Bangkok. They cabled on August 21, 1945: "Thai dilemma aggravated by their fear of British which seems fully as great as fear of Japs. They seem particularly concerned not to do anything that might annoy or offend Mountbatten and we have impression while they sincerely welcome and appreciate American support our government could easily get into the position of seeming more pro Thai than the Thai themselves as far as relations with the British concerned" (File 2575, Box 150, Entry 154, RG 226, NA). In fact, Pridi and the bulk of the Thai cabinet ministers were inclined to accept the British terms and bargain later, while Seni, whom Pridi—much to his subsequent regret—installed as Prime Minister, doggedly opposed acceptance. The drawn-out haggling not only delayed the restoration of relations and trade with the British but also intensified domestic political differences.

64. "Problems and Objectives of United States Policy," Apr. 1, 1945, Box 15, President's Secretary's File, Truman Library. Edmond Taylor wrote in *Richer By Asia*, p. 40: "The political reaction which began to develop in the United States after Roosevelt's death and the revolution in colonial policy which marked the advent of socialist leadership in Great Britain both reached Southeast Asia with too great a lag to have any discernible effect on Anglo-American relations in that theater up to the time of my return home in January 1946."

65. On Washington's intervention and the subsequent jousting between the British and Americans, see *FRUS, 1945*, 6: 1304–1415.

66. The OSS evaluated even the rescue of POWs in terms of its impact on the Thai. A "Chief of Mission Report" of Aug. 1945 (File 219, Box 20, Entry 110, RG 226, NA) noted that the U.S. support and supply of the underground and "the manner in which we brought out our American POWs out of Bangkok (for instance, landing there with eight planes and bringing almost all of them out on the first day), have impressed the Thai like no amount of publicity could."

67. On the end-of-the-war intelligence agenda, see "Notes on Intelligence Requirement for Thailand," Aug. 8, 1945, File 2660, Box 157, Entry 154, RG 226, NA. Many of the post-surrender OSS intelligence reports are found in the "XL" file in RG 226. Of particular interest are XL 22760, XL 23034, XL 23037, and XL 34351. Also, see: "General Impressions of the Situation in Bangkok," Oct. 9, 1945, File 274, Box 24, Entry 110, RG 226, NA. On the reasons for the lack of hostility toward the Japanese, see the author's "After-

math of Alliance: The Wartime Legacy in Thai-Japanese Relations," *Journal of Southeast Asian Studies* 21: 66–87.

68. Life for the victors in postwar Bangkok is well described by Dillon Ripley in "Incident in Siam," *The Yale Review* 36: 262–276; Jorges Orgibet (then of OWI) in *From Siam to Thailand* (Bangkok, 1982), pp. 13–15; and Alexander Mac-Donald in *Bangkok Editor* (New York, 1949), pp. 1–10. A list of personnel in Bangkok on Sept. 5, 1945, is found in File 2610, Box 153, Entry 154, RG 226, NA. Further information was obtained from an interview of Dilworth Brinton (Bangkok, Oct. 31, 1987) and Arlene B. Neher, "Prelude to Alliance: The Expansion of American Economic Interest in Thailand During the 1940s," Ph.D. diss., Northern Illinois University, 1980, pp. 19, 26–27.

69. William Warren, *The Legendary American* (Boston, 1970); MacDonald, *Bangkok Editor*; R. Harris Smith, *OSS: The Secret History of America's First Secret Intelligence Agency* (Berkeley, 1972), pp. 273, 308, 312–313; and Neher, "Prelude to Alliance," pp. 21–22, 49–51, 54–55.

70. *War Report of the OSS*, vol. 2, *The Overseas Targets*, intro. by Kermit Roosevelt (Washington, DC, 1976), p. 413. The "several hundred fliers" cited in Donald E. Nuechterlein, *Thailand and the Struggle for Southeast Asia* (Ithaca, NY, 1965), p. 80, appears to be drawn from James V. Martin, Jr.'s "Thai-American Relations in World War II," *Journal of Asian Studies* 22: 463, which states: "The Underground smuggled into these [isolated] fields, and onto American transport planes some 400 Allied fliers forced down in Thailand, plus Allied prisoners of war." Martin, in turn, cites an article in the *New York Times*, Jan. 19, 1946, which more accurately stated that one of the underground's achievements was "to help fly out about 400 American prisoners to freedom." This article, however, greatly exaggerated the frequency of secret flights in and out of Thailand, describing them as "almost nightly." John B. Haseman first questioned such claims in *The Thai Resistance Movement During the Second World War* (DeKalb, IL, 1978), p. 138.

71. The best summary documents of the Thailand operations are found in File 2569, Box 150, and File 2600, Box 153, Entry 154, RG 226, NA. On the POWs at Petchaburi, see "PATTERN Operational Report," Sept. 28, 1945, File 2609, Box 155, Entry 154, RG 226, NA.

72. This is notable in Smith's re-creation of conversations with OSS guerrilla trainers during his stay in Bangkok. By not revealing that the majority of them had arrived in Thailand after Smith himself, the reader is left with the impression that their operations had been under way for a much longer period of time than was actually the case. Smith and Clark, *Into Siam, Underground Kingdom*, pp. 271–272.

73. Alsop and Braden, *Sub Rosa*, p. 110.

74. The MAGIC diplomatic intercepts, for example, even included bomb damage assessments reported by the very large and active Japanese Embassy in Bangkok.

75. Brookhart to Moffat, Nov. 7, 1945, Box 51, Records of the Foreign Service Posts of the Department of State, RG 84, NA.

76. Letter from Timberman to his wife, Jan. 20, 1946, Box T-4, Timberman-Fiske Family Papers, USAMHI.

THE LEGACY OF
THE OSS, 1945–91

Overleaf: Gen. William J. Donovan, whom President Roosevelt appointed in 1941 to organize the first U.S. national intelligence agency, directed the OSS from 1942 to 1945. (Record Group 226)

The concluding session of the conference took place on Friday, July 12, in the National Archives Theater. Ambassador William Colby, an OSS veteran and former Director of Central Intelligence, directed his attention to the OSS's impact on modern American intelligence. Weaving together examples and lessons of intelligence operations in World War II—some drawn from his combat experiences—Colby substantiated that the abolition of the OSS in 1945 did not, in fact, end its impact on postwar intelligence institutions. He pointed out the importance Donovan placed upon analysis, especially that oriented around geographic areas, and the need for the objective and independent judgment of that analysis. The second featured speaker, Professor Bradley F. Smith, the author of a perceptive study of OSS, *The Shadow Warriors*, urged attendees to widen their boundaries of research and include many other records and sources in addition to those of the Office of Strategic Services. He also challenged the conventional view of why President Harry Truman abolished the OSS in September 1945. A perceptive and articulate commentary on the theme of the session was provided by Elspeth Davies Rostow. This former OSS veteran and professor at the University of Texas at Austin pointed out that the contemporary perception of the role of the OSS in American history textbooks is not negative or positive—rather it is not even mentioned as a part of this American wartime experience. She urged the audience to correct this defect. Rostow also provided other contributions to this legacy. Ray S. Cline, a leading student of 20th-century intelligence, chaired the session, introduced the speakers, and moderated the discussion that followed.

THE LEGACY OF THE OSS

William E. Colby

This National Archives conference has examined a fascinating piece of American history: how a fine leader and a dedicated group of subordinates hurriedly assembled an organization to conduct some of the most sophisticated and complex of operations, under the complications of secrecy, in a frantic wartime atmosphere. We of the Office of Strategic Services (OSS) appreciate the attention to our efforts of long ago; but we of the more recent intelligence profession appreciate even more this effort to identify our beginnings and the basic themes, developed during World War II, which shape our character today.

Many of us—and many of the later leaders of American intelligence—learned our trade and fashioned our concepts in the OSS. We may have been involved in only one of the many sharply compartmentalized activities of the OSS, but we knew that there was a strategic concept being shaped, and that the whole was very much more than the sum of the individual parts in which we may have been engaged.

We had good teachers, particularly some of our British cousins who patiently exposed us to the craft of intelligence in some of the stately homes they borrowed for the war from some of the great families of England. One such teacher may have overstated the process when he referred to "receiving the fresh-faced young Americans to be indoctrinated into the arcane ways of Europe's long-established intelligence brothel," but there was something to it, for example, as Major Fairbairn of the Shanghai Police Force taught the most effective way of plunging a knife into the side of a German sentry with a hand over his mouth to prevent alarm to his fellows. (No, I never saw one used except to open ration cans!)

We had good partners in the great crusade against Nazi and Japanese aggression: French, Belgian, Dutch, Norwegian, Danish, and yes German, Austrian, Italian, Greek, Czech, Polish, Burmese, Thai, and Chinese patriots, whose dedication to their countries' freedom inspired the Americans helping them and gave personal meaning to the commitment until death or victory that our association entailed. The cause of struggle against totalitarianism not only characterized the wartime period, it was to continue to be the guiding spirit as a new totalitarianism threatened freedom during the ensuing years of the cold war.

Perhaps the most significant lesson American intelligence learned from the OSS came from the character of its leader, Gen. William J. Donovan. His physical courage displayed in France during World War I won him the Medal of Honor and the Distinguished Service Cross, the two highest American decorations for gallantry, and gave him full credibility when he sent OSS men and women into perilous circumstances behind enemy lines. He insisted on renewing this credibility by attending the Normandy landings and flying high into Burma in a small plane to visit his troops. His example stayed with American intelligence over the years and inspired new generations to assume the risks and agonies that inevitably characterize intelligence operations.

Donovan was also what the modern world would term an intellectual. He was a spectacularly successful lawyer, founder of a fine New York law firm (with which I am proud still to be associated), and an indefatigable student of international affairs through his rapid reading, extensive travels, and interviews of the great and not-great of many continents. He saw that the most vital aspect of modern intelligence is not mere information but the analysis of its meaning.

When President Roosevelt asked him to form the wartime OSS, Donovan put these qualifications into practice. He developed the concept of central intelligence, of a center at which all information could be collected and analyzed. Donovan did send operators to parachute into hostile territory on missions of information collection or sabotage, but he backed them up with a corps of the best brains he could assemble here in Washington. These analysts reviewed what the operators reported and used all the information available from libraries, multinational industries, and open sources to reach conclusions regarding the problems and opportunities that faced the nation. Ray Cline was one of these pioneers, of course, and he went on to a distinguished career in intelligence analysis.

Perhaps the culmination of our nation's recognition of the primacy of analysis in the intelligence process is the present nomination of Robert Gates to become Director of Central Intelligence, the first analyst to supplant the operators like Dulles, Helms, Casey, and myself who dominated the agency for so many years. Curiously, part of the blame for this slow recognition of the importance of analysis belongs to those who failed to follow Donovan's organization of the analysts by their geographic specializations, a situation finally remedied by Bill Casey in the early 1980s. The reason for this error over so many years was an undue identification of intelligence analysis with the academic process. Central Intelligence Agency

(CIA) analysts followed the academic model of organizing themselves by their disciplines—politics, economics, military, science, etc.—as universities are organized. Donovan's practical approach recognized that while universities teach such disciplines, the function of intelligence is to warn. However much intelligence shares the academic dedication to objectivity, its subjects arise in the real world of geographic nations and regions.

There is an inherent contradiction in the analytical process, of course, since if the analysts accurately predict a certain prospect harmful to our nation, the policymakers hopefully will move to bring about a better result, in which case the prediction will be proved to be wrong, but wrong for the right reason. This is one of the frustrations of building up a record of success for intelligence, but Donovan clearly viewed analysis as the real contribution intelligence might make to a better world.

Donovan's OSS had another institutional heir in the modern military Special Operations Command and its component forces, as William Henoeffer, former Curator of the CIA Historical Intelligence Collection, has pointed out in his pamphlet "If Donovan Were Here Today," published by the CIA. Donovan's concept was to keep intelligence operations and unconventional warfare in the same organization (along with "morale operations" against the enemy) so they could provide each other the best possible mutual support. With the greater scale of unconventional warfare today, this function has been passed to the American military. After many years of treating the special forces as poor relatives, the military has finally given their function the priority their potential contribution justifies, as we saw in the recent Persian Gulf war. The CIA retains a paramilitary function and a close liaison with the special forces in order to contribute its political sensitivity and flexibility on occasion. When this relationship works well, as it did in the later stages of our effort in Vietnam, both sides benefit. When it does not, as in some of the earlier years of that conflict, the result is worse for all.

The OSS was wisely limited to the "strategic services" of its title and made no pretension of supplanting the military's tactical intelligence functions. This example still prevails, and while a tactical commander such as General Schwarzkopf will still complain about the shortfall of intelligence (what commander won't?) or the differences and caveats conscientious analysts will insist on in the face of uncertainty, the improvements in both strategic and tactical intelligence have reduced the proverbial "fog of war" that earlier commanders faced. Can they both be improved? Yes. Will they be? Certainly. But the separation of the functions is a real one, to be recognized as such while strengthening the links of communication and responsiveness between them. What we do not need is to merge them in one direction or the other, as Donovan wisely saw (and realized was practically impossible in the interbureaucratic jungle of Washington).

One of my early lessons was the need to integrate expert knowledge with courageous enterprise. My mission was to attack the Norwegian rail line carrying German forces from Finnmark in North Norway to join the forces fighting the Allied armies in Germany. Tunnels seemed an appropriate target, and we developed a complex tactic of explosive charges in the tunnels to cause them to collapse. Only years later did I realize that we had used a technique meant for constructing tunnels in rocky mountain areas and that the charges we planned to detonate on their ceilings would only have added a few inches of rubble to the trash along the tracks. The trains would have continued comfortably through them. Consultation with a few tunnel engineers would have saved my brave troops much unneeded effort, and produced a better result, if the secrecy of our operation could have been expanded to include such analytical resources. (We finally did not use the tactic because the German defenses were too imposing, but we did expend a large amount of effort preparing to do so.) We learned the same lesson later at the Bay of Pigs, when our stress on secrecy for the venture excluded the analysts who did not "need to know." The *operators* needed the analysts in order to make better evaluations of the prospects of success or failure.

The CIA has remedied one of the OSS's (and Donovan's) failures by providing for close consultation with Congress. Donovan saw his agency (correctly at the time) as reporting only to the Joint Chiefs of Staff and his friend President Roosevelt. He apparently put little time into cultivating a relationship with an obscure Senator from Missouri, Harry Truman, even after Truman became Vice President. Truman made quite apparent his distaste for Donovan when the war ended (and a flood of heroic tales from the OSS appeared in the press). He disbanded the organization. Truman soon found that he needed a central intelligence function and gradually rebuilt what he had dissolved. He even oversaw its resumption of covert action to meet the challenges of the cold war (despite a bit of revisionism in his later memoirs on the subject).

The new CIA, under Dulles, McCone, and Helms, noted the lesson and quietly kept in touch with the power centers of Congress to inform them of the agency's activities and to generate their support. They benefited from the same sense of patriotism in the face of the cold war that had served Donovan during his "hot" one. When this atmosphere of acceptance dissolved as the cold war began to ebb and Congress began to assert its constitutional privileges much more forcefully, later directors had to develop a much more intense and complex set of relationships with Congress, sometimes at considerable cost in terms of sensationalism and confrontation. Today, this process seems to have calmed to a regular procedure that may not always produce unanimity but at least does achieve courtesy, frankness, and confidence. Donovan might be startled to see how the process works today, but he would certainly appreciate its necessity.

One final lesson from the OSS faces us today. With the end of the cold war, and the resulting sea change in the strategic situation the nation faces, some say we should dissolve the CIA and fold even its remaining functions back into other departments. That is what the nation did at the end of World War I ("Gentlemen do not read each other's mail") and what Truman did after World War II. In each case, we found later that we needed a professional intelligence service, as Donovan pleaded for even before the end of World War II. This lesson does not need to be repeated.

The United States still needs professional intelligence operators and analysts to face the remaining "enemies": terrorists, the haters of the "Great Satan" and its citizens and institutions, the drug lords, ethnic and religious extremists, and the would-be developers of secret mass destruction weapons. Intelligence will still be necessary to help achieve and to monitor further reductions in the weaponry that is all too extant in the world and to protect our nation's technology and economic efforts from those who would secretly damage them. The fine corps of experts assembled over the years since the OSS must continue to serve our nation with the skills the OSS may have initiated but which have developed to levels we in those early years could hardly have envisioned.

THE OSS AND RECORD GROUP 226: Some Perspectives and Prospects

Bradley F. Smith

The sessions of this conference have presented a multitude of interesting papers and discussions on the Office of the Coordinator of Information and the Office of Strategic Services (COI/OSS), featuring both scholarly inquiries and vivid memories of William Donovan's organization. In this final session as well, there is a mix of scholarship and memory because my two colleagues bring to us a happy blend of OSS experience and distinguished careers in research, reflection, and writing about modern history and politics.

I am primarily an archival researcher, on the other hand, and although I have written about the OSS, I believe that I can contribute most to this concluding session by focusing on the importance, the implications, and some of the limitations of the new National Archives collection of OSS records. The size of the Records of the Office of Strategic Services (RG 226) and their range, depth, and completeness obviously mark them out as an important addition to the holdings of the National Archives. The devotion and hard work of many archivists and Central Intelligence Agency (CIA) officials, with John Taylor and Larry McDonald in the forefront, have left scholars and the public permanently in their debt. The imaginative use of volunteers to make possible the processing of this collection must be one of the most courageous and farsighted initiatives in the history of record depositories, if not of modern governments, and we are all grateful to them. The relatively small number of withholding slips that one encounters in the boxes of this collection—a veteran of years of warfare in British records is speaking now—indicates that the custodial agency tried to be generous, and scholars should extend thanks to the CIA for its part in making this success possible.

Each of us, pursuing a special interest, or astride a particular hobby-horse, will be delighted with what we receive from RG 226, or perhaps grumble about this or that deficiency. But the most basic fact is that this is a revolutionary archival accession. For the first time in the life of the planet, a nearly complete body of records produced by an intelligence organization of a great power—or of any country for that matter—has been placed in the public and scholarly domain. This is a totally unprecedented event—one which leaves those of us who wrote about the OSS in the pre-McDonald-Taylor days rather like fish beached by a surprisingly high tide—for it opens the way to a wide range of in-depth research projects, such as those which have been chronicled or charted during this conference.

The significance and the implications of RG 226, however, stretch far beyond the specific embryonic research projects that it makes possible. Never before have scholars been able to see, study, and ponder the raw record of what an intelligence/covert operations organization did and how it did it. Until now, all of us writing on such questions have had to play by different rules than those individuals studying other organizations and governmental activities. Scholars pursuing serious intelligence history have been compelled to content themselves with memoirs, memories, documentary traces in the records of other agencies and countries, and the trickle of original intelligence papers found in the files or wrestled free by the Freedom of Information Act. All of our work has been lamed by second handedness and the impossibility of ever judging particular features or facts against an overall pattern of the activities of the organization we were trying to study. Without having the broad range of records of a department or agency available to us, we have been one-eyed squinters with dim lamps, compelled to pick up solitary bits and pieces and then puzzle out of them whatever meaning we can.

Therefore, this collection is most important to historians because it provides organizational context and will make possible more complete, complex, and "normal" historical examinations of the OSS than have previously been possible for any intelligence organization. I would hazard a guess that, as Churchill said, "in days that I shall not see," those responsible for the records of other intelligence organizations, both here and abroad, may well come to realize that it could be in their interest to follow the example of the OSS and RG 226. A large body of open historical records, and an expanding pool of respectable and responsible scholarship, may extend the public's understanding and tolerance for "secret agencies," and support for them might well increase. Secrecy, all pervasive and unswerving, has not always served intelligence organizations well, especially not at budget time or when an operation has gone badly awry. Serious scholarly work based on more records may help everyone to put such matters in a sharper perspective, and an era of more accessible intelligence materials may therefore become the wave of the future. If it does, RG 226 will certainly have been the genesis of this process.

Even if that does not happen, and we stick with the hard Dickensian facts, the appearance of RG 226 launches a new phase of serious historical study of intelligence activities and organizations. On many counts, the COI/OSS is a highly suitable organization with which to begin this era. The time frame of the COI/OSS is especially significant, ranging as it does from the pre-Pearl Harbor era of partial neutrality, on through the roaring changes of the war era, and up to, but not quite crossing, the bridge into the postwar and cold war periods. The COI/OSS is also an unusually fruitful object of study because between 1941 and 1945 it evolved from a blend of earnest effort and slapstick comedy to the well-honed intelligence and military support machine that functioned worldwide in the spring and summer of 1945.[1] The history of such a dynamic organization may, of course, raise more historical issues and problems than it solves. But the OSS can surely also help to tell us much about the processes of mid-20th-century intelligence gathering and collation as well as much about the special dynamics that affect such organizations. The history of the separate branches of the OSS, such as the Secret Intelligence Branch and the Morale Operations Branch, is therefore vitally important in its own right because no one has ever before been able to make in-depth explorations of such specialized intelligence departments. The same can be said of the relations of these branches with each other and of their individual and collective relations with the OSS leadership. Much has been written over the last 50 years about the struggles between the OSS central administration ("The Colonels") and the activists in the branches, as well as the subplot tensions between OSS personnel overseas and the branch organizations in Washington. Only now will it be possible to wrestle with these intriguing matters on the basis of a large body of documentary evidence.

One may also use RG 226 to wrestle with identity and relational questions within the OSS. Many passionate arguments have occurred since the death of the OSS over the relationships that should exist among various aspects of central intelligence, such as special operations, black propaganda, secret intelligence, research and analysis, and counterintelligence. Such matters are so personal and emotional for American intelligence practitioners that one hesitates to raise them in mixed company. To outsiders like myself, the passion, longevity, and intricacy of these matters recall the controversies between medieval scholastic philosophers: enticing in their complexity, but too remote from the everyday world to captivate this son of a day laborer. Even British practitioners with whom I have discussed these arguments, while granting that British intelligence yields place to no man in the matter of territorial battles, insist that passionate theorizing about intelligence organizational relationships is a peculiarly American, post-OSS endeavor. Careful study of what actually happened in the relations between the pathfinding branches of the OSS during the years 1941–

45, as well as the writings on such matters by the organization's leaders, could illuminate this mysterious realm and provide fresh insight into the internal dynamics affecting the development of intelligence agencies.

While citing all the wonderful things which RG 226 may do for the future of intelligence history, it is important to consider what it cannot do, at least not on its own. In my view there are now at least three permanent overarching questions regarding the COI/OSS: namely, how did it affect American military operations and overall decision making during the war, how and why did it change so drastically in the course of its short life, and why, despite the passionate loyalty of many of its personnel, was it abruptly abolished at war's end? If we examine these three questions in light of the current state of our knowledge, I think some of the inherent limitations in what RG 226 can be expected to do for us will be obvious.

Judging the value of particular intelligence and covert activities is notoriously difficult. On some occasions, body counts have been used to indicate the success of covert operational activities, and box scores listing the number of reports prepared and distributed have been made to substantiate the significance of intelligence activities. But all such efforts to impress carry the marks of special and imprecise pleading, in part because higher OSS leaders vigorously and assiduously sought to promote the virtues and triumphs of their organization (especially during its later stages) by preparing just such reports to set forth their achievements. Items so obviously intended to impress will certainly raise the hackles of suspicion among historians when they are found in RG 226.

Therefore, although RG 226 surely holds some clues to the value of OSS operations, these will not necessarily suffice to demonstrate convincingly the worth of the organization or of its subsections. Even when the RG 226 materials are supplemented by occasional testimonies made by the consumers of OSS "products," the results may still not be very satisfactory because much of the evidence is scrappy, and some consumers such as U.S. Army Intelligence (G-2) and the State Department were often jealously critical of Donovan's organization or nervous about its innovative activities.

The uncertainties that will inevitably remain regarding the overall wartime significance of the COI/OSS (despite the appearance of RG 226) are paralleled by serious and probably permanent difficulties in determining how and why the COI/OSS changed so radically and so often in the course of the war. In oversimplified terms, the COI/OSS began as an attempt to centralize American strategic intelligence and to create embryonic shadow warfare activities. The organization did not stay in that or any other form for long, however, and it ended up primarily as a secret intelligence and covert operations organization, with its center of gravity resting on direct support for ground and air combat operations.

Obviously, this evolution was prompted in part by the changing demands imposed by the war itself, but it was also caused by shifts in the shape, activity, and importance of organizations such as G-2, the Office of Naval Intelligence (ONI), the State Department, and the Joint Chiefs of Staff (JCS). All these groups impinged on the existence and form of the COI/OSS; their records are nearly as germane to the issue as those of the OSS itself.

Aside from external influences, it seems obvious that the nearly continuous changes in the organization and "mission" of the OSS were occasioned by the personality and dynamism of its founder and only Director, William Donovan. Little in RG 226 is likely to tell us why the Director ran where and when he did, nor are journeys to Carlisle Barracks likely to provide much enlightenment on this matter. I would therefore urge all of you who worked directly with William Donovan and are interested in how the OSS will fare in the hands of future historians to put your reflections about the general onto paper and deposit them in an open archive, because the mysteries surrounding William Donovan, especially those touching on the repeated changes in the organization of the COI/OSS, are never likely to go away.

To further complicate the question of what made the OSS run in differing directions at different times between 1941 and 1945, there is the significant and intriguing matter of General Donovan's relations with President Roosevelt. The Donovan-Roosevelt relationship was certainly crucial for the creation of the OSS and probably had some bearing on most of the important turns in the history of Donovan's organization. But in this matter, as in many other complex and often mysterious happenings in the Roosevelt administration, there is no quick explanatory fix.

It has generally been assumed that in most of the crucial OSS battles the President supported the innovative, or wilder, side of William Donovan, while G-2 tried to corral the general. In consequence, when Wild Bill lost a major bureaucratic battle, such as that in 1942–43, which gave the bulk of foreign propaganda activities to the Office of War Information (OWI) and not to the OSS, it has been customary to conclude that this was a triumph of the orthodox bureaucrats over Mr. Roosevelt's inclination toward innovation. However, a document has recently surfaced from the U.S. Army Staff files held by the National Archives that suggests that the relationship between the White House and the OSS may not have been as simple as that which portrays Mr. Roosevelt and General Donovan as innovative buddies. On February 18, 1943, G-2's Assistant Chief of Staff, Maj. Gen. George Strong (the G-2), was summoned to the White House to meet with the President. Immediately following the meeting, he sent a memorandum to Gen. George Marshall recounting the peculiar events which had befallen him there. After a few warm-up remarks in which the

President declared his view that "psychological warfare was primarily propaganda" and that "he had no sympathy with planning committees or advisory committees to planning committees," Mr. Roosevelt turned to the squabbles between the OSS and the OWI. The President stated, according to Strong's report, that the "psychological warfare" program of the OSS should be given to the OWI and that since "he was too busy to be annoyed with picayunish questions arising out of the administration of OSS," and since he thought "the Joint Chiefs of Staff should not be required to devote attention to such things," the OSS should "be placed under the War Department" because its interests were "primarily military."[2]

Champions of the OSS may be tempted to dismiss this document as irrelevant to a serious examination of Mr. Roosevelt's views either on bureaucracy or the OSS because the remarks have a "pop off" tone and because George Strong was far from being besotted either with the OSS or William Donovan. The G-2 himself seems to have realized that even General Marshall might have doubts about his reliability as a witness on OSS matters, and he therefore carefully noted that during the White House meeting he did "no talking except, first to confirm certain factual statements the President made, and second at the close of the conversation to suggest to the President that the steps which he decided to take would involve a change in the executive order establishing the OSS as an agency of the Joint Chiefs of Staff."

Given the care and caution General Strong used in his account of this meeting with the President, the extant record probably closely parallels what actually occurred. If that is true, then what we have here may indicate that in midwar the White House was turning away from innovative, free-floating, OSS-type administrative methods, and that the President was a major force in pushing the OSS into a "primarily military" direction. Or perhaps this is a sign that the bureaucrats had cornered the President and were nudging him into playing by more traditional rules. Or it could be that Mr. Roosevelt himself was already being ground down by his responsibilities and was on the lookout for shortcuts as early as February 1943. Whatever scenario one selects to elucidate the document and the White House events of February 18, 1943, the simple and oft-repeated tale that FDR was always in Donovan's corner both during the bureaucratic battles and in support of his innovative ideas needs to be handled with great caution, no matter what apparently relevant data exist in RG 226 or elsewhere.

Regarding the last, and probably most volatile, of my three basic questions that are unlikely to be effectively answered by the materials in RG 226—namely the termination of the OSS in September 1945—a conventional, and to my mind oversimplified explanation has had general currency since 1945. Many believe the OSS died simply because it was hijacked and killed by the traditional intelligence agencies, led by G-2, who feared the competition and the innovative capabilities of the OSS and William Donovan. This murderous conspiracy was successful, it has been claimed, because Franklin Roosevelt died and was replaced by the inept, bureaucracy-minded, traditional, naive, and unimaginative Harry S. Truman, who had a personal antipathy to William Donovan.

I have already put forward my caveat about assuming FDR was a consistent partner of William Donovan. It also needs to be stressed that although organizations like G-2 were extremely territorial, and often akin to dinosaurs in their unwillingness to change, it is also true that in 1944–45 both the ONI and G-2 carried through more significant internal reorganizations than had occurred at any time since World War I. During the spring and summer of 1945, the two service intelligence departments even overcame their ancient rivalries sufficiently to achieve much closer coordination of their cryptanalytic activities, which I think we will all concede was to the mind of American leaders the most sensitive of all intelligence matters. Furthermore, during the summer of 1945 the Army and Navy Departments steadily pushed forward to their goal of extending ULTRA/MAGIC-type cooperation with the British beyond the end of hostilities. On September 12, shortly after V–J Day, the Secretaries of War and Navy, in conjunction with the Secretary of State, persuaded the President that the Anglo-American cryptanalytic partnership should continue into the postwar period.[3] Mr. Truman authorized the Anglo-American cooperation in an environment saturated with JCS worries about the effect that "new weapons," i.e., the atomic bomb, might have on American security, and efforts of ONI and G-2 to increase the reliability and volume of Western intelligence regarding the Soviet Union.[4]

Given these developments, and the general impression in the highest levels of the U.S. government that cryptanalysis had been one of the most vital wonder weapons of the Second World War—and might continue to be in the postwar era—it should not be totally surprising that 1 day after authorizing the prolongation of Anglo-American cryptanalytic cooperation, President Truman would remark to his budget chief, Harold Smith, that he "should recommend the dissolution of Donovan's outfit even if Donovan did not like it," and that 1 week later the President would sign without comment the OSS dissolution order.[5]

The ULTRA/MAGIC factor, and its relation to the abolition of the OSS, suggest that there were more dimensions to the demise of "Donovan's outfit" than Trumanesque idiosyncrasies or bureaucratic jealousies lurking in G-2. Without entering into the ancient revisionist versus traditionalist argument about who started the cold war, it is clear that deep worries about postwar security were bubbling away in high places in Washington during the late summer and early autumn of 1945. The two armed services were much more effective than Donovan in advancing proposals to meet this situation, and this factor certainly worked to their institutional advantage. The deep secrecy and low price of the cryptanalytic proposals meant that there was no direct clash between them and the American public's craving for "normalcy," which was waxing strong during the last weeks of the conflict.

Whether the ultimate triumph of the War and Navy Departments over the OSS was merely due to good fortune and a more effective exploitation of the situation at the end of the war is difficult to say. But it should be noted that Donovan had opted from the beginning against sharing agreements with the British, except in the field of counterintelligence, in favor of establishing agreed zones of influence. On the other hand, beginning with the cryptanalytic agreements of 1942–43, the American military and naval authorities had opted for a policy of broad Anglo-American intelligence sharing and interdependence. This choice left the Army and Navy much better placed than the OSS at war's end to make mutually advantageous and cheap deals with Britain that would serve the postwar security interests of the U.S.A.

All of this shows that the abolition of the OSS was the product of a more complex combination of factors than has often been supposed. It suggests that RG 226 is probably not the best place to go in search of the dominant reasons why the OSS died and cryptanalytic cooperation survived. Even so, RG 226 may help answer the question of why, following the bushwhacking of its central intelligence plan in February 1945, the OSS leadership marched blindly on toward its fate, failing to try to check the factors that would ultimately give eternal life to the cryptanalysts and death to the OSS in September 1945.

Thus RG 226 will have at least some role to play in virtually every historical inquiry regarding the OSS. But researchers must be careful not to fall so completely in its spell that broader perspectives and other sources fail to receive their due. We are very appreciative of the gifts that RG 226 bestows upon us, but without falling into ingratitude we must go on practicing our craft both by continuing to ask questions and by snooping under every accessible rock in hope of finding answers.

NOTES

1. Memorandum, Dec. 15, 1941, for G-2, 350.05, Box 64, Entry 57, Records of Headquarters Army Ground Forces, Record Group 337, National Archives and Records Administration, Washington, DC (hereinafter cited as RG 337, NA).
2. Strong to Marshall, Feb. 18, 1943, Box 346, Entry 175, Records of the War Department General and Special Staffs, RG 165, NA.
3. B. F. Smith, "A Note on the OSS, Ultra, and World War II's Intelligence Legacy for America," *Defence Analysis* 3 (1987): 184–189.
4. Memorandum, Sept. 7, 1945, CCS 334, CIA (12-6-42) Sec. 1, Records of the U.S. Joint Chiefs of Staff, RG 218; Lt. K. W. McMahan to Capt. Joseph Wenger,

May 25, 1945, SRH 200, Pt. 2, Sec. 2, Records of the National Security/Central Security Service, RG 457; Col. Alfred McCormack to Brig. B.P.T. O'Brien, July 21, 1945, Box 782, Entry 203, "British Participation" file, RG 165, NA.

5. Sept. 13, 1945, Conferences with the President file, Box 15, Harold Smith Papers, Franklin D. Roosevelt Library, Hyde Park, NY.

BIOGRAPHICAL SKETCHES OF CONFERENCE PARTICIPANTS

Dušan Biber

Dušan Biber is a Fellow of the Institute for Modern History, Ljubljana SFR, Yugoslavia. Dr. Biber was born in 1926 and joined the resistance movement in the Yugoslav National Liberation Army. He is the holder of UNESCO, Fulbright, and Ford Foundation fellowships. His publications include *Nazism and Germans in Yugoslavia, Tito-Churchill, Top Secret,* and many contributions to journals and edited works. He currently serves as president of the Yugoslav National Committee for the Study of History.

Richard Breitman

This Phi Beta Kappa from Yale University is currently professor of history at the American University in Washington, DC. Dr. Breitman is the author or co-author of four books and numerous articles and book reviews. His most recent book. *The Architect of Genocide: Himmler and the Final Solution,* won the Frankel Prize for Contemporary History. Dr. Breitman's works are characterized by extensive use and careful evaluation of archival sources.

Sir Robin Brook

Robin Brook was educated at Eton and King's College, Cambridge. Between 1941 and 1946 he served as an officer in the British Army. Part of this time was spent in the Special Operations Executive, where he was liaison with OSS and other Allied intelligence organizations. He was responsible for Western Europe SOE operations. Among his many military honors, he was awarded the Order of the British Empire (OBE) in 1945. He went on to a very successful career in government and business, serving as a Director of the Bank of England and later Chairman. In recognition of his outstanding service, he was knighted in 1974. For many years he has served as Chairman of Leda Investment Trust Ltd. in London.

Fabrizio Calvi

This French journalist is well known in Europe for his writings relating to the work of secret societies in western Europe. His fifth book, *The OSS in France*, involved 3 years of research in archival repositories such as the National Archives and interviews with over 200 former OSS, French Resistance, and Gestapo members. This book is scheduled for translation and publication in English in the coming months. Mr. Calvi has directed television documentaries on terrorism and the Mafia.

Carolle J. Carter

Carolle Carter is a professor of history and political science at Menlo College in Atherton, CA. In 1991 Professor Carter made a trip to China at the special invitation of that country. Her work in progress is "Dixie Mission: American Intelligence with the Chinese Communists, 1944–47." She is the author of *The Shamrock and the Swastika: German Espionage in Ireland in World War II* and several articles and presentations relating to World War II topics.

Ray S. Cline

This conference participant has many accomplishments to his credit. After receiving his third degree from Harvard, Dr. Cline went to work for the U.S. Navy in its codebreaking operation and then joined the OSS in 1943. The next year, he became chief of the Current Intelligence Staff and remained there until 1945. His scholarship is impressive, and his publications are numerous. His book, *Secrets, Spies, and Scholars,* should be read by all interested in the basics of intelligence. Dr. Cline was Deputy Director for Intelligence at the Central Intelligence Agency during the Cuban Missile Crisis, and from 1969 until his retirement in 1973 he served as Assistant Secretary of State. He currently is Chairman of the United States Global Strategy Council and Vice-Chairman of the Veterans of OSS.

William Colby

In 1940 William Colby graduated from Princeton University, where he was elected Phi Beta Kappa. During World War II he joined the OSS, and he parachuted into France with a Jedburgh team. In 1945 this 24-year-old headed an operational group that dropped into Norway to assist the resistance forces. After graduating from Columbia University Law School, he joined the firm of Donovan Leisure Newton & Irvine for 2 years and praticed in Washington, DC. Colby served in several U.S. embassies during the 1950s and then became chief of the Far East Division of the CIA in

1963. In 1968 he was named Ambassador and Deputy to the Commander, U.S. Military Assistance Command, Vietnam. In 1973 he was appointed Director of Central Intelligence. He resigned in 1976 to return to the practice of law. He is the author of two books, *Honorable Men* and *Lost Victory*, both recognized for style, grace, and candor.

George C. Constantinides

Mr. Constantinides is a careful student of the broad field of intelligence literature. He is the author of the widely used *Intelligence and Espionage: An Analytical Bibliography*. His professional writing reflects his 25-year service in various intelligence and national security assignments. During World War II, Mr. Constantinides served in a cryptographic unit attached to the French in Europe.

Max Corvo

In Augusta, Sicily, young Max Corvo helped his father print an anti-Fascist newspaper during the 1920s. His family moved to America to escape the Italian political situation. Upon the outbreak of war, Corvo volunteered for service in the U.S. Army but soon was moved to the OSS because of his interest in and talents concerning intelligence planning. Corvo worked in the Italian Section of the Secret Intelligence Branch in the United States and in the field for the duration of the war. His book, *OSS in Italy*, draws upon his extensive OSS experience and expertise.

Gordon A. Craig

The publications of this distinguished American historian have won numerous awards and prizes. In 1956 Craig was awarded the prestigious Herbert Baxter Adams Prize for *The Politics of the Prussian Army, 1640–1945*. In addition to many years of teaching at Princeton and Stanford, he has lectured extensively around the world. In 1981 he served as president of the American Historical Association. Dr. Craig is a member of the American Academy of Arts and Sciences, a Fellow of the British Academy, and honorary Fellow of Balliol College, Oxford University. Dr. Craig is widely recognized as an outstanding articulator of European political throught.

Helene Deschamps-Adams

The daughter of a French officer, Helene Deschamps joined the Resistance in 1940 and served as a courier and counterespionage agent in southern France. In November 1943 she joined the OSS as a field operative for the network "Jacques," better known as Penny Farthing. Working behind and crossing German lines became part of her life between 1943 and 1945. The successful invasion of southern France in August 1944 must be in part credited to OSS operatives providing information, sabotage, and encouragement to Allied and French patriot forces. For almost 5 years Helene Deschamps served the Allied cause. At the conclusion of the war, she married an American officer and came to the United States in March 1946. A successful speaker and writer, her first book was *The Secret War.*

Harold C. Deutsch

This well-known historian has contributed much to the teaching and scholarship of 20th-century European history. In addition to teaching students for four decades at the University of Minnesota, Dr. Deutsch has written 7 books and contributed to 11 collective works. During the war, Deutsch held several responsible positions in the Research and Analysis Branch of OSS. During 1944–45, he served as supervisor in charge of the transfer of R&A personnel to London and was later in charge of the Paris R&A unit. Upon retirement from Minnesota in 1973, Dr. Deutsch directed European studies at the National War College and then served on the faculty of the Army War College for an additional 11 years.

M.R.D. Foot

Born in London in 1919, M.R.D. Foot served with distinction in the British military between 1939 and 1945. In 1942 he was transferred to Combined Operations Headquarters, where he served until 1944. He then served in the Special Air Service Brigade in the field, where he was taken prisoner by the Germans. His publications are marked by the high quality of scholarship and the sensitivity to the grim realities of war. Among the many books to his credit is *The SOE in France,* the official British government history of an important operation to free the French people.

Arthur L. Funk

Arthur L. Funk was born in 1914 in Brooklyn, NY, and received his B.A. degree from Dartmouth and advanced degrees from the University of Chicago. During World War II, Dr. Funk served in the U.S. Navy and, upon discharge in 1946, resumed his teaching career at the University of Florida, where he spent most of the next three decades teaching history. He has written or edited seven books and numerous articles, many of which relate to World War II topics. His book *The Politics of Torch;* his biography, *Charles de Gaulle: The Crucial Years, 1943-1944;* and his forthcoming work, "Hidden Ally: Special Operations, the French Resistance, and the Landings in Southern France, 1944," represent considerable expertise in this aspect of World War II operations.

Waldo Heinrichs

Waldo Heinrichs is Dwight E. Stanford Professor of American Foreign Relations at San Diego State University. This prominent American diplomatic historian took his Ph.D. from Harvard in 1960 and has since taught at several leading universities. His publications focus on the prewar period and American-Asian relations in the 20th century. Professor Heinrichs's recent book, *Threshold of War: Franklin D. Roosevelt and American Entry into World War II,* is an excellent synthesis of events related to American entry into the conflict. His writings are rigorously supported by careful assessment of primary as well as secondary sources of documentation.

Richard Helms

Richard Helms graduated from Williams College in 1935, having been selected to Phi Beta Kappa during his junior year. Between 1935 and the attack of Pearl Harbor, he worked for United Press in London and the *Indianapolis Times.* In 1942 Helms received a commission in the U.S. Naval Reserve. After a year of active duty in the Navy, he was transferred to the OSS in Washington. In addition to serving in headquarters, Helms was posted to London, Paris, Wiesbaden, and Berlin between 1943 and 1945. Helms joined the Central Intelligence Agency in 1947, the year of its establishment, and in 1966 President Johnson appointed him its Director. He resigned in 1973 to accept appointment as Ambassador to Iran. He resigned this post in January 1977 and has since been president of Safeer Company, an international business consulting firm.

Henry Hyde

Henry Hyde was born in Paris, graduated from Cambridge University with an M.A., and then entered Harvard Law School, where he received his LL.B. in 1939. Hyde began practicing law in 1940, but in 1942 he was attracted to Washington to serve in the OSS. His talent and management of Secret Intelligence Branch affairs in Algiers brought praise to OSS overseas operations. Hyde was then placed in charge of the OSS unit attached to U.S. Seventh Army forces. In 1947 he returned to New York City and to the practice of law.

David Kahn

At the age of 13, David Kahn read Fletcher Pratt's *Secret and Urgent* and became an avid student of cryptology. He joined the American Cryptogram Association and started writing for *The Cryptogram,* its official publication. After graduation from Bucknell University, he became a reporter for *Newsday* and in his spare time wrote articles on codes and codebreaking. In 1967 his book *The Codebreakers* was published and has gone through 11 editions. In 1972 Kahn went to Oxford to study and in 1974 received his doctorate of philosophy. His most recent book, *Seizing the Enigma,* tells how the Allies, by capturing documents from U-boats and German weather ships, solved the German Enigma cipher machine and defeated Hitler's submarine warfare.

S. Peter Karlow

Peter Karlow, a graduate of Swarthmore College, was one of the "early on board" OSS veterans and performed a wide range of intelligence functions. He went to North Africa in 1943 to establish a Research and Analysis Unit. He was later wounded and decorated for an operation on Corsica. At war's end he was responsible for preparing the *War Report on the OSS*, edited by Kermit Roosevelt. While living in St. Louis after the war, he was international affairs director for the Monsanto Chemical Company and served that city as chairman of the St. Louis World Affairs Council. Karlow is now a writer and business consultant in San Francisco.

Barry Katz

Barry Katz received his B.A. from McGill University in Montreal, his M.S. from the London School of Economics, and his Ph.D. from the University of California at Santa Cruz. He is currently the Senior Lecturer in the Program in Values, Technology, Science, and Society at Stanford University. Katz's second of three books, *Foreign Intelligence: Research and Analysis in the Office of Strategic Services 1942-1945,* and a forthcoming article on the OSS in the *Oxford Companion to the Second World War* relate to his investigations of scholars, their ideas, and their work within the OSS.

J. Kenneth McDonald

Since 1981, Dr. McDonald has been Chief Historian of the Central Intelligence Agency. He has served on the faculty of the George Washington University, the Naval War College, and was visiting fellow in history at Yale University. Following graduation from Yale in 1954, he was on active duty as a Marine Corps infantry officer until 1958. McDonald holds a doctorate from Oxford University and was also a senior associate member of St. Antony's College. He has several publications relating to 20th-century military history. His research, "Secrecy, Accountability and the CIA: The Dilemma of Intelligence in a Democracy," is a contribution to a forthcoming publication, *The United States Military under the Constitution, 1789–1989,* edited by Richard A. Kohn

Lawrence H. McDonald

A native Washingtonian, Larry McDonald received his B.A. and M.S. degrees from Georgetown University. He received his Ph.D. from the University of Maryland in 1974, at which time he joined the National Archives, where he has worked in several units of the Office of the National Archives. Since 1985 he has worked on the arrangement and description of the records of the Office of Strategic Services and directed a team of volunteers providing description and greater access to these records. He has served as a review editor for the *American Archivist* and has written several articles on the OSS and its records.

Elizabeth McIntosh

On December 7, 1941, Elizabeth McIntosh was hired by the Scripps Howard Newspapers to provide on-the-scene coverage of the Pearl Harbor attack and the war in the Pacific. In 1942, McIntosh, a graduate of the University of Washington School of Journalism, transferred to Washington, DC, to cover the White House and prepare feature stories. In 1943 she joined the OSS and was sent to Burma, where she conducted morale operations against the Japanese in Burma and China. In the latter country, she operated behind Japanese lines. After the war, McIntosh held several senior assignments with government agencies including the CIA, from which she retired in 1973. She has written two children's books and *Undercover Girl*, a story of her OSS experiences during the war.

Timothy J. Naftali

This Harvard doctoral candidate has made extensive use of OSS records during the past few years and has a book contract with Oxford University Press to publish a study of the counterespionage branch (X-2) of the OSS. His B.A. is from Yale, and his M.A. is from the School of Advanced International Studies of Johns Hopkins University. A native of Canada, Naftali has been a speechwriter and policy analyst in the Office of the Premier of Quebec. He was recently named a MacArthur Scholar at Harvard and has also written several articles and made presentations at professional meetings.

Neal H. Petersen

Born and raised in Milwaukee, WI, Neal Petersen holds an undergraduate degree from Princeton University and advanced degrees from Georgetown University. Between 1964 and 1988 Petersen was a historian in the Historical Office of the Department of State, where he compiled or directed compilation of 14 volumes of the *Foreign Relations of the United States*. In 1988 Dr. Petersen retired as Deputy Chief Historian and has since served as a historical consultant. He is currently preparing for publication a documentary collection of Allen Dulles's wartime intelligence reports and a bibliography on American intelligence.

E. Bruce Reynolds

Dr. Reynolds is assistant professor of history at San Jose State University and director of the East Asian materials and Resources Center there. He received his undergraduate and M.A. degrees from Central Missouri State University and his Ph.D. from the University of Hawaii at Manoa. He has published several articles on Thailand's role in World War II and is working on a history of Japanese-Thai relations in the 1930s and 1940s.

Aline, Countess of Romanones

As a graduate of Mount St. Vincent College in 1943, Aline Griffith was recruited by the OSS and, after some intensive training, was dispatched to Madrid. While in Spain, she performed undercover work and conducted espionage for the United States. As the Allied front advanced toward Germany, she was stationed in France and, after the war, in Switzerland. Leaving intelligence work in 1947, she married the Count of Quintanilla in 1948 and raised three sons while earning an M.A. in 1952 from the University of Madrid. She was recruited for intelligence by the CIA in 1958 and worked until 1980 on a special basis. Her first espionage novel, *The Spy Wore Red*, based upon her field experiences in Spain, became a best-seller and was followed by two additional popular espionage novels based upon her later experiences. The Countess is in demand as a speaker on espionage as well as on the politics of El Salvador.

Elspeth Davies Rostow

Elspeth Rostow is currently professor of government at the University of Texas at Austin. Having relinquished her position as Dean of the Lyndon B. Johnson School of Public Affairs, she continues writing as a columnist for the *Austin American Statesman*. President Reagan appointed her to the Board of the United States Institute of Peace, where she now serves as acting chairman. Professor Rostow was a research associate in the Washington Research and Analysis Branch of the OSS between 1942 and 1945 and specialized in French intelligence. After the war, she taught at several universities including Sarah Lawrence College, Cambridge University, Massachusetts Institute of Technology, and Georgetown University. Her publications include *Europe's Economy After the War, America Now,* and *The Coattailless Landslide.*

Walt W. Rostow

Walt Rostow's contributions to the field of economics and politics include 31 books and numerous articles stretching through four decades. A Rhodes Scholar at Oxford and Yale Ph.D. recipient in 1940, Rostow taught at Columbia University until World War II interrupted. Rostow, a major in the OSS, was sent to London as part of a small unit, the Enemy Objectives Unit, which studied a vast amount of data to prioritize German targets for Allied bombing. In 1946–47 he returned to teaching as the Harmsworth Professor of American History at Oxford University. In 1950 he became professor of economic history at the Massachusetts Institute of Technology. In 1961 President Kennedy appointed him Deputy Special Assistant to the President for National Security Affairs. That same year, however, he moved to the Department of State to become Chairman of the Policy Planning Staff. In 1966 Rostow returned to the White House as President Johnson's Special Assistant for National Security Affairs. In February 1969, Rostow returned to teaching at the University of Texas at Austin. In 1969 he received the Presidential Medal of Freedom.

Michael Schaller

Michael Schaller received his Ph.D. from the University of Michigan in 1974 and has since taught in the history department of the University of Arizona. He is currently the head of the department. Schaller's major publications relate to 20th-century United States-Far East relations. His book *The U.S. Crusade in China, 1938–45* won the Bernath Book Prize of 1980, awarded by the Society for the Historians of American Foreign Relations. His latest of four books is *Douglas MacArthur: The Far Eastern General.*

Arthur M. Schlesinger, Jr.

Arthur M. Schlesinger, Jr., has been the Albert Schweitzer Professor of the Humanities at the City University of New York since 1966. After graduation from Harvard in 1938, he became a fellow at Harvard until serving in the Office of War Information from 1942 to 1943. In 1943 he moved to the Research and Analysis Branch of OSS located in Washington, DC. As London OSS operations became more vital, Schlesinger transferred and worked for a time under another historian, Harold Deutsch, until moving to Paris late in 1944. He served in the U.S. Army in 1945 and after discharge joined the Department of History at Harvard. His second work, *The Age of Jackson,* won the Pulitzer Prize for History. He also won two prestigious historical prizes, the Francis Parkman Prize and the Bancroft Prize. Between 1961 and 1963 Schlesinger served as Special Assistant to President John F. Kennedy. In 1965 came publication of the masterful *A Thousand Days: John F. Kennedy in the White House* and another Pulitzer Prize.

Bradley F. Smith

Professor Smith is a scholar whose publications are based upon careful research and are noted for impressive synthesis. *The Shadow Warriors: OSS and the Origins of the CIA* drew upon an array of materials even though the operational records of the OSS were not yet available in the National Archives. Many of his nine books have gone through several editions and have been translated into other languages. This Phi Beta Kappa from the

University of California at Berkeley has won Woodrow Wilson, Fulbright, and Horace Mann fellowships. He currently teaches at Cabrillo College, Aptos, CA.

Peter Tompkins

At the age of 20, Peter Tompkins interrupted his education at Harvard in 1939 to join the *New York Times* bureau in Rome. During the next 2 years, Tompkins covered the European war for the Mutual Broadcasting System, *London Sunday Times,* National Broadcasting Company, and Associated Press. In 1942 Tompkins returned to the United States and joined the Office of Coordinator of Information, where he was trained to parachute into Italy. During 1943 he was landed in Salerno to organize intelligence and partisan activities. Tompkins spent 5 months behind German lines relaying intelligence and recruiting 25 agents. In 1945 the OSS transferred Tompkins to Berlin for espionage operations. After the war, Tompkins resumed work as a correspondent, movie script writer, and director of television shows for the Columbia Broadcasting System. Tompkins's 11 books include *A Spy in Rome,* describing his espionage activities, and *The Murder of Admiral Darlan.*

James R. Ward

James Ward graduated from Boston College in 1940 and was attending its night law school when Pearl Harbor was attacked. He left his job and school and enlisted in the Army. In September 1943 the OSS recruited him because of his proficiency in foreign languages. Upon completion of special training, he was assigned to Detachment 101 in Burma, where he spent more than 13 months in combat leading guerrilla forces behind Japanese lines. After World War II, Ward served with the CIA and Department of State.

Robin W. Winks

Since 1957 Robin Winks has taught at Yale University, where he specializes in the history of the British Empire, conservation history, the theory and development of intelligence, and as an avocation, detective fiction. His regular column on mystery fiction appears in the *Boston Globe.* Dr. Winks has published 17 books including *Cloak & Gown: Scholars in the Secret War,* which won the National Intelligence Study Center prize for the best book on intelligence published in 1987. He has served as an adviser to the Department of State, the U.S. Information Agency, and the National Park Service. From 1969 to 1971, while on leave from Yale, he served as cultural attaché to the American Embassy in London. His B.A. degree was awarded from the University of Colorado, and he holds double M.A. degrees in history and anthropology. His Ph.D. was awarded by Johns Hopkins University.

INDEX

Abramowitz, Moses, 44
Abwehr, 192, 222, 235n.5, 249, 257-
59, 271n.13, 280-81
Adun Adundetcharat, 331, 338
AFHQ. *See* Allied Force Headquarters
Agents: Allied, 293; Burmese, 321-22;
code names for, 106; French, 140-
64, 270; Italian, 122; Japanese,
122; Soviet, 112; Thai, 330-31,
333-34
Agents, German, 122; and French OSS
agents, 249; in Italy, 218-21, 224,
235n.5, 236n.6, 236n.7, 239n.37;
in Spain, 127-28; in Turkey, 279
Agents, OSS, 121; in France, 140-64,
248-50; in Germany, 278-79; in
Mediterranean, 167; training of,
123, 125, 170, 175, 184-85, 249-
50. *See also* names of agents
Aircraft, for OSS, 169, 172, 250, 322-
23, 338
Airmen, rescue of, 197-98, 323, 326,
338, 343, 350n.70
Air Transport Command (ATC), and
Burmese operations, 322
Alexander, Sir Harold, 131, 135, 192,
213; quoted, 295
Alexander, Sidney, 44
Algiers, OSS operations in, 166-80,
188
Aline, Countess of Romanones, 121;
The Spy Wore Red, 109
Allied Expeditionary Air Force, and
EOU, 50

Allied Force Headquarters (AFHQ),
71; in Algiers, 166-67, 169, 173-
74, 178-79; and Italian campaign,
185-86, 188, 190-92; OSS at, 169-
70; and Penny Farthing, 255; and
proposed German negotiations,
205
Alsop, Stewart, *Sub Rosa*, 110
Americans, national characteristics of,
295-96
Analysis: importance of, 355-56; of
intelligence information, 28-29,
34, 37, 44; political, 63-64, 66-68
Anderson, Frederick L., 50-51, 54
Anderson, Hartvig, *The Dark City*,
110
Angleton, James Hugh, 224
Angleton, James J., 113; and
counterespionage, 91, 93, 191,
236n.9, 237n.13, 237n.15; quoted,
237n.17, 240n.54; and X-2
operations, 165, 218-34
Anstey, John, 174-75
Anzio, 129-39, 171, 189-90, 255
Archives: CIA, 86; German, 73; OSS,
84-85
Ardeatine Caves, massacre at, 138
Ardennes offensive, 283-84
Army Intelligence (G-2): in China,
302, 304, 308-9, 312; and EOU,
50; in France, 146, 149-51;
inadequacy of, 56; and Italian
campaign, 186-91; and OSS, 179,
362-65; OSS coordination with,

Kolbe, Fritz (GEORGE WOOD), 278-80
Kramer, Ellsworth R., 201, 210
Krieger, Leonard, 24, 44

Labor groups, Italian American, 184-85
Lalich, Nick A., 198
Landon, Perry, 336
Langer, William L., 20, 25, 110, 303; and R&A, 32, 44, 62-63, 89, 91
Languages, and intelligence work, 8, 23, 37, 43
Latin America, 30, 79, 122, 126, 298
Legge, Barnwell, 260-62, 265, 267-69, 275
LeHand, Marguerite, 13
LeMay, Curtis, 312-13
Lemnitzer, Lyman, 286
Lend-Lease Act, 11-12, 209
Leontief, Wassily, 45
Lescanne, Jean, 255-56
Levy, Walter, 45
Liaison: and counterespionage, 223-30, 233-34; OSS-Abwehr, 258-59; OSS-military, 178-79
Lindsay, Franklin, 208
Lisbon, 87
Literature, OSS, 109-17, 166, 249
Livermore, Russell, 170, 189, 192
London: intelligence activity in, 41-42; OSS in, 41, 82; R&A in, 62-64; SOE in, 69-73
Loofbourow, Frederick, 275
Lord, Walter, 63
Lovell, Stanley, *Of Spies and Stratagems*, 111
Lowry, W. McNeil, 61
Lubell, Sam, 61
Lucas, John P., quoted, 131; 134-135

MacAdoo, Dale, 183-84
MacBain, Alastair, *Cloak and Dagger*, 110
MacDonald, Alexander, 342
MacDonald, Elizabeth, *Undercover Girl*, 111
McDonald, J. Kenneth, 77
McDonald, Larry, 77, 104, 106, 359
McDowell, Robert, 194, 196, 200-214
McDowell mission, 165, 194-214
MacFarland, Lanning, 200
McGarry, W. D., 338, 347n.43

McGreggor Mission, 188
McIntosh, Elizabeth, 301
McKay, Donald, 62
Maclean, Fitzroy, 198, 202, 209
MacLeish, Archibald, 83
Macmillan, Harold, 199, 212
Madrid, 87, 121-28
MAGIC, 12-13, 14, 125, 296, 365
Malfatti, Franco, 130-32
Mangold, Tom, *Cold Warrior, James Angleton*, 236n.9, 244n.100
Mansfield, Walter, 194
Maquis, 70-71, 126, 140, 144-45, 176-77
Marcuse, Herbert, 24, 45
Marine Unit (OSS), 224-25, 239n.37
Marret, Mario, 249-50, 252-55, 257-59, 270
Marshall, Gen. George C., 17, 319
Martin, FFI chief, 143-44
Martin, Guy, 309
Mason, Edward S, 44
MASSINGHAM, 167-68, 170, 174-76
Masterman, Sir John, 91
Materazzi, Albert, 192
Mauch, Christian, 246
Mayer, Gerald, 275, 278
Mediterranean theater, OSS operations in, 165-80
MEDUSA, 168
Mellon, William Larrimore, 124, 126
Menzies, Sir Stewart (C), 251
Mero, Peter S., 168, 171
Merrill's Marauders, 323-24
Methodology: EOU, 49-50; R&A, 32, 44, 46, 89; for record research, 103-6
Meyer, Albert, 264-70
Mihailović, Draža, 165, 194, 204, 206-13
Miles, Milton E. (Mary), 303, 330
Military, German: and opposition to Hitler, 281-92; and peace negotiations, 284, 291n.21
Military, U.S.: and CIA, 356; and COI, 80; and OSS, 22, 28, 30, 170, 362; and postwar security, 365-66
Mills, Frank, 95
Milodragovich, John R., 201, 208
Mission Jackal, 95
Mockler-Ferryman, Eric T., 298
Moffat, Abbott Low, 336